Fate and Fortune in the Indian Scriptures

Sukumari Bhattacharji

FOUNDATION BOOKS

FOUNDATION
BOOKS

Foundation Books is an imprint of Cambridge University Press, India.

Cambridge House, 4381/4 Ansari Road, Daryaganj, New Delhi 110 002

www.cambridgeindia.org

First published 2014

Printed in India at Sanat Printers, Kundli, Haryana

ISBN 978-93-82993-88-9 Hardback

This book was first published in 1995 with the title 'Fatalism in Ancient India' by Baulmon Prakashan, 28 Ballygunge Gardens, Kolkata 700019.

Contents

Preface

IN 1981 I attended a conference on religion in Winnipeg, Canada. My paper was on Fatalism in Ancient India. In the course of my discourse, I had mentioned that the theories of Karman and rebirth were two of the most vicious ever invented by man. I was attacked vehemently by all and sundry; I realized that fatalism with which these theories were intrinsically linked was a vested interest, or, the apathy and passivity it produced were. It was then that I resolved to work on this theme. It took me many years and a few trips abroad as to use foreign libraries on the relevent matter, however slowly and surely the ideas emerged.

The Spalding Fund made it possible for me to use the Oxford and Cambridge libraries twice, the Maison des Sciences de l'homme at Paris kindly assisted me to use the French libraries twice. I am also grateful for the B.M. Barua Senior Research Fellowship at the Asiatic Society for making it possible to work on and complete the book.

Scholars here and abroad have helped me in my study and preparation of the work. Of them, I am most grateful to Professor B. N. Mukherji who unstintedly gave me his time to discuss certain facts and also lent me books out of his personal library. Dr Tapodhir Bhattacharya gave his time and energy to go over the manuscript and give it a shape. I feel a deep debt of gratitude to him. Dr Shyama Prasad De, as always, helped me arrange the unwieldly manuscript, revise the typescript and arrange alphabetically the bibliography. Sri Dibakar Karmoker, despite his ill health and other pressing duties, kindly typed out such a difficult manuscript. I am grateful to them all.

The subject itself is rather vast and baffling and I am sure that a better equipped scholar would have done a better job of it. I felt the subject posed a challenge, a threat to academic and practical existential life in India. So, I decided to probe it with whatever equipment I managed to muster. 1 have been encouraged by Dr Tanika Sarkar and Professor Sumit Sarkar—my daughter and son-in-law, in carrying out this work. Aditya Sarkar, my grandson, by his very presence inspired me a lot. My friend Bani Bhattacharya offered unfailing encouragement throughout the long years of its preparation, I feel deeply grateful to her. Professor Jasodhara Bagchi offered two useful references which Professor Jyoti Bhattacharya kindly tracked and sent me; I owe a debt of gratitude to both. I also appreciate the faith of other friends and ex-pupils in me and in the work. I was moved by two facts –that this work had not been undertaken before and that it needed to be tackled.

Undoubtedly, the book has many errors of commission and omission, all due to my ignorance and inefficiency. If these provoke a better scholar to do a better work on the theme, then I shall feel that I have not worked in vain.

Introduction

FATALISM, the belief that fate is an unseen, incalculable and uncontrollable power which controls human affairs, is ubiquitous and a very old belief. In Vedic times, says Klostermeier,[1] "It was apparently a fairly marginal existence which was possible under the given circumstances; survival was precarious and threatened by famine, disease, enemy and wild animals. Every catastrophe was necessarily attributed to a break in the powercircuit that connected the devas with the world of men."[2] Yet in India, the earliest texts, known as the early Vedic literature, the Sarphitās and Brāhman, do not have any trace of fatalism. Life was more exposed to dangers and unforeseen calamities of nature than it was half a millennium later, but the tone that pervades this literature is that the Gods in heaven control human life and man can always placate them with laudatory, hymns, delicious oblations and libations in sacrifices. Generally, the Gods were benign and well-meaning, life was very much worth living as long as possible, nature was beautiful and bountiful and life was a joyous affair. Slowly but steadily with the inflow of plenty in agricultural production, cattle tending, resumption of maritime trade via the Middle East to the Graceo-Roman world, wealth increased. "The total complex[3] indicates that the people of the PGW[4] culture at the site had developed iron technology from the very beginning. They were also able to mine iron ore in a considerable quantity which enabled them to produce tools and implements in abundance. They were thus able to clear the land of tropical vegetation and bring it under extensive cultivation and started cultivating wheat in addition to rice, barley and pulses. They also engaged in trade without which they could not have acquired so much metal or beads of semi-precious stones. These observations, thus further strengthen

---

1 In his article 'Ecological Dimensions of Ancient Indian thought.'

2 Jash (ed.), 1984, p. 351.

3 at Atranjikhera.

4 Painted Grey Ware.

the view that the period represents the culture of the Aryans at least of the later Vedic period."[5] This affluence sharpened the class division and more clearly underlined the irrational fact of one section in society enjoying a greater measure of plenty and enjoyment than the toiling masses.

Tribal life disintegrated, the joint family emerged as the social unit. When the Aryans had defeated and chased away the pre-Aryans from northern India, they captured many of the defeated people and forced them into slavery. Much of the heavy manual labour devolved on these slaves leading to the creation of a leisured class at the top. Society had been divided into the four varṇas (brahmins, kṣatriyas, valśyas and Sūdras) much earlier. With time, the combination of the various professions with the several varṇas gave rise to castes, 'jātis', which connoted both birth in a particular group and the practice of a particular profession. Now with the accumulation of wealth in the hands of the non-producing leisured section there was a further division - classes came into existence. The leisured masters devoted themselves to intellectual pursuits while the subordinate class did manual labour. The first were a handful compared to the vast numbers of the tillers and craftsmen whom they controlled. Relevant to this topic is the subject, how evil entered the society; there is a curious statement in the Dīgha Nikāya Suttanta[6] which says that in the beginning society was peaceful and harmonious. Evil entered it through greed and invention of agriculture, private property, trade, theft, falsehood and every other kind of wickedness. It seems possible to assume that this passage portrays the Indian society of the eighth and seventh century B.C. or perhaps somewhat later—say the early sixth century B.C. when widespread agriculture, trade and commerce brought in surplus wealth in the hands of the few, while the masses remained poor. Inexplicable actions and experiences did not tally, hence a space was created which demanded clarification. "Bafflement, suffering and a sense of intractable ethical paradox are,... if they are intense enough, or long enough, radical challenges to the proposition that life is comprehensible and that we can, by taking thought orient ourselves effectively within it—challenges which any religion, however 'primitive' which hopes to persist must attempt somehow to cope."[7] Herein

[5] Ghosh (ed.), *An Encyclopaedia of Indian Archaeology*, p. 26.

[6] Nos. 26, 27; also in Chinese Taisho No. 1, sultas 5 and 6.

[7] Geertz, 1973, p. 100.

lies the initial surrender of the common people to a section of society which assumed the role of its mentor. It is not true to say that the people swallowed every concept that was served to them. Some of their protests and questions have found place even in the corpus of the orthodox text. Thus the *Taittirṣya* Saṃhitā retains a very significant question regarding life after death: "It is not easy to pass from this world of men, they say, who knows if it exists in that other world or not."[8] The *Kaṭha* Upaniṣad also expresses scepticism regarding the existence of the next world: "This doubt among men (regarding) life after death. Some say it exists, others, that *it does not* ..."[9] Belief in life after death, the very starting point in most religions, thus becomes controversial. There are hundreds of cryptic or clear statements of doubt (as Tennyson says, "There lives more faith in honest doubt." In Memoriam XCV st 3) which contains faith in life and these not only gave rise to some materialistic schools of philosophy but challenged dogmas propounded by the hieratic authors and later, as we shall see, challenged fatalism itself.

> A conviction that the mystery that surrounds human life will never be completely unveiled appears again and again... at times they[10] convey pessimism and even a sort of natural sceptism. Their core question seems to be whether or not it is possible to say true words about the beyond, the universe of the Gods or one's survival of death.[11]

This scepticism and the scriptures framed by priests and lawgivers created a tension out of which slowly grew what is known as Hinduism, the religion which incorporates doubts and faith, pessimism and optimism or in other words life-negating and life-asserting views. This creative tension is at the base of the faith in human effort, 'puruṣakāra' which seriously challenged fatalism. Meanwhile, many changes in the conceptual world were generated by changes in the material life of the people.

With slaves taking over most of the manual labour in the affluent families, women were released from much of the heavy household chores as well as work in the fields. Besides, quite early after the advent of the Aryans, intermarriage between Aryans and non-Aryans began. As Aryan men married

---

8 VI: 1: 1: 1.

9 I: 1: 20.

10 Such convictions.

11 *Macmillan Encyclopaedia of Religion*, Vol. 9, p. 404.

non-Aryan women, the investiture ceremony of die holy thread (*upanayana*) was denied to women presumably for fear of the Aryan lore being shared by non-Aryans. As this ceremony granted the right to education, women were naturally debarred from education. So there was a further division of privilege—this time, gender-based. Education became the right of the affluent males of the three upper castes. This was the time when priestcraft became an exclusive province of the males of the privileged educated brahmins. All compositions were Initially orally composed and orally transmitted, preserved as a treasure in the top echelon of the society. Priests promulgated social laws and liturgical rules for sacrifices.

Most possibly there was a section among the pre-Aryans who lived as mendicants, either roving or stationary; these did not follow the rules of the customary four āsramas.[12] There must have been interaction between the dominant population and the nonsacrificing hermit orders. People living in society noticed the wealth-based dichotomy and the discrepancy in the allocation of power. The quality of life for the vast majority was poor, bordering on destitution. Now, the priests and social lawgivers had to explain the anomalies. These religious lawgivers took upon themselves to comment on existential evils in terms of religion which really began to be clearly formulated in the later Vedic age. "Religion is (1) a system of symbols which acts to (2) establish powerful, pervasive and long-lasting moods and motivations in men by (3) formulating conceptions of a general order of existence and (4) clothing these conceptions with such an aura of factuality that the moods and motivations seem uniquely realistic."[13] In the late Brāhmaṇas and in the Upaniṣads we hear of recurrent 'deaths' which gradually assumed a more delineable contour and emerged as the theory of transmigration. "When the entire social structure and even the cosmos is felt to be inauthentic, as in late antiquity, mediumistic ecstasy may lend to apocalyptical predictions of the end of the age, the united protest becomes radical and explicit ... the speculative effort must usually begin in court and *priestlycircles*, for it depends on a cumulative effort of generations and a specialized learning of which in most early civilizations, only centralized priesthood was capable."[14]

---

12 Four stages of life: student, house-holder, forest-dweller and roving hermit–brohmacarya, garhasthya, vanaprastha, yati or sannyasi, of these the last two were added in the later Vedic period.

13 Geertz, 1973, p. 90.

14 *Macmillan Encyclopaedia of Religion*, p. 378, italics added.

When religious leaders and lawgivers rose to prominence, they expounded religion to the people to suit the needs of the poor masses seeking spiritual consolation, an affluent minority seeking assurance against protest or molestation and for security, also for the priests themselves to profit in pelf and power. Why would the common people accept the teaching of the priests? "Religion must be viewed against the background of the insufficiency or anyway *the fell insufficiency of common sense*, as a total orientation toward life; it must also be viewed in terms of its formative impact upon common sense ; the way in which by questioning the unquestionable, it shapes our comprehension of the quotidian world of what there is, in which whatever different drummers we may hear or may not hear, we are obliged to live."[15] Because religion makes the everyday life better explicable to man that man heeds its tenets.

The same thing happened among the Jews. The first urbanization led to rise of cities with a more organized priestcraft. "Whatever conditions permitted, rabbis sought to institutionalize their authority over the community. In the early period, this meant reaching an accomodation with the real rulers of the community. Later it meant assuring that internal Jewish courts should be dominated by rabbis."[16]

The role of priestcraft is, however, much less pronounced because intermediation between the Gods and men did not figure so prominently. Nearer to magic than the city-based orthodoxy of the Great Tradition, "a crucial ingredient in the folk religion is *the immediate presence and access to a God or goddess...* which may be aniconic or iconic. The God exists here and now."[17] It is this very intermediary's role which enhanced the significance of the urban priesthood which multiplied its own hierarchy and its functions; villages around cities were influenced by the growing magnificence of the hieratic class; imbibed and imitated them.

If the common people could see a direct correspondence between their actions and their experience of good and evil, there would be no spiritual space left for this intermediary section.

Even in the pre-urban stage socio-ethical authorities were vested in the priesthood along with many other functions and privileges, "...the embryonic

15 Geertz, 1988, p. 95, italics added.

16 *Macmillan Encylopaedia of Religion*, Vol. XIV, p. 259.

17 Sonthelmer and Kulke (ed.), 1989, p. 4.

structure of the city already existed in the village. House, shrine, cistern, public way, agora... all first took form in the village... The beginnings of organized morality, government, law and justice existed in the village council of Elders... In an oral culture only the aged have had enough time to assimilate all that is to be known."[18] From among the aged came the lawgivers. Respected because of superior experience they were regarded as equipped with the necessary spiritual depth, knowledge, foresight and hindsight, they were invested with the task of laying down rules for the smooth running of the government and society. These elders[19] later from among the upper castes were held responsible for (a) guidance in the quotidian life and also in crises and (b) to spell out the teleology and ontology to justify their mandates. In other words, to frame a religio-metaphysical paradigm which would justify their mandates and make them acceptable to the people.

Feudalism has a disputed connotation in the context of India. If we agree to admit that in an incomplete and rudimentary form it existed after the arrival of the Aryans and even after the racial and cultural amalgamation between them and the pre-Aryan peoples and that there emerged a crude form of feudalism, then this had a different character; caste played a significant role in it. The brahmins, custodians of socio-religious law were at the helm of affairs. "In the period of feudalism the source of support for the majority of Brahmins became not so much the fulfilment of priestly obligations as service in the administrative apparatus, the courts and land ownership."

"It is beleived that the oldest class society existed in the Indus Valley in the second half of the third millennium B. C. and lasted somewhat longer in Gujrat. ...In the society of the Vedic Aryans there was private ownership of cattle, movable property, slaves and household plots. There was a tribal aristocracy that gained increasing power over the common members of the tribe."[20] The additional socio-political power enjoyed by the brahmins at the court and in society endowed them with a charisma which 'validated' their claims of justifying the ways of God to men. True, the earliest Upanisadic evidence asserts that the theory of rebirth originated among *Kṣatriyas* but quite early the brahmins assimilated and usurped the idea; they worked on it, expounded and embellished it and within a couple of centuries augmented

[18] Mumford, 1961, p. 19.

[19] From 'sanal—old, long-lived, of Latin 'senatus', council of old men.

[20] *Great Soviet Encyclopaedia*, Macmillan, Vol. IV, p. 50.

the theory of karman to it, thus attributing to it distinct characteristics which later lent themselves to fatalism easily. But of that later. There may be some truth in the idea that rebirth is a product of agriculture; a seed sown in the ground sprouts up as a plant after some time—this may have engendered the belief that death is not the final stage of life. The seed-plant regeneration may have been easily transferred to the human level and rebirth was formulated and accepted. Death as the ultimate end is difficult to accept, the human mind cannot handle the void. Besides rebirth may have been part of the creed of the agricultural Indus Valley people from whom the Aryans may have imbibed the doctrine gradually and slowly after learning the art of agriculture. By itself, at first it offered consolation and life with an additional mystique. It was only when karman was attached to transmigration that an elaborate doctrine was posited which brought other issues in its train.

The first significant premises was the formulation of the rebirth and transmigration theory. The early Upaniṇads rest with the idea of transmigration with the new emphasis on life being continued beyond death in different bodies. Then in the next age, to transmigration was added karman which was linked not only with the successive births but happiness and misery, the events of life. On one plane it was more satisfactory as it boosted the human ego by positing that man was the architect of his own fate although there was no clearly delineable direct correspondence between man's karman and its effect on the course of his life, "...the non-historical, timeless notion of external existence in the form of millions of successive incarnations, is morally less satisfying than the determinist or fatalistic teachings of the Mediterranean religions which when the chips ire down, uphold the notion that God chooses some and rejects others. ...On the purely religious side...the Indian alternative is rather more palatable in the explanation of human suffering and in assigning moral choices to the individual rather than to some divine decree."[21] But once karman was linked to rebirth the resulting theory landed in real metaphysical and ethical difficulties. Hence the earliest Indian fatalist Gosāla says, "There is no such thing as exertion or labour or power or energy or human strength; all things are unalterably fixed."[22] Not only Ājṣvikism but Cārvāka and his followers also questioned some early priestly premisses. "It is... also important to note that the Cārvāka materialists

[21] Bharati, 1978, p. 42.

[22] Uvāsagadasāo i: 97: 115.

did raise significant objections against the idea of necessary relation between the antecedent and the consequent as the basis of the idea of causality. They point out that there is no ontological or logical connection between them. It is merely imagined to be there as a habit of thought."[23] But classical Indian thinkers hold that the causal relation between karman and effect is firm and thus fate can be ruled out. "It is wrong to identify the doctrine of karma with fatalism. Karma is not an external destiny driving man to his doom, nor a blind mechanical framework from which there is no escape."[24] But if fate is not a valid assumption, then the prior dogmas of karman, its effect and rebirth also become uncertain. But 'Karma', says Karl Potter, "must be an assumption and *cannot be proved by any of the valid means of knowledge...* The last problem for which karma offers a solution is the one most frequently pointed to: the problems of inequality and evil, of why there are such great differences among men in spiritual and mental capacity or why men occupy different places within the socio-economic order. The spiritual and intellectual differences between jīvas are the result of their conduct. The place in society they occupy at any time is the result of their past action."[25] But actions do not produce uniform results, hence the assumption of an unknown quantity viz. fate, under the deterministic aspect of fate, "...every deed is recorded separately, and each must result in a reaction (reward or punishment) suited to the nature of the deed. Good deeds cannnot cancel bad deeds, although the greater the number of good deeds, the greater the number of pleasant events to be ordained by the head-writing. The role of the head-writing in theory, is to determine what karma will be activated, that is, attain fruition, in a particular life-time. Not all deeds performed in one life-time bear karmic fruit in the next life-time. Some are deferred to several lifetimes."[26]

Buddha declared that there can be no wiping out of intentional deeds done and accumulated without experiencing the result thereof and these may mature either in this present state or in some other state hereafter. There is no end of evil resulting from intentional deeds done and the fruits accumulated thereof.[27] So that to work off the accumulated karmans, rebirth

23 Balaslev, 1983, p. 20.

24 Mahadevan, Vol. I, 1954, p. 179.

25 Potter, 1963, p. 219, italics added.

26 Kayes and Daniel. 1983. pp. 39–40.

27 *Aṇguttara Nikāya,* VCC VI: 1–2: 13.

became an essential pre-requisite. By the seventh century B.C. this entire syndrome of karman—rebirth was in the air. What the Ājīvikas repudiated was the role of karman in the revolving wheel of rebirth.

Jainism, Buddhism and Brahmanism accepted the vital role of karman in moulding the pattern of rebirth. Yet there was a question of residue and the inexplicable element, the hiatus between the karman and its effect. This led to the inception of fatalism. Hence even the results of karmans are left indefinite, thus a faith in a dark force which controls human destiny is referred to in almost all religions and mythologies. Even in Meso-American literature signs of this belief are evident. "A conviction that the mystery that surrounds human existence will never be completely unveiled appears again and again in these compositions... at times convey pessimism and even a sort of natural skepticism. Their core question seems to be whether or not it is possible to say true words about the beyond, the universe of the Gods, or one's survival of death."[28]

M. Anesaki writing on transmigration in Buddhism says, "Theoretically Buddhism teaches neither the existence of the soul nor its transmigration but insists on its revolution or stream (saṃpsāra)... It amalgamated everywhere with the animistic conception of the soul whether human or other... it impressed the popular mind with a degree of fatalism, the belief that every event in one's life was the result of past deeds."[29] G. Dotten writing on Celtic religion says that there are two passages which dearly assert the belief in metempsychosis among ancient Celts. Caesar[30] tells us that the soul does not perish, but after death *passes from one body into another*. Diodorus completes the evidence of Caesar and states it precisely. "Among the Calatae the doctrine of Pythagoras prevails, that the souls of men are immortal and after a fixed number of years begin to live again, the soul entering into a second body (v: 28)[31] "... the same breath directs their members in another world."[32]

We know Empedocles' famous claim, "ere now have I been a youth, and maiden, a bush and a dumb fish in the sea." Scholars find cryptic and overt references to metempsychosis of various shades in the writings of the Orphics,

[28] *Macmillan Encyclopaedia of Religion*, Vol. 9.

[29] *Hastings Encyclopaedia of Religion and Ethics*, Vol. VII.

[30] *De Bell, Coll*, VI: 4.

[31] Lucan in *Pharasalia* I: 449–456.

[32] *Ibid.*, Celtic, p. 430; italics added.

Gnostics, pythogoreans, Dionysian, Eleusinian and other cults. From the end of the third millennium B.C. to the early Centuries of the Christian era, the belief in transmigration was in the air all over the Mediterranean world and also in Egypt. In India it survives through these millennia, arising with the first urbanization, lying dormant for about three or four centuries in the first millennium B.C., only to resurge in the Upaniṣads.

But before this happened, northern India had experienced the Greek, Pahlava, Scythian and Kushan invasions. All the invaders brought their own social order and religious beliefs and practices. The sixteen mahājanapadas which rose by the sixth century B.C. slowly disintegrated until the Maurya empire rose a couple of centuries later, after Alexander's invasion. The Scythians and after them the Kushans built up kingdoms; the Kushans actually built up a vast empire with communication with many peoples outside India. "The time between the composition of the *Satnpatha Brāhmana* and the rise of Early Buddhism saw extensive demographic and cultural changes in Magadha and the adjacent territories. Brahmanical penetration and dispersal in these areas have proceeded apace and within the Brahminical group great diversities in occupations and philosophical pursuits had taken place. Early Buddhism itself had seen a gradual but continuing change in the social composition of its votaries."[33] This was a melting pot, ideas, dogmas, beliefs and practices blended with each other, giving rise to an atmosphere seething with discontent, doubt and probing. Sacrifices continued sporadically but pūjā became the order of the day. The religio-philosophical area was rather sprawling, now expanding now shrinking, ever changing and absorbing new influences, building up a composite construct. The two steady verities were karman and rebirth. But even these accrued the third component, fate, in some theories, even though some others dispensed with fate. In Hie graph of fatalism at the apex is Gosāla's Ājvīkism which is absolute fatalism, where fate moves in its own mysterious way, totally independent of karman. At the base is Buddhism which, like the Semitic religions, does not believe in God or Gods. Brahmanism stands between these two positions: it has a mobile pantheon where new Gods come and old ones leave, but it firmly holds the theory of karman and rebirth. And fate. This fate as we shall see is both dependent on and independent of karman.

[33] Narain (ed.), 1980, p. 68.

Socially it is a concomitant of the rise of the city, which in India first took place some time during the third millennium B.C. We have no record of that stage but it could not have been basically different from other countries.

> As far as the present record stands, grain cultivation, the plow, the potter's wheel, the sailboat, the drawloom, copper metallurgy, abstract mathematics, exact astronomical observation, the calendar, writing and other modes of intelligible discourse all came into existence at roughly the same time, around 3000 B.C., give or lake a few centuries. Together with the city, grew a whole complex machinery of many institutions.

Not merely the priesthood, but a new intellectual class, thus came into existence, the scribes, the doctors, the magicians, the diviners "as well as the palace officials who dwell in the city and have taken an oath to the Gods."[34] Once the city began to function as the nerve-centre of a complex of villages, the priests and the intellectuals, released from primary production became the ideologues for the masses. Since, in however rudimentary a form, laws were framed for the administration, conceptually the backlog of bad karmans appeared like unpaid debts which had to be repaid, if not in this life then in some future life. By the same token, since reward and punishments were meted out by the judges, the good or bad karman also earned happiness and misery to be experienced in this or in some other life. Heaven and hell were but imaginary replicas of the rewards and torments which the subjects experienced from the landlords or kings.

From the Kushan times or possibly from a century or two earlier, a new composite religion had come into vogue, with its icons, temples, different oblations and libations, pilgrimages, vows, etc. Gods were slowly but steadily changing their Vedic function of granting mundane bliss—longevity, cattle, children, wives; victory, plunder, health and a happy and prosperous life on earth. All this and liberation. Not only did the object and manner of worship change but the objective of life also changed: from a desire for a long and cheerful life on earth[35] people now sought release from the chain of births. This indirectly proves that for the majority, life had become miserable. With the class division and with wealth and prosperity becoming the share of a handful, the masses chafed in misery. The primary producers passed their lives in grinding poverty while the leisured class-whether priests, nobles or intellectuals—who

---

34 "As George Contend quotes a letter," Mumford, 1961, pp. 33, 38.

35 Incidientally this still remained in the catalogue of blessings solicited.

were divorced from actual productive activity now sneered at manual labour and became parasites who lived on others' labour. This set-up wait eminently conducive to the flowering forth of the theories of karman and fate.

The solemnity of the written text which accompanied the first and also the second urbanization is attested by the admonition of Ipu Wer(?2300–2050 B.C.) which reads, "The writings of the august enclosure (the temple) are read... the place of secrets... is (now) laid bare ... Magic is exposed." In Sumer magic came to be connected with medicine at a later period. Earlier medicine was an independent science: "Our ancient medical document... is entirely free from the magic spells and incantations which are a regular feature of cuneiform medical texts of later days; not a single deity or demon is mentioned in the text."[36] It is tempting to presume that in the earliest texts Kramer speaks about belonging to a pre-urban stage when magic, fate, demonology were kept outside the scope of medicine. Later, with the full floruit of urbanism of which the cuneiform writing is associated with magic, came into its own. And with it Gods and demons and fate. Magic or miracle is "a violation of the laws of nature" supported by human testimony and sustained by belief as Hume says in his *Concerning Human Understanding* (p. 10). St. Augustine says, "when anything is done outside the order of created nature by a power unknown to us it is called a miracle as regards ourselves."[37] We must bear in mind that the early man's knowledge of nature was based on observation and a large sector of nature remained beyond his ken. When something is unexperienced before or inexplicable to his range of knowledge he would call it a miracle and look upon it with awe and wonderment. With time and with the enlargement of the horizon of man's scientific knowledge, the number of miracles dwindled, ghosts and spirits faded away and 'magic' became scientifically explicable. But in those early days belief in magic was widespread; We are now talking of the first urbanization when magic had entered man's quotidian life, so to speak.

This is an age when oral composition and transmission of knowledge were being replaced by writing, when written documents were jealously guarded, when magic ensured the priests of an abject acceptance by the people; when disregard of the priests' authority was truly a sacrilege whose enormity is comparable to the divulgence of top state secrets today. These priests prophesied, acted as oracles, interpreted dreams and omens, performed

[36] Kramer, 1963, p. 97.

[37] *Sumuna Theologine,* 1: 110: 4: 2; also in *City of God* 21:8.

as haruspices, augurs and necromancies. They claimed to be clairvoyant and this drew absolute obedience and surrender from the people, endowed the priests with awe and charisma. And the priests, in most cases were hand-in-glove with the king and the nobility; this mundane power augmented and magnified their spiritual authority.

In their attempt to explain fate they introduced fate, the unknown and unknowable, man's experience of the discrepancy between his conduct and his portion of luck and ill-fate, made him prone to accepting this explanation.

> City life and its ever greater differentiation between the fortunes of families and individuals and those of other families and individuals encouraged feelings that special success was due to a God's personal interest in a man and his family, while conversely, misfortune would seem to be due to the God's abandonment of his ward for some reason or other. Thus the term for having luck became 'to acquire a God'. Since no achievement necessarily implied such intervention, the close connection between the personal God and success could not but raise problems, for experience showed that virtue was not always rewarded, rather a virtuous man might fall ill or suffer other miseries such as should have happened to evildoers only. The obvious solution, that the virtuous man unwittingly must have offended his God, was accepted in a measure and prayers often asked for enlightenment as to how a sufferer has sinned, so that he could do penance and mend his ways; but as a general explanation, it did not carry full conviction and the vexing problem of the righteous sufferer arose.[38]

This account of Babylonian history of the connection between city life, the priest's role and fatalism is clearly brought out.

"Fate ... the absolutely inscrutable power to which all men arc subject and may be either personified or represented as Impersonal. It is a conception which prevails whenever the mind of man is unable to frame the idea of rational necessity or of a supreme purposive will, and it survives so long as either of these, though within the field of consciousness is imperfectly realized."[39]

The first social schism which slowly but steadily ushers in a new parameter, the division between spirit and flesh was essentially ethical-

---

[38] *Macmillan Encyclopaedia of Religion*, Vol. 9, p. 456.

[39] *Hastings Encyclopaedia of Religion and Ethics*, Vol. V, 'Fate'.

metaphysical in character. "... a second parameter, the parameter of hierarchical subordination, the letter is subordinated to the spirit... Here the danger is that the element of subordination may be pushed to the point that the inferior may lose its autonomy and in quasi-monophysitic fashion be absorbed by the hierarchical superior."[40] In a class-divided society spiritually controlled by a priestly section, the subordination of the inferior by the caste–class superior often likes the form of intellectual, ethical and spiritual subsumption. If the spiritual powers posits fate as the ultimate explanation of all experiential anomalies, then fatalism does become an accepted dogma. The śūdra, dāsa, mleccha, śavara, niṣāda, pullnda and śvapāka had been the underdogs for a long time. To these were added those of lowly professions and meagre means who could not, for the life of them understand the causal relation between their acts and their social existence. Lest their sense of discrepancy rouse them to rebellion, an apparently comprehensive and acceptable theory had to be formulated. This was done in three stages. First was rebirth. This life is not the last word about existence, so men had something to look forward to. Next was added the theory of Karman: as you sow, so will you reap; man is the architect of his own fate. Apparently, this has a more optimistic message. Man could mould his future lives. Scriptures told men, "this life is the fruit of your own karman. Born as a śūdra, dāsa, caṇḍāla? Never mind, serve the upper castes with abject servility and you will surely be reborn as one of those you covet." This bait worked. The third stage saw the accretion of the doctrine of fate. The obvious anomalies thus had a two-fold explanation: one's own work and what fate had in store for him. This unknown element was attempted to be subsumed under karman, but to make assurance doubly sure, it was postulated that, unknown to him a man accumulates a backlog of evil works which, like unpaid debts, had to be paid at some point, in some life. Or a store of unknown good works may shower fortune and felicity like a windfall on some because like the discovery of a hidden treasure-trove, these reward man for his own unknown merits and virtues. Together they inculcate the twin lessons of (a) acceptance of one's own fate, however miserable it may be as repaying old debts of evil karman and (b) not feeling malicious or even jealous of those whose evil ways do not prevent them from enjoying a gorgeously affluent and fortunate life. The unuttered lesson is: try and improve your lot through unquestioning service to the 'right' people and

---

40 Caspray, 1979, p. 113. italics added.

since nothing is final, you also may enjoy a windfall in some future life. The carrot of mundane pleasure is dangled so cleverly that it is difficult not to conform. As man saw it, fate brings undeserved misery to the innocent. It was the experience of the toiling masses who lived on bare subsistence and were forced to forego many of the necessities of life, that slowly engendered the belief that their fate was to toil and their social and religious superiors had the fortune to live on the labour of the masses. An Akkadian myth narrates the archetypal prototype in its primordial version. It is the tale of Atarhasis "... in the beginning the Gods themselves had to work for their food, digging the needed irrigation canal. They eventually rebelled, and Ea thought of the solution: *creating wan to do the hard work.* To that end a God was killed and his blood mixed into the clay from which man was to take form. The mother goddess gave birth to him and there was general rejoicing... Ninmah who had assisted Namma at childbirth, drank and boasted that she controls man's fortunes, determining whether they will be good or bad."[41] This account is a product of the first urbanization with its concomitant division of classes and the resultant attitude of sneer of the upper echelons of society for manual labour. The creation of man should be read as the creation of the toiling man whose labour the upper class exploits. And flourishes in the process. So the archetypal relation between man and God is one of servant and master, it is for manual service that the Gods created this lower order of workers. Not only that, the goddess Ninmah boasts that she holds the clue to man's fate which she controls absolutely. In this theology fate as a goddess is accomodated in the pantheon.

Why are we so keen on connecting fatalism' with urbanization? Because historical evidences testify to the simultaneous emergence of these two. There is "no evidence of any religiously central preoccupation with fate *in cultures preceding the earliest civilization* based on cultivation of cereals nor can we demonstrate any special religiously significant place provided for notions of fate in hunting cultures."[42] Fatalism thus is a concomitant of urbanization. The city provided some measure of physical security for its inhabitants but, as we know now, that by its very definition, at least three quarters of its population was divorced from primary production and were therefore, dependent on the tillers, mostly living outside the city. And inside, there was

41 *Macmillan Encyclopaedia of Religion*, Vol. 9, 456; italics added.

42 *Macmillan Encyclopaedia of Religion*, 'Fate', italics added.

class division and caste stratification which was increasingly getting stiffer. Then along with the chance of crop failure and natural calamities there loomed a large prospect of insecurity, the prospect of insubordination, even open rebellion by the masses.

We have noticed how the first urbanization in the ancient world brought in its train, first, a rudimentary, mythological fatalism. In India it has not left any direct trace because, the Indus Valley civilization has not left a large corpus of text and secondly, what has been left is not likely to yield any significant information; it seems the undeciphered script would only throw light on their material life; the seals, plaques, cylinder seals being primarily connected with production, trade and commerce. Invisibly, the ideas of the Indus civilization must have percolated through oral transmission and been assimilated in the composite Brahmanical culture.

"For her next cities her 'second urbanization', India had to wait for over a thousand years after the disappearance of the Indus cities—till the middle of the sixth century B.C.; which saw simultaneously the beginning of her historical period... The sixth century B.C. which was indeed a turning point for north India... the establishment of the janapadas itself was the result of the new society of the later Vedic age in which economic and political factors both played their part with the former perhaps remaining in the background to boost up the latter."[43] In India this age of the second urbanization saw the use of writing the dissemination of monastic ideas of various brands, the accumulation of private property, the disintegration of tribal society and its concomitant—a new type of social, ethical and spiritual unrest and a sense of insecurity. All this prepared the ground for the emergence of new ideas, beliefs, cults, sects and ritualistic practices. It took some centuries for the full flowering forth of what was in a rudimentary form at this time. But the spiritual turmoil that prevailed all over northern India was such that many mendicant sects arose out of the people disenchanted with the sacrificial religion. Mendicancy in some form or other had presumably been a latent legacy from the period of the first urbanization. Now with the sacrificial religion held at a discount, alternative forms of worship with their distinct texts and ritual raised their heads within a few centuries. But of that later. The prevalent mendicant tradition which flourished outside cities i.e. in the forest and among some roving sannyasin groups was a reaction to the sacrificial

[43] Ghosh, 1972, pp. 2, 13, 22.

religion which in their turn also interacted with these forest dwelling hermits, so that the last two stages (āśramas), 'vānaprastha' and 'yati' were evidently incorporated within the brahmanical.

> The śramaija tradition is intimately linked with the cities which rose on account of new technological developments, surplus agricultural produce, and resultant growth of trade and commerce. This urbanism led to material prosperity, conflict situations arising out of the problem of demand and supply, reaction against mechanisms of affluence, suffering on account of tensions of life and insecurity of the person, and also to a concern for the preservation of the fauna and flora, which were being destroyed by the rise of cities and self-indulgent savage rituals and games... some of the earliest descriptions of the planning and architecture of the cities of this second period of urban growth are found in Buddhist and Jain sources, not in the Brahmanic.[44]

The resistance to wanton waste of cattle wealth and in animal sacrifices at a time when because of the widespread use of the iron ploughshare more wealth could be generated with plough animals, the resistance to burning forests to gain arable land, the resistance to a large section of the deflated non-Aryan populace being reduced to slaves and servants around this time accounts for a new orientation in religious, metaphysical and social thinking and the introduction of new values and ethos. Foreign invasions between the fourth century B.C. and the third century A.D. also accelerated this transformation. "The blending process... had begun certainly by the sixth century B.C. which saw the rise of the Persian Empire and since then had passed through several distinctive phases. By the Lime one gets to the second century A.D. the large scale migration of ideas had been going on for so long, and often, so unobtrusively that in cases there is no awareness of 'taking over' anything at all."[45]

Gordon Childe in his article 'The Urban Revolution'[46] gives an account of the first urbanization dwelling on the size of the cities, their dense population, the transport of workers, merchants, officials and priests. The city centred around a palace and/or temple to which flowed the tiny surplus of the primary producers. One significant feature was the construction of

44 A. K. Narayan, Introduction to Har Dayai's *The Budhisutva Doctrine in Buddhist Sanskrit Literature*, pp. xxvi–xxvii.

45 Grant, 1961, p. 34.

46 In *The Town Planning Journal*, Liverpool XXI, April 1950, pp. 3–17.

monumental buildings which 'symbolize the concentration of social surplus'. The non-producing (except the craftsmen and at times a tiny section of agriculturists) population lived on the surplus generated by temples or royal granaries. Priests, war leaders and eminent citizens used a major share of the total surplus and together they formed the ruling class. This class in their own interest invented systems of recording and other 'practically useful sciences', like arithmetic, geometry and astronomy. The art of writing was invented in direct response to the new needs of society in Egypt, Mesopotamia, the Indus Valley and Central America. According to Childe the city provided its craftsmen with raw material. It had "greater homogeneity, more complex division of labour, more secular professional specialization, greater development of economy based on money, less organized kinship, less stringent social control and greater dependence on impersonal control institutions."

Most of these traits resurged at the second urbanization in India around the sixth century B.C. The process, once started kept rolling until the fifth century A.D. by which time it has assumed a definite shape. More precisely, between the Kushan and the Gupta age it went through a sea-change, especially during the second Bhārgava interpolation of the *Mahābharāta*'. It was this particular section composed by sectarian priests who wished to endow the theories of karman and rebirth with a final and abiding shape by augmenting them with the theory of fatalism. What could not be explained by either of the former fell within the scope of fatalism which together with those two created a paradigm which still persists in India.

Eschatology, heaven, hell, theories of liberation, meditation, expiation, pilgrimages, vows, temples with iconic worship in the spirit of devotion to a persona! redeemer God—as distinct from the earlier collective worship either as sacrifice or pūjā, charity, as a merit-earning gesture, exorcism, prophecy, oracle, the śrāddha, offering spiritual benefit to the departed, curses and boons as mediatory forces between the 'hagios' and the people, transference of merit, all these appeared one by one during roughly the four centuries when the Bhārgava interpolation was slowly accruing in different regions of India and assuming a composite shape in this redefined Brahmanism which went on being further elaborated in the Purāṇas. And through all this, fatalism has lasted for over a millennium and a half.

Fate by its very definition is inscrutable, but man as an intelligent animal has assiduously sought to pierce the veil of its mystique. His efforts in this direction are of two kinds; first, to gain presages and prognoses and secondly, to deflect the moves of fate through expiatory, placatory and vicarious moves. If fate is immutable, as theoretically it is, then all such efforts are "bound in shallows and in miseries." Yet they afford consolation to those afflicted by fate and also strengthen the moral and ritual hold of the hieratic section on the populace.

All through the epic-Puranic literature and through the Dharmasastras and Nibandhas the scriptures perform a three-fold task relentlessly: first, they emphasize the immutability of fate discursively and through tales and anecdotes and secondly, they prescribe methods of gaining foreknowledge of what is predestined; and thirdly, they lay down ways and means of appeasing, placating, thwarting and deflecting the course of fate. The inherent contradictions of these tasks is obvious, but man in his utter helplessness, pitted against an irrevocable fate refuses to admit such abject defeat. Hence these measures in the scriptures.

The second urbanization brought in its train the break-up of the tribal system, the rise of the joint family, 'kula', the prevalence of the monastic schools of different shades, surplus in agriculture leading to greater prosperity in trade and commerce, inland and maritime, the rise of an affluent class which together with the priests and intelligentsia had full command over the common people and for whose convenience exact sciences like arithmetic, geometry, astronomy and medicine, etymology and grammar originated and began to be cultivated. The city-dwellers were dependent on the supply of their food mainly on the villagers. The palace and the temple—with their individual entourage—joined hands in the administration of the city-centred principalities. In the field of ideas sacrificial religion was slowly but increasingly supplanted by pūjā and the scripture composed for this emergent religion—sectarian, cultic, soteriological—were the proto-Puranic section of the Bhārgava interpolation of the *Mahābharata*, the Purāṇas and Dharmaśāstras. The new antennae of this religion, vow, pilgrimage etc. were all subsumed under the vitally significant concept of fate—a characteristic of both the first urbanization around 3000 B.C. in the Mediterranean world. Egypt and China, as well of the second urbanization in India and elsewhere. It was a powerful weapon in the hands of the religious and secular rulers aiming at reconciling man to his fate—a fate which was increasingly deteriorating into a hostile force for the greater bulk of the population while the affluent power-wielders of society indulged in conspicuous consumption. The latter lived in mansions, ate, dressed and lived well; the resources of this well-being came from the toiling masses. The glaring discrepancy in the life-style had to be explained to the people to their satisfaction. To reinforce the karman theory and to strengthen it, late was brought in as the most powerful agent, an intermediary between Gods and men. The apparent injustices were thus ascribed to fate whose mysteries could not be unveiled or remedied. This clever device pacified the otherwise bewildered and potentially rebellious sufferers of injustice and enhanced the prestige and pelf of the priests and lawmakers. Cities generated this vicious narcotic presumably because city-life spelt greater threat of insecurity and misery of the bulk of the people.

But the heroic part of man refused to be daunted by the verdicts of fate. And these same scriptures give us instances—again discursively and anecdotally—of man asserting his own endeavour against a hostile fate. He emphatically asserts that he enjoys the freedom not only to will, but to execute what he wills and defeat fate in the process. Scriptures and priestcraft did their utmost to break his inherent pride of manhood and they have been largely successful in their effort: man has not clear-sightedly detected the mutually contradictory doctrines, or even if he has, he could not muster the courage to challenge the joint strength of priests, scriptures and the pressure of public opinion through the centuries. Again it is true, that although with the enhancement of man's knowledge of nature and mankind, much of what formerly was designated as fate is now known differently and is to some extent controlled by man, there is still the element of the unforeseen and unforseeable 'accident' over which man has no power. Natural calamities, wars and the commoner quotidian accidents will largely remain beyond the scope of man's power. So there will ever be an area where unforeseen dangers will lurk unobserved and overtake man unawares. But if we look at how much of the phenomena that a third millennium B.C. man took for granted as operations of fate, is now known to be otherwise and is under man's control, we feel amazed. In every generation the collective efforts of man defeats and banishes many so called incurable diseases, the individual will and effort achieves wonders in so many spheres of human life. What is really lacking is the collective goodwill and determination to banish misery from human society. Vested interests stand in the way and man will never stop hoping that with concerted effort, some day, fatalism as a formidable and insuperable force will be vanquished. Fatalism as an ideology is rooted in vested interests of the economic rulers of society, priests and lawgivers, whose threats and baits hold the ignorant man enthralled, who win in this game of power by fanning man's worst superstitions. These superstitions assume different forms in different regions and in different ages and go on multiplying. Here if anywhere, knowledge is power. And the right will is power. Once man sees through the dirty game of the religion's lawgivers and crafty politicians and determines to strive against their foul motives and put up a brave, and collective-fight, fatalism's fang will be broken. As a theory it is riddled through and through with fallacies, but in practice it still wields considerable power. Man has first to shatter the mystique that envelopes it by pointing out the basic illogic and self-contradiction. With this diagnosis the disease is half conquered. For the rest, man has to assert that except for accidents—which undeniably can assume formidable proportions at times—man's life is not predetermined, that he lives only once and carries no backlogs of karman and the course of his life is determined largely by himself and his social milieu, that there is no inscrutable power which decides his destiny, that his freedom of will is an unquestionable' and inalienable right which none can usurp. Once he takes this stand, he stands for the freedom which also entails the knowledge of limitations but which entirely frees him from the bogey of fate. His pride in himself, his power to him from the bogey of fate. His pride in himself, his power to will and achieve, is a boast he makes on behalf of all mankind, the glory of each bit of his success in defeating fate will redound to the glory of the human race.

CHAPTER 1

Inception

THE concept of fate is ubiquitous although it bears many names in different countries and ages possibly with subtle shades of difference in the connotation of each. Ancient India knew it as Daiva, Bhāgya, Niyati, Kāla, Vidhi, Vidhāna, Vidhilipi, Diṣṭa[1] Bhāgadheya[2], Bhavitavya (tā), Krtārita,[3] Acintya, Adṛṣṭa,[4] Yadṛcchā and Bhāvī. The *Atharvaveda* equates Kāla with Rohita. In Daṇḍin's *Daśakumāracarita* the Maskarins of the Ājīvika school call a fortune-teller, maskarin or kārtāntika.[5]

Early Sumerian literature calls fate Me or Mu; in Akkadian mythology Shimtu stood for fate. At the end of the second millennium B.C. the Mesopotamian epic; *Enutna Elish*[6] mentions the 'tablets of destiny' which it calls Tup Shimati or Dup Shimati. Babylon has a name for the natural order. 'Ma'at', Egypt knows destiny as Hathor Shai Rennet[7] who is a partial personification of destiny. The owner of the 'tablets of destiny', and hence, the final arbiter of fate was the foremost God in the pantheon. The God Anzu stole these tablets; this act disturbed the balance and harmony of the universe which was restored when the tablets were recovered. Enlil of Nippur was the arbiter of destiny for a time; later, when Marduk usurped the pre-eminent position, he possessed the tablets of fate. In Assyria the national God Ashur inherited the traits of the supreme God and automatically became the arbiter of human destiny. 'Ming' in ancient China was 'something spoken.'[8] or

1 More commonly in the instrumental from diṣṭyā, from diṣṭi.

2 *Cf Mbh* XII: 28: 18 ff, III: 273: 6.

3 Which, like Kāla also means death.

4 Can it be cognate of the name of the Greek Goddess Adrasteia?

5 Lit, he who can predict death.

6 Written down by 1000 B.C.

7 Shai is derived from the verb 'śa', the decide. But in Egypt the major gods like Re, Amon, Plah, Thoth, Khnum were all lords of fate.

8 Cf fate > 'fatecum' past participle of 'fari', to peak.

decreed; Ming meant to forecast the future. But there fate was not irrevocable; it could be escaped through divine intervention.

The Pahlavi language has the word 'bakhi' for fate; its cognates are 'bhakta' (Sanskrit meaning 'divided') > bhāga < (share) the root 'bhanj', to divide. The Persian word 'baghōbakht' also means fate. Here the meaning derives from the concept of sharing by casting of lots, and 'lot' is a synonym of destiny of fate, in the sense of what is allotted (by some superior power or arbiter), as the tribal leader shared the kill or the plunder among the members of the tribe by casting lots. 'Lot' comes from old English 'hlof portion'; it also means choice or decision. The concept may be reminiscent of nomadic tribal life of hunting plundering folks. The kill or the loot was shared by casting of lots. It was here that the tribe first learnt to associate 'lot' with the irrational share of good or bad falling to them un-accountably. These associations lingered in the unpredictability, unexpectedness, irrationality and irrevocability of fate. German 'Los' also meant casting of lots. The primitive hunters and plunderers knew that there would be the 'best' 'better' 'good' 'not-so-good' and 'bad' portions of the meat and the loot and that there would be no voluntary takers for the last two categories, so, to avoid bad blood inside the tribe, the people agreed to this lottery, hoping that today's ill-luck would be remedied by tomorrow's good luck. And if that did not happen, there was no one to blame but the lot which was blind, irrational and capricious. These conceptual associations persisted even after 'lot' had changed its semantic meaning from the tribal sharing to the invisible 'lot' sent down by a capricious mysterious power or 'God' from above. As in the primitive days, food or plundered articles changed the meaning of existence, so, later, what lot or fate ordained for men made visible modifications in human existence. People came to impute the tribal leader's function of casting lots to an invisible arbiter of human joys and sorrows who sat somewhere allocating shares of happiness and misery to the deserving and undeserving alike. Thus there was no expectation of a fair deal because fate was beyond justice and injustice.

Arabic calls fate 'Nasīb'. German Schicksal, fate, is derived from the root 'schicken' to send. Fate is thus that which is sent from above for mortals to enjoy or suffer.

Analysing the common characteristics of fate as it was believed in the ancient civilizations we find that whether they called it fate, fortune, chance or destiny it was regarded as (1) beyond human control (2) controlled by a superior cosmic power operative in the universe but particularly manifested in human experience (3) generally ineluctable, immutable, irrational and unaccountable i.e. not causally linked with any obvious action or event.

"Hesiod was the first Greek to give the fates names, a lineage, and a particular function. At one time he makes them unnamed daughters of Night and the sisters of Death; at another the daughters of Zeus and Justice, calling them Clotho (the spinner), Lachesis (the assigner) and Atropos (the unbending one) who snips the thread of life. They are said to dispense good and ill to mortals at birth, but like their sisters the Horae they also represent the principle of cosmic order."[8a] "The parcae or Tria Fata, as they were known in Rome, were invoked at a child's birth to write down his destiny in life."[9] In the many names with slightly differentiated functions, the Greek goddesses of fate resemble the many-faced image of fate in Indian mythology. The Roman Tria Fata perform the function of the Indian Great Tradition God Vidhātr or the Little Tradition goddess ¨aṣṭhī, who on the sixth day after birth writes the child's fate. Providence or Vidhi, a semi-abstract theophany of the Great Tradition is really in charge of the head-writing, hence, 'Vidhilipi'.

The equation of Kala with fate is brought out clearly in a passage, "All misfortunes and accidents are controlled by Kāla, and if Kāla is adverse and angry, how, then shall we escape?[10]Again, " it is impossible to know (what happens to man after death), not even the sages know it, let alone ordinary mortals."[11] The inscrutability of fate is here recognized in its darkest and most sombre aspect, viz. man's experience, if any, after death (Kāla). This very inscrutability again combines Time (cf after death i.e., after crossing that span of time which is known to man, his life) and Adṛṣṭa. Hence Kāla becomes one of the synonyms of fate. The first passage emphasizes man's complete ignorance, even the wisest man's epistemological limitations, and his total helplessness in the face of adverse fate.

Greek Atropos, Iranian Zurvan are conceptually linked with the Indian Kāla, Antaka and Kṛtānta (all of which mean time and death). Time has one yardstick of mensuration in human life viz. death, Kāla. Death thus becomes an essential conceptual constituent of fate. We shall return to this later. But

---

8a Greek 'Eileithiya' – 'Parca' (Roman).

9 *Encyclopaedia Americana*, Vol. II, p. 46.

10 Matsya P. 210: 5–7.

11 *Vāya*, p. 55: 63.

let us bear in mind that the *Matsya* Purāṇa, a late antiquity scripture, equates fate with death and time, in a series of names it catalogues.[12]

The first reference to the Erinyes, the vindictive aspect of fate is as old as the fifteenth century B.C. in the Linear B tablets of Knossos in Crete. Then comes Hesiod in the pro-classical Greece, as we have seen, he was one of the earliest authors to mention fate. He also calls them Moirai and at one place equates them with Clotho, Lachesis and Atropos. Spinning and weaving were two of the earliest arts civilization invented and which women practised; hence the identification of the three sisters who spun, measured and snipped off symbolized the span of human life as alloted by fate. The span is the length of material which was arbitrarily discontinued at one point by fate. A slight variant of the meaning of the imagery connected with 'fate as time' is noticed in the *Taittirāya* Brāhmana.[13] 'Two sisters weave tins cloth, eternal, spread over six rays, one throws out the filaments, the other catches them, neither does (the one) weave nor does the other finish (weaving)'.[14] The Moirai were, for that matter, also known simply as the spinners' Klothos'.[15]

Greece also had other divinities who represent fate. While Dike symbolizes justice and Themis stands for right dispensation, Hymarmene is simple fate just as Adrastaeia is. Tyche is derived from 'tynchano' to happen by chance.

Democritus explained life and creation by atomism but also admitted 'eudaemonia' or 'hedone' within his scheme. Later Diogenes Laertius equated God with 'nous', reason, fate that is Heimarmene and Zeus. Cleanthes staled that though all that corned through Providence is fated, yet this proposition cannot be inverted simply: all that is fated does not come from Providence.

Perhaps a real equivalent of the Indian concept of fate is Nemesis, entirely unpredictable yet prominently retributive in character. "Nemesis, of whom the violent rape by Zeus is recounted. The very name of the goddess referred to her character as an enraged avenger of the violence suffered."[15a]

---

[12] 102: 22; 107: 27; 135: 76; 136: 5. See also *Mārkaṇḍeya* P. VIII p. 80.

[13] A text slightly later than the samhitas.

[14] II: 1: 4; p. 60.

[15] Odyssey, VIII p. 197.

[15a] Jesi: 1964, Vol. 3, no. 2, p. 268.

To Aristotle, Tyche was subjective, so he distinguished between 'eutuchia' and 'dustuchia' according to whether it was fortune or fate. To Plato Tyche was a goddess, Theia Tyche; but, then, most synonyms of fate are conceptually personified and literature treats them as divine agents. Ananke, though not a proper deity, together with Asia, Ate, Themis and Phthos signifies envy or jealousy of a man's good fortune; they may not exult in man's good fortune. These theophanies bring man misfortunes till he is properly cut to his size. Ate and Alastar represent the spirit of the murdered one crying for revenge and retribution. It is interesting to note that in Greece as also in Sumer, Akkad, Assyria and Babylonia there is not a single God who represents all aspects of fate. A multitude of theophanies collectively function as fate. The reason may be sought in both time and place. Kingdoms and petty principalities which rose and fell periodically, introduced corresponding changes in the pantheon where yesterday's supreme God became subservient to today's chief God. Also, allegiance to Gods shifted and changed with time. In Vedic times there was not one God who symbolized Fate completely. Rudra-Śiva, Kāla, Yama are the three who come nearest to representing fate, but later literature abounds with abstract names of fate and with time, these abstractions dominated the conceptual scene, although the earlier Gods lived on. No one God or concept was adequate or comprehensive enough to satisfy the composite figure of fate which multiplied its attributes with rime. So, the concept of fate, wholly absent in the Saṃhitās,[16] makes its first appearance in the subsequent literature and by the time of the Purāṇas its name becomes legion.

Latin 'fatum' literally means something spoken with a shade of meaning bordering on the oracular. 'Fortune' in Latin literally means chance, although, with time, this sense shifted from 'fatum' and while the latter signified ill-luck, the former represented good luck. The Germanic Valkyries (nine in number) servants to Odin and the 'Uradr' (Urd) in Norse mythology have some connotative similarity.

In Iran Mazdeism acknowledged the supreme role of fate. "The activity of the whole world is carried on by Destiny... mid time and decision of fate which is itself Zurvan, the sovereign and long continuing ruler."[17] Manicheism which inherited much of Mazdeist ideas also held fate responsible for the good and evil which befall mortals. "In late antiquity gnosticism's doctrines of salvation

[16] With the dublous exception of 'Rohita, Kāla', in the *Atharvaveda*.

[17] Winston, *History of Religions*, Winter 1966, no. 2, p. 192.

show patterns with very striking resemblance to a fate beyond God."[18] Although in some religions and mythologies fate and the Gods interact, fate is commonly acknowledged to be a supreme power, superior to and beyond God. The logic behind this belief seems to be that if fate were amenable to placatory, laudatory or expiatory actions dedicated toward the Gods, then it would cease to be Fate. In this age we confront one of the many paradoxes associated with Fate. Strictly speaking, Gods and Fate cannot co-exist; one cancels the other out. But man's response to life and its experiences has always, everywhere been so confused that mutually contradictory entities have conceptually co-existed. We shall have occasion to explore such obvious anomalies regarding the concept of fate later in our study.

In the Orphic doctrines arising in Hellenistic Greece, fate was the law that controlled the conditions of man's birth, death and reincarnation, but by the fifth and fourth centuries B.C. Tyche is goddess became increasingly important. Pliny, too, admits of fate, "we are much at the mercy of chance and chance herself lakes the place of God."[19] Chance connotes probability, randomness, coincidence, contingence, accidence, incidence, fortuity, hazard, risk, opportunity, fortune, fate and automaton i.e. Tyche. All these terms have very thin lines of connotative demarcation between them, but they all presuppose, albeit negatively, that the universe as a rule functions according to some norm. This can be natural, ethical or religious, but chance connotes the absence of such a norm.

What is fate? There is not one definition, but all over the world and down all the ages of history there is a considerable area of agreement regarding the concept of fate. When a man is happy, when life is easy and pleasant for him, or he has some kind of windfall, he does not talk of fate but of fortune. Fate is thus inseparably connected with the reverse situation, mainly connected with suffering. The concept originated in experiences which appeared to man as underserved suffering, suffering that was prolonged and/or acute and essentially, not causally linked to any action of the agent. The concept was reinforced in a negative way, i.e., at the sight of an evil man enjoying a happy and prosperous life and of a righteous man suffering a miserable existence. Since neither the suffering nor the happiness could be causally related to the agent, both fate and fortune were recognized as fortuitous.

---

[18] *Macmillan Encyclopaedia* of Religion, 'Fate'.

[19] *Natural History*, II; 22.

Fichte, the German philosopher defending fatalism said that any fortuitous consequence is fatalistic, Schelling defines fatalism as a system which sees action and history as blind and predetermined, while to Schopenhauer fatalism is a basic truth.[20] Thus the three philosophers do not agree; while Fichte calls it a 'dogmatic sequence', Schelling regards it as 'a system', and Schopenhauer as a 'basic truth'. The West like the East was not only familiar with fatalism, it also thought of it as a 'system' or 'a basic truth'. In our investigation we shall see that most ancient cultures took fatalism quite seriously. India created a vast literature on fatalism that took various forms and assumed many names which kept growing in bulk.

Ājīvikism, possibly the first metaphysically propounded fatalism, was absolute and final i.e. fate to it was the ultimate referent regarding any event or even the entire course of human life. Its tenets hold that "there is no such thing as exertion or labour or power or energy or human strength; all things are un-alterably fixed."[21] Again, "there is no cause for depravity of lyings; they become depraved without reason or cause. There is no cause for the purity of being; they become pure without reason or cause... In short nothing depends on any human effort ... Their varying conditions are... due to fate."[22] Gosāla was thus the one and only true fatalist, a believer in the immutability of the principles which determine all things. Possibly around this time the *Śvetāśvatnra* Upaniṣad says, 'Kālahsvabhāvo niyaliryadfcchā'. Time, Nature, Fate and Determinism.[23]

Fate is a creation of man's imagination but it is a creation which is a direct outcome of many of his experiences and is, in turn, shaped by it. "If the power of destiny is regarded as impersonal, it is possible to enter into any kind of relationship with it ... the belief in a personal determiner of destiny produces religious behaviour ... But both of these attitudes occur together in one and the same person. In Greek and Teutonic religions destiny becomes acute." ... "It is man's reactions to what happens to him that forms the very kernel of the religious experience; he feels dependant, powerless and guiled; he seeks and finds perhaps a purpose or a meaning behind the events as personal, the result is a God; if not

[20] Ritter, *Historischer, Worterbuch des Philosophie,* p. 914.

[21] Uvāsagadasño 1: 97: 115.

[22] *Dīghamikāya* (PTS), Vol. 1, p. 53.

[23] 1: 2; Suśruta, in his section on sarūrasthāna quotes it in I: 11: 3.

it is fate or chance ... It is often not only its inexorableness but its capriciousness that gives destiny its character. In reality theism and fatalism are intertwined".[24]

We have seen that not only in the monotheistic Semitic religions but also in the polytheistic religions of ancient Sumer, Egypt, Mesopotamia, Greece, Iran and later in India, Fate and one or more providential God or Gods co-existed. In some religions these Gods act subserviently to fate; in others, fate under one or more names occupies a position in the pantheon, and in still others, Gods and fate share the ultimate power over human destiny. The desideratum common to all is the inexorability and the inexplicable capricious nature of fate, ubiquitously present in all climes and in all times. These two characteristics make fate a supremely formidable force, higher than man and virtually higher than most Gods. It is believed in most countries that any attempt to challenge or fight fate is doomed to failure, although everywhere human endeavour continues alongside the belief in fate. This is one proof that fate is but a projection of man's helplessness in the face of untoward, unexpected, undeserved occurrences for which he is wholly unprepared. So he calls fate capricious and yet challenges this caprice when he chooses so as not to have to surrender unconditionally to fate.

Most accounts of folk religions bear testimony to the existence of a belief in fate. The *Popol Vuh,* the *Florentine Codex,* Chinese folk religion texts all share this belief. Ichiro Haro corroborates this idea from the Japanese folk religion. "The idea of Mappō, according to Anesaki was based on a group of predictions offering a pessimistic view of fate long fashionable among Buddhists."[25] Thus whether in the Great Tradition or in the Little Tradition fate held sway. Whether the two traditions can really be separated distinctly is problematic, because of the continuous vital interaction between the two so that the one constantly influenced the other. Yet, if the written-down official religion is distinguished from the set of beliefs which was current, floating orally among the non-literate masses, the available evidences point to the existence of fatalism in both.

As we have stated in the beginning of this chapter, the four Saṃhitās are quite silent about fate, as are most of the Brāhmaṇas. The prayers in the Saṃhitās generally assume the existence of a benevolent pantheon: Gods could be placated with hymns, suitable oblations and libations and induced

---

24 Ringgern, 1967, pp. 8, 10.

25 A Neoaki, 1974, pp. 101–2.

to bless and help men, see them through critical situations like battles, diseases and natural calamities. They could be persuaded to grant fertility in crops and cattle, plenty of wealth—much of which came from plundering the pre-Aryans—longevity and in the latest section of the *Ṛgveda*, a happy dwelling place after death. Life was good and covetable and ṛta, a rational norm controlled the universe; hence the general attitude was one of hope, faith, buoyancy, reliance and optimism. Such a view of life did not offer much scope for fatalism.

Other ancient civilizations especially Sumer, Akkad, Assyria, Babylonia, China, Iran, Mexico and Greece, even during the age when the Saṃhitās were being composed in India, offer plenty of evidence of a belief in fate—a power which controls human life but which was itself beyond human control. These civilizations testify to the first stage of urbanization which produces a different ethos, a different set of values and a different attitude to life. The pastoral nomadic Aryans cherished and carried with them the new ethos when they arrived in India. From the joyous optimism which prayed for 'a hundred-year span of a happy life', so that they could 'see the rising sun every day', it is a long cry to the pessimistic terror-stricken attitude imbued with awe and apprehension about a formidable power whose operation was incalculable, hence fearsome. If the Indus Valley people believed in fate—as a people of the first stage of urbanization they most probably did—we have no record of their creed. "One might guess that the pre-Aryan occupants of the Valley of the Ganges were believers in something like a primitive notion of rebirth."[26] This belief may have been more widespread than merely over the Ganges Valley and could have earlier encompassed the Indus Valley also, although when we first meet it in the later Brāhmaṇas the Aryan's were already present in the upper Ganges Valley and they could have imbibed it there from the indigenous people. The Indus Valley people have left no written literature and the oral literature which they must have cultivated was swamped and slowly but surely assimilated by the invading Aryans. There is an indirect proof to this; within half a millennium after the advent of the Aryans they absorbed this belief which surfaces in the later section of the Brāhmaṇas and more palpably in the Upaniṣads. But let us not forget that during this time northern India experienced the second urbanization—one of whose concomitants was fatalism, as the first urbanism in the Middle East,

[26] *Macmillan Encyclopaedia of Religion*, Vol. VI, p. 128.

the Mediterranean and China testifies to. It is arguable that ideas of fate may have grown independently of the influence of the indigenous people who lived in bronze age urban culture, but at the same time the Aryans also slowly imbibed urbanism. Huts made of kiln-baked bricks, agriculture, primary trade and the slow but steady break-down of the tribes and tribal values, the emergence of a parasitic cluster of people who controlled cultivation, arts, crafts, plied trade and commerce but who did not till and grow food crops and, therefore, had to depend on people living in areas surrounding the townships for their subsistence. These areas—whether in agriculture or in cottage industries and crafts—became divided into two sharply different groups: (i) primary producers and (ii) users, buyers, sellers and traders of the primary products. This was the class division, unknown to the invading pastoral nomads but steadily recognizable in the contours in the society of the townships which were reflected in the later Vedic literature.

With the introduction and later with the widespread use of iron ploughshares in the middle of the first millennium B.C., the rise of townships, especially the sixteen big kingdoms (the ṣoḍasa mahājanapadas of the early Buddhist literature) became an established fact. The Aryan ethos changed sharply; the tribal values gave way to the values of the joint families (kulas) which was now the social unit with its individual holding of arable land, a certain number 'owned' cattle with a grazing lot assigned to each family i.e. private property in cattle tending. Agriculture became easier with the use of the iron ploughshare, larger 11 ids were brought under cultivation so that surplus arose and the class division became sharper with time. Now the values which dominated this amalgamated population of pre-Aryans and Aryans were shared by both. One by-product of these new emergent values was a belief in fate. We shall come back to this. But for the present let us bear in mind that in the Saṃhitās we do not have a trace of fatalism; it surged in the succeeding period.

When Lewis Mumford says: "... the most precious collective invention of civilization, the city, second only to language itself in the transmission of culture, became from the outset the container of disruptive internal forces"[27] he has a wide connotation for disruption. One of its disruptive functions was class stratification with the formation of a leisured class entrusted with the spiritual guardianship of the people. Although the village, too, had its priests,

---

[27] Mumford, 1961, p. 53.

the city priest was qualitatively somewhat different, enjoying closer contact with the ruler and nobility, performing collective sacrifices with pomp and splendour, directing the people in their mundane and religious life, for both of which his mandates multiplied rapidly. One of his contributions was to give shape to the peoples' inherent dark fears about a force which controlled their lives. The priest gave it a name, 'fate,' and reserved a dark impenetrable area in the invisible divine and chthonic realms where man's destiny takes shape.

CHAPTER 2

Rebirth and Transmigration

OF the two major formative ideas viz. rebirth and karman which constituted the core or basis of fatalism in India, the first to appear was rebirth. And, interestingly enough, at its inception it was not recurring births, but recurring deaths. And even more strangely, this conceptual chapter opens not for man but for the Gods and has an element of teleology inherent in the episode. The *Śiatnpatha* Brāhmana broaches the subject: "Now indeed the Gods were at first mortal, only when they gained the year did they become immortal."[1] "Through the sacrifices the Gods became immortal. Death was scared: 'what shall be my share?' They reassured him, 'From now on none shall be immortal in the body... They who know this or do this holy work come to life again, when they have died; and coming to life, they come to immortal life. But those who do not perform this act come to life again and again."[2] "If one does not offer these oblations then one gets (i.e. meets) death in the different worlds."[3] More concretely this age knew one form of death, namely hunger. Hunger is a living death, "by death, by hunger was everything pervaded, hunger is death."[4]

So we have a few basic tenets regarding rebirth: (1) it first threatened the Gods and when Death was alarmed at the prospect of losing his share of food viz. the victims of death, (2) the Gods laid down two principles (a) the gaining of the year and (b) the performance of certain sacrifices, by which (3) they became immortal with a solemn assurance to death that 'from now on none shall be immortal in the body.' Needless to say, this applies to men alone because the Gods had already attained immortality. So men could perform sacrifices and gain immortality after they had died at least once. One

1 XI: 1: 2: 12.

2 *SB* X: 4: 3, 9, 10.

3 *TB* III. 9: 15: 53–56

4 *SB* X: 6: 5: 1.

remembers that the God Yama also died in the body before attaining heaven: 'Yo mamāra prathamo martyāhām.'[5] And finally, hunger was one form of death; it is not for nothing that the Upaniṣads keep harping on *aśanāyāpipāse,* hunger and thirst, as two of the most formidable enemies of mortal men. Food was scarce for the masses, so hunger was a bitter reality and it carried many to death in those days of inadequate production.[6]

But with one physical death the fearful experience of death could not be overcome. "Even after dying (a man) is subject to further death, being devoured by his own works."[7] "A man leaving this world is born again; that is his third birth."[8] "Know him with the mind and the heart, O wise man, so that, you are not subject to death any more."[9] The *Śatapaihta* Brāhmaṇa mentions recurring lives;[10] the *Kaṭha*-Upaniṣad mentions recurring deaths[11] for those who believed that there was nothing after death. Rebirth could be either in the human shape or in a sub-human shape.[12] "Man dies like crops and is reborn like crops."[13] "Rebirth is inevitable for those who die without realizing Brahman."[14] "The next life and one's station in it are determined by one's desire."[15] The prolonged imagery of the fig, the pipal and the mango tree renewing their life after senescence[16] or the water-worm leaping from the edge of one leaf to another are brought in to prove rebirth as an accepted tenet.

After the Brāhmaṇas and Upaniṣads which posit the theory of rebirth for the first time in the history of Indian thought and literature come the Pāli

---

5 *Atharvaveda* XVIII: 3: 13.

6 The *Śouva* Upaniṣad in the Chhāndogya comes to mind where a pack of hungry dogs perform a mock rite to stall hunger.

7 *TĀ* 1: 8: 6.

8 The first is physical, the second *upanayana* and rebirth after death is the third. Ait. Ār. 11: 5: 1.

9 *TĀ* X: 63.

10 III: 1: 2: 21.

11 1: 2: 6, 11: 34: 11: 27.

12 *Katta* V: 3: 37.

13 *Ibid.,* I: 1: 6.

14 *Ibid.,* II: 3: 4.

15 *Ibid.,* III: 2: 2.

16 *Ibid.,* I: 2: 9.

Jātakas composed towards the end of the first millennium B.C. These, by and large accept rebirth as a part of the credo and offer many and various instances of rebirth of (1) Buddha in different forms and stations and (2) other beings being reborn in various shapes in successive births. The Jātakas also theorize on rebirth. The very first jātaka, the Āpaṇṇaka says that the righteous are never reborn into hell but are released from rebirth into states of suffering, they pass into the realms of the Gods. The *Āditta* jātaka generalizes saying, that lowly duties i.e. works, win in the next birth, a man a princely fate on earth; middle duties win him heaven and the highest duties win him a pure state.[17] The *Kaṭha* text which says that a man is reborn according to his desire[18] is borne out by the *Śaṅkhapāla* jātaka (no 524) where the Mithilā prince saw his father's nāga friend and desired to be born as a nāga in his next birth, as *Śaṅkhapāla*. Again, the childless pious queen of Kāsī, Caṇdādevī prayed for a pious son. Sakka was looking about for a suitable station for a Bodhisattva who had suffered eighty thousand years in hell and he sent him as the queen's son.[19] Again, there was a rich brahmin in Vārānasī who was childless. His wife prayed hard, Buddha descended as her eldest child. Buddha was once born as a servant who gave away his own food to a Paccekabuddha with great reverence and begged that he be not born as a servant again. In the next birth he was born as a king.[20] Once again Buddha, born as a poor servant, practised extreme austerities and died with the desire of becoming a king. In his next birth he was born as prince Udaya.[21] Buddha told an ogre 'your past sins have made you an ogre.' On being slain the ogre was reborn and was shown five evil courses and chose a pious life.[22] The king of Vārānasī was so fond of meat that one day his cook, at a loss for procuring meat cooked a corpse. The meat sent a thrill through the king's body because he had been a yakṣa in the previous birth.[23] This brings out that attributes of a previous birth are carried on into the next. Similarly, a Kāsī queen who had been extremely vain about her beauty was punished by being reborn as

[17] No. 424.

[18] III: 2: 2.

[19] No. 538 *Temiyakumāra.*

[20] No. 415, *Kumamāṣapiṣḍa.*

[21] No. 421, *Gttagānātā* jātaka.

[22] No. 55, *PaÛcnbuddha* jātaka.

[23] No. 536, Kuṇāta jātaka.

a dung-worm in her next birth.[24] A rather unusual and not quite authentic jātaka says that Buddha 'was born under the star of a robber', so he robbed but escaped arrest as the famous prostitute Sāmā fell in love with him and procured his release in a cruel and inhuman way.[25]

Analysing the assumptions behind these and various other instances of rebirth in the jātakas we realize that they do not add anything to the views current about rebirth except expressing for the first time, that a man's works determine the nature and station of his next life. These jātaka stories all assume that (1) rebirth is inevitable for a man who is not completely detached (2) he can to some extent control his next life by (a) desiring and (b) deserving through appropriate actions (3) man can be reborn as man, animal or God and the reverse is also true.

The reason we devote so much space to the jātakas is because they, as early contemporary literature of the two great epics, formulate for the first time the connection between a man's deeds and his rebirth. A passage in the *Mahūbhārata* enunciates rebirth in its most rudimentary form, emphasizing, albeit suggestively, that man does not live only once. It says "man dies again, is born again, declines and grows old again, solicits and is solicited again, mourns and is mourned for again. Happiness, sorrow, being and not-being, profit and loss, death and life—one touches all these in turn, hence the heroic soul neither exults nor grieves."[26] By the same logic, caste system is obliquely justified; when a śūdra properly worships brahmins, kṣatriyas and vaiśyas and when these are pleased, the śūdra on relinquishing his body ceases to suffer and enjoys heavenly bliss.[27] And again, a soul moving through different lives, being born again and again, in due course and at some point is born as a brahmin.[28]

The Buddhist work *Madhyamakosūtra* has an anecdote about a tax-gatherer who lived a dishonest life. When he realized that death was imminent he sent for Buddha's disciple Sariputta and begged to be told what he needed to do to be born again in the world of Brahman at his next life. The apostle told him to cultivate the right frame of mind for this. He did so and was

---

[24] No. *207, Assoka* jātaka.

[25] *No. 318, Kāuavera* jātaka.

[26] Mbh V: 36: pp. 44–45.

[27] Ibid., V: 40: 26.

[28] Ibid., XIII: 28: 5.

reborn in Brahmaloka.[28a] This reduces the role of karman in the determination of the station in rebirth to a ridiculous minimum; many later Puranic texts go still farther as we shall see later. But one thing it establishes emphatically and that is, rebirth is determined by action, karman, whether life-long or a last-minute change of heart.

Much depends on the state of the mind immediately before death. Even Vaiṣṇavas, if they harbour the desire in their hearts, go to heaven but return to India and are born among brahmins.[29] Apparently such an idea reinforces the claim that in transmigration a man is the architect of his own fate. G. Obeysekere, however, says, "I suggest that in the ideal rebirth eschatology there is no ethicization: morally wrong actions are not religiously good actions... Since ethicization implies the religious evaluation of moral action, actions that are morally good or bad are transformed into actions that are also religiously good or bad; that is why the notions of sin and religious merit must develop... Both (Pythagoreans and Orphics) believed in the purification of the soul through successive births."[30] Apart from the Pythagoreans, the followers of the Orphic cult also took rebirth seriously, "Orphic view... anticipated an ultimate escape from the wheel of birth into an Elysium of heavenly light."[31] This is clearly not the same as being born on earth in human or subhuman forms. Yet Orphism did subscribe to this common concept of transmigration.

Another such single reincarnation is found in the myth of Attis: nagged by Kybele, his angry mother, her son Attis died of self-castration and then returned to life in response to his mother's intense mourning.[32] The Orphic theology did believe in transmigration although only as a mere tenet of theology, but scholars hold that the theory of transmigration which Pythagoras (c. 572–500 B.C.) propagated was borrowed from the Orphics. The Orphics also believed in a retributive rebirth. "The Orphic priests explained that punishments in this life were warded for transgressions in a previous life."[33]

[28a] Jataka, 81.

[29] *Brahmavaivarta* Purāṇa, Prakrti Khāṇḍa, p. 26: 30.

[30] O' Flaherty (ed.), 1983, pp. 146, 147, 151.

[31] Champbel, 1968, p. 266.

[32] *Macmillan Encyclopaedia of Religion,* Vol. VI.

[33] Pollard, J., 1965, p. 100.

Plato writing in the first century B.C. says, "Seeing, then, that the soul is immortal and has been born many times and has beheld all things in the world and in Hades, she has learnt all things."[34] Elsewhere he says, "The laws of fate are divine decrees whereby the animal universe is produced out of successive reincarnations of man, who, however, determines the nature of each successive reincarnation by the manner of his actions and volitions."[35]

The Greek words for transmigration are 'metensōmatōsis' (lit. passage from one body to another, whence the English word metempsychosis) and 'palingenesis' (lit. to begin again). Pythagoras not only believed in transmigration but also that one could remember his past lives.[36] Heradeides Pontiens tells that Pythagoras said that he was born once as Aethalides, the son of Hermes and received from Hermes the boon of remembering his past lives. He remembered being wounded by Menelaus and in his life as Pythagoras he could still remember the shield which Menelaus had hung up in the temple of Apollo at Branchidne. Subsequently he was born as Hermotimus, and then as Pyrrhus, a Delos fisherman.

In Buddhist and Brahminical literature we have many tales where some characters claim to remember their past lives. Buddha tops the list; the jātaka tales (in nearly five hundred of them) bear testimony to this. Evidently the jātakas are used to string these different tales together. The theological objective behind this literary device was to supply credibility to the theory of rebirth. It did help to entrench the transmigration theory and to earn acceptance in the popular consciousness. Numerous brahminical tales in the epics and Purāṇas and the incarnation myths of several Gods served the same purpose.

Macmillan Encyclopaedia says in the section on 'Metempsychosis':

> "The belief in one form or another is found in tribal or non-literate cultures all over the world... may be that this belief arose contemporaneously with the origins of human culture *per se.* The Zulu hold that the spirit of each person undergoes numerous rebirths in the bodies of various beasts... until at long last the spirit enters a human body where it is fated to undergo yet another birth. Finally, after reaching the pinnacle of human existence the soul is unified with the supreme spirit from which it originated... According to Australian aboriginal religious beliefs, a deceased ancestor after a

---

34 *Mamo,* 81c also 50, A.B.

35 *Timaeus,* 41 E.

36 Jātismara in Sanskrit.

sojourn of an unspecified length of time in the land of the dead, returns to the world of the living by entering the body of the mother at... conception.[37]

Regarding the shapes assumed by the spirit at rebirth, J. Bruce Long in his entry "Reincarnation"[38] says "(Beings are) customarily human or animal in nature but are in some instances divine, angelic, demonic, vegetative or astrological.

Michel Hulin says "dans la mythe grandiose de la transmigration (saṃsāra) indefinie des âmes śincarnant dans des corps animaux, devins ou humains de leursactes (Karman) il est permis de reconnâitre l'intersection de notions brahmanique relations au mecanisme de l'actesacrificiel (cense produice infalliblement son fruit à condition dêtre correctement execute) el d'une certaine systematization par les renogan ts de conception repetitive qu'ils se font de la vie à l'interieur de la caste."[39] This is true of a later period in Indian theology where rebirth is vitally linked with action, but there was a time before the middle of the first millennium B.C. when rebirth was posited independently. Regarding the length of years which a spirit spends in his wanderings from body to body. Empedocles (582–507 B.C.) thought that sinners transmigrate for thirty thousand years through various kinds of incarnations and are affected in different ways by each of the four elements. A long process of purification ensures escape from this dismal destiny.

The 5 *Nārada* Purāṇa says that the soul after travelling through a crore of lives finally attains human life;[40] it also gives detailed description of the results of sin suffered at death, in the womb, at rebirth and thereafter.[41]

The Jain *Bhagavatīsūtra* says that eighty four thousand mahākappas for all seven births, seven groups, seven sentient births, seven abandonments of transmigration, five lakhs of kammas, sixty thousand and six hundred and the three parts of Kamma. Then being saved, awakened, set free and reaching nirvāna, they have made or are making or will make an end of all sorrow. One notices the attempt to push the time to such an antiquity as to make liberation nearly unattainable. The real aim is to emphasize the difficulty of the task.

37 Macmillan, *op. cit.*, Vol. XII.

38 Macmillan, *op. cit.* p. 265.

39 1978, p. 38.

40 11: 6: 36.

41 II: 4: 1–25.

The *Acārāngacayanikā*[42] is a collection of some *Acārānga* sūtras. One of them says, "When the karman is not known (which is bearing fruit), the man moves in this direction or the other directions, in all directions and sub-directions and suffers from many different forms with which he connects himself... The man with desires, one indulging in desires, returns to the womb (i.e. is reborn). Man has to suffer the effects of his own works."[43]

In the Buddhist *Angutlara Nikāya* when non-violence is preached with many admonitory passages, it gives a moral justification: "one who takes life, takes what is not given."[44] But along with logic and ethics it predicts evil consequences of violence in this life which the perpetrator of violence suffers in the next life. "It is that guilty dread, housefather, which he who kills in this same visible stale as a result of his killing."[45] The socio-economic reasons operative behind the rise and preponderance of non-violence around the seventh-sixth centuries B.C. now sought reasons to justify non-violence by admonitions, to which were attached the dreadful consequences of violence to be suffered in some future life. With the theory of rebirth steadily gaining ground around this time, this suited the propounders of rebirth and its consequences.

Why was this theory of transmigration formulated? One simple answer would be man's love of life prompted him to prolong it beyond death and, therefore, logically, before birth. Secondly, it ensured varieties of experience not possible in a single life-time. Thirdly, such a view affords man an opportunity to rectify errors and improve his status in the subsequent lives and fourthly, it removes the fear of finality, a fear which has haunted man everywhere throughout the ages. But obviously, rebirth by itself cannot guarantee an ascent in either the spiritual or the mundane level. The will to improve is what matters vitally and that also is influenced by various factors beyond human control.

Above all, transmigration is, in a vital sense, a negation of death. Hajime Nakamura says that the belief in metempsychosis means that: souls do not die but pass at death from one body to another–a great incentive to virtue, for

42 ed. by Kamalachand Somani.

43 Sūtra Nos. 6, 108 and 170.

44 VII: (81).

45 ii (92).

the fear of death was disregarded. The Brahmana literature has put forward two distinct paths for the soul of the dead. One was through the moon to rebirth, the other through the sun to release, Pitṛyāṇna and Devayāna, respectively.[46]

Most accounts of the countless lives through which the soul wandered aim at the attainment of release at the end. Theologies, like the Eddie or Germanic or Gaulic which do not hold transmigration as a theological tenet portray this release as located in heaven, as does the early Indian theology of the Ṛgveda. We read: "Un ensignement du ṁeme ordre se donnait à Eleusis. Sans vouloir exagerer la spirituality des mysteres, petit ou grands in leur attribuer I'idde d'une renaissance à la filiation divine, il faut reconnoitre la force de I'impression produite sur les initios: ils crovaient transported dans la beatitude d'outre- tombe... le parfait initie se sentait libre, il pensait "vivre avec les hommes purs et saints."[47] Whether heaven, Eleusis or Bihisht, the aim is unmixed and unending happiness; moksa or nirvana qualify them so they are not tinged with happiness as such, but merging in the supreme bliss in moksa and being released beyond experience in nirvāṇa. But both these presuppose a series of rebirths before the end is reached.

Finally, one asks what is it that transmigrates? The soul? What does it carry from one life to the next? A.L. Herman says, "What transmigrates is a set of individual dispositions which are nonetheless non-spirit but personal in some sense... There must be some mechanism or a vehicle whereby to identify. Individuality or personality is maintained from life to life, or else there is no rationale behind the justice with which the law of karma is going to work."[48]

In so far as rebirth is concerned, we have seen that it is a prior theological tenet which for some time existed independently and which, in many other theologies remained dissociated from karman. Even in India, the Ājīvikas believed in rebirth but not in karman, some other minor systems also totally denied the influence of karman on rebirth. Hence karman was not an inalienable concomitant of rebirth, although within two centuries after the postulation of rebirth, karman was associated with it in a causal relationship and has remained so for the last two millennia. Bruce long says, "Once this

---

46 Similar ideas are found in Caesar: De Belto Galico VI: 14.

47 Dictionnaire de Spiritualite, 1967.

48 O' Flaherty, W.D. (ed.), 1983, pp. 171, 190.

cosmic life system with its multitudinous creatures was propelled into motion, it has continued to gyrate in a cyclical pattern from death to rebirth, either under the creator's influence or by the action of fate, time or human action or by combination of these factors."[49]

The ineluctability of rebirth is brought out very prominently by subjecting the Gods under the scheme. One would imagine that Gods would be immune, outside the scope of rebirth, as they are in most mythologies, as they were in the Sarphitās Brāhmaṇas, Āranyakas and Upaniṣads. The new trend

> to bring the Gods under the laws of transmigration set in with the codification of the Jātakas where Budha is reborn again and again. Later, other Gods from the epics-or to be more precise, from the later interpolated sections of both the epics-came to be reincarnated when the contingency arose. These deities who are reborn as avātaras, if the assumptions for rebirth are not to be held in temporary abeyance for them, must be reborn under the same rules as other beings: Thus they must have souls, must be karma-laden with desire in some sense e.g., the desire to save the suffering world... This of course implies that the Cod who incarnates is not perfect because he still possesses a trace of desire which must be worked out in an earthly locus and in a human form ... As many historians have pointed out ... the law of karma is a principle which is regarded by the Indians, without exception as an unseen principle which holds sway even over the material atoms and brings about objects and events in accordance with moral principle.[50]

The reincarnation of Gods, increasingly depicted as a matter of course in the late Purāṇas and Upapurāṇas, gave the theory of rebirth a fillip and a surer ground for assuming repeated rebirths for men as the normal course of the human soul.

---

[49] O' Flaherty, W.D. (ed.), 1983, p. 80.

[50] O Flaherty, W.D. (ed.), 1983, pp. 210, 237.

CHAPTER 3

Karman and its Consequences

IT was in the middle of the first millennium B.C. that rebirth came to be associated with karman: a man was reborn according to what he did in his life on earth. This association had many facets. In the first phase rebirth had reference only to the future, but with karman it was a two-ended position: a man's past karman determines his present station and his present station decides how he will fare in the future. Now, with the Jātakas a man could be born as a God or as subhuman being, a sondergötter-a yakṣa, piśāca, gandharva, kinnara, rākṣasa, nāga, any animal, bird, serpent, insect, aquatic or atmospheric creature. "Sin and piety in this life result in birth in hateful or covetable stations (in the next)."[1] As tree-spirits and river-spirits they could, to some extent, be identified with aspects of nature. The scope and possibility of rebirth thus widened to illimitability. Secondly, now there appeared a pseudological chain of causality: certain karmans yielded certain results. Thirdly, divine intervention and the role of the supernatural in controlling the course of a man's life was admitted. Fourthly, now fate became a myriad-named divinity. We shall deal with most of these aspects in the following chapters, but karman opened up a large vista which rebirth by itself could never do. One of the earliest inklings of the connection between action and its effects is found in the *Brhadāraṇyaka* Upaniṣad where we read that "as a man decides, he acts, and as he acts he gets the fruits of the action."[2] This idea is repeated in many other Vedic passages.[3] The *Manusaṃhitā* also has a long discourse on karman and its consequences[4] but this text is late, of around the second century A.D. It discusses the threefold origin of karman the mind, words and the body. Action, then, begets fruits in the form of consequences. In the *Macimillan Encyclopaedia of Religion,* the entry on

---

1 *Matsya Purāṇa* 39: 19.

2 IV: 4: 5 of also *kausītaki* I: 1 ff; *juiminīya* I: 18; *chhāndogya* V: 10: 6.

3 *Kausītaki* 26: 3. *Bṛhadāraṇyaka* Up. 1: 5: 17; III: 2: 3, *Taittirīya* Up. 2: 8.

4 XII: pp. 1–82.

Karman by W.K. Mahony says, "Originally (karman) referred to properly performed ritual activity, the notion was ethicized to include the large meaning of any correct activity in general. Granting this view, the religious, social and medical philosophers of India, particularly those intrigued by the doctrines of rebirth and the origins of suffering (but also the related problems of the sources of personality and the justification of social states) expanded the meaning of the term."[5]

We have seen in the last chapter that there was a socioeconomic background which gave rise to the doctrine of rebirth, the same factors gradually consolidated and there were other religio-philosophical factors which operated to form and fortify the theory of karman so that together they became a formidable force. When Buddha set out in search of truth he met a number of mendicants, each with a distinct metaphysics and a following. It was in this atmosphere, heavily charged with religion and metaphysics that the karman theory was formulated and adopted by Buddhism, Jainism and Brahmanism. Though the theory of karman has an appearance of scientific regularity; what it led to in society, metaphysics and theology was a belief in fate.

What is karman? Put simply, it is action, any action, good or bad; any action, in other words which involves a moral decision. But occasionally an unwitting action also counts for karman - both for good and bad.

Although the Mīmāṃsā mentions apūrva, it is the *Nyāyakusumāñjali* which mentions adṛṣṭa, fate and has a special chapter called apūrva adhikarana. The analogy used by this text to explain the time-gap is that between sowing and reaping; this is the time taken for 'the maturing of adṛṣta (adṛṣṭa-paripāka)'. Again, commentators on the Mīmāṃsā, like *Rāmānuja* and Kumārila and those who came between these two use the analogy: the time that elapses between the administering of a medicine and the recovery. Let us not forget that even in the Upaniṣadic age the sacrifice is compared to an unstable leaking boat (cf plavā hyete adṛḍhā yajñarūpāh. *Muṇḍaka* Up I: 2:7). Later by the time of Yāska and still later in the Mīmāṃsā doubts are cast on the efficacy of sacrifices, one of the reasons being this time-gap which, unreasonably long, would lead to the natural interpretation as the non-delivery of the goods. Besides, experience told men that many properly

5 Vol. VIII, p. 267.

performed sacrifices failed to yield expected results; hence sacrifices were not quite dependable.[6]

How did the theory of karman originate in India? Let us not forget that the basic tenet that a man reaps the harvest of his own action is common to all peoples throughout the ages. But the theory of karman in India has the additional appendage of rebirth according to karman. "Possibly originating... in the agrarian experience of aboriginal India, the notion of an impersonal law of cause and effect subsequently pervaded (often decidedly un-agricultural) ideology of vedic ritualism, yoga and vedānta, Āyurvedic medicine and sectarian theism and it stands as a central theme (in Jainism and Buddhism). There is no single south Asian notion of karman."[7] Each action is supposed to generate a proportionate result either in this life or in a future life. A heritage of the concept of time-gap later known as apūrva between karman and its fruit derives from Śaṅkara's commentary on the Mīmāmsā."[8] "Apūrva is a conceptual device designed to keep off or circumvent empirically oriented criticism of the efficacy of the sacrifice, to establish a causal nexus not subject to the criterion of direct, observable sequence... Karma cannot be the moving force behind the whole world process in the theistic Vaiśeṣika or in the 'atheistic' Sāṃkhya context. Vaiśeṣika adṛṣṭa-the retributive potency of past deeds stored as a quality of the soul has served as a model for the explication of apūrva by subsequent authors."[9] As actions are many they give rise to many apūrvas, "the distinguishability of the various apūrvas or 'units' of apūrva accounts for the multiplicity and variety of the results."[10] The Mīmāṃsā philosophy in its exploration of the mechanism of the sacrifice yielding the desired result observed the time-gap, that the result does not appear immediately after the performance. Hence they had to postulate a power which they called apūrva which was generated immediately out of the sacrifice. This apūrva, although it begins to be operative at once, does not furnish the fruit immediately, but at a suitable time. This suitable time remains

6 cf *Muṇḍaka Up* 1: 2: 7.

7 *Macmillan Encyclopaedia of Religion*, Vol. 28, p. 267.

8 In Jaimini's *Pūrvamimaṃsā* Sutra itself, the word apūrva which accounts for the time-gap does not occur; only in Śaṅkara do we meet it.

9 O' Flaherty (ed.), 1983, pp. 279, 281.

10 O' Flaherty (ed.), 1983, p. 304.

a mystery. Now, the first religiously significant karman is the sacrifice.[11] Later, when the karman theory was propounded, this apūrva concept too, came as a legacy and gave rise to the concept of adṛṣḍa, the unseen. What is unseen? That particular karman in the past whose fruition takes place in the present; similarly those karmans done in the present which shall bear fruit in the future would be regarded asadṛṣḍa. In Jainism, "The transmigrating soul is said to be housed by a body as well as by a so-called body."[12] Karl H. Potter says in his *'Karma theory in some Indian Philosophical Systems,'* "As Karmic residues mature they re-operate with what are called 'traces' and 'impressions' (vāsanā) to determine the way in which the Karmic potentials will in fact be worked out. Here there is a partial explanation of the time-gap between action and reaction: there is a process of maturing involved."[13] "As far as the physical and cosmological usage of adṛṣṭa is concerned, its primary function seems to be to account for strange and extraordinary phenomena in nature which would not be explicable otherwise... as well as for phenomena which seem to be signs or to contain an element of reward and punishment... Adṛṣṭa, on the one hand serves as a kind of gap-filler in the realm of physical causality providing a principle of explanation where other visible and, therefore, preferable causes, fail."[14]

There is an inherent fatalism in many of the basic texts of Jainism. For example, Abhayadeva commenting on *Uvāsagadasāo*[15] says: "What is not to be, never happens; what is to be, happens even without effort. That which is not fated to be, gets lost even though it comes within grasp." Then the famous *Syādvādamañjari* is quoted by Mallisena: there is one verse which says: "Even when destroyed (it, the body) comes again if the faith suffers injury."

An early contemporary of the Buddha's, Maskarin Gosāla, the founder of Ājīvikism said: "There is no cause, no proof of the suffering of creatures."[16] Jñānavimala's commentary to the *Pras'navyākaranasūtra* says: "Some babble that the universal is produced by fate, saying Destiny is everywhere the

---

[11] From which the later concept of karma- kāṇḍa , sacrificial religion, derives its name.

[12] O' Flaherty (ed.), 1983, p. 231.

[13] *Op. cit.*, p. 249.

[14] *Op. cit.*, 1983, pp. 285, 288.

[15] VI: 165.

[16] *Dīgha Nikāya,* I: 53

stronger as in 'For what reason does a man obtain that thing which he must obtain? Inevitable fate'. Therefore, I do not grieve or despair that (destiny) which is ours is not that of others. Fate suddenly bringing out what is desired even from another continent, even from the end of the world (in any) direction, makes (it appear) before one's face. Age is one's destiny, so is one's intellect successful, so is one's resolution, so are ones companions."

These texts have such a strong predilection for fatalism that action in them is rendered futile. What is destined to happen thus happens, despite man's effort to achieve a different result.

Śaṅkara's *Brahamsūtra-bhāṣya*[17] defines the 'prārabdha' karman which attains fruition within a given life-time . Jaimini's view is that the act produces the operative power, called apūrva in the commentary, which leads to its outcome i.e. the residue of action from a previous birth or births (sañcita karman) which works itself out automatically in a given life-time. Vādarāyaṇa, the author of the *Brahmasūtra* holds that the act itself is powerless to produce effect in the next life, because it does not last long enough to travel from one life to the next. He also holds that apūrva itself cannot do so because it is an unintelligent agent and thus incapable of determining suitable time, place and mode for the resultant experience. Hence both the author and the commentator of the *Brahmasūtra* have to posit a God who supervises the process so that the effect is appropriate and adequate to the cause. This God leaves scope for man's own moral choices; he only supervises the proportionateness of the action and reaction.

> There remains the question whether, even with God superintending the proportionateness of action and reaction, there is real justice in the transaction. If the law of Karma is just... (one) would get exactly what's coming to him, his due, no more, and no less. Could there be an overcompensation or undercompensation?... No such prediction is possible with the law of Karma, apparently, nor should we see any... If there is indeed a cosmic force Karma and cosmic results of this force, saṃsāra, operating independently of the will of God, then, Cod's power would seem to be curtailed. ... God is in control of the law of Karma, then he is involved with the suffering and misery dispensed through or by way of the law... And if God is not in control of the law of Karma and it works independently and autonomously of God, then either God is not all- powerful or we are involved with TPE (transferable personal

[17] III: 2: 38–41.

> entity), or both ... But if God is either implicated in the end (hence blameable) or merely a pawn in the hands of uncontrollable cosmic process (not all-powerful), it would seem He is also involved in both these ways in the beginning of the creation or the origin of the universe ... Under the rebirth solution and the principle of Karma there is no (moral) pure chance that can befall man in the sense that some eyil acts will go unpunished or some good acts unrewarded.[18]

The inherent paradox, one of many with regard to the question whether the doctrine of karman is an adequate or just explanation of human experience, is well brought out in the above quotation. With or without God as the supervisee there are dilemmas out of which there is no escape. G.W. Kaviswar says, "The Vainayikas seek a rebirth in heaven and not complete mokṣa by fourfold good conduct in mind, word, body, in giving toward Gods, kings, ascetics, kinsfolk, elders, inferiors, mother and father."[19] This author asks many pertinent questions but the solutions offered are feeble, conformist and unconvincing. Among such questions are— "Does the grace of God cancel or abrogate the Law of Karma in some cases at His will? If yes, will it not undermine the common man's faith in the law, and also result in temptation to show repentance and offer surrender? ... While justice can be claimed as right, grace differs from it... (it) is the conferring of some special benefit which the recipient is unable to secure on his own strength, and also may not demand or claim, and yet deserves it if and when granted by the giver of his own accord."[20] With a God supervising the karman and its fruit, the question of grace naturally arises, but this God is not the all-powerful, merciful one; he functions only in a specific official capacity: meting out retribution.

Then there is the question of the agent, the doer of the fruit bearing karman. Desire, say both the Buddists and the brahmanical philosphers, is at the root of being and, therefore, of suffering. Desire inheres in the soul which moves from one life to another. "Il ne se présente pas comme un désir particulier, mais plutôt comme le resort profond de tous le deśirs prealable a toute connaissance actuelle, apparait avant tout comme un "appetit d´être" une spontaneite vitale qui se specifiera suivent le corps dont on herite par

---

[18] O' Flaherty (ed.), 1983, pp. 275, 278, 290.

[19] 1974, p. 31.

[20] *Ibid.*, pp. 32–3.

le Karman."[21] The question of the agent is really persistent esp. when the fruits of a person's karma are experienced after his personality has undergone a change of identity in time, place, milieu and ther formative factors. To claim that the fruits are tasted by the same person— whether as a man, beast, demon or demi-god—seems to stretch the point a little too far. "The revulsion of the prop,[22] the prop is the individual's psycho-physical complex; it is understood by some schools in a matter-of-fact manner as a change of personality operated by karma, as in the case where a woman is reborn as a man or a man becomes an animal."[23] Karman and the resulting effect, to all appearance, function in a mechanical way with no apparent scope for grace or any other mitigating factor. "Karma as a mechanical process cannot forgive and cannot stop itself."[24]

The fundamental problem regarding karman is that despite its appearance of rational causality what it produced was the totally irrational notion of fate. Delving deeper into the problem one may say that this apparent paradox stems from a lack of clarity regarding the actual mode of operation of karman- through or independently of apūrva.

Ninian Smart has an extremely cogent account of this.

> The theory or rebirth together with its twin, the concept of Karma, presents certain difficulties to the various viewpoints about the mechanism whereby rebirth, etc. occurs. Thus ... the Logic- Atomists because of their belief in rebirth were obliged to suppose that causality at a distance could occur, at least in the spatial sense. Moreover, their concept of the unseen force as determining the destiny of living beings in effect constitute an evasion of the problem of how Karma actually opérated. On the other hand, the common doctrine in the Indian tradition that the self or soul is all-pervasive helped to make the concept of causation at a distance acceptable; since it is a determination via the all-pervasive soul of the moral forces left over from a prior embodiment. However, the early Indian view of Karma (doubtless of non-Indian provenance) was that it operates as a kind of natural law, and that really there was no further problem once one had stated that this was how the world was. Later metaphysicians tended to ask how Karma operated... the theists argued

21 M Biardeau (ed.), 1973, p. 76.

22 āśayaparāvṛttl i.e., the reintegration of the personality, after the revulsion of the prop.

23 Tucci, *East and West,* Vol. 38, Nos, 1–4, Dec. 1988, pp. 16–17.

24 R. Panikkar, *East and West,* Vol. 38, Nos. 1–4, Dec. 1988, p. 100.

> that the operation of Karma was used as a 'theistic proof.' But... the concept of a self-regulating moral law was so deeply ingrained in the Indian imagination, that such a proof was hardly likely to be persuasive and unpersuaded.[24a]

"The dominant view... was that the 'selves' or souls are all-pervasive... it accounts for the way in which karmic effects worked out at a distance."[25]

The question of time-gap between an action and its consequence has reference to the effect of action experienced some time (1) in the same life or (2) in some future life. The analogy of apūrva being generated through the power of mantras uttered during the sacrifice and apūrva yielding a fruit of the action— is based on a time-gap between the utterance of the mantras and the appearance of the fruit. As Hajime Nakamura says: "Some Karmas bear fruit in the same life in which they are committed, others in the immediately succeeding one and others in more remote future lives. The individual is the result of a multitude of causes carried over from his past existences and is intimately related to all other causes in the world. The explanation can always be reversed to correspond to the present fact. It fits the facts because it is derived from them. And it cannot be disproved (though it can be verified from experience) for it lies in a sphere beyond the reach of human enquiry. The reason why the doctrine was retained in Buddhism is because it thus provided a moral cause."[26] The individual as a moral agent is thus a product of his past actions, some of which mature and bear fruit in the present life, and unless he succeeds in freeing himself from all attachment he acquires some more actions and desires, to experience the fruits of which he has to take birth again and again until both sides of the ledger are clean i.e. he has no unfructified karman and no unfulfilled desire carried over and no karman performed in this life to be carried over. The individual responsibility of the fruit of the action is carried over to the next world.[27] The *Majjhima Nikāya* says that what it (the soul) does, determines what it becomes and the impressions which it gathers. In the *Dhammapada* we read, "By oneself evil is done, by oneself one suffers, by oneself evil is undone, by oneself evil is punished." (165).

[24a] Smart, 1964, p. 163.

[25] Smart, *Ibid.*, p. 168.

[26] Nakamura, 1986, p. 264.

[27] *Samyatta Nikāya* III: 12: 10: 9–10: III: 1: 4: 6 *Aṅguttara Nikāya* VCC VI: 1–2: 13 III: 35: 1; where Yama says that a man will pay for evils dons in deed, word and thought.

Buddha declares that there can be no wiping out of intentional deeds done and accumulated without experiencing the results thereof and these may mature either in this present state or in some other state hereafter. There is no end of evil resulting from intentional deeds done and accumulated without experiencing the result thereof.[28] The new emphasis is very significant—'the intentional deed'; this makes man a moral agent and we can guess that the result flows not so much from the deed as from the intention itself. It also exonerates the agent from guilt for unintentional deeds. This is a new overtone introduced for the first time in theology; now ethics becomes the desideratum. This also leads to a corollary; since acts are done by an individual, the retribution also can only concern the individual; hence a natural calamity like a plague, famine or epidemic, a train or plane disaster, a car accident which involves the fate of many cannot be explained by group action or past collective guilt, but by individual actions fructifying accidentally at the same time. "There is thus conclusive evidence that the concept of collective Karma is foreign to Indian religious tradition and in fact is negation of the classical doctrine of Karma."[29]

Peter Berger has remarked: "Through reification the world of institutions appears to merge with the world of nature. It become necessity and fate, and is lived through as such... Roles may be reified in the same manner as institutions. The sector of self-consciousness that has been objectified in the role is then also apprehended as an inevitable fate for which the individual disclaims responsibility."[30]

The Vedic sacrificial religion was mainly collective, even the domestic rites were attended by all the members of family and the family was 'kula', a large joint family. The collective sacrifices yielded fruits which, with the exception of a few, benefited the entire community. From this until the time of the Upaniṣads there were many changes. One concomitant of the rebirth theory which appeared in the later Brāhmaṇas was that rebirth was a recurring evil, release from which was the supremely desirable end. With this the focus of religion shifted from the community to the individual: he it was who would have been reborn repeatedly; therefore, he would be who would gain from the cessation of rebirth. The Upaniṣads clearly emphasized the role, duty

---

[28] *Aṅguttara Nikāya* VCC VI: 1–2: 13.

[29] *East and West* Vol. 39, Nos. 1–4, Dec 1989, p. 193.

[30] Berger, 1970, p. 108.

and goal of the individual. Large collective community sacrifices were still being performed and continued for over a millennia, but the trend shifted from sacrifices to 'tapas' leading to realization on the one hand and to pūjā, on the other. The new goal was liberation. Whose liberation? Not of the masses who chafed under grinding poverty and were hankering for a measure of economic sufficiency and stability, but for the individuals of the elite who were worried about the means of gaining salvation for themselves. Thus the theological unit was the individual. Heesterman says, "Many factors will have contributed to the rise and elaboration of the Karman doctrine, but it would seem to me that the pivotal point is *the emphasis on the individual.* The life-death alternation which was to be realized through the agonistic cooperation with the others must now be worked out by the single individual in his successive lives. Dispersal of impurity becomes a hereditary speciality. In other words, we touch here the principle of caste ideology."[31]

By about the seventh century B.C. all around in the Mediterranean world in Greece, China and India slowly but steadily great changes were setting in, one of whose contents was the concept of rebirth. When within a century or two the theory of karman came to be appended to it, the change was, to all appearances complete. In other words, a viable metaphysics was formulated which appeared to be cogent, explaining the hithreto inexplicable anomalies of life. One's station in life, one's griefs and joys, losses and gains were traceable to one's actions done in some earlier life. Since this could not be proved, the naturally credulous common people who chafed under the anomalies suffered misfortunes for which they could not even remotely be held responsible were now conditioned to accept that the evil deeds accumulated in some previous life or liveswere accountable for their present misfortune. Needless to say, there were many loopholes to the theory which the common man could not detect and therefore accepted. What was offered to them as an apparently all-comprehensive theory, a neat frame in which their experiences fitted. One of the anomalies was pointed out by L. de Vallêe Poussin: "The Indian solution of *the great riddle of the origin of suffering* and the diversity of human condition is to be found in the word Karma. This solution of the great riddle is not altogether satisfactory as we get no answer concerning the very beginning. It (the theory of Karma) gradually broke away from Vedic naturalism, mysticism and piety."[32]

---

31 Heesterman *WZKS*, 1963, p. 16. Italics added.

32 'Karma' in the *Encyclopaedia of Religion and Ethics*, Vol. VII, pp. 673–76.

The theory of karman and rebirth is riddled with fallacies. We shall discuss only a few. In the *Mahābhārata* when Indra seduced Ahalyā, Gautama, her husband, refused to blame either (presumably because the major culprit was no less a person than Indra, the sovereign of the Gods) and said that the fault was due to karman. No one asks or answers the valid question: whose karman.[33] Clearly, the theory of karman here exonerated a crime. Again, the *Matsya* Purāna says, "what Gods do, bears no fruit, good or bad as it does for man."[34] We notice the anomaly between the two passages. The theory of līlā, sport, explains the actions of Gods on earth. Līlā is not judged morally. And this would account for Rāma's killing Vālin unheroically in an un-kshatriya-like manner through a subterfuge, his rejection—twice— of the wholly innocent Sītā, his cold-blooded slaughter of Śambūka. Again, if the Gods' actions do not bear fruit, then, why did the innocent Sītā spend much of her time on earth in miserable suffering, false accusations and burning humiliation? She was a goddess and as such was not paying off a backlog of earlier sins. She was puzzled at her own suffering when she said, "What heinous crime must I have committed in another life so that I have to suffer this cruel heart-rending grief."[35] She speaks here like an ordinary mortal, forgetting that she had not been born before and therefore, could not have committed any crime. In the last book of the Mahābhārata, the Svargārohoṇa parvan, we hear from an angel that Draupadī had been Laksmī in heaven. We are never told why a goddess who had committed no crime in heaven was so humiliated publicly in the royal court and had to live through so much hardship, bereavements and suffering. The theory of karman and reincarnation for retribution thus leaves many strings hanging loose. Later, such puzzlement disappears; in the *Mārkṇḍeyu* Purāṇa a brahmin's wife on being separated from her husband said, "the fruits of my karma ripened, hence I was separated from my husband." It is interesting to note that as the theory becomes entrenched in the popular mind, people try to draw consolation from it. Kauśalyā and Sīta felt bitter, but with time this bitterness gets less, to some extent and only in some cases, where belief in fate eventually helps grow a callus and makes acceptance a cruel but inevitable necessity.

---

33 *Mbh* XII: 258: 42.

34 IV: 6.

35 Rāmāyana, V: 25: 18.

Explaining the anomaly of Gods and the theory of fate, the *Devībhāgavata* Purāṇa says "Brahman, Viṣṇu, Rudra and Indra and the other Gods, demons, yakṣas and gandharvas are all under the power of karman; otherwise how could they have bodies and experience happiness and sorrow as embodied creatures do?" "Kṛṣṇa performed all his great manly deeds (pauruṣa) by the power of predestination."[36] Gods in the Purāṇas are portrayed almost as mere human beings. Thus the *Skanda* Purāṇa says that Bṛhaspati consoled Indra who had sinned and said "do not grieve. All this universe is in the sway of karman."[37] Another such consolation in the *Linga* Purāṇa to one whose father was killed by the demons reads, "The demons did not kill your father, it was fated to happen to him thus. Who is slain by whom? Man experiences the fruits of him own karman."[37a] The interesting point here is that fate is equated with the fruits of karman.

Generally, however, most systems of philosophy which discuss karman, its effects and liberation hold that no one knows how karman moulds one's course of life, Jainism perhaps makes a truly extreme statement when it says: "Even after attaining to the station of a minor God, one does not know which act performed by him has yielded this fruit."[38] The same text which puts such a premium on knowledge of one's actions and the results thereof understandably states that "liberation comes after one knows one's previous sinful acts, and that the knowledge redeems the sinner."[39] It is the ignorance of one's previous acts and the fruits they bear that leads to the bondage viz. rebirth. As long as one cannot understand the import of his past sinful acts and the retribution that follows these, one is attached to the chain of successive rebirths.

Why did Kṛṣṇa, the incarnation of Nārāyaṇa, give dishonest counsel to the Pāṇḍavas to bring about the deaths of the Kaurava heroes? That he lied and cheated is borne out by Gāndhārī's curse to him which would not have come true if the charges were baseless. Kṛṣṇa, a God, thus stands condemned. By introducing the theory of remote fructification of karman thus pushing it notionally beyond several births, karman is truly rendered an unknown and

---

[36] IV: 10: pp. 17–19.

[37] II: 7: 23: 10.

[37a] I: 64, pp. 109–111.

[38] *aśaveyāliya* sulla V: 47.

[39] Culiya 1: 18.

unknowable quantity, virtually nonexistent but conceptually ineluctable. It appears as wholly intransigent and those who interpret an experience in terms of a karman beyond several lives act either as dishonest criminal lawyers or arcane soothsayers. Theoretically, it invalidates the retributive character of the effects of karman since a person, even with a heavy load of sin, can live quite comfortably and happily for many lives before recompense is introduced. The remote reaction by which a deed is separated from its effect has posed a problem for ascertaining which deed generates which effect and it is a serious hurdle in the logical structure of causality.

Maskarin Gosāla, however, did not subscribe to the theory that each Karman has a corresponding and equal effect; according to him experiences are fortuitous, bearing no direct correspondence to actions which can be regarded as their causes. "Evil in deed, word and thought is not a necessary consequence of depravity. Neither is the good consequence of goodness."[40] This theory began in the Mīmāṃsā-bhāṣya which was much later than Jaimini's Sūtra. Meanwhile Buddhism faced it and was hard put to finding a convincing solution. What it constructed is best demonstrated in the *Aṅguttara Nikāya.* Punishment in the *Aṅguttara Nikāya* for two categories of faults is defined: "those with their result in the present existence and those whose consequences are to be in a future state of further action, which may prove deleteirous in the long run." A.K. Warder comments on the doctrine of precise retribution in Buddhism: "It is the doctrine on which the authentic Tripiṭaka has very little to say and which perhaps had not been elaborated in more than a very general way by the Buddha himself, but which the schools of Buddhism later worked out in much detail, seeking, no doubt, to make their teaching to laymen more perfect by inclusion of circumstances, particulars of the destinies attending every kind of action."[41] The same desire for a full, symmetrical explanation, to construct a complete paradigm is operative in each school of ethical and theological thought.

Buddhists believed that each karman matures independently and that the same karman could lead to different results to different persons; the difference in fruit was related to the already collected karman of the individual, that good action was more powerful and its effect lasted longer. Some karmans had greater power; good acts could be transferred by the agent to another, the

---

40 *Uvāsagndasāo* appendix II.

41 'Karma and problem of rebirth in jainism' in O'Flaherty (ed.), 1983, pp. 228–229.

time taken by actions to mature cannot be specific. Jainism which had evolved a substantial literature by the third century A.D. faced the same problem. Padmanabha S. Jaini remarks: "At least one hundred and eight souls become emancipated in each period of six months and eight months ... in Jainism the model of a Karmically ordered universe, in which the soul's position could be improved or worsened by action did prevail over the kind of fatalistic determinism accepted by the Ājīvikas."[42] A comment on the Jain theory says that good and bad actions do not eradicate each other, their effects are inexorable. But actions need to mature before they can bear fruit the doctrine of kammavipāka in Jainism also suffers from (the) same impreciseness and confusion. Kammavipāka is the maturing of action until its fruition, literally, the ripening of karman.

"In certain Indian texts, most conspicuously in the Dharmasūtra literature and in some Purāṇas, we find elaborate lists of actions and their Karmic results, specifically, forms on Karmic punishment for prohibited acts, that is, undesirable modes of existence in this world or in the underworld ... Explanation of this kind is not explanation in the modern scientific sense, but something much closer to theodicy."[43] We must remember that even faulty explanations bear testimony to man's desire for explanation, his desire to discover a recognizable pattern where none exists. In Tibet also there is the idea of a direct correspondence between action and its consequence. The Tibetan *Book of the Dead* presents a long catalogue of karman and the corresponding rebirth. Similarly in the Āśvamedhika *parvan* of the *Mahābhārata,* the sage Kasyapa holds a long dialogue with a brahmin which is but a list of queries and replies on the nature of karman and its effect or the absence of such effect on birth and death.

A discussion on karman and fate necessarily introduces nature. In fate thwarted or promoted by a karman, how is nature related to karman and fate? Is there a separate entity called nature? If so, does it affect human action? If so, how? Nature or Svabhāva entails (I) belief in a natural niyati (2) in a supernatural niyati. The first, says G. C. Pande, is a result of reflection over the regularity of phenomena while the second, that of reflection over the accidents, especially in the sphere of human matters. "Since the accidental is merely that the cause of which is unknown, in earlier times when curiosity ran very much ahead of knowledge, the idea of a supernatural necessity is likely to have impressed the

[42] *Numen*, Dec., 1983, p. 207.

[43] O' Flaherty (ed.).

minds of men forcibly. In accordance with the probability, therefore, Niyativāda should in general be taken to have reference to this type of Necessity."[44] The vehement denial of the freedom of will and the non-mention of any divine agency suggest that Niyati itself was considered an ultimate principle.

> The denial of any reason or cause behind the saṃkilesa or visuddhi of men shows that destiny was considered blind i.e., as equivalent to a causeless necessity... once earned, the inheritance of karma was held to be independent of individual will and supposed to work its way along its own logic... will itself is denied... This absolute determinism did not preclude a belief in Karma, but for Makkhali Gosāla the doctrine had lost its moral force, karma was unaffected by virtuous conduct, by vows, by penances or by chastity but it was not denied... All beings, were developed by Destiny (Niyati), chance (Saṃgati) and nature (bhāva)... progress and change are completely controlled... Bhāva... suggest, below the fundamental category of Niyati, sets, of conditions and characteristics in each entity which acting as factors, subordinate to the great principle, control growth, development and rebirth... It would seem that the Svabhāvavadins differed from the Niyativādins in that while the latter viewed the individual as determined by forces exterior to himself, for the former he was rigidly self-determined by his own somatic and psychic nature. These ideas have much in common and we suggest therefore, that Svabhāvavāda was a small subsect of Ājīvikisin.[45]

Nature entered as a factor modifying the course of events in the outside physical world as well as the course of human life; it was soon made into an abstraction and identified with Niyati or fate in the non-conformist systems. When the theory of cosmic illusion entered the scene, it swamped even a Niyati.

> This concept of process, the slow evolution of all entities along rigidly determined lines is clearly stated in Pāli and Ardhāmagadhī. Not only are all things determined but their change and development is a cosmic illusion... with the decline of Niyati in importance, the idea of the futility of human effort probably slipped in the background also... Indeed, it is possible that the rigid determinism of Ājīvika theory never greatly affected Ājīvika practice and that its influence on day-to-day life was negligible... Gosāla believed in an immutable principle which determines all things, Karman is unaffected by good conduct, by vows, by penances

---

[44] 1974, pp. 339–40.

[45] Pande, 1947, pp. 225–27.

> or by chastity... Thus to the Ājīvikas Niyati is the ultimate cause of this universe, it is the first cause, saṃgati and bhāva are but illusory modifications on Niyati.[46]

Long before Gosāla propounded his theory the *Śvetāśvatara* Upaniṣad had formulated a similar tenet *Kālah svabhavo niyatiryadṛcchā* (1: 2). The word yadácchā qualifies the content of niyati: it is capricious and unpredictable. This rules out any attempt at finding a coherent pattern of the workings of fate, niyati.

Some call this the ultimate supremacy of fate, ākasmikavāda, fortuitousness. Balaslev refers to their views. "A number of views termed as ākasmikavāda, sudden occurrence, yadrcchāvāda, haphazard happening, svabhāvavāda, naturalism attributed to the materialists must have been current at a very early date. Whatever subtle difference the views may have from one another, what they all seem to advocate in common is, that the occurrence of an event is without any invariable cause (niyatakāraṇa), that the happening has no necessary dependence on anything else. These theories of spontaneous indeterminate origination were obviously challenges offered by the sceptics against any explanation of the universe through the idea of causal operation."[47]

While the Ājīvikas snapped the causal link between fate and karman, mainstream brahminism did the opposite: it sought to tighten the link between karman and fate. So quite soon in its history karman became closely associated with that part which is beyond human cognition and assumed the name adṛṣṭa, the unseen. Buddhaghoṣa commenting on the *Sāmaññaphalasutta*[48] section of the *Dīgha Nikāya* in his commentary *Sumaṅgalavilāsinī*says: There is neither cause nor basis for the sins of living beings; they become sinful without cause or basis. Neither is there cause or basis for the purity of living beings; they become pure without cause or basis. There is no deed performed either by oneself or by others (which can affect one's future births), no human action, no strength, no courage, no human endurance or human prowess (which can affect one's destiny in this life). All beings, all that have breath, all that are born, all that have life, are without power, strength or virtue, but are developed by destiny, chance and nature and experience joy and sorrow in the six classes of existence.

---

46 *Op. cit.*, 235ff, 471ff.

47 Balaslev, 1983, p. 19.

48 PTS, London, 1975. Vol. I, pp. 53–55, section 21.

"There are fourteen hundred thousand chief uterine births, six thousand and six hundred; five hundred karmans, three karmans, a karman; and a half a karman, a karman sixty-two paths; sixty-two lesser Kalpas, six classes of human existence; eight stages of man; four thousand nine hundred ascetics, four thousand nine hundred dwellings of nāgas, two thousand faculties, three thousand purgatories, thirty-six places covered with dust, seven sentient births, seven insentient births, seven births from Knots, seven Gods, seven men, seven piśācas, seven dreams and seven hundred and eighty four hundred thousand great Kalpas through which fool and wise alike will take their course, and make an end of sorrow. There is no question of bringing unripe karma to fruition, nor of exhausting Karma already ripened, by virtuous conduct, by vows, by penance or by chastity, "That cannot be done, Saṃsara is measured as with a bushel, with its joy and sorrow and its appointed end. It can neither be lessened nor increased, nor is there any excess or deficiency of it. Just as a ball of thread, when thrown, unwinds to its full length, so fool and wise alike will take that course and make an end of sorrow."

The above long quotation brings out clearly the surrender of all reasonable assumptions of causality. Nothing is of any lasting value, good or bad, foolish or wise–all are playthings in the hands of a blind fate. Buddhist literature betrays a jejune partiality for numbers which soon becomes astronomical and even when they are within human comprehension, they are arranged in a way which is wholly inexplicable. But what makes the whole passage somewhat fearsome is the total indifference to causality or any logical structure, its divorce from reason. And this pattern not only came to stay but to be multiplied in its incomprehensible details. Man truly appears as a passive agent to whom things happen, things over which he has no control.

> Karl. H. Potter sums up this state of things beautifully: "... on the one hand, skepticism, the doubt that events are regularly connected and consequently that there is a sufficient condition for getting up and not getting off, and on the other hand, fatalism, the doubt that is not free from a predestined fate *determined by impersonal forces* independent of his control. The parallel fears are, on the one hand, the fear that nothing one can do can bring about a hoped for result and on the other hand, the fear that nothing one can do can alter *what is bound to occur...* Complete freedom is the removal of *Karma,* and if one believes that no real distinction can be found between the renunciatory routes of activity or resignation which beget partial freedom... the fear of the

absurd within man, the fear that there is something irrational that is natural to man such that his capacity in any particular situation as well as in general cannot be gauged by himself or by any other."[49]

Gradually an atmosphere was being created in which the unseen, the unknown element which was at first tentatively posited, notionally gained in significance and soon became so formidable that human action with its rational proportionate sequence became subservient to it. "The concepts of dharma and adharma themselves appear under the title adṛṣta in the list of the qualities (guṇa) i.e. as instances of the second category of Padārtha of the classical Vaiśeṣika system of Praśastapāda ... the doctrine of Karma and rebirth which explains and justifies the current caste status and allows for a future ascent to higher stages."[50]

Adṛṣṭa assumed various shapes, means and associations, but functionally it was fate, the ineluctable force. Among the various names and shapes it took, one was lalāṭalipi, the writing on the head which in Greek was presented in a different form.[51] In ancient Iran Immana the chief God "ist also ein ausgesprochen Sehicksalgott, zugleich gut und bosc, und wollkommen unberechenbar."[52]

What happens to man—good and evil—is determined beforehand by a God above. This belief was spread all over the world. The village mythical tradition in India holds that on the sixth day after the baby's birth, God in the shape of Vidhi, Providence, comes to the new-born baby at night and in invisible letters writes out the events to take place in the course of the baby's life, his destiny. One remembers that Satyavat was fated to die within a year when Sāvitrī wished to marry him, which was why her father had vehemently opposed the match. True enough, death came to fetch him on the appointed day. But such was Sāvitrī's persistence in deterring Yama that he had to relent and Satyavat was restored to life. The head-writing then was not so irreversible as it is made out to be. There are a few other instances of such deviation from the preordained fate. Kaṃsa said about his doom, "People like me can override

---

[49] Potter: 1963, p. 23.

[50] Halblass: 1991, pp. 29, 70.

[51] cf kores burning the baby Triptolemus in her charge to make it immortal; Athena dipping Achilles in water with the same intention; Fileithiya tending new-born babies and deciding their fate.

[52] Widengren, 1938, p. 47.

fate and turn it to advantage by the right conduct, by spells, herbs and incessant endeavour."[53] He could not, however, change his fate, presumably because of the lack of right conduct. Others could, as we shall see later. To add to the external constraints on a person there is the problem of the original, arbitrarily assigned head-writing which showed the fate of all entities in a positive or a negative direction. "The first head-writing has no basis in former deeds and hence decreed events were in.some sense un- derserved. Given the powerful influence of fate one must ask whether a person ever has a chance to alter his head-writing, to correct a negative trend initiated by the first head-writing, to override bad karma assimilated from other or to resist the influence of the head-writing in order to chart a destiny which he desires and controls"[54] "... every deed is recorded separately and each must result in a reaction (reward and punishment) suited to the nature of the deed. Good deeds cannot cancel bad deeds, although the greater the number of good deeds, the greater the number of pleasant events to be ordained by the head-writing. The role of the head-writing in this theory, is to determine what Karma will be activated, that is, attain fruition in a particular life-time. Not all deeds performed in one life-time bear Karmic fruit in the next life-time. Some are deterred to several life-times."[55] Apparently it may look as if "Karma is a thing that can be.... never entirely destroyed."[56] But this view is erroneous as we shall see in the last few chapters of this book. Many and various are the prescriptions in a whole bulky literature composed over the last two millennia whose sole aim is to destroy, totally eradicate or substantially modify karman. "What can be more rightly asserted is that Karma and its consequences have been presented as so intractable and so inexorable, precisely to construct a complicated and elaborate schemata for the destruction of Karma together with its effects. The Kāpālikas and the liṅgayets negate Karma and rebirth."[56a] The vast Puranic literature presents the effects of past karman as adṛṣṭa, unseen; only a handful of wise men gifted with arcane knowledge or clairvoyance presume to interpret the effects and trace it back to the karman. A much earlier Buddihst text, *Milindapñha,*

---

[53] *Harivaṃśa* XL VIII: 39.

[54] The deterministic theory.

[55] Kayes and Daniel: 1983, pp. 35, 39.

[56] O' Flaherty, W.D.: 1974, p. 14.

[56a] Sontheimer and Kulke (ed.), 1989. p. 190.

states that the maturing and fruition of karman is incomprehensible;[57] the Jain sage Haribhadra Suri calls fateadṛṣṭa.[58]

Brahmanism, Buddhism, Jainism all agree that one sure result of sins committed in this life is birth in an inferior station or in a subhuman species in the next or in the subsequent birth or births. Being born as a man is a prize for good conduct in some previous birth. In Jainism, we read: "An animal may have experienced the existence of hell... A God, circumstances permitting, may materialize as a serpent, a precious stone or a tree... plant-souls come from the animal or man-stage, though it has to be noted that here the emphasis is on simultaneity of the incarnation partly basing on the fact that certain plants are the bearers of several or many souls."[59] "Brahmanism only rarely spells out birth as subhuman or inanimate objects as being the result of karman, so clearly. Jainism is in this respect more comprehensive in its approach to the entire universe. As the universe comprises both the animates and the inanimate objects so the soul may assume any of these shapes at rebirth. Besides, a God being born as 'a serpent, a precious stone or a tree', all this has its parallel—although rare—in Brahmanism."[60] But while in Brahmanism such myths are woven around these doctrinal points, Jainism puts them forward rather baldly as tenets of faith. The conceptual worlds of Buddhism and Jainism have much in common; Gods fall from their heavenly station through sins in both, more than in Brahmanism.

"Of the Gods belonging to the centre world, only the stars are quoted in the acknowledged quaternary number though apart from them, we have numerous local deities. Even individual places of the Jambudvīpa have a God of their own, bearing their names and for us mostly leading a wholly vague existence ... To a sinful heretic God it may happen that he attacks a spiritually advanced monk most certainly because in exercising magic he thinks him to be his like."[61] All this falls within the scope of karman and its fruit, because although the very idea of 'a sinful heretic God' is wholly foreign to us, it is

---

57 IV: 4: 1.

58 *Sāstravārtāsamuccaya*, 91, 107.

59 Schubring, 1962, pp. 191.

60 cf Balarāma as Vāsuki the serpent, Tulasī the beloved of Nārāyaṇa becoming a plant and Nārāyaṇa himself as the śālagrāma stone, Śiva as the Bāṇaliṅga stone, etc.

61 Schubring, 1962, pp. 231, 243.

clearly possible in Jainism where Gods reap that fruit of their karman and take birth as inanimate objects. The doctrine of karman is a central concept in Jainism and even the Gods are subject to it. Whereas in Buddhism, for the Gods, birth on earth as human beings and even as beasts and inanimate objects is the result of karman, in Brahmanism it is generally the result of some curse, in Jainism it is the result of their own karman.

Kauśalvā mourns after Rāma's banishment saying that in vain has she observed vows, given gifts, performed austerities and practised penance all for a son since that son was snacthed away from her by fate.[62] When Sītā was touched by Rāvaṇa (thus socially polluting her) it was fate which was to be blamed.[63] Where an obvious morally responsible and guilty agent is present, fate is brought in extraneously to explain a phenomenon.

Yet the *Mahābhārata* says people suffer joy and sorrow through their own faults;[64] by this logic Sītā in suffering humiliation and insult, paid for her own fault. This personal accountability is counteracted by another passage which says, 'joys and sorrows are meted out by fate and are not controlled by the individual.'[65] Even the Pāṇḍavas experienced their own fate.[65a] An individual wanders from one birth to another, goaded by ignorance, karman and desire.[66] When such confusion seems rampant, a compromise formula is framed: 'Something through fate, some by accident, and some through his own Karman does a man get the fruits; there is no fourth'.[67] This idea is repeated in the *Brahtnuvaivarta* Purāṇa where we read, "Some say that on this earth (experiences are due to) one's own action some say that it is through Fate, and others, through their nature. These are the three views in the Vedas... (when) oneself is the agent of action, that is caused by fate, and men's disposition is born of their earlier works."[68] The *Bhāgavata* Purāṇa reiterates this idea: "Some say it is karman, others that it is one's own nature, others, that it is time; others, that it is fate and (still) others, that it is a desire

[62] *Rāmāyaṇa* II: 20: 52.

[63] VI: 80: 8.

[64] I: 74: 29.

[65] *Mbh* II: 44: 1.

[65a] J: 84: 7.

[66] *Mbh* III: 2: 67.

[67] *Ibid.*, III: 33: 32.

[68] Prakṛti khaṇḍa LX: pp. 25–28.

... 'The cause of man's birth and death is fate (daiva)'."[69] This jumbled idea is repeated in many passages, onesuch is: "Some say that the soul is the supreme substitute of the self, some regard it as fate, others as Karman, still others as Nature (or constitution). Some conclude that it is beyond argument arid is quite inscrutable. Hence, sage of a king, sort it out with your own intellect."[70]"Karman cannot be ultimately counteracted by Karmans; both proceed from ignorance, like a dream within a dream."[71] "There is no power superior to fate."[72] Curses and boons are all determined by fate."[73] "Again, "what will happen will happen, what is to occur, occurs."[73a] Thus in text after text, in scripture after scripture, fate is magnified as the supreme controller of human experiences. It is evident that logically this is an untenable position. It confuses individual ethical responsibility by bringing in the extraneous element, fate. Also it is ludicrous to say that these views are there in the Vedas which are quite innocent of the complexity of rebirth, Karman and Fate. This really is confusion worse confounded, and yet it is the nearest to reality. The inscrutability of the power that controls human destiny is most powerfully brought out here. What is not noticed is that there is an inherent contradiction between fate and karman. Of that later one can be born as a human being, or live in heaven or be born as an animal, there is no fourth fate.[74] But we have numerous references of birth as monster, fairy, ghost, demigod and even a full God. When a text says that fate is powerful and the accumulated action is difficult to cross, this is the fault of sinful acts done in the past;[75] it is not at all clear what the mutual relation between past acts and fate is. In one breath the text utters: "man is the agent of good and evil deeds, and experiences the fruits of these; why should God be the agent?"[76] And in another it says, "What fate allocates from before (as) sin is just the 'nimitta',"[77] the excuse or a peg; we (humans) are but the mere automaton authors of such deeds.

[69] The commentator Śrīdharasvāmin, a theist, glosses on 'daiva' and calls it Isvara, God.

[70] *Bhāgavala Purāṇa*: I: 17: 19, 20.

[71] *Op. cit.*, IV: 29: 34

[72] *Brahmavaivarta Purana*: 44: 73.

[73] *Ibid.*, 23: 146.

[73a] *Ibid.*, 27: 57.

[74] *Mbh* III: 178: 9.

[75] *Mbh* III: 198: 86.

[76] *Mbh* III: 18: 7; VII: 41.

[77] *Mbh* III: 199: pp. 2–3.

Acts performed before cling to the 'Soul'. Providence has laid down this law of discriminating among many acts.[78] Such passages are innumerable, strewn all over the epic and their total effect is blindfolding a moral agent regarding his actions and their effects.

Thus "from accident, from fate, from nature (or constitution), what a man receives is but the fruit of earlier action."[79] Again; "none else undergoes the experience of the fruits of actions performed, he alone is the agent, the recipient of joys and sorrows. Whatever karman he has performed, he experiences (the fruit of) it himself; there is no destruction of deeds done."[80] "When you depart none will follow after you; good and evil deeds alone will pursue you."[81] "The familiar image of sowing and reaping is expressed in the kind of seeds a tiller sows, he receives the same kind of harvest—good or bad,"[82] "A man reaps the harvest of his own karman in the self-same bodies (again). A deed done is not destroyed."[83]

The *Bhagavadgīa,* regarded as the quintessence of the *Mahābhārata,* also bases itself on a firm belief in rebirth and karman, the two corner-stones of epic philosophy. "It seems possible to suggest," says Arvind Sharma, "that the various conclusions suggested earlier, namely, that the Gita opts for predetermination or that it never quite makes up its mind about the issue can be seen as fragments of a larger mosaic provided by the trichotomy of karma with kriyamāṇa or āgāmī karma; sañcita karma and prārabdha. In terms of this trichotomy the death of the Kauravas has become prārabdha, but participation in battle by Arjuna is yet sañcita karma which is being provided with the cutting edge āgāmī or kriyamāṇa karma by Kṛṣṇa's pep-talk to render it fully operational or prārabdha, something which in Kṛṣṇa's view Arjuna could, should and would do."[84] One can interpret the cardinal metaphysics of the *Bhagavadgītā* as also of the *Mahābhārata*—at least of the core story—as an object lesson of the theory of karman and its consequences. This is true also of almost all the Purāṇas.

---

78 *Mbh* III: 199:16.

79 *Mbh* III: 33:18.

80 *Ibid.*, III: 200: 27.

81 *Ibid.*, XII: 316: 35.

82 *Ibid.*, XIII: 6:6.

83 *Ibid.*, XIII: 7: 3, p. 5.

84 1979, p. 53.

The late text, the *Yogavāśiṣṭha Rāmāyaṇa* also corroborates the tenets of karman rebirth experiences as fruits of karman, with fate thrown in for good measure. "Previous desires prompt me (in this life)."[85] "One should endeavour in attempts which of themselves will counteract the evils."[86] "As a jar or a cloth, has a specific size, even so the desires of man is of a specific limits."[97]

Fatalism was such a ubiquitous and all-pervasive doctrine that even the medical text of *Caraka* (a third century author) had to take cognizance of it and use it in connection with his own subject in hand. He clearly says that, "Fate should be considered as brought on by oneself from over the previous life, although a person performs actions in this life also."[88] A little later he distinguishes between weak and strong fate: "weak fate is thwarted by a man's action, but at the same lime his action is thwarted by predetermined fate."[89]

Mitchell C Weiss writing on *Caraka* says on the Saṃhitā passage (III: 3:30): "Fate is to be regarded as self-inflicted , an action of a prior incarnation, there is also a person's action that he does here".[90] Weak fate is impeded by individual action, on the other hand, one's action is impeded by pre-eminent fate. Weiss says, "By shifting the emphasis on etiology from previous lives to the present, *Caraka*, effectively redefines aspects of an immutable karma doctrine as mutable." On *Caraka* IV: 2 he continues: (p. 95) "Due to defects of the seed, the residue of one's own karma and the season as well as the mother's food and activities, the various polluted doṣas produce malformations." On 11: 7 "Neither devas, nor gandharvas, nor piśācas nor rākṣasas afflict the man who is not self-afflicted." From these passages it would appear that Caraka preferred to find natural causes for natural defects and diseases and did not ascribe malformation to sins committed in an earlier life as we have found the Purāṇas do. But unfortunately when it comes to therapeutics he says: "Thus any malady is cured when the influence of both the doṣas and karma are dissipated."[91] The apparent anomaly is rather puzzling: the author

---

85 Mumukṣu, V: 10.

86 *Mum.* V: 11.

87 *Mum.* V: 24.

88 *Caraka Saṃhitā* III: 3: 30.

89 III: 3: 33 cd–347.

90 *Caraka Samhita* III: 3: 33 cd–34.

91 O' Flaherty (ed.), 1983, p. 117.

who takes a scientific view regarding malformation which the doctrine of karman clearly ascribes to the effect of past evil acts, who says only the affliction within oneself torments one while the Gods and semi and subdivine beings cannot touch him, suddenly changes his stand regarding the cure of disease. But this is not an isolated instance, the entire *Caraka* Saṃhitā is riddled with such contradictions: a purely scientific attitude prevails over the whole work but frequently such hopelessly obscurantist stance vitiates the tenor of the otherwise wholesome and bold attitude. The only valid explanation is that such passages are conciliatory; the tremendously powerful authors of the Dharmaśāstras who were propounding the karman doctrine and fatalism could not allow such a purely naturalistic and scientific explanation to percolate to their clientele and counteract all their preaching. Hence these rulers of society had to be placated; which explains these apparent concessions. Needless to say, other authors of science and nonconformist philosophy also faced the same problem and solved it the same way. By making occasional concessions, they not only saved their skin, but also saved their works from being suppressed, banned or abolished. Besides, when fate or karman is made responsible, even though partially, as cause or remedy for a disease, priests or shamans and witch-doctors were summoned and paid to perform expiatory rites. Such concessions to non-scientific elements thus provided loopholes through which these people could make some money and gain social prestige.

The supreme mystery regarding karman and its effect is that although scholars have attempted to give it an appearance of causality like clouds bringing showers or seeds sprouting into plants, such a theory clearly holds no water because karman and its result do not belong to nature and therefore do not function naturally. This is the theory of *Karmuvipāka,* fruition of karman. Many texts espesially the Purāṇas, have long passages with catalogues of 'which karman bears which fruit'.[92] Despite these lists, the appearance of causality in a non-physical level requires an intelligent and efficient arbiter, whose discretion is above all suspicion and whose judgment can thus be relied upon. The fallacy of such an assumption lies in the absence of a true

92 cf *vāyu* P. 101: 115–45, 175–192. *Brahmāṇḍa* P. pt III: 4:2: 145–191, *Viṣṇnu* P. II: 6: 1–10m, 32. *Agni* P. 352; *mārkaṇḍeya* P. 11: 22–25; the whole of ch. 12; 14: 16–18; 23–31; 39–95; the whole of chapter 15. *Garuḍa* P. II: 32; 72–80; 125–26; *Bhāgavata* P. 3: 30; 4: 5, 20–27. 32 *Brahmavaivarta* P. 26: 11; 31; 39 : 1–16. *Vāmana* P. chapter 12 et al.

Indian surrogate for Christian Providence, Judaic Jehovah or Islamic Allah.[93] A polytheistic religion like Brahmanism has no one divinity who disburses results of karman, whose judgment is indisputable and therefore, acceptable to all. For the Sumerians "there was a judgment of the dead by the Sungod Utu and that the moon-god Nanna, too, decreed the fate of the dead."[94] This judgment was applicable even for the Gods, "Enlil sinned and in accordance with fate decreed by the Gods he had to depart in the direction of the Sumerian Hades."[95] This kind of all-encompassing divine dispensation has an incontrovertible authority. In Indian theology, Brahmanical, Buddhistic and Jain, there is no such dispensing authority. Texts are full of contradictions, discrepancies, anomalies, inequalities and imbalance between reprievals, aggravations and nullifications of karmans and fruits. In other words, there is no parity between cause and effect so that this lack of uniformity creates problems of credibility. We have a divine clerk, in later mythology, viz., Citragupta, but no judge. So, man's inherent expectation of a just retribution of his actions—past, present and future meets a void or a chaos of multiplicity of standards and authorities. This chaos constitutes the happy hunting ground for both the upholders of fate and the subscribers to the karman theory.

T. N. Madan condemns fatalism really harshly when he says: "Fate informs the parent child relationship at every step: from the initial step of Kanyādāna (giving the daughter away)... through the interminable step of garbhādhāna (begetting of a child) to the ultimate steps of piṇḍadāna (the food-offering for the departed soul)".[96] This actually is the impression one gets from the cumulative evidence of the Purāṇas. Let us look at some such passages. "Fate cannot be gauged, hence all action is based on human endeavour."[97] This, clearly is a ease of nonsequitor, but the important idea is that if fate cannot be gauged and the human endeavour is karman, then fate would be obliterated. Even in the *Mahābhārata* Yudhiṣṭhira could not be dissuaded from accepting the invitation to the game of dice; his feeble argument was, "I cannot disobey his word because of the irresistible power

[93] Not even the Christian concept of Providence has solved all theological problems, or that of Jehovah in Judaism and Allah in Islam.

[94] Kramer, 1963, p. 132.

[95] *Op. Cit.*, p. 147.

[96] Madan, 1987, p. 29.

[97] *Devībhāgavata* IV: 21; pp. 5–7.

of fate."[98] This reads like a conscious and voluntary surrender to fate, an abdication of moral responsibility.[99]

Sometimes specific evil deeds are mentioned with their effects. Thus "receiving dakṣiṇa (ritual fees) from caṇḍāla or other inferior castes causes both the sacrificer and the priest to be born as worms in stones."[100] "If your fate is strong, you will again gain wealth; (for) wealth diminishes when fate declines and increases (when fate) ascends."[101] Kalkin introduces himself to Jina (Buddha), "Know me to be fate, the bestower of good and evil fruits."[102] The most repeated formula regarding fate is, "One must necessarily experience the imperishable fruits of karmans. Karman is not eroded without being experienced even in hundred crores of kalpas.[103] The God, the lord of the world, who indwells the spirits of all men, experiences all the fruits of all action."[104]

The *Brahma* Purāṇa harps on the theme of the ineluctability of fate: "who can escape what is ordained by fate?[105] "Of those in human form, who knows fate?"[106] And yet although in these two passages fate is presented as supreme, action and its role are also magnified. "AH men experience everywhere and at all times; none can do anything good or evil to anyone else."[107] One notices the obvious confusion in the statement, the unaccountability which is at the back of the positing of nebulous and uncertain causes. "As a man has acted previously, so he experiences the fruits."[108] "Of the three causes, action is the first, then the agent and then something else."[109] "Of piety, wealth, desire and release, the action itself is the cause."[110]

---

[98] II: 67: 3, 4.

[99] The supremacy of fate is harped on repeatedly in the *Mahābhārata* cf I: 109: 10, 11; 43: 32; 45: 55 ff; 67: 3–4; 71: 35, 176: 26ff; V: 159–64; VI: 76: 19; 135: 1, VIII: 9: 3.

[100] *Vāmana* Purāṇa 12: 36.

[101] *Ibid.*, 79: 27–28; XII: 6: 1 ff *et al.*

[102] *Kalki* p. II: 7: 15.

[103] Creationn Annihilation= akalpa.

[104] *Nārada* II: 3, pp. 69–70.

[105] II: 1: 69.

[106] II: 3: 10.

[107] II: 12: 49.

[108] II: 23: 25.

[114] II: 27: 10–25.

[110] II: 27: 22.

The Purāṇas alternately emphasize the roles of fate and action. "This entire universe, (with the) movable and immovable is under the dominance of fate."[111] Also the whole of chapter eight in the same text, an account of Hariśćandra is a long story of unmerited misfortune like that of Job in the Old Testament and like Vessantara in the Jātaka, although a demand for poetic justice brings redress in all three cases. The slogan that nothing is mightier than fate is repeated *ad infinitum* in all the Purāṇas.[112] The attitude of surrender to fate is abundantly clear in the epics and Purāṇas. "After an effort is made, what will happen will happen."[113] A preordained fate is accepted as the major premises; it is the writing of destiny which determines the nature of experiences, "When through the agency of time a soul assumes a body, even then everything is written beforehand— joy, grief and death. "In whatever manner a man is fated to die, he dies in that same manner, there can be no alteration. Men's lives and deaths are completely under the power of fate, none in the three worlds can counteract it."[114] "A righteous man performs penance for long. The bestower of the fruit are the Gods, regarding the truth of this there can be no doubt."[115] "Fate is irresistible, there is none mightier than fate."[116] Sometimes a balance is sought to be struck between fate and karman. Thus "Providence unites, but karman brings about separation."[117] In an irreversible way karman was associated with fate; the links in the chain get forged stronger and stronger, although the logic of the link is nowhere explained with any precision.

Fate is glorified as the supreme entity: "Those perfect in wisdom who know this mortal body in its true essence do not consider whether it is stationary or moves upwards. (They regard it as) arriving through fate or through the dominance of fate as the drunk person regards his clothes as dirty."[118] "This is the limit of folly that when people talk of acting or eating,

---

[111] *Nārada* P. IL: 13: 107.

[112] *Brahmavaivarta* P. 11: 17.

[113] *Devibhagavata* P. V: 5: 51.

[114] *Ibid.*, V: 1110; 38, 39, 11: 44.

[115] *Brahmavaivarta* P. Brahmakhaṇḍa 14: 30.

[116] *Devībhāgavata* P. IX: 16: 31.

[117] *Brahmavaivartaa* P. 13: 46.

[118] *Bhāgavata* P. XI: 3: 36.

they (really) talk of fate and time."[119] "This visible world which is seen in its expanse is the soul's dance hall, hence he dances away here. The third (force) is Kṛtānta, the fierce one. Fate dances in the world in the shape of a Kāpālika."[120] "Of this form (of fate), before it dances Destiny, the eternal feminine, without abating her gestures she dances all around (it)."[121] And "Destiny, because she is feminine is by nature ever flighty and ever forward."[122] "Works are rooted in fate, the whole world is under the sway of fate. Fate protects the good and punishes the evil."[123] If only things were like this in real life! Since they are not, we can see through the subterfuge: the proposition, inverted simply stands: Those who suffer do so because they are evil, and those who are protected are good. Such assertions are thus extremely tendentious and ultimately false. "Victory and defeat are controlled by fate."[124] "Time is but a contingent, fate is the mightier of the two. Everything is fashioned by fate, hence nothing can be altered. Fate is the supreme power, fie upon human endeavour: (fate) is the victor over all the Gods."[125] "The result of what one does, good or bad, has to be experienced without fail, by the strongest, just as by the weak, whether much (is) done or whether a little. Truly in all respects (such fruits) have to be experienced by the Gods, demons as well as by men."[126] "No soul is under his own power, but ever under fate."[127] "Men's union and separation are always under fate."[128] At the end of Hariścandra's patient suffering the Gods offer him a ready reward, he was to ascend to heaven with his wife and son.[129]

Despite the supremacy of fate asserted in innumerable texts, karman, a newly fledged idea of this early Puranic age is emphatically stated to be all powerful. "Karman determines birth, death, pleasure, pain, fear, and

[119] *Yogavāśiṣṭha Rāmāyaṇa* Viragya, section 25: 1.

[120] *Ibid.*, vai. 25: 5.

[121] *Ibid.*, vai. 25: 10.

[122] *Ibid.*, vai. 26: 5.

[123] *Brhamāradīya* P. 8: 58.

[124] *Ibid.*, V: 7: 18, 19.

[125] *Ibid.*, VI: 7: 22; also 23.

[126] *Ibid.*, VI: 7: 18, 19.

[127] *Ibid.*, VI: 10: 29.

[128] *Ibid.*, VI: 30: 16.

[129] *Ibid.*, VII: 27.

bereavement; a creature becomes Indra through karman, Brahman's son, a servant of Hari, is immune from birth, etc. By one's own acts one may attain all success and become immortal. Through karman one obtains being in the same sphere (sālokya) in intimate communion (sāyujya) proximity (samīpya), and equality of rank (sārṣṭi) with Viṣṇu. Through karman (one attains) brahminhood, liberation godhead, manhood, supreme overlordship, supreme sainthood or mendicanthood, kṣatriyahood, vaiśyahood, śūdrahood, an untouchable existence, a hill, tree, animal, bird, a small creature, worm, serpent, gandharva, monster, kinnara, yakṣa, kuṣmāṇḍa, spirit, gnome (vetāla), ghost, a demon, ḍākinī, daitya, dānava, a holy creature or a great sinner, handsome, healthy, very sick, blind of an eye, ugly. He goes to hell or heaven, to Sūrya's, Candra's, Indra's domain: fire, air, Varuṇa's station, Kuvera's, Dhruva's, Śiva's and the stars', of truth, 'jana', 'tapas', 'mahas', the nether worlds or to Brahman's; to India coveted by all, to Vaikuṇṭha, Goloka, free from diseases, a long-lived person, a short-lived one, one who lives as an embryo for a moment only and then dies."[130] This comprehensive catalogue of life in various stations and experiences of various kinds actually seeks to cover all forms of life and then trace them to karman as their cause. Not that there is any real compatibility of this idea with other contradictory ones. And what is more, this passage itself is riddled with contradictions if we take into consideration later, especially Vaiṣṇava texts which declare that certain spiritually exalted stations can never be attained by karman but by devotion. Then again, the Upaniṣadic—and later Vedāntic texts assert that neither by good karman, nor by sacrifices can one attain Brahman, nor even by deep and wide knowledge; grace of God bestows the right frame of mind which renders a man into a fit recipient of the realization that alone leads to liberation.

Another passage says,

> the good never boast because creatures are formed by their own work. Some ride carriages while others draw them, the king receives taxes because of karman (sic) others pay it. Some sit on thrones, some are courtiers, others are various categories of servants because of karman,some ride horses, some on elephants... some are carriers, others, are carried because of karman some enter a sow's womb, others Śacī's, some become yours (i.e., Brahma's, to whom Mohinī was speaking), some through devotion to Hari become his courtiers. Because

[130] *Brahmavaivarta* p.: Pṛakrtikhaṇḍa: 24: 17–37.

> of fate (daivadoṣatah) some become dung-worms; because of karman, some emperors go to heaven, while others go to hell and wallow in dung and urine there. Because of karman, some become the lords of Gods, even Indra, some Gods, some men, some small animals. Because of karman some are born in the highest caste, even as brahmins on earth, others kings, vaiśyas, śūdras and outcastes. Because of karman some become wise, all-seeing through knowledge, while others (become) stupid, blind and of defective limbs. Because of karman some teach the scriptures to disciples, others study everything and learn from teachers' mouth. Because of karman, some in their stationary or mobile bodies become mendicants or murderers, or a chaste woman while another, a prostitute.[131]

The Purāṇas build up an edifice of the karman theory; it rests on rather shaky ground and is full of self-contradictions, yet increasingly growing in bulk and complications. One of the major Purāṇas, the *Padma* Purāṇa has an interesting passage.

> (The soul) comes to the earth.alone and leaves it again and again, because it experiences the fruit of his karmans. Creatures are born through (their) karman and perish through karman, Happiness, sorrow, fear, grief—all (these) he experiences through karman. With the remainder of karmans creatures are born (on earth) and appear and disappear repeatedly ...(The fruits) of actions performed whether good or evil have to be experienced without fail. Godhead, manhood, birth as animals and birds lower creatures or inanimate beings—all these happen according to one's karman. Deeds performed in a previous existence, no man can alter on this earth either by might or through wisdom.[132]

Again, the *Brahmavaivarta* Purāṇa enunciates the position: "the agent experiences the soul, the individual spirit is ever the one to go through the experience."[133] These passages clearly state two things: (1) the fruits of actions are inescapable, (ii) they must perforce be experienced by the agent himself, " the realm of saṃsāfa of transmigration and of retributive causality ... is governed by factors (such as adhikāra, aḍṛṣta/apūrva, etc.) that are themselves not amenable to worldly ascertainment and explanation..."[134]

---

[131] *Brahmavaivarta* P. : Śrīkṛṣṇajanmakhaṇḍa 32: 42–54.

[132] II: 81: 43; II: 94: 94, 15.

[133] Prakṛtikhaṇḍa, 25: 16: see also 26: 30; 28: 10; 37: 14, 17, 60: 64. Gaṇeśa khaṇḍa 12: 19; 27: 62, 66; 34: 65, Śrīkṛṣnajanmakhaṇḍa 6: 30, 31; 32: 42–54.

[134] Halbfass, 1991, p. 152.

Besides being a jumble of illogical *non-sequitors* and pseudo-causality what is interesting in the passage is that although karman is here posited as the root cause of all stations of life, all its conditions and of all manner of experience, yet one sentence where a person becomes a dung-worm, the cause mentioned is not karman but "due to daiva (fate)'s fault"; yet the sentence continues in the vein of its earlier and later statements; there is no real reason why fate should be brought in there in place of karman. The obvious conclusion is that behind this whole passage there is a conceptual equation of fate with karman. We shall discuss this point later.

In the *Devībhāgavata* Purāṇa when Sāvitrī asks Yama "which action leads to what kind of deformity, disease, state of mind, success and stations in the next world she receives a lengthy reply which has an appearance of one-to-one correspondence between an act and its effect."[135] In the second passage a Caṇḍāla who touches the Tulasī plant remains pure for seven successive lives and a mleccha who touches Gaṅgā-water, for five lives, the dung-worm touching the Śālagrāma stone (remains pure for) seven successive lives. This book lists the effects of good and bad karmans which lead to many sons, childlessness, still-born infants, long-lived sons, meritorious, defective or deformed sons, many wives (sic), wifelessness, handsomeness, piety, sickness, disease and recovery and ends with, "karman, therefore is the Veda of all Vedas." Not only is such a concept of karman incompitible with fate, it also negates many other positions stated before, and contradicts much of later bhakti theology.[136] Earlier the same text says that through karman man deserves and gets birth , death, happiness, grief, fear, misery (which rise and disappear according to karman). "Gods attain still higher stations or honour, the mleccha is born as a mleccha because of his karman, people are born as trees, stones, monsters, beasts, insects and worms according to their deeds."[137] "if one eats without sharing his meals he becomes childless, a malicious person is born blind (in the next life), a stealer of books is born to be childless."[138] One notices the total lack of parity between action and its effect; so logical causality is trodden underfoot in passage after passage of such tenor.

---

[135] IX: 29: 15–33; IX: 35: 41–42.

[136] IX: 46: 29–31.

[137] *Ibid.*, IX: 27: 17–24.

[138] *Garuḍa* P, Uttarakhaṇḍa 44: 14, 15.

Karman can be accumulated from the past (sañcita), be performed now (kriyamāṇa), and also be karman of the past which bears fruit in this life (prārabdha). When the prārabdha is just about to bear fruit, it is technically known as 'niṣeka'; and "everything (that is accomplished) is accomplished by niṣeka. Niṣeka is mightier than Providence... who can deter (or prevent) niṣeka."[139]

Fatalism is not an invention of India, it was present in some form or other all over the ancient world. Helmer Ringgern translates a Persian couplet from the Persian epic *Al lailah wa la'ilah*[140] which says: "We tread the path where Fortune hath led. The path Fate writ we fain must tread."[141] In his book *Studies in Arabian' Fatalism* he writes, "One of the general words for Destiny is the verb *hamma* and its derivatives. Generally used in the *passive form* to indicate that something is determined or assigned or, as by gambling, falls to a person's share arbitrarily.[142] That which is destined or decreed is firm and unchangeable as if it were already existing in advance ... Who it is that decrees or determines is never said... the cup of fate as written in a book or on tablets."[143] "Thus in the early medieval period, Persian epics and Arabian texts present a clear picture, of fatalism despite the dominance of monotheism in those regions. Fatalism was a very old belief prevailing in the Middle East and we now know that this fatalism survived many forms of opposition.

In China "A fatalistic *T'ien* equivalent to the concept of fate (ming), a term applied to all those events in human life over which man himself has no control"[144] About Mencius this author says, "At times he seems to designate a fatalistic heaven."[145] And about Lao-Tzu, "All things, howsoever they flourish, return to the root. This return to the root is called quiescence (ching) which is called submission to fate, and enlightenment."[146] Regarding

---

139 *Brahmavaivarta P.*, Kṛṣṇajanmakhaṇḍa 46: 58.

140 ed. By Macnaghten and translated by Burton, Vol. I, p. 77.

141 Ringgern, 1952, p. 20.

142 Especially for death, the day is predestined.

143 1955, pp. 6, 7, 18 and 48.

144 Fung yu Lan: 1952, p. 3.

145 *Ibid.*, p. 129.

146 *Ibid.*, p. 181.

Mo Tzu, we read: "Now those who hold that there is a Fate say whoever is rewarded was destined by Fate to be rewarded and it is not because of his virtue that he was rewarded ... This heaven and Fate both denote something that is beyond the scope of human power," Mencius' view was "That which is done without man's doing it is from Heaven. That which happens without man's causing it to happen is from fate."[147] Chinese civilization is very ancient and from all the evidence we have, the belief in fate goes back to its first period of urbanization and has persisted regardless of Buddhism, Islam and Christianity although the area and the degree as also the social stratum of the really enlightened people now limits its sway.

In the first chapter we have noticed that early Greece as well as the classical i.e. mid-first millennium Greece knew fatalism and had invented a number of Gods in charge of different aspects of fate. It must be added, however that some of the multiple theophanies of fate may be explained by regional variations. But later we have noticed that Greek philosophers not only subscribe to fatalism but sought to rationalize and bring it in line with the metaphysics they propounded. Thus "in both *Timaeus* and *Republic,* in conformity with divine will *through the compelling power of the stars (Plato) fixes the course of successive reincarnations.*"[148]

Jacob Neusner writes, "It would be difficult to doubt that what one does, determines the effect of what one does. But that position is rejected. The very valence and result of a deed depend, to begin with, on one's prior intent which leads a person to do a deed governs the culpability of the deed. There is no intrinsic weight to the deed itself."[149] Thus the Mishnah internalizes karman, placing the sole emphasis on the intent rather than on the deed itself, and here it is the intention which determines the result of the karman. Karman thus is governed by the ethics of the volition more than by the actual performance, the action itself. In his *Jesus the Magician* R. Morton Smith writes, "The second century Church Fathers refer to Christian heretics called Gnostics, people who believed among other things that salvation came from *insightful knowledge of a God beyond the* creator-god and of a fundamental flaw in creation revealed in the revealed scriptures of Moses."[150] The Gnostics'

---

[147] *Ibid.*, p. 127.

[148] Vincenzo Cioffari, 1935, p. 36.

[149] Brock, Baarde, and Mansfield (ed.), 1988, p. 277.

[150] 1976, p. 37, italics added.

dogma was a very different one from the Great Tradition Christian dogma; they believed the creator-God failed in his task, so that creation is incomplete and imperfect. Deliverance was thus to be obtained not through works, karman, but through the recognition of this faulty creation of a creator and hence through seeing, realizing the other God above the laws of Moses. Their rejection of the validity of karman as such resembles that of the Ājīvikas and like the Upaniṣadic seers they placed their faith on knowledge, gnosis, for salvation.

In the ancient world many sects repudiated faith in salvation through karman; one corollary of such rejection was fatalism "A l'epoque romaine, quand, par application d'une idée facile à reconstituer, on eut rangé la roue parmi les attributs de Tyche-Fortuna, elle-même parfois assimilée à Isis, on ne vit plus dans le roues egyptiennes au temoignage de plutorque qu'un symbole de I'instsbilise les choses humaines."[151] This loss of faith in the stability of things human was another path which led to fate. It could also lead to God as it most frequently did but "most ancient mythologies assimilated Tyche-Fortuna in their pantheons." So fate co-existed with the Gods and sometimes assumed distinct names, shapes and roles and operated with, under or above the Gods. The respective roles of fate and karman were often confused; some texts made fate the superior agent, others maintained that since what man experiences is directed and caused by his own karman, there was no gain saying its supremacy. The two are not only incompatible but wholly irreconcilable. Yet scriptures often attempt to fit the square within the circle and fail.

[151] Comte:, 1911, p. 30.

CHAPTER 4

Karman, Fate and Free Will

BOTH rebirth and karman stem from death, the trauma and uncertainty associated with death. The excavation of prehistoric burial sites bring to light man's worries and concerns regarding death, his attempts to offer comforts to the departed soul. Life can never accept death, the negation of life. "Man has always reacted to death. He did not accept it, convinced as he was that it did not belong to the original plan of human life. So we find several myths explaining how death came into the world."[1] One reaction to man's spiritual rejection of death was application of magic for prolonging life, necromancy, attempts at rejuvenation through pseudo-chemistry etc. Underneath such endeavours is the belief that death is extraneous to the schema of life. Man held that the ultimacy of the termination of life in death was unacceptable. Also the appearance of the departed in dreams assured him that the essential man i.e. the spirit lived on, despite the death of the body. Hence the universal belief in an existence of after-life: in heaven, paradise, purgatory, hell, an astral body or the spirit form. "The care taken over the disposal of the dead indicates a deeply held conviction that provided the appropriate steps are taken, death could be regarded as a transitional slate... The oldest astronomical texts now known are found on the lids of wooden coffins dating from the Ninth Dynasty (c 2150 B.C.). They are called 'diagonal star clocks' or diagonal calendars and they give the names of the stars associated with the respective decans."[2]

All over the world men have sought to understand death, to interpret it, to assimilate and place it in the paradigm which they constructed for life. Because understanding death was part of understanding the significance of life and this quest for knowledge or realization of life was universal. It was a dire spiritual need for man—to penetrate the mystery of life and therefore,

---

1 Blacker: 1963, p. 135.

2 Whilrow: 1988, pp. 23, 28.

of death. In the period when metaphysical enquiry was couched in the language of mythology and mythology was enacted in the ritual, "The transcendent authority of the Brahmins who sacralize the social order, is reinforced by the theory of death as a cosmogonic sacrifice, for this theory locates, the ultimate source of regenerative power in the ritual sphere and places its control in the hands of those who operate the sacrifice."[3] The obsequial service, the crematory ritual thus becomes regenerative in potency; *antyñeṣṭi* is a *grhya* rite, a sacrifice, *(isti),* of the corpse in the funeral fire to reassure regeneration, just as inhumation makes sure of the body waiting until the trumpet shall sound and the dead are called up to eternal life. Yet practical experience of death as the inescapable end was too obvious to be negated. All must die: this is a recurring theme of the epics and Purāṇas. "There is none immortal among the mortals, man has a specified span of life."[4] "Some become immortal through their work, some deny the existence of death. O King, listen to me since this is so, don't be scared. Both these are right, when a ksatriya makes no endeavour, then death is his delusion, approved of by the poets, I call death an error, to be ever alert is to be immortal."[5]

Death can be violent, sudden, slow but is always certain. In all its forms it strikes terror not only in the one who dies but also in those who watch and survive. Regarding the origin of death, the *Mahābhārata* has a myth of divine anxiety to control over-population. Brahman created a woman and commissioned her to destroy men and so reduce population. She declined, went and sat meditating. Summoned again, she pleaded inability to oblige him, and shed tears of compassion for creatures and terror at the cruelty of the mission. Brahman had her catch the teardrops in her palm and said these would be diseases which would bring death to men.[6] She, Mṛtyu, escaped the task of killing man outright, the killing became indirect. This element of compassion in Mṛtyu herself is rather new. Everywhere else, in the epics, Purāṇas and in literature Death is portrayed as a man of fearsome aspect. Trinetrā, a monstress in Rāvaṇa's palace enclosure has a dream of the impending death (of Rāvaṇa); Death in her dream is fierce and awe-inspiring.

---

3 Block & Paryy (ed.), 1982, p. 41.

4 *Mbh* III: 136: 5.

5 Sanatsujāta lo Dhrtaruslra, *Mbh* V: 41 3, 4; continued to 14.

6 *Mbh* XII: 274.

In the *Harivaṇśa,* Viṣṭi, wife of Adharma (impiety) gives birth to Fear (Bhaya), Great Tear (Mahābhāya) and Mṛtyu; Death here has evil and unholy associations, she is daughter of impiety. The *Matsya* Purāṇa presents Viṣṭi as a personification of Kāla— time or death[7] Some myths conceptually equate Śiva, the God of cosmic annihilation as representing Death or destruction. The true identity of Śiva dawned in Brahman's heart who passed it on to lndra who in his turn communicated to Mṛtyu from whom the (eleven) Rudras received the knowledge and they finally handed it over to a human, Taṇḍi.[8]

The real God of death in Indian mythology is Yaina who was at first a mortal and who, on his death went over to a happy region. In the Ṛgveda he welcomes and looks after the dead, with whom he enjoys food and drink. It is noticeable that there is no element of fear or fierceness associated with this God. Once a mortal himself, he is kind to those who pass through death and come to him. But after the doctrines of rebirth and karman were firmly entrenched in the theology, Yama changed perceptibly and totally: from 'a God of the dead' he now became 'a God of death'—fierce, awesome and cruel.[9]

The Creek God of death is Ker; Thanatos is another personification of death. The Orphic hymn to Thanatos says: "for you alone is the judgment of all brought to pass: / you alone are not swayed by prayers of supplications."[10] The Celtic parallel is Morrigan. In Ireland "Death's coach had a headless driver, black or headless horses." In Brittany the "Coach of Ankou" is driven by Death "who is but a tall lean skeleton."[11]

The *Yogavāśiṣṭha Rāmāyaṇa* equates death with Kala who like a rat marks the old burrow, and dire poisonous diseases finally rest in the hollow of the body. "The life is thus drunk up as venomous serpents drink up the woodland breeze... A man is sighted by death as a rat is by a cat... Happy is a man when he foolishly wishes to enjoy the earth, to catch the moon from the sky; how can he attain happiness? Senility destroys the body as does the

[7] XI: 32.

[8] *Mbh* XLII; 17.

[9] For a mythological account of Yama see the author's book *The Indian Theogony*, Anima Publishers, Chambersburg USA and Motilal Banarassidass, 1968, Chs II, III and IV.

[10] No. 8718.

[11] *Hasting's Encyclopaedia*: 'Fate'.

river (uproot) the tree on its banks."[12a] Thus life is cheated surreptitiously by death hunting for a prey. Of Kalkin, the last incarnation due to bring about a cosmic holocaust to end this aeon, it is declared, "Whence is Kāla, whence Death, who is Yama, where is the God; the God Kalkin has been multiplied (into these) through illusion."[12] This apocalyptic vision is also repeated in other myths.

In the *Rāmāyaṇa* when Lakṣmaṇa become senseless after Rāvaṇa has hurled the Śakti spear on him, Rāma laments: "What sinful act have I done in an earlier lite, so that my righteous brother lies dead before me."[13] " When we remember the text which says to Rāma, "Sīta is Lakṣmī, you are Viṣṇu and Kṛṣṇa is Prajāpati,"[14] we feel puzzled, because as Viṣṇu how could Rāma sin? But both he and Sīta suffer long periods of misery although since they were incarnations (born for the destruction of Rāvaṇa and the monsters) they could not very well have sinned themselves as Lakṣmī and Viṣṇu while in heaven. Rāvaṇa's queen Mandodarī lamenting for her dead husband says. "The agent is bound to receive the fruit of sinful acts, my husband; when the time arrives, there is no doubt about it. The doer of good receives good and the doer of evil, evil."[15] While the wicked Rāvaṇa reaps a harvest morally due to him although he dies after a long happy and prosperous life; it is difficult to explain an incarnated divinity's sinful deeds in another birth, the fruits of which, dire distress and prolonged misery he suffers in life. Nowhere does the text say that he pays for unethically killing Vālin and the innocent Śambuka and for twice abandoning the innocent Sītā or even that theseare sinful acts. It would, then, have made sense for his suffering; but what about his pure, devoted wife Sītā's sufferings? Except wrongly upbraiding Laksmana under terrible mental stress—which almost mitigates the sin—she never committed any other sin, yet pays a much more heavy and unaccountable penalty than Rama. The Gods are shown to be pleased at the slaughter of Śambuka and at Sītā's entering the fire, they come and vindicate her piety but do not say a word blaming Rāma for his rejection of his innocent wife. One would imagine that Rāma incurred the Gods' displeasure at committing these

[12a] Vairāgya Section 16: 17: 19.

[12] *Kalki* P. III: 1: 36.

[13] VI: 101: 1, 2.

[14] VI: 107-27.

[15] VI: 111: 25, 26.

unethical acts during his incarnation for which he would pay in the next life. But no, at the end of his life here he goes straight to heaven and is received there as Visnu with due pomp and splendour.

When the righteous Uttānapāda saw his end approaching, it appeared to him "with its foot placed on death ascending the house... He gave himself to penance, studied the Vedas for millions of years and worshipped Hṛīkeśa and finally overcame the fierce, almost invincible Death."[16] Death is here presented as something which can be conquered or averted with good works and with devotion to a saviour God. But for ordinary mortals it is the immutable end. The *Devībhāgavata* says that even "the Gods like Brahman, Viṣṇu and Śiva were devoured by Death, so what should one say of lesser ones?"[17] We, however, find no scriptural reference to these Gods' death except for Viṣṇu when he was incarnated.

Kāma, desire and Māra—Death in Buddhism are sometimes equated with death. In "Pour une problématique nouvelle des religions Indiennes anciennes", G Fussman says of Māra "les Kafirs de 1' Hindo Kouch, qui attribue à Māra le dieu oblige à poser la question suivante: si Māra est un dieu mineur... les theologiens bouddhiquess out et£ obliges de placer Māra audessus d'lndra? La response est, je crois evidante: ces legends sont nèes dans un milieu qui faisait de Mara le souvrain des dieux."[18] So, among a certain people, at a certain period, Death or Māra was the sovereign God. This becomes evident when we think of the inevitable defeat life suffers at the hands of death. Also when we think how desperately men have in all countries and in all ages sought to get the better of death. And failed. This attempt is best brought out in the world's first epic The Gilgamesh "... in creating mankind the Gods allotted death to men; they kept life firmly in their own hands."[19] Gilgamesh went to the ancient ancestor Uta Napishtim for procuring ambrosia. He passed many hurdles before arriving before the ancestor, the latter sought to dissuade him from the pursuit. But when Gilgamesh was adamant in his supplication, the former gave him the desired object. Happily he descended from that region and on the way back, placed it on the grass at the bank of a river where he went down for a dip. A serpent

[16] Bhāgavita P. IV: 12: 30, XII: 8: 11.

[17] X: 13: 51.

[18] *Journal Asitique*, 1977; 1 and 2 p. 52.

[19] Bleeker: 1963, p. 138.

came up from the water, ate it up and immediately cast its slough."[20] Very deviously Uta Napishtim had his way: he deprived mankind of immortality which he had reserved for himself.

Death then is the portion of humanity. The *Bṛhadārṇyaka* Upaniṣad says that Prajāpati, a mortal created the immortal Gods. "Since being a mortal himself he had created the immortals, therefore he surpassed in creation."[21] This is one of the rare occasions where Prajāpati is designated as a mortal, for, except Yama the Vedic texts do not give direct human antecedents of any other God.[22] This difference between the Gods and men—mortality and immortality—turned them into two distinct species, mutually dependent yet with an inherent resistance in men towards the Gods.

One reason for this was that man's fate to a large measure, especially as adrsta, was in the hands of the Gods, Draupadī said to Yudhislhira, "God is a magician, man is a mere puppet. Man knows nothing and exercises no influence over his own happiness and misery ... God's actions should be seen as arising from the same selfish motivations as man's... God, like man, is pursued by the tainted fruits of his own actions and, therefore, vulnerable in the same ethical judgment as men".[23] Here Draupadī basically takes a correct stand; there is precious little difference in motivation, actions, suffering or enjoying the fruits of their actions, their impulses are equally selfish. Yet the Gods are above men, controller of their destinies. Hence, "In doctrines of predestination, theistic religions softened the ruthless quality by subsuming the facts of inevitable necessity under the will of God."[24] Although apparently there is a contradiction between fate and the Gods or God, in most religions they coexist peacefully. And, consequently, the Gods' relation to fate is taken to be a deep secret. "Of actions, pious or wicked, the fruition, rise and decline are secrets even to the Gods."[25] Before the second game of dice Yudhisthira,

---

[20] One remembers the image in the *Bhagavatgītā* of shedding the old body like an old garment. Behind the image we see the serpent casting off its slough and gaining a new lease of life.

[21] 1: 4: 6.

[22] Although inferentially we gather the human antecedents of Indra and the Asvins who were later deified.

[23] *Mbh* III: 31: 21–39; Abo in the *Bhagavatgītā* in the same vein in II: 18: 61.

[24] *Encyclopaedia of Social Sciences*, pp. 146–148.

[25] *Mbh* III: 32: 33.

drawn to it irresistibly says, "Creatures receive good and bad from divine dispensation"[26] thus denying his own responsibility, shifting it to the Gods. A similar famous statement is 'He whom the Gods wish to destroy, they deprive him of his wisdom and he sees everything distorted.'[27] Dhṛtarāṣṭra attempting to deny his responsibility says to Vyāsa: "Sir, I do not enjoy this game of dice, I think, I have been forcibly made to act so by Providence."[28] At another place Vyāsa says: "(Of actions) either God is the agent, or man. Man acts, but the fruits go to God. Accidents happen in this world or the fruits are remembered as of actions (men perform) good or bad deeds, appointed by God."[29]

The particular story of Sāvitrī and Satyavat[30] begins with a prophecy of predestination: Satyavat's span of life was to be over within a year and it was going to happen that way. Death had come to take his soul away. Then began the antipodal movement; Sāvitrṣ argued, pleaded, coaxed and cajoled, quoted scriptures, took the role of a spiritual enquirer and finally wrested such boons from the God as could not be fulfilled without Satyavat's revival. The God here who represented Satyava's fate relented so that the predestined fate was nullified. But apart from the sociological interest served by the episode it is a rare exception.

There is thus an inherent contradiction between the belief in God/Gods and fate: Yama deviated from his role as 'fate as just' and became a boon-bestowing God, the contradiction lies in the thematic justification of his presence in the episode. "Man cannot be expected to take the same attitude when he considers the righteous Cod to be the Determiner of Destiny and thinks that he is guided by moral principles in distributing fate, as when he believes in Destiny as an impersonal and mechanical power... If we stick to the definition of fatalism as the belief that man's destiny is determined by an impersonal fate, it is evident that in theory at least, fatalism excludes every belief in God as the author of destiny."[31] Real fatalism has no room for a God; there is a metaphysical contradiction between the two. "Tout absolument tout

---

26 II: 67: 3.

27 *Mbh* II: 72: 8.

28 *Mbh* III: 10: 1.

29 *Mbh* XII: 32: 11, 12.

30 *Mhb* III: 281.

31 Ringgern: 1955, p. 124.

dans le nature, dans la societê, dans les actes et les pensêes des hommes est place sous la responsibility et la controle d'un dieu."[32]

But if instead a God is posited to account for the anomalies of the universe and human life, then an altogether different picture comes before us. The best example is the Apocryphal passage 4 Ezra: 3: 20 on which Edward Stone writes: "It is primarily the attempt to establish Cod's responsibility for the state of the world... For not only did God create human beings with a weakness which led to sin, but having done this, he then proceeded to punish mankind and Israel for sinning... It is a challenge to God's justice... it reapplies the telling of God's gracious acts to God himself so that it becomes the summons calling him to account before the bar of his own justice. This striking reversion of the matrix... emphasizes the author's theological daring ... by its end he comes to accept the role of determinism in the divine conduct of the world."[33] We have seen how an idea of God or Gods as dispensers of fate conflicts with the notion of fatalism. But fatalism also conflicts and contradicts any just and logical system of causality. The simple logical premise that a cause precedes and generates an effect is so logically rounded up, neatly and completely, that it leaves no scope for fate. Yet, fatalism and causality have co-existed in most theologies: "Tyche, although always operative is particularly obvious in the case of those occurrences in which we see no other cause. Aristotle's *Phusis* (a passage) deals with the terrestrial Tyche demonstrates its validity and had nothing to do with cosmic automation."[34] *Adrasteia* sets down the laws operative above the Gods as well, *Heimaitnene* indicates the law which operates in the material world, and the three Fates are the ministers of Zeus whose job is to determine and record his mandate ... "She (Fortune) interferes with the recording Fates by introducing sudden and unforeseen outbursts. Not satisfied with the unforeseeable occurrences she claims some control over predictable causality, thereby becoming identified with *Nemesis,* the goddess of retribution. In the Epicurean system events were not causally connected and happened either as a result of chance or undetermined free will."[35]

32 Duverger: 1987, p. 113.

33 Brock, Buarda, Mansfield (ed.), 1988, pp. 133–34.

34 196 a 12.

35 *Dictionary of Ideas,* Vol. II, pp. 228–29.

It is interesting to note that most of the fatalistic deities operated under Zeus. But Zeus is nowhere presented as the ultimate arbiter of fate, nor is he portrayed as personification of cosmic or human justice. Fate thus remains the domain of these Gods and Goddesses who function practically independently relying on their own sense of justice and retribution.

Because their judgement and the logical cogency of the judgment is seldom explained to mortals, the Gods' function remains an inspissated, dark mystery to mortals. This trail is universal, common to all mythologies in which fate and the Gods cohere.

The early Greek Gods and Goddesses of Fate and Fortune are many. If we turn to a late phase of Greek culture, the Orphic Hymns provide us with instances of some of the Greek Gods in connection with man's fate. The poet Pluto addresses thus: "You alone are the rewarder of deeds, seen and unseen."[36] To Herakles: "and drive away ill fate with poisoned arrows."[37] To the Moirai, the traditional divinities of fate: "where glory persues the earth-holding chariot beside the boundary of justice and hope and cares."[38] To Nemesis, another famous theophany representing fate 'in you is the justice of mortals.'[39] Dike, also a goddess of fate is addressed with, "for all things which are come to mortals, by evil opinions, /difficult of judgment, to mortals who wish the greater part by unjust counsels, / you alone, stepping in, raise up justice for the unjust /enemy of injustice, may you kindly reward the just."[40] The Hymn to Nomos says, "abiding harmlessly with ail / the lawful, bringing dire evils upon the lawless."[41] To the goddesses of revengeful justice, the Erinyes, "who ever look upon the numberless /races of all mortals /with the eye of Justice, judges who are forever. /But goddesses Fates, serpent-tressed, of many forms."[42] Somewhat similar in role and function are the Eumcnides, "who look upon the life of all impious mortals, /punishers of the unjust, standing near necessity."[43] To Mellinoe "who drive mortals to madness with frightful

36 No. 18, 16.

37 No. 12, 16.

38 No. 58, II 8–9.

39 61, 9.

40 62, 6–9.

41 69, II 10–11.

42 69, II 10–13.

43 70, 4–5, 18 says 'of many fates'.

imaginings /showing forth the shape of form by means of strange images, / sometimes manifest, sometimes shadowy, nocturnal with hostile attacks during the murky night."[44] To Tyche another well-known Goddess of fate "for to some you bring a prosperous wealth of possessions / to others evil poverty which raises up anger in the soul."[45] In these hymns different poets, on behalf of their society praised the various epiphanies of the Gods and goddesses of fate. The praise is prompted by awe and the fear of the unknown and is accompanied with prayers for the divinities' favour and clemency. Both the attitudes are classical and ubiquitous.

To an earlier period belong the Homeric hymns to many Gods which bring out their mythic character. Thus to Demeter,[46] "Mother, what the Gods send us, we mortals bear perforce, although we suffer, for they are much stronger than we." The third hymn addressed to Pythian Apollo says "but now we are come on shipboard to this place by *no means willingly*—another way and other paths—and gladly, would we return. But one of the deathless Gods brought us here against our will."[47] In the fourth hymn Hermes is invoked; Apollo speaks "As for man/*will harm one and profit another,* sorely perplexing the tribes of unenviable men. Whosoever shall come guided by the *call and flight of birds of sure omen,* that man shall have advantage through my voice and I will not deceive him, but who shall trust *idly chattering birds*, and shall seek to invoke my prophetic art contrary to my will and to understand more than the eternal Gods, I declare that he shall come on one idle journey."[48] To Pan the half-man-half-goat shaped God, "luck-bringing Hermes."[49] To Earth the Mother of all, "To you it belongs to give means of life to mortal men and to take it away"[50] And finally, to the Dioscouroi "who are deliverers of men on earth, and of swift-going ships when stormy gales rage over the restless sea."[51]

---

[44] 71, II 6–9.

[45] 72, II 7–8.

[46] Callidice to Demeter.

[47] III: II 470–74; italics added.

[48] IV: II 541–45; italics added.

[49] XIX: 140.

[50] XXX II, 7–9.

[51] XXIII: 11 5–7.

In these passages we notice that men depended for justice on these Gods whom they frequently equated with fate. In other words, fate or the unseen power which meted out justice to men was governed by the Gods. The anomalies did not disturb them. Yet to a modem author who takes a comprehensive overview of the role of the Gods in the Creek epics and dramas the picture is very different. "At no time are men *anything but the playthings of the Gods.* Hecate and Calliope take an interest in men. The first protects nurslings but for the rest distribute her favour *quite arbitrarily* among competitors in war and sport... The second gives eloquence to wise princes which helps them politically. Some men evidently receive favours from the Gods which accounts for inequality in fortune and talents. Mankind's lot is not substantially improved by these intercessions."[52] Hesiod's Theogony bears this out. "In his heart he, Zeus thought evil against mortal men which also was to be fulfilled."[52a]

What strikes us forcibly is the undercurrent of hostility, almost rivalry, between the Gods and men. Not only do the Gods act capriciously but in a positively hostile manner towards men. And what becomes all the more gruesome and terror-inspiring is that the Gods' hostility is not provoked by any apparent misdemeanour or remissness on the part of men. It is truly motiveless malignity, hence all the more fearsome. And all these traits become attached to fate—this motiveless malevolence, this capriciousness, this lack of balance between men's action and the Gods' award of good or ill fortune. Slowly but surely a nebulous—and therefore all the more awesome—figure emerges, whose will is law and whose will has no bearing on any ethical justice. The Gods act with supreme indifferences to mens' interest or their just portion. All over the world this divine indifference has puzzled men. The doers of evil are not punished just as the doers of good are not rewarded; therefore, fate is anything but just. To account for life's anomaly brahminical theology has invented the neat paradigm of the theory of karman. What cannot be balanced between karman and its effect in this life is cleverly pushed back into the past, or forward into the future. A wicked man flourishes? He was pious in a previous life or he will be punished in the next. Since both these are beyond human ken, karman assumes the vital characteristic of fate, viz. inscrutability. For over two millennia, authors of the Puranas and

---

52 Geertz (ed.): 1971, p. 133.

52a *Ibid.*, p. 119.

Dharmasastras have worked assiduously to build up a bulky literature based on the non-apparent aspect of fate, the life or lives beyond the present. The hostility of the Gods is frank hostility in Greek theology and mythology; the issue is cleverly dodged and manipulated in brahminical theology. The entry on 'Fatalismus' in the *Brockhaus Enzyklopaedie* says, "Die Schieksalmacht kann aber auch persönlich vorgestellt und über den etwa verhandenen anderen Göttern stehend gedacht werden, wie die Moiren in. Grichenland. Die tritte möglichkeit findet sich in Islam. Hier ist der Wille Allahs allbestemmend unabṇnderlich, aber oft auch undurchschauber."[53] "The fatalism in Islam is, strictly speaking, not a belief in destiny but presupposes the predetermination of almighty God... The pre-Islamic Arabs as well as the ancient Teutons had a certain preference for passive verbal forms in order to express the predetermined lot."[54] That Muhammad introduced monotheism as one of the measures for unifying disparate groups of polytheistic and often mutually hostile tribes is well known. But these tribes carried over their pre-Islamic heritage of beliefs. Whenever misfortune befell, rather than blaming the almighty being, the father-figure of Allah, they blamed it on fate. In *Islamic Fatalism* Ringgern says, "It may be a consequence of the purely secular character of this poetry that Fate stands out much more clearly than theism ... It is characteristic that most of the fatalistic verbs are entirely missing in the Koran", where Allah is the allotter. "God creates the acts of a man, but the man 'acquires' them and makes them his own and becomes responsible for them."[55] It is interesting to note the use of passive verbal forms which had preference in pre-Islamic Arab literature as well in Scandinavian literature. In both the cultures man was more acted upon than acting, a more passive agent than fending for himself. The casuistry of 'acquiring' action which Allah has already allotted him is, to say the least, a clumsy and metaphysically and ethically untenable position, an attempt to combine free will and predestination, which many theologians all over the world and throughout the ages have attempted. The only way out of this impasse is in mysticism. Ringgern mentions this, "in the mystic, this feeling of absolute dependence does not create indifference and paralyzing apathy. Predestination is liberating." "It is an interpretation of destiny that expresses man's feeling of

[54] Wiesbaden 1968.

[55] Ringgern: 1967, pp. 10–11.

[56] 1967, pp. 53, 55.

total dependence, not on an impersonal power or universal order but on an omnipotent God."[56] We may add a note on the fatalism in the Edda, E Neumann writes in *Schicksal Notwendigkeit:* "(1) what happens had to happen (2) a kind of superwill wants it to be this way." "The first type belongs to a primitive people and corresponds to the Gods called *Vanir* while the second type is connected with a more civilized and politically organized people and matches the Aesir Gods."[57] The Aesir were nearer our notion of divinity while the Vanir were intractable and nearer the concept of Gods of fate, generally belonging to a camp hostile to the Aesir.

The Sumerians, one of the world's most ancient civilized peoples, were like most other ancient peoples, polytheistic. "There were several deities who had the supervision of the moral order as their main function... Unfortunately, although the leading deities were assumed to be ethical and moral in their conduct, the fact remains that, in accordance with the world view of the Sumerians, they were also the ones who in the process of establishing civilization had planned evil and falsehood, violence and oppression—in short, all the immoral and unethical ... modes ... of human conduct." "Gods were like mortal rulers and no doubt had more important things to attend to."[58] Gods in ancient pantheons had to perform heroic feats, conquer alien people, succour their devotees at all costs. And they could not lead puritanic or ethical lives. Their lapses are many and varied. Quite in keeping with such an image is the capriciousness in their conduct as dispensers of justice. Since-the myths portray that their own behaviour was far too erratic and unpredictable, people could not and did not expect strict justice from them.

We notice that the concept of fatalism was well developed in the ancient civilizations which flourished between the third and the latter half of the second millennium B.C. One common factor of these civilizations was that they were predominantly urban, with class divisions clearly recognizable. With land and sea trade controlled by a handful who exported agricultural and craft goods and who organized the manufacture of these goods at home, tills oligarchy enjoyed unprecedented privileges.

Under them, directly or indirectly laboured the primary producers who subsisted on a mere pitence. The class bifurcation of these societies whose

[56] 1967, p. 62.

[57] Glessen, 1955, pp. 1, 70.

[58] S N Kramer: 1963, p. 124–126.

elites lived in the cities was sharp. The craftsmen lived inside on just outside the cities while the vast majority of the people, lived in the less advanced, mostly primitive villages. The tribal cohesion which was a protection for the poor tillers was either gone or on the way out the cities enjoyed the army protection of the the city-states. There was thus a major gap in life-style, wealth or plenty. No wonder, fatalism flourished in such unequal distribution of the amenities of life. On the other hand, storms in the ocean, pests, droughts, floods, epidemics, etc. effected the affluent even though sometimes indirectly or marginally. Because of the fatalism was formulated in the upper, priestly sections of society in different degrees of submission. In the final analysis, the earliest appearance of fatalism in the Middle East, Egypt and China is co-incidental with primary urbanization.

In a jātaka tale perfect being from the world of the thirty- 'three fell in the a lotus and grew up as girl.'[59] In another a golden light emanated from Siri, she said that the favoured the ethically pure the virtuous people.[60] But in actual fact Gods did not always favour the good, many a time a very wicked person got through to the would of the Gods or received high spiritual station through a minimal gesture of devotion to Buddha, a Buddhisativa or a Pacekabuddha. Another divine reaction quite common throughout the jātakas is: whenever men excel in austerity, charity, self-sacrifice, or in any extraordinary merit, Sakka's throne in heaven feels hot and he descends to succour or reward them. Also in the face of extraordinary moral excellence he become jealous and seeks to tempt them and deflect their austerities, but more frequently he actually assists or rewards them.

Gods, then, in most mythologies are not morally perfect, they do not bear exemplary character. They interfere in human affairs and sometimes embody justice, but more frequently, capriciousness and injustice. This is their role as distinct divinities, but in some myths they bear the names of the different aspects of fate and act as agents of capricious and very infrequently of the just fate.

There is an anomaly not only between karman and fate, between the Gods and fate but also between the laws of causation and fate. If causation is accepted as a cosmic and natural principle, then it becomes immutable and irrevocable and leaves no room for fate. A. Long referring to the Hellenistic

---

[59] No. 38, *sankā.*

[60] No. 382, *Siri Kālakamni.*

myths says, "the stories were committed to determinism by the properties which they ascribed to Nalure itself. As the all-pervading pneuma or logos, Nature is the intelligent director of everything. If some events were fortuitous or fell outside the scope of Nature's power, the world could not be analyzed entirely by reference to Natural Law... divine providence, which the Stoics strenuously maintained, presupposes a capacity in God or Nature lo bring about good works."[61]

With the change from Vedic sacrifice to the notions of rebirth and karman with their concomitant concept of fatalism there was a greater emphasis on karman and fruits of karman. Madame Biardeau writes. "En un mot, e'est la distribution de valeurs qui est changée, non les valeurs ellemêmes, et la morphologic sociable reste immuable en ses principes sinon dans les fruits."[62]

When Nature and causation are taken together as inter-dependent forces working in conjunction, then a cause is the necessary immediate antecedent of the effect. But reality often belied such presuppositions. "It is... also important to note that *Cārvāka* materialists did raise significant objections against the idea of necessary relation between the antecedent and the consequent as the basis of the idea of causality. They point out that there is no onlological or logical connection between them. It is merely imagined to be there as a habit of thought."[63] Causation, therefore, is not accepted as an essential dogma in explaining natural phenomena, chiefly because it has been observed to be erratic and, therefore, undependable. Nature's movements cannot invariably be accounted for by the operation of the law of causation. Hence some room is made for fatalism, which, essentially as an unknown and unknowable quantity, explains what cannot be explained by Nature or the law of causation. In the human world also there is imbalance between karman and the fruits of karman. Robert Alter in his article, 'Sacred History of Prose Fiction' says, "...the tension between the divine promise and its ostensible failure to be fulfilled; the other is a tension between God's will, His providential guidance and human freedom, the refractory nature of man... the double dialectic be-tween design and disorder, providence and freedom . . ."[64] It took centuries, even millennia to observe the discrepancies

---

[61] Long: 1985, p. 164.

[62] Exister, no. 2a, 1981, p. 9.

[63] Balaslev, 1983, p. 20.

[64] Freedman (ed.) *Near Eastern Studies*, Vol. 22, p. 14.

between what was expected and what really happened. Between early Brāhmaṇas and the *Muṇḍaka* Upaṇisad which describes ritualistic religion as 'a leaky boat', no more than four or three centuries had elapsed, but the frustration of 'non-delivery' of goods promised by rituals as assured results was palpable already. But to experience the much greater frustration of finding Nature behaving erratically, even capriciously, to experience that no immutable law governs nature and that man's conduct was punished and rewarded arbitrarily was much deeper, with a more abiding despondence.

A natural corollary of this experience was a questioning of man's own responsibility in shaping the course of his destiny. The *Matsya* Purāṇa has a relevant passage: fate cannot be gauged; so all action is based on human endeavour, (paurusa). One's own karman is called fate earned from another existence, therefore, wise men say that manly effort is more important. An adverse fate can be counteracted by endeavour, by those who engage in ceremonies and try to rise higher. By endeavour men receive the result they seek: men who lack wholly in manly vigour believe in fate. Fate, man's own action and the fruits of the past, present and future—these three bring about the fruits of karman for a man."[65] Zoroaster, however, "believed... that man has an inescapable moral responsibility for his own actions."[66]

The question of man's moral responsibility and therefore, that of the extent of the freedom of his will is a cardinal one which has plagued mankind for millennia... the notions of moral guilt or blame, of moral responsibility are inherently confused and... we can see this to be so, if we consider the consequences either of the truth of determinism or its falsity... Just punishment and moral condemnation imply moral guilt and guilt implies freedom and freedom implies the falsity of determinism."[67] The dichotomy of freedom of will and predestination or fate has been clear to thinkers for ages. Possibly the confusion centres on the degree of both these elements. Absolute freedom of will is countered by real, unforeseen, sudden accidents and natural political, social or even familial disasters. Similarly, absolute determinism is falsified by experiences where a man wills and then accomplishes something, subsequently enjoying or suffering from the effects. It may be pointed out here that there are schools of thought like the Ājīvikas or Calvin which are

---

65 221: 1: 12.

66 Whiltrow: 1988, p. 34.

67 Strawson, 1974, pp. 12.

absolute determinists. But there is no school of thought which upholds the total sovereignty of the human will; experiences of accidents of various kinds contradict such a position.

If absolute determinism is fate, then completely fatalistic thinking has not dominated either theology or metaphysics. Qualified determinism is an area where the dispute between fate and free will is much less acutely pronounced. In the last chapter we shall come back to the respective relevance of these two positions.

"There is no problem in reconciling determinism with freedom of action ... Hobbes (is) the originator of the compatibility thesis but he ... denied the truth of free will."[68] If the action is compulsive with no freedom of choice and therefore, of moral obligation, then determinism becomes compatible with freedom of action, but since this action is not preceded by a moral choice, freedom of will is denied. The gloss on the Jain *Bhagavatīsutta*[69] says that 'man suffers from the consequences of his own actions prompted by desire; this is the worst evil viz. desire'. But even with desire the action it prompts can be avoided, the moral choice or option is there. But once man yields to desire and acts evilly, he lands in hell, continues the exposition. Hence freedom of will is not precluded.

What opposes fate in action is independent human endeavour (puruṣakāra) impelled by free will. And here is an inherent contradiction of a very long standing. Ninian Smart says, "It is interesting to observe that in so far as Indian philosophers discussed freedom of will (and this was bur slightly), the topic arose in connection either with karma or with God's controf of us." For the thesis that all human acts are the result of prior causes, almost inevitably interpreted by reference to the self-regulating law of karman, this problem of free will takes on the form of the question, *"Is it possible by present or future acts to alter the causal sequence already set in train by our previous deed*? The answer is generally agreed to be 'Yes', on account of the fact that we can perform good deeds which make our future more favourable and more importantly, in various ways annihilate existing karma or neutralise its effects."[70] What is not tackled here are the problems (i) whether rebirth

---

68 Raphael, 1981, p. 7.

69 The Chūrni on No. 2.

70 Ninian Smart: 1967, p. 164; italics added.

can be proved, (ii) whether there is a continuity of the identity of the self across births, (iii) whether good and bad deeds can be transmitted as if these were reified and finally, (iv) whether, therefore, the good or bad consciousness, which causes the deeds and which, then, becomes an essential concomitant of such deeds also travels across death. All the texts, Buddhist and brahminical, agree that the reward of good deeds is birth in a famous wealthy family of a high caste and in a healthy male body. Frequently, such well-born and prosperous people are mean, deceitful and corrupt in character. The question naturally arises, can the good self which reaps the harvest of its past good deeds turn into its moral opposite and yet enjoy the fruits of its past actions? Did it leave its goodness somewhere on the way to rebirth? Besides, there is no proof of the questions posited before. Only surmises, with serious fundamental metaphysical doubts dogging them at each step.

The *Dictionany of the History of Ideas* says, "The patterns of life are submitted for selection to the souls present for exercise of their free will. Their choice is determined by lot. This chance element viewed subjectively from the point of view of the soul becomes Fortune. Following Fortune which is the law and order of the Universe, the soul is transformed as a result of its free choice of life, but that free choice may itself be limited by the individual's Fortune... when Fortune attaches itself to the cause, it is Mind itself in so far as accidents are causes... As such, chance negates the possibility of predicting the outcome, but does not affect the human or religious values of the outcome. In the *Eudemian Ethics* luck is analyzed as operating through a personal instinct which guides man to a desired success at the opportune moment and under the most favoured circumstances and does so in defiance of good reasoning, or rather by making bad reasoning come out right. The naturally lucky man is the one, therefore, whose desires are prompted and guided by the deitv. The scholastic view of his divine Luck as Providence is introduced into the world as good Fortune in general."[71] The author then asks two questions, "(1) How is it possible for the deity to bring luck to the undeserving? and (2) why is bad luck visited upon those who deserve good luck?" Among the Stoics in particular, the necessity arose to account for bad luck in a providentially ruled world. In Seneca, God and nature become identical and Destiny was identified to both. Fate was the 'Word of God' which once spoken had to be obeyed *(De Providentia)*.[72] In Apuleius,

---

[71] 1247b 34ff.

[72] De Platone et eius dogmate 1: 12: 205.

Providence was the divine plan and fate itself is necessity and order. In *Simplicius* fate is the chain of causal concatenation which is inherent in the seed and, therefore, considered the *ratio seminalis*. It is the law of individual aberration made to control human actions. The Stoics considered fate as an incomplete comprehension of causal concatenation. However, fate is defined as a cause unknown to human understanding; it can have no reality of its own. As such it can no longer be suspended from God.

"The problem of maintaining both free will and causality was at the root or explanation of the fortuitous in a providential universe. Fate operates in human conduct on condition that we deduce it from certain antecedents. These postulated antecedents are our merits. There is freedom of choice at the start, but once a choice is made necessity comes in control. Events can be regarded as fateful only when free will is exercised without which there could be no rewards or punishments and, therefore, no moral law. Divine prescience does not imply determinism, for, knowledge on the part of God is proportionate to the thing known. This is a basic concept in reconciling free will and the element of chance in the Christian doctrine."

In St Augustine — "Providence controls all things, for it is inconceivable that God who provides for everything should wish that any part of it escape the rule of Providence or any astral determinism independent of God's will cannot possibly exist... The Augustinian Providential system does not question the existence of causality."[73]

Since fortuitous events involve human choice, the manner in which human choice raises the claim of causality is significant. (3) Volitions and choices are disposed immediately by God without an intermediary, (2) Human knowledge is disposed by God through the medium of angels.

Bernard Berofsky says in *'Free Will and Determinism'*: "A choice is free, therefore, if it is the product of deliberation involving free judgments... An act is free if the predominant composition in its determination is the man's reason or intelligence. Freedom in fact is the essence of morality. For, if freedom is determination of will by the laws of its own reason, then, freedom is autonomy, legislation by the self, for the self... Now how can man qua noumenon freely determine the will to perform a specific act that is necessitated by antecedent conditions to perform (Kant)."[74] This idea is

[73] *De Civitac Dei,* Bk V, ch II.

[74] Vol. II, pp. 227–229, 239, 240.

borne out in the *Dictionahe de Théologie Catholicim* – "ce principe de predestination est absolumment universal Les semi-pélasgiens ont objecte: śil y a une prédestination infallible, je suis predestiné ou non. Si oui, je fasse je serai infalliblement sauvé; sinon quoi que je fassse je serai infalliblement dammné."[75] Here the crux of the paradox is expressed in a crisp and inescapably logical form: 'if 1 am predestined to be saved, do what 1 may, I shall definitely be saved; and if I am not predestined to be saved, do what I may I shall definitely be damned. Logically it is an irrefutable dilemma, "Quant à la cause de la prédestination, il ne le voit point dans la prescience de nos mérites mais dans une misericorde speciale de dieu... le motif de predestination en general est done la manifestation de la bonte divine, sous la forme de la misericorde qui pardoune; celui de la predestination de tel homme plutot que de tel autre et la bon plaisir divin. S'il en est ainsi, comment forrnuler exactment le motif de la reprobation soit positive, soit negative."[76] For predestination it is not at all necessary to note merits or men, but God's special grace that He can pardon. It depends on the divine pleasure. Thus, predestination affords God the special privilege of forgiving i.e. showing special favour to whom he pleases. Man is thus reduced to a passive recipient of divine grace.

In Egypt, Fate was connected with birth and/or rebirth and when the gift of a son is sent, Hathor spins his fate around him— again fate offers the Gods an opportunity to manifest their special powers.[77] The Egyptians knew that fatalistic misfortunes befall or meet men but also unexpected luck can be sent to him. They differentiated in this regard the quality of the day (i.e. the astronomical concatenation of asterisms).[78] Tracing all human experiences good or bad to fate was the way of the ancient world's thinking process, at least from the period of primary urbanization. It coloured the thought systems of different theologies in different ages.

---

75 Entry on 'Predestination', Paris, 1932.

76 *Ibid.*

77 "Die Ansicht daß Schicksal irgend die mil Ger Gebürt verknupft ist ... Auf tein Gebet bin shenckteh die Göller ihn cinen Sohnn ach dessen Geburt die Hathoren kamen um ihm sein Shicksal zu bestimmen."

78 "Die ṁgypter wufilen, daß schicksalhaftes Ungliick den Menssehcn treffen, aber auch unerwaricles G'uck ihm Geschenkt werden kann Sic un-Icrschieden in dicscr Hinsicht die Qualitat dor Tagu." Numen (j fase 1–2 "Shicksal in der all-Agypllschen Religion", pp. 113, 118, 128). AL Oppcnheim, 1964, p. 201, 2M, 206.

About ancient Mesopotamia we read "Customarily Simtu is translated by the Assyriologist as 'destiny' or 'fate', a translation that is inexact and misleading ... quite generally speaking, Simtu denotes a disposition originating from an agency endowed with power to act and to dispose such as the deity, the king or any individual may do, acting under specific purposes. Such a disposition confers in a mysterious way privileges, executive power, rights and—when originating from a deity—even qualities (attributes) upon other gtxds, persons and objects deriv-ing its effectiveness solely from the power and the right of disposition inherent in the acting agency ... Just like Simtu, isqu has a wide semantic range, extending from lot, fortune, fate to nature, quality and even office (the Greek klaros) ... usurtu (Sumerian giś hur) which means drawing or plan, design apparently referring to some kind of divinely predetermined— outlined, even 'blue-printed'—course of events that determines all happenings". In old Persian *melammu* corresponds to *hvarena* which in turn represented in contemporary Aramaic Lexts by *gndia* i.e. 'luck.'[79]

One interesting point emerges out of the early part of this quotation: the concept of fate as an arbiter was an idealized reflection of an earthly potentate who wielded apparently unlimited power, who decreed the rewards and punished the guilty according to his caprice. Just as in the pre-legal kingdoms, the kings and/or priests sometimes administered true justice but quite frequently satisfied their unjust whims and desires simply to strike terror and awe in the subjects because the lord's wish often came to be declared and satisfied in an unexpected manner at unexpected hours with no recognizable rime or reason; similarly when unexpected experiences of joy or grief came to men they ascribed it to the unknown and unknowable power operating invisibly. Fate thus was an abstraction of the unaccountable conduct of an earthly overlord who exercised limitless power to do good or harm to his subjects.

In discussing these Western philosopher, we confront some basic assumptions which are open to question: (i) God is gracious to all creatures, (ii) He gives man a free choice, (iii) Once the initial free choice is made, the rest follows automatically, (iv) Freedom involves the determination of the will by the law of its own reason and becomes autonomous. But this is just not compatible with the presence of God. Then again, man's intellect is operative in the exercise of free will but if a Providence is allowed who acts

[79] A L Oppenheim, 1964, pp. 201, 204, 206.

independently, then there is precious little scope for the independent human intelligence. Then, Fate and Providence are, delightfully confused. The first presumably standing for ill-luck and the second for good luck; but even that is not tenable in the final analysis.

At best it is a strenuous, sincere attempt to build such a paradigm which will contain mutually contradictory ideas and at worst, it is a veritable hodge-podge because it seeks to reconcile such mutually incompatible tenets as can never be reconciled. The trouble can be analysed only historically. Slowly but steadily and gradually the human intellect came to take cognisance of certain facts of experience: Free will, fate, God and/or Providence. Mercifully it keeps away the most complicating factor, viz. rebirth. But even then, chance or fate which is conceptually blind or capricious can hardly be expected to behave in a logical, coherent fashion. And if a God or Providence, benign towards humanity, whose movements and judgments are at least rational and to mortals he is introduced in this schemata, it is like seeking to make fire and water co-exist. Since this is a conceptually unsound proposition the pattern is riddled through and through with fallacies. So we now see another anomaly, a benign Providence cannot co-exist with fate. Can free will co-exist with fate? It is the moot question. Maskarin Gosāla thought that the concept of free will was a vulgar error. "The free will perspective... rests (on) the responsibility with the individual for it is believed that he has the ability to resist the control of the head-writing over his 'will' and to initiate karman that can reverse unfavourable events. If unexpected suffering befall him because of his head-writing, he is still considered responsible because they are thought to represent a just punishment for deeds freely willed in a former life time."[80] This is the irony of trying to accomodate free will in a scheme where fate dominates. To say the least, it is less than metaphysically honest to juxtapose two mutually exclusive entities. If fate is predominant then all occurrences, good or bad, in this life, in former or succeeding lives—are governed by fate. Maskarin Gosāla's first premise is completely compatible with this stand: human effort is not worth anything, things happen fortuitously and there is nothing that man can do to achieve anything or to alter what is predicted or arranged by fate.[81]

---

[80] Keys and Daniel, 1983, p. 41.

[81] Gosala's second premiss, however, is dictated by a vague optimism regarding the ultimate destiny of man: after 84,00,000 births a man is automatically liberated. Such liberation is a withered carrot dangling before the ass—it is too remote to enthuse any one and the liberation is too vague to affect man's ethical attitudes or decisions. He lives and dies a plaything in the hands of fate.

In Christian theology, we know how the controversy over freewill and predestination dominated the theological field for a long time and that even now there are those who follow the rigid predestination theory of Calvin. But by and large, it raged over sometime and has abated since. "Two aspects are to be clearly distinguished from the start: the divine prevision which belongs to the order of knowledge, and predestination which involves much more. In the latter, God is envisaged as the creator and conserver of the world, the primary mover who moves all secondary causes, including the human will. He moves the will in such a way that its free decisions are ultimately effects of God's primary causality. This is as true of any human life as a whole, as of each individual decision."[82]

"As a consequence of original sin, mankind is assigned to perdition but God saves from this *massa damnata those whom he his* marked out for salvation and these are infallibly saved. The number of the elect is predestined from eternity. God does not positively reject the rest, but *permits them to assign to perdition* because of their sins. What appears primarily as an abstract metaphysical truth is in fact the concrete field of the subtle interplay of grace and freedom."[83] Theologically, this statement is wholly untenable because of its many self-contradictory statements, God has decided whom he will save; therefore, the rest will not be saved, but damned; so logically they are automatically doomed from the beginning of time i.e. long before their birth. How does God permit them to earn the doom through their own sins? A verisimilitude of free will is introduced: men get doomed through their own sinful actions. But by the very logic of the first premise, viz. God's prior selection of whom he will save, the rest are pushed to sinful acts. They never had any real option from the teleological point of view; their option was essentially fate. Hence this pre-selection is not only a prevision, but a predestination which goes all the way from the doomed man's pseudo-choice of moral action, his inevitable sinful choice and then his ineluctable doom. There is neither fair play nor grace in the cases of those who even before they commit one single sinful act are preordained to destruction. Free will is a mere eye-wash; it fails to take in any logically thinking mind. "It is man's power of reason which is the basis of his free will, and free will is found in

---

[82] *Sacramentum Mundi: An Encyclopaedia of Theology* (ed.), 1969, Vol. V. p. 88.

[83] Karl Rahner, 1969, pp. 88–90.

neither plants nor animals,"[84] This power to reason is an essential prerequisite of freedom of will and this is what is tacitly denied in fatalism. Neither a benign Providence, nor kindly Gods, nor a mechanism or power which dispenses justice would allow blind fate to co-exist with the freedom of human will which is pre-conditioned by human intelligence.

With regard to Islam we have seen that despite injunctions to the contrary, fatalistic ideas had prevailed from the pre-lslamic period and continues till today. How does free will fit in, in this frame of belief? "From the early days of Islamic society the question of free will began to exercise the minds of men." A tradition, the authenticity of which is very much doubled was circulating to the effect that Muhammad had said, "The proponents of free will are the Magians of my people. Opposed to free will is rigidly enforced predestination. Those who maintained that chained to a fate decided for him by Providence, in-capable of free choice were known as *Miyubbiruh or jahriyyah—believers in forceful fate... When toe ascribe action to man it is figurative.*"[85] The *Enzyklopaedie Brockhaus* says on the subject, 'Prädestination'. "In Islam ist der Gedanker der 'Prädestination' besonders deutlich vertrete. Da der Koran hinsichtlich der Prädestination keine eindeutige Meinung vertritt (wenn er ihr audi zuneigt) kam es schon in 8 Jahrhundert zu lebhaften Auseinandersetzungen zwischen Anhṇngern and Gegnern der Prädestination spater wandten sich vor alien die orthodoxe Lehre von dor Prädestination (Kismet) durchgesetzt. Die mabgebende Theologie baut auf ihr auf' The *Lexikon für Theologie und Kirche*[86] has on 'Fatalisms', "die Annahme eines blindwaltenden Schicksal das die Gottesvorstellung verdrṇngt oder beeinflubt aus den Menschen einer siene Freiheit nicht achtenden vomerbestimmung unterwirft ... besonders in der antiken Mythologie der Stoa, dem Islam und dcr Prädestination, Schicksal Religiongeschichtlieh. Die universal Erfahrung des menschen, da er in dem ihm wiederfahrenden höheren Gewelt abhangung. 1st prṇgte sich auf verschiedene Weise aus. Das Schicksal kann entwider als von einer unpersönliche über allem (auch den Göttern) stehenden Macht oder als von personlicher Gottheilen gevvirkt gelten." We find that in early times there was no uniformity of opinion regarding predestination. Only with time the opposition was subdued and the orthodox religion grudgingly accomodated predestination within its scheme.

---

84 Boughton: 1946, p. 13.

85 A M Balyuzi, 1976, p. 225.

86 Freiburg, 1960.

Almost the same thing happened in Brahmanism. Free will was never questioned but had been assumed as an accepted dogma in Indian religion. Later with the rise of fatalism the inherent dichotomy, even opposition between the two fate and free will surfaced. In India predestination is subsumed in fate, or is one aspect of fate. While in Islam and Christianity God or Allah as Providence dispenses man's destiny, in Brahmanism Vidhi/ Vidhātr is the nearest approximation, because unlike the Christian God or Allah, Vidhātr is an abstraction. But whatever the name or form assumed by predestination or fate it counters free will. As Schopenhauer said so succinctly, "Man can do what he wills but he cannot will what he wills." "The Deterministic perspective generally treats an individual as responsible only in the sense that, because he is the agent of the deed and there is no one else to blame or reward, he must bear the circumstantial responsibility for the action. Yet this perspective usually elicits pity for those who suffer or commit crimes and support summary dismissals of the accomplishments of those who have been successful. It is the head-writing that is ultimately responsible, since the good or bad intentions of the person are only the by-product of the influence of the history."[87]

The obvious conclusion from such a position is that since the ultimate responsibility of deeds and man's course of action in life are pre-ordained, he as an individual has no real responsibility either for what he does or for what happens to him. The simple corollary is that man is an amoral creature, his head-writing or 'vidhilipi' or 'Talāta-lekhana' maps out his course of life at the moment of or even prior to his birth. In this sense it condones man's iniquitous actions and refuses to give him the praise due for the good, selfless and noble acts he may perform. Now if this head-writing is linked to the karmans performed in a previous existence then in a tortuous way responsibility attaches to him. But since in this life he cannot undo or wish away his previous actions, the residual action in the shape of his head-writing is the prime determinant not only of all his acts but of all that happens to him. Within this framework the acknowledgement of free will is superficial and so constricted as to be virtually non-existent by this logic Rāvaṇa could not help being the wicked monster because he was fated to be so and fate was his earlier karman over which he had precious little control in his Rāvaṇa incarnation. And by the same token Sītā's goodness even in the midst of

[87] Kayes and Daniel (ed.), 1983, p. 40.

unaccountable suffering does not evoke praise because she was what fate made her and her quota of suffering was determined by her acts in a previous life. And there's the rub, for the *Rāmāyaṇa* says that she had been Lakṣmī, the virtuous wife of Viṣṇu in heaven. How could she commit heinous crimes to earn an almost life-long suffering, humiliation and agony? The scriptures choose to be silent on such crucial questions, because any attempted answer would upset the theologians' neat little applecart of rebirth and retribution.

A verse in the popular literary text the *Pañcatantra* says that five things are decided for man even when he is but a foetus: his span of life, actions, wealth, learning and death. In other words, the formative and final terms of his life are beyond his control, determined before his birth. Noticeably it leaves 'character' out i.e. the external elements are predetermined but his inner spirit is shaped by his own effort. But then this character cannot modify his financial status, his activities in life or his learning—things that vitally affect human life. I quote this popular stanza to indicate the widespread belief in the power of fate. Fear and trauma were attached to this concept. The 'fearless subduer of all, fate, preordained.' It is the attribute of 'pre-ordained' that generated 'the fear', because against the decree of fate there was no appeal, Human action could frequently be traced to a cause; this did not deprive man of his freedom of will. Bergman asks: "... is it self-evident that an act cannot be free because it has an antecedent cause? ... regardless of whether the act is strictly caused or not caused, if whatever causes it or generates it in some other fashion is not me, the action is not free."[88] In other words, unless the agent himself wills an act and performs it, he does not exercise his free will. In his *Hellenistic Philosophy* Long writes. The Stoics were committed to determinism the properties of which they ascribed to Nature itself. As the all-pervading *pneuma* or *logos,* Nature is the intelligent director of everything. If some events were fortuitous or fell outside the scope of Nature's power the world could not be analysed entirely by reference to Natural law ... divine providence which Stoics strenuously maintained, presupposes a capacity in God or Nature to bring about good works; notwithstanding apparent imperfection here. Nature so organizes each part that harmony is present in the world ... The karman, fate and free willno-called problem of free will arises primarily out of two conceptions—belief in God's omnipotence and predetermination and beliefs in the absolute

[88] *Orphic Hymns* no. 10, 26.

continuity of physical causation, ... Carneades held that sufferings of the virtuous and the flourishing of the malefactors prove that the Gods are quite indifferent to human affairs ... Here, as elsewhere Carneades is picking out a Stoic tenet, the Gods' providential care for mankind and citing evidence which seems to be wholly inconsistent with it."[89]

Now Carneades was a pre-Christian defender of human dignity and freedom of will. He maintained that even Apollo could not know in advance what men were going to do. This statement is an ultimate expression of the supreme dignity of man's freedom of will. In Rickaby's '*Free Will and Tour English Philosophers*' (1966) Hobbes holds, "Liberty is the absence of all the impediments to action that are not contained in the nature and intrinsical quality of the agent." For Locke "So far as man has power to think or not to think, to move or not to move, according to the preference or direction of his own mind, so far a man is free." And to Hume, "chance which is universally allowed to have no existence ... If voluntary action be subjected to the same laws of necessity with the operations of matter, there is a continued chain of necessary causes pre-ordained and predetermined reaching from the original cause of all to every single volition of every human creation." Mill says that the religious metaphysicians in favour of the freedom of will maintain it to be consistent with divine fore-knowledge. A fatalist believes or half believes not only that whatever is about to happen will be the infallible result of the causes which produce it—which is the true necessarian doctrine—but moreover that there is no use in struggling against it; that it will happen however we may strive to prevent it. According to all these philosophers it becomes clear that fatalism is quite incompatible with freedom of human will and that theistic philosophers admitted of divine pre-ordination, which to mortals on earth appear as fate, since both are equally unknown to man and come as unmerited experience over which they were not free to exercise any will. Campbell arguess thus: "Is the act of decision ... determined solely by the self and capable of alternative forms of expression? If it is, then we have a free act which serves as an adequate basis for moral responsibility ... There is no question ... of a free will that can will just anything at all ... one experimental situation in which there is any possibility of the act of will not being in accordance with character ... a course in conflict with the agent's moral ideal."[90] Belief in God militates with the acceptance of fatalism because

[99] Bergman: 1977, pp. 232, 237.

[90] Long: 1986, pp. 60, 101, 164.

it is opposed to belief in freedom of will. "True, the Ājīvikas the Cārvākas and, technically also the Jains and Buddhists, did not believe in God but with the exception of the *Cārvākas* and the Ājīvikas, the other two, as well as many other non-conformist systems accomodated karman and/or rebirth and also admitted of an irrevocable fate. "The ritualist (and his āstika progeny), in order to safeguard man's transcendence subjects his freedom to transcendent injunction. The nāstika, on the other hand surrender's transcendence in favour of man's freedom."[91]

In India from the very early post-Saṃhitā period there was a dichotomy between fatalism and freedom of will. In the conflict between fate and human effort this dichotomy receives a forcible expression in the epics and Purāṇas. The *Bhagavadgītā* says that "natural propensities drive a man forcibly to action."[92]Again "All men are under the control of nature and they will follow nature, chastisement avails little."[93] Kṛṣna says to Arjuna: "Out of pride you decide 'I shall not fight'—this is but a false pride, Nature will impel you. You are bound by your own action springing from Nature. Now that you refuse to act; what you do not wish to do, through an illusion (that same task), you shall perform like an automation."[94] "All this—the world of the mobile and the inanimate—is under (the domain of) fate. There is no creature who is under his own control, but under the control of the fruit of his action."[95] This dependence on fate or the fruit of one's unknown action can render a person inert, insensitive to pleasure or pain. "Fate, I deem as supreme, fie on human effort Even Viṣṇu's head was cut off with all the Gods watching."[96] "Clndra, what is pleasure or pain to a man governed by fate? Time does (with him) just as it pleases."[97]

Time, then, is another face of Fate. We know Time shares some synonyms with Death—Kāla, Antaka, etc. The *Matsya* Purāṇa says that Kāla, Mṛtyu (death), Antaka (ender), Yama, Vaivasvata and Dharmarāja are all the same.[98]

---

[91] Campbell: 1967, pp. 44, 46.

[92] Heeslcrman: *Wiener Zeitschrift für die Süd and Ostasiens*, 1968–69, p. 184.

[93] III: 5.

[94] III: 33.

[95] XVIII: 59–60.

[96] *Devībhāgavata* P. III: 20: 35: 36.

[97] *Op. Cit.* 1: 5: 42.

[98] *Op. Cit.* 1V: 14: 55.

The same text also says that all misfortunes and accidents are controlled by Kāla; if Kāla is adverse and angry how, then, shall we escape?[99]Kāla, action and Nature—the supreme soul used these as it found them and used them to become (himself)·[100] "From Kāla inhabiting man and from Nature arose the conflicting attributes, their result, the birth of karman and of Mahat."[101] That kāla, the creator of eternity, without a beginning, yet the maker of a beginning, the just, creating man from man and destroying the Ender (Antaka) with Death."[102] "This independent form will kill brigands, and (destroy) heaven, too, in the shape of the ruler of the subjects as Kāla, (becoming) of different attributes he will (do this) to negate (destroy) everything."[103] These words were spoken on the episode of the serpent King Takṣaka killing its enemy in the shape of a small worm dinging to his neck; at that point Takṣaka became fierce of form, even Kāla.[104]

Kāla thus has his *alter ego* in death, destruction, the end. The *Mahābhārata* says, 'Kāla cooks creatures', presumably in the sense of ripening them;[105] the verb to cook 'pac' has the sense of ripening also. How long does Time cook and ripen and why? To make creatures ready for death: the ripe fruit falls.

Nārada narrates a sinister tale of one of Kāla's daughters roaming about looking for a suitable husband. None pleased her, finally, at Nārada's counsel she went and chose as her husband Bhaya, Fear.[106]At another place another daughter of Kāla is said to be Jarā, senescence, who pleases none. The Yavana King Mrtyu took his sister Jarā for his destruction (or to his house, for the word 'ksaya' may mean both 'ruin' and 'house'.)[107]

"This supreme Lord Kāla of great valour, his inner self is made up of might, power and the strength of character and the senses, Brahman and the other Gods are under his control."[108] "Kāla is mightier than the mighty, the

---

[99] 213: 3–7.

[100] 210: 5–7.

[101] *Bhāgavata* P. II: 5: 20.

[102] *Op. Cit.* 1I: 5: 21.

[103] III: 26: 45.

[104] *Op. Cit.* VIII: 14: 9.

[105] *Devībhāgavata* P. II: 1: 62.

[106] The text: Kālah pacati bhūtāni *Mbh* I: 1: 188–91 XII: 206: 13, 220: 2.

[107] *Bhāgavata* P. IV: 29: 22: 23.

[108] *Op. Cit.* IV: 29: 22: 23.

Lord God, the endless. As a shepherd kills his (own) herd so he slays his (own) subjects."[109] The passage echoes Shakespeare's 'As flies to wanton boys are we to the Gods/They kill us for their sporf.[110] But is really more sinister in import because the shepherd tends the flock and then kills one of them. Kāla is the (supreme) Spirit, the unreachable region. Nature and righteousness—among a cluster of conflicting attributes (men) thus characterize them variously."[111] "All activities are connected with Kāla, for the experience of their fruits[112] —auspicious (things) joy, happiness, sorrow, fear, grief and harm. Trees grow in time, throw out branches in time, in time do they blossom and bear fruit. And they perish also in time."[113] Time bestows kingdom, time (decrees) death and rebirth. Time creates this universe, (again) time destroys it. Kāla as Janārdana (Kṛṣṇa) protects in the shape of Kāla. Śrīkṛṣṇa is the end of Time, the Creator of the creator, the destroyer of Destruction, the Preserver of the preserver, the maker or niṣeka, a karman whose fruition is imminent. With fate he himself gives the fruits of meditation as Niṣeka. Which creature is killed by whom without the ripened fruit of action?"[114] "Everything perishes in time, time cannot be bypassed. Śrīkṛṣṇa is the Kāla of time, the creator of the Creator of the creator."[115] "It is Kāla which brings friends together and again separates them, causes hostility or affection between them... Joy and sorrow, fear, anger, senility, death and rebirth, all happens according to karman, brought about by Kala."[116]

"As cows tied through their noses move about in control, so are all the Gods controlled by Kāla's noose."[117] "Kāla is the maker of piety or impiety."[118] "Kāla may not be transgressed."[119]"Kāla is the author of equality and inequality, it bestows defeat, honour and respect. Kāla causes a man to be a

---

[109] *Bhāgavata* P. VII: 8: 8–9.

[110] *Op. Cit.* X: 51: 19.

[111] *King Lear,* Act IV, scene I, II 36–7.

[112] *Bhāgavata:* XI: 10: 34.

[113] The gap between an action and its fruition is time.

[114] *Brahmavaivarta* P. Prakṛti Khaṇda 17: 55–57.

[115] *Brahmavaivarta* P. Gaṇeśajanmakhaṇḍa 34: 66–68.

[116] *Op. Cit.* 40: 46, 47.

[117] *Op. Cit.* Kṛīṇajanmakhaṇḍa 90: 70–73.

[118] *Devīblāgirvata* P. IV: 20: 17.

[119] *Op. Cit.* VI: 11: 14.

donor and reduces (a man) to a supplicant. Observe the conduct of Kāla."[120] "Universes arise in time, and in time are they destroyed. The creator creates out of time, the preserver preserves in time; the destroyer destroys in time, they move in steps. The creator, preserver and destroyer is the Soul, the dancer in the time."[121]

In the *Rāmāyana* Jatayu told Rāvaṇa, "you are caught in the noose of Kāla, where will you flee to get free?"[122] Rāma says to Lakṣmaṇa, "Laksmana, note the exceedingly great might of Kāla in all creatures."[123] "Kāla steals, destroys, makes, consumes and kills. Kāla dances the dance of this (passing) world (saṃsāra) in various forms, like an actor."[124] "The God Mahākāla is the playful cuckoo fledgling."[125] "This Kāla, the barbarian, ever eager to gobble up, always throws the world in the ocean of danger."[126] Kauśalyā tells Rāma, on the eve of his departure to the forest, "Kāla verily may not be crossed... The ways of Kṛtānta, my son, are always unpredictable on this earth."[127] "Kāla alone is the lord of the being and non-being of the creatures."[127a] "Heroic, and mighty, well-armed soldiers collapse in the battlefield like sand-hills."[128] When Vālin breathes his last, his wife mourns saying," It must be Kāla who terminated your life."[129]

An oft-quoted couplet in the *Mahābhārata* expresses an eternal truth: "Kāla does not raise his weapon aloft and lop off anyone's head. The might of Kāla lies in this that it makes one see things in a contrary fashion."[130] One notices a surfeit of imagery in the texts on Kāla; this seems to be due to the ever-present sense of death, the inescapable end which is sought to be expressed in diverse images, primarily because death symbolized fate in its most relentless

---

120 *Op. Cit.* VI; 30: 19.

121 *Op. Cit.*VII: 22: 19, 20.

122 *Op. Cit.* IX-16: 53, 56–58.

123 III: 51: 27.

124 III: 69: 48.

125 *Yogavāśiṣṭha Rāmāyṇa,* Vairāgya.

126 *Op. Cit.* 24: 8.

126a *Op. Cit.* 26: 3.

127 *Rāmāyṇa* II: 33, 35.

128 *Bhāgawta* P. IV: 12: 3.

129 *Rāmāyṇa*III: 69: 50.

130 *Op. Cit.* IV: 20: 14.

131 *Mbh* II: 72: 11.

and ineluctable form. Kāla is seen as the greatest destructive force, the best weapon of fate which strikes terror in the hearts of men because it is wholly incalculable. Natural calamities like drought, ravaging tempest, conflagration, flood, etc, are all brought on by Kāla. At the end of an aeon such things take place because then Kāla, as Kali closes the aeon. Kṛṣṇa in the transfiguration scene in the *Bhagavadgītā* describes himself a Kāla, grown as the "destroyer of the earth."[131a] Quite frequently we are told that the decrees of Kāla are irrevocable, that Kāla is insuperable, no one can afford to bypass or disregard its verdicts.[132] The Vamana Purāṇa[133] makes a feeble attempt at portraying Kali as reverted or inverted time, as akāla, vikāla, duṣkāla and Kāla. Clearly this seeks to paint time as out of joints, but no picture emerges since the passage is based on far-fetched and hopelessly vague abstractions. The *Brahtmāṇḍa* Purāṇa[134] describes Kali and the cosmic holocaust at the end of the aeon. Strangely enough, the most vivid descriptions of Kali are metaphysically impotent; they describe a social turmoil, confusion of norms and values and some natural disasters leading inevitably to a situation when a Noah is commissioned to build an ark or Viṣṇuyasas' son Kalkin appears to destroy the wickedness rampant in society by waging a righteous war with the now powerful demons and to put things right so that there is a new heaven and a new earth; the birth of the next aeon. Kāla thus degenerates into Kali and creates an agent in Kalkin to rectify things so that Kāla rolls on again cyclically, smoothly.

In the famous and in a sense cardinal episode on the subject in the Mahābhārata, Gautamīs son dies of snake bite. At her complaint the snake confesses that it was but an instrument Death used. 'I was goaded on by Kāla', says the serpent. Death says that Kāla was at the back of this death and Kāla reveals that actually it was the boy's karman in his previous life which is responsible for his premature death.

This is a neat paradigm which contains the disturbing and apparently mutually exclusive concepts/entities within a whole. Death caused by snake bite—an accident, a manifestation of fate—is explained by Kāla-here vidhilipi

---

131a *Mbh* VI: 33: 32.

132 We hear more about Kali in *Matsya* P. 270–272, and *Kurma* P. chapters 28 and 29.

133 47: 125–26.

134 I: 86: 120ff.

or head-writing- which is further traced to the victim's own previous action. The contrariety of fate, time or predestination and karman is glossed over. The story succeeds in giving the questionable juxtaposition an appearance of coherence. "All is Kāla-centred, O serpent, this whole world's indentity is Kāla."[135] Everything is created by Kāla and destroyed also by Kāla."[136] Kṛṣṇa explains existence to Arjuna: "All this is rooted in Kāla, the seed of this world, O Dhanañjaya. Kāla alone takes away again at his own sweet will."[137] At this point Kāla is time, death, fate i.e. predestination all rolled into a single entity.

The *Harivaṃsa,* a much later sequel to the *Mahābhārata* harps on the theme: "Kāla, indeed is mens' enemy, Kāla, too, is the consequence. Kāla takes away everyone, people like me are but means (used)."[138] In the Bhavisyaparvan section of the same book we are given a description of the gradual degradation and decadence in the Kali aeon.[139] Kāla there fought the demon army in a fierce shape; armed with various weapons he defeated the demons."[140] Of death which is but Kāla we are assured that none dies before time.[141] Now this is just a case of begging the question: saying that 'none dies before his time is up,' is but saying that a man's span runs out when he dies. It is, at best an idle consolation and at worst, dishonest casuistry, and/or tautology.

When Arjuna mourns over the death of his numerous kinsmen, Kṛṣṇa consoles him with, "Do not give in to sorrow, O Pārtha, Kāla is insuperable."[142] Even though an act has been planned in a certain way, it transpires differently—in this (is seen) how strong is Fate. Kāla, too, is invincible.[143] And a portrait of Kāla "who always plays fair has no favourites, no enemies... neither is Kala indifferent, it forcibly pulls everyone."[144]

---

[135] *Mbh* XIII: 1: 46.

[136] *Ibid.*, verse 49.

[137] *Mbh* XVI: 933.

[138] *Viṣṇuparoat,* 4: 53.

[139] Ch. 3.

[140] Ch 59: 74–100.

[141] Nāprāptakālo mrylatc—*Mbh* IV: 62: 13; IV: 80: 10–133, IV: 81: 1–178, IV; 82: 1–143; IV: 84: 1–114.

[142] *Mbh* VII: 57: 6.

[143] *Mbh* VHI: 5: 45.

[144] *Mbh* XI: 2: 14.

"Everything happens in the ripeness of time, nothing before or after"[144a] "The fierce, awesome aspect of Kāla is brought out in: Kāla roams about and visits everyone's house, always a fierce bald-pate, a ruddy, dark man."

A feminine concept of this formidable figure is Kali. Since Tantra assimilated her, her Time aspect was enveloped in a complex, mystic and symbolic aura, yet this black woman "laughs at night baring her white teeth."[145]

What is the essence of Kāla? That which cannot be resisted from any quarter, at any time, that is the divine Kāla which is come before us all."[146] The essential trait is that it is irrefutable and irrevocable. Then normally the question arises, "If Kāla is the cause of joys and sorrows, what is the point of purifying oneself, or becoming numb or active?"[147] This is a very serious corollary which admits that it is Kāla which governs not only our activities but their fruits as well: it reduces the agent to a passive onlooker, an insensate automaton.

Kāla has reference to the past, present and future. Man is intensely and immediately aware of the present in which he acts; the future lies in his desires, but of the past his awarencss is rather dim. "Kāla, time, is no longer seen as an independent ordaining principle, but becomes a function of karma."[148] So there was a paradoxical situation between time and karman, time as Kṛtānta is an aspect of death and hence essentially related to fate. Now in order to stretch karman backwards through the ages illimitably, karman and therefore rebirth, could stretch backwards to a limitless antiquity; ... by the third century B.C. previous cycles have had their respective Buddhas."[149] In the same journal Dower says: "The history of Man on earth is divided by the Mandaeans into four epochs. At the end of each, mankind was destroyed with the exception of one human couple."[150] This closely resembles the Indian concept of the four aeons, Kṛta, Tretā, Dvāpara and Kali which comprise a lcalpa, at the end or which there is a cosmic holocaust after

---

144a *Mbh* XII: 26: 5–12.

145 *Mbh* XVI: 4: 1.

146 *Brahmāṇḍa* P. I: 13: 19.

147 *Bhāgavata* XI: 2355.

148 Halbfass: 1991, p. 294.

149 R Panikkar: In *East and West*, vol. 38(1–4) Dec. 1988, p. 2.

150 p. 92.

which there is fresh creation in the same order. Hence it will be true to describe the Indian view of time as cyclical because the kalpas continually repeat themselves. But within the kalpas time is linear and regressive, if not progressive but proceeding lineally. Regressive because there is a gradual ethical and physical degeneration from one age to the next until it becomes so corrupt, sinful and degraded that total destruction followed by a fresh creation seems to be the only option left. With the archaeological excavation unearthing grave goods (food, utensils, ornaments, etc.) of around 3500 B.C. in the Sumerian plains scholars knew of the great devastating floods in Sumeria c 4200 B.C. This flood must have had tremendous repercussion on the survivors and their progeny in the Mesopotamian city-states. It is quite possible that this last of the major deluges produced a peculiar unrest in the minds of men. This and occasional earthquakes, eclipses, droughts, floods, incessant rains, locusts, epidemics, unusually fierce tempests — all added to man's sense of insecurity. The Sumerian Kinglists of about 2000 B.C., the Epic of the Gilgamesh—the oral version current among people—the ancient Chinese texts, the *Enuma Elish,* the Mesopotamian version of the Great Flood, recorded in the Bible and the Manu-and-the-fish anecdote in the *Śatapatha* Brāhmaija all bear testimony to this unrest. And this sense of insecurity prepared a fertile ground for the rise of fatalism. There were other reasons also and we shall discuss them later.

Since man could not by the widest stretch of imagination account for these apparently supernatural phenomena, they took to studying the celestial phenomena and concocted a system of astronomy which was made to bear a close relation to astrology and with this man tried not only to explain the 'fatalistic' disastrous phenomena but also to predict—and if possible, prevent future misfortunes. "There was assumed to be a counterpart in human events to every celestial phenomenon. This belief led the priests to make careful systematic observations of the heavenly bodies."[151] Astrology, as we shall see later, is one of man's many efforts to penetrate the veil of the unknown—karman and fate.

The concept of time in Iran was dualistic. "Throughout Iranian thought there was a tendency to dualism, and it is, therefore, not surprising that the two distinct forms of aspects of time were recognized: indivisible time that is the eternal 'now' and time that is divisible into successive parts. The former

[151] Whitrow: 1988, p. 31.

represented the creative aspect of time and was fundamental. It was called Zurvan akarana, or infinite time and was the progenitor of the universe and of the spirits of good and evil. Associated with the universe was the other form of time called Zurvan daregho-chvadhata, that is, time of the long dominion of finite time. This was the time that brought decay and death."[152]

Plato thought that the universe produced time, Aristotle rejected this theory. In the Denkart we are told "Time was originally limitless; then it was subjected to limitation; at the end, it returns to limitlessness."[153] The Old Persian approach is extremely interesting: Time is hostile to man; its hostility, manifests itself in misfortunes... Inexorably, ruthlessly and meaninglessly does Fortune act towards men... those concepts of destiny are rooted in older Iranian ideas. In the Pahlavi religious texts... we often meet with the idea of man's life associated with time... Zurvan exhibits the characteristic duality of the God of destiny; Zaman, on the other hand, is still an entity that is in the service of the good and that will not be finished by Ahriman."[154] The same author in his *Studies in Arabian Fatalism* has a chapter, "Time as the Agent of Destiny." There his views are: "It is remarkable that Allah plays such an insignificant part in the 'fatalistic'passages of poetry... Casket even thinks that the government of the world in poetry belongs not to Allah but to time. And if God intervenes he does so quite arbitrarily thus appearing in this respect as similar to Fate or Time."[155]

In the Persian and Arabic fatalism we meet an apparently strange but metaphysically quite expected phenomenon which is not spelt out clearly in Indian texts, viz. the almost subterranean yet real identity of Time and Fate with the connivance of God or the Gods. In the story of the untimely death of Gautamī's son we see fate, time and the death (or the God of death) almost in collusion—and they all converge in a flourishing theory of karman. Although in a true theology fate and Gods cannot co-exist (though they do in most ancient theologies) or if time is the dispenser of good and evil, as it is presented in most cases, it yet precludes fate. If karman determines the good or evil that befalls man, then strictly speaking, there cannot be a significant role for Providence or God or for fate either. And finally, if the freedom of will is admitted then neither God, nor fate nor 'Time the sovereign' can have any real function.

---

[152] *Ibid.*, p. 35.

[153] p. 282 17ff.

[154] Ringgern: 1952, pp. 21, 22, 23, 30 & 101.

[155] 1955, pp. 29, 47; Ringgern also speaks of 'Destiny in the shape of time', 1955, p. 64.

CHAPTER 5

Fate, Eschatology and Liberation

WHAT happens to the man who dies? Christian theology as expressed in the lexicon says that eschatology means the four last things: death, judgment, heaven and hell.[1] Of these, Brahmanism does not have a judgment *per se*. In this chapter we shall look at the fate of the dead man which in brahmanical terms has many more alternatives than the lexical meaning of eschatology in English. A man may go to heaven or hell temporarily and then shift to the other place according to the length of time he has earned himself in either place through his karman on earth. He can attain liberation: mokṣsa or nirvāṇa; he can be reborn in a human, subhuman or inanimate state. He can become a disembodied spirit—good or bad and hover in the upper or lower regions doing good or harm to men according to the nature of the spirit. He can also hover in an astral body.[2] It is clear that these post-mortal fates are mutually exclusive but can be experienced successively or in different births.

The most usual and frequent fate of the dead soul is rebirth. But man's first inkling of the ancient man's belief regarding post-mortal existence is born out of excavations. The gravegoods, especially for the affluent—servants, wives, necessary and luxury items, coaches or chariots and draft animals—prove beyond doubt that man then believed in (1) the existence of the departed soul in some form after death, (2) its capacity to enjoy the good things of life and, conversely, to suffer from lack of these items, (3) some fear or obligation felt by the survivors to serve the departed kinsman which prompted the provisions. Clearly the soul's departure to heaven or hell or liberation or movement in an astral form was not visualized as a long-term possibility—hence the gravegoods.

1 *Shorter Oxford Dictionary.*

2 Which some schools of Christianity and some other religions also admit in some of their later and sometimes less important scholiasts.

The Jains do not perform the śrāddha ceremony because according to Jainism the soul of the dead is reborn immediately after death. The *Mahābhārata* also says that "no time intervenes between death and rebirth."[3] Āpastamba and Gautama, authors of Dharmasūtras think that rebirth occurs after an intervening period.[4] Maṇḍana Miśra, the philosopher, a contemporary of Śaṅkara says in his *Brahmasiddhi* that those who go to the region of Brahman remain there until the time when they are reborn. Speaking about Zoroastrianism, Whitrow says, "This doctrine of 'last things' was the first systematized eschatology in the history of religion and it profoundly influenced Judaism, Christianity and Islam."[5] Clearly, Whitrow speaks of the Semitic religions and Zoroastrianism; but even in ancient Sumer, Egypt and China eschatology developed quite early. In India we know nothing about the beliefs connected with the first urbanization—in the Indus Valley period, but during the second urbanization these ideas assumed a quite clearly discernible contour, however, blurred they got at times owing to conflicting notions being juxtaposed.

Hulin speaks of two perceptions of the object which are forever separated by an interval—antarāla—where the conscious soul having 'consumed' the preceding object and not yet having entered in contact with the following, rests in its pure undifferentiated essence.

"Deux perceptions determines d'object sont toujours separées par un intervalle—antarāla—ou la citi, ayant "consumée" l'object precedent et n'étant pas encore entree en contact avec le suivant, repose dans sa pure essence indifferenciée."[6] About the Mandaeans we read, "The souls of the devout dwell upon this earth as in a foreign land. Here, meanwhile, evil spirits reign, akin to the powers of darkness now immured—the deities of other people and other creeds ... At the hour of death a divine being takes the soul from the body and bears it upwards through the celestial spheres to the world of light and Great life."[7] All, that is except warriors fallen in battle or women dying in childbirth. About the Mexicans we read, "Man's destiny was submitted to the all powerful Tonalpohuatli (the calendrical round); his life in the other

3 III: 181: 23, 24.

4 Āp. D. S. II: 1: 2-2, G. D. S. II: 29-30.

5 1988, p. 34.

6 Hulin, 1979, p. 308.

7 *Encyclopaedia of Religion and Ethics*, Vol. VIII, p. 387.

world did not result from any moral judgment. His duty was to fight and die for the Gods and for the preservation of the world order."[8] Here then is a truly fatalistic approach to eschatology. The calendrical round symbolized time which decided a man's fate according to whether he fought and died for the Gods. This was the criterion of one's well-being in the next world. The Mexicans believed that except for warriors fallen in battle and women dying in childbirth, all the other dead went down to Mictlan the skeleton-masked God of death. There they travelled for four years until they arrived at the ninth Hell where they disappeared altogether. Offerings for the dead continued for eighty days after the funeral, then one year, two, three, four years later, the link between the living and the dead snapped. But the victors who crossed over to the heavens in the retinue of the sun came back to earth after four years as humming birds... Divine women used to appear at night at cross-roads and strike the passer-by with palsy. Here the theology differs widely from the Indian, where those who joined the retinue of the sun were liberated and were spared rebirth; those who followed the moon-path known as the way of ancestors (pitṛyāṇa) were subjected to rebirth. Besides, the poetry of being born as humming birds is totally absent in Indian eschatology which is hyper-serious and wholly matter-of-fact. But "Across Fast Asia, a millenarian aesthetic developed within contexts far less adversarial, and we find no figure antiphonal to the universal perfect."[9] In Babylon "If one had no son to make the funerary offerings, one lived like a beggar, but with many sons one could enjoy a degree of comfort. Reasonably well off were also young men killed in battle and the small children."[10] What strikes us here is the emphasis laid on the son who could offer obsequial offerings which helped the father's status in the next world. Such an emphasis is all-pervading in India. Through the daughter the father gleans no spiritual benefit, it was the son who really mattered.

In the region of the Great Unknown, the life after death, conjectures regarding the soul's future were framed and modified according to the prevalent metaphysics, sociology and social ethics. These were directly or obliquely reflected in the paradigm of future existence. The son was the channel through whom property was held and hence transmitted his superior

---

8 *Encyclopaedia Mactopaedia*, Vol. 2, p. 551.

9 *Macmillan Encyclopaedia*, c. 522.

10 *Macmillan Encyclopaedia*, c. 462.

right to aid the departed father's spiritual well-being. In a society perpetually engaged in tribal warfare where the tribe's well-being was the summum bonum, those who died in battle were promised happiness after death as also women in childbirth. This becomes clearer if we remember that progeny was a treasured possession, therefore, the woman who died carrying, brought fertility and greater well-being to the tribe. In Mexico after four years the link between the dead and living snapped; in other words, the survivor was exempted from obsequial duties; this was a way for life to go on after the ancestors had been duly honoured for four years; then there was no more obligation; so life on earth could go on. But since a God of time made the decision not on the way he passed his life, but on how he died, it became more or less fatalistic compared to most other systems, for, it may not be given to all to fight and die for the Gods. A similar vision of the next world and man's station there in St. Augustine: "Despite the union of all men in the love of God, Augustine's heaven will not be an egalitarian society, a hierarchy of merit obtains, though Augustine cannot foresee precisely how the different degrees of honour and glory will be awarded ... In the *Phaedrus* Plato accepted into his own myth of the soul an Orphic doctrine, not unlike Pindar's, of the three incarnations and a final release of soul, for the philosopher without guile... The common fable of the fifth century Athens had a wish fantasy of a sensuous paradise ... closer to the Orphic poets than to Plato's philosophical heaven of the soul. Plato of Alexandria preferred to paint the God of Eden spiritually after Plato. Allegory became the typology for the future paradise in heaven. The Gnostics of the first century... resorted to extravagant fantasy."[11] Men weave dreams where there is a vacuum in knowledge. Life-after-death is one such vacuum, so all kinds of fanciful pictures were painted by the different authors to fill it up with.

In China, "Popular values are sanctioned by revelations from the Gods and by belief in the purgatory, where one's part of the soul goes after death to be punished for its sins according to the principles of karmic retribution. There are ten courts in the purgatory, each presided over by a judge who fits the suffering to the crime. Passage through purgatory can be ameliorated through the transfer of merit, money for Buddhist or Taoist rituals, when its guilt has been purged the soul advances to the tenth court, where the form of its existence is decided."[12] "By the third and fourth centuries C.E. it was believed that there was a subterranean kingdom within MtT' ai where judges

[11] Geertz, 1971, p. 105.

[12] *Macmillan Encyclopaedia of Religion,* Vol. HI, p. 282.

decided the fate of the dead."[13] "In an inscription of 165 C.E. Lao Tzu is described as a creator deity equal in status to the sun, moon and the stars. A contemporary text assures his devotees that *he has manifested himself many times in order to save mankind*."[14] Here the rebirth theory reaches a legitimate fulfilment in his reincarnation which is nothing but the rebirth theory transferred from man to God. With the Gods it is the philanthropic necessity "to save men, altruistic desire of which urges them to be incarnated." As in China, so in India.

It is a karmic necessity to work off the effects of accumulated karman or to earn some more karman. In other words, for men it was inevitable to be reborn as frequently as their karman demanded. "Although rebirth... has to be viewed with a much larger framework; there is no doubt that for the compilers of the Dharmaśāstras it ranked as the first and most importantresult of action."[15] There is a theory in India that at death the "sense organs merge in different elements of nature; a man's speech goes to fire, his eyes to the sun, his mind to the sky, his ear or hearing to the quarters and finally his breath to the wind."[16] Śvetaketu comes as a pupil to Pravahaṇa Jaivali. On his return Śvetaketu comes to his father, and to whom Jaivali had expounded death and eschatology in terms of ritual mysticism. He says, "Then when he dies they carry him to the fire. His fire is the fire, fuel the fuel, smoke the smoke, flame the flame, sparks the sparks. In this fire the Gods offer man. From this oblation, man arises having the colour of light."[17] Psychologically, it affords the dying man some consolation: he is sacrificed and then assumes an effulgent body. The idea of the various component parts of the human body dissolving in the various elements of natural phenomena have already been anticipated in the late Brāhmaṇas. For example, the *Śatapatha* Brāhmaṇa expressed this very idea around approximately the seventh century B.C.[18] Before any definite ideas of eschatology were formed, man saw the corpse on the funeral pyre go out in smoke and possibly conjectured that the constituent elements of the human body finally dissolved in natural elements. "The path

---

13 *Op. Cit.*, Vol. V, p. 267.

14 *Ibid*., p. 268. italics added.

15 O' Flaherty (ed.), 1983, p. 78.

16 ŚB X: 3: 3: 8.

17 *Bṛhadaraṇyaka* Up. VI: 2: 1ff.

18 X: 2: 6: 8–33: 8.

to the south, the moon, the moonless night, the plants and creepers, food and semen... is the path of fathers and of rebirth. Fire, the sun, daytime the forenoon, the bright fortnight ending in a full-moon night, perfect independence—this is known as the path of the Gods where one passes the stages one by one."[19]

While the Upaniṣads lay down the path to liberation through knowledge, this Devayāna does not mention it; its terminus is the sun while in mokṣa the individual soul merges in the supreme soul, Brahman. Rebirth according to Upaniṣadic theology is caused by residual desire, but pitṛyāṇa ignores it. This same Upaniṣad defines the path of the righteous man through the sun to liberation—devayṣana; and the other path through the moon to rebirth.[20]

The Bhagavatī sutra[21] says about the soul of the righteous dead: "Gautama: He does go up to four or five heavenly abodes by dint of his own power and beyond that by dint of assumed power." The assumed power is obtained through the grace of the Gods in higher abodes of bliss who help these up. Thus heaven can be won through piety up to a height beyond which the soul needs grace from the Gods above. Varuna's son Bhrgu visited the land of the dead.[22] So there is a land of the dead; as yet in the Upaniṣads this has not been compartmentalized into heaven or hell and the duration is not specified which may lead one to think that one's stay in the land of the dead was forever. The *Bṛhadāraṇyaka* Upaniṣad, however, specifically mentions a post-mortal transition to a heavenly life.[23] Of these passages the one which says that man's sense organs merge in the elements appears to deny eschatology altogether, presumably because it disposes of the mind also and one cannot imagine a soul without the mind. There are other later passages which support this view. Bhṛgu's visit to the land of the dead has echoes in Homer, and Virgil; in the *Rāmāyaṇa,* however, the dead visit the land of the living. This static, unqualified land of the dead is a direct heritage from the RV bk X where the dead are handed over to Yama who is supplicated to look after them and keep them cheerful.

---

19 *Bhāgavata Purāṇa*; VII: 15: 51, 55.

20 VI: 2: 15, 16; also *Chhāndogya* Up. V: 10: 7–8.

21 Ed. Lalwani, SBE, Vol. IV, p. 128.

22 ŚB XI: 6: 1: 1.

23 IV: 4: 3–4. This Idea is also found in I: 5: 17; and repeated in *Kauṣīakī* Up. II: 15.

"The ideas of the fate that will meet man in 'yonder world' are not very fixed."[24] Actually until the end of the Upaniṣads, eschatological ideas were extremely nebulous and hazy. And despite the ardent, elaborate and many-pronged efforts of the Purāṇas—where these ideas are spelt out in diverse ways—they remained mutually conflicting and got irritatingly vague with the passage of time. The *Bṛhannāradīya* Purāṇa, a late work, Mates categorically that Yama is the great arbiter of good and bad deeds and the allocator of respective stations in the next world.[25] Then the entire content of the Garuḍa Purāṇa has for its theme death, the rites immediately after death and all obsequial rites up to the annual śrāddha ceremony and tarpaṇa (for the peaceful existence of the departed in the next world). Incidentally, the soul's progress from the moment of death occupies a considerable amount of space and interest in the text. It describes the soul's difficult path, the obstacles in its way until it reaches Yama's domain and eventually, hell. It describes the newcomers' arrival there and his plight. Then the soul is given an account of the sins it has committed on earth. Hell torments are described at length. We then hear of the rules and obligations which should govern human life. A discussion follows about the 'true' son, the rightful heir who may perform the obsequial rights and the śrāddha ceremony. We are next treated to the glories of the satī, the wife who immolates herself on the husband's funeral pyre. Next there is a dialectical section where questions are answered about the obsequial rites. One of the more important aspects of these rites is the quantity and quality of gifts given to brahmins on this occasion because such donations not only increase the merits of the donor but help improve the soul's condition in the next world.

It becomes clear that the soul's course and condition in the next life largely depends on acts performed by others subsequent to his death, on mertitorious and pious acts and on the largesses of the survivors. We are then given an account of the gradual fashioning of the human body, from inception to the growth of the foetus in the womb. Then follows another description of hell and of the various paths to hell. This is followed by directions for giving obsequial gifts to brahmin recipients and a glowing description of the glories of a properly performed śrāddha, as well as the five defects arising out of the ritual remissnesses of the śrāddha. The next section is devoted to the

---

24 Rodhe, 1946, p. 113.

25 The whole of chapter 29.

determination of the true progeny and of paternity. This is followed by trivialities like giving pitchers to brahmins, the Nārāyaṇa 'bali', the offering of a bull and other gifts which help the soul cross the Styx, Vaitaraṇī. The primary preoccupation is with the amelioration of the soul's suffering, until rebirth, through appropriate gifts to brahmins given by the survivors.

In the *Brahma* Purāṇa, too, there is a long section on the different stations after death.[26] The soul experiences stays in different regions for the duration of an aeon—the firmament, the region of the Gandharvas, of the sun, moon, stars, the Gods, Indra and Prajāpati. In the reverse direction the soul travels from the world of the ancestors to this world, then to the region of Hari, Varāha, Narasiṃha, Viṣṇu, Brahmā, Nārāyaṇa and the cities of Aniruddha and finally of Pradyumna. This clearly is a Viṣṇuite work following the vyūha theory; two of the descendants of Kṛṣṇa here enjoy the superior status of having their special regions. The *Nārada* Purāṇa presents the stages from death through the soul's movement along difficult paths—then its transformation as a foetus and the subsequent months of pain until it is reborn and starts the next existence on earth.[27]

'A man who performs the duties allotted to him by the scriptures, after passing through a hundred lives, become Viriñci and then Rudra. The Bhāgavata region of Viṣṇu defies description.'[28] When a man breathes his last, he leaves his earlier body and enters another according to his karman. The oft-quoted line, "when men's merits fade, they enter the earth" occurs in the *Devībhāgavata Puraṇa.*[29]

One improves one's caste status by living righteously. "The pious śūdra, dying, attains vaiśyahood, the pious vaiśya after death becomes a kṣatriya, and the kṣatriya, a brahmin. The brahmin who is quiet and has shed all desires is liberated."[30a] Just as there is no double promotion, so also, the carrot of a single post-mortal caste promotion is dangled before him. Patience, piety and appropriate service to the upper castes does it.

Another passage says that 'in the Kṛta era people having done good works go to heaven; brahmins, kṣatriyas, vaiśyas and śūdras, performing their

---

26 II: 40: 10–50.

27 II: 4: 2–7.

28 *Bhāgavata* P. IV: 24: 9.

29 Kṣīṇe puṇye martalokaṃ viśanti, III: 12: 62.

30a *Op. cit.*, IV: 1: 18, 19.

caste duties go to their respective (i.e., next higher) stations. Truth, compassion, charity, fidelity to one's own wife, non-violence to all creatures, equal regard to all—abiding by these common virtues even the low caste people like the washerman—go to heaven. In the Tretā age and in Dvāpara and Kali, the wicked go to hell and remain there until the aeon is over. Then they are born again as men on earth. When at the end of the Kali age a fresh Kṛta aeon begins, then the doers of good come down from heaven and are born as men on earth. When Dvāpara ends and Kali begins, sinners from hell are born as men on earth.[30]

A strange kind of rebirth anecdote narrates how Vaśiṣṭha in anger cursed his own son Nimi to instant death. At Nimi's request the sages kept him artificially alive and performed a sacrifice. Pleased with this sacrifice, the Gods offered him a boon. Nimi desired, 'I wish to live in all creatures' eyes'. The Gods advised him to worship Pārvatī, with her boon he became the 'wink', nimiṣa and lives in all creatures' eyes.[31]

Man's fate after death is nowhere stated clearly or categorically or irrefutably. The strange and somewhat amusing thing is that many mutually contradictory views are strewn all over the vast religious literature, but each statement has an air of finality or irrevocability. Attaining heaven is said to be the fruit of life-long piety yet whoever builds a house (i.e.) temple for any God lives in heaven for as many years as there are specks of dust there (i.e. in the temple).[32] 'Whatever is offered (to guests or hungry men) is enjoyed, one enjoys nothing that has not been given. Having enjoyed the bliss of living in heaven, one is born in India, and is born in stages in the 'vipra' families (i.e. brahmin, kṣatriya and vaiśya).'[33] A common refrain is: all the fruits of karman have to be experienced, karman does not diminish unless it is experienced yet innumerable actions are prescribed, as we shall see later, which destroy the fruits of sinful acts, not only one's own but for several generations. In eschatology and theories of karman, its fruits, rebirths in various stations and forms, the sufferings of the effects of sinful acts or the pleasures following pious acts, their duration and consequences constitute a vast puzzle which no scripture even attempts to solve. And that—leaving

[30] *Op. Cit.*, VI: 11: 19–26.

[31] *Op. Cit.*, VI: 5: 20.

[32] *Devībhāgavata* P. IX: 29: 52.

[33] *Op. Cit.*, IX: 29: 65–66.

many loose strings hanging—is precisely part of the programme. Man will never realize clearly what act results in what experience and will live his life in perpetual terror and awe. Priest-ridden religion abhors clarity, a large measure of uncertainty which can, whenever necessary, be ascribed to inscrutable and immutable fate, suits it perfectly. It is thus idle to seek a one-to-one ratio between action and consequences; it was never intended to be offered. So, in its place we have a complexly structured conundrum, a maze with no exit.

Eschatology of individual human beings is enveloped in the deep mystery of the karmans he has performed in another life, according to the merits and demerits of which his fate after death is determined. And each strand of eschatology challenges fatalism; for, if man reaps the fruits of his karman after death then fate has no scope to determine his existence after death. Formulas of piety differ but piety is essential for happiness in postmortal existence. And yet fate, the unknown quantity in-vades this neat paradigm and upsets all calculations. If one is reborn in a lowly status after a pious life, then fate comes in. But more fully than this there is no way to prove what kind of acts the man had performed in his earlier existence. Hence one begins to calculate from what is obvious, the seen or known, i.e. the present life and even in this existence an element of incalculability creeps in. We call it fate, forgetting that eschatology is either controlled by the incalculable fate or by a man's acts, it cannot be both.

Besides, the numerous options of post-mortal existence militate against any neat or acceptable pattern: the soul can be reborn, go to heaven or hell or purgatory, hover in thin air as an astral body or be liberated. Each is a valid possibility, each depends on past karman, yet there is no schemata affirming which karman leads to which result. Thus, there is an inherent contradiction in the case of the individual's eschatological status.

When we regard the group fate, or the ultimate future of mankind, the *Agni* Purāṇa predicts a cosmic holocaust which will end this creation.[34] So does the *Matsya* Purāṇa; the transformation at the end of the aeon is described vividly in the *Kūrma* Purāṇa.[35] The cosmic cataclysm is described stage by stage: the destruction of creatures is a permanent and continuous annihilation; it is called 'Nitya' (permanent), the destruction of the living creatures is a

---

[34] 368–69. 35 ch. 165.

[35] Chs. 43; 44; 50.

'naimittika' (exigent) of Brahma pralaya, the holocaust at the close of thousands of the four aeons touches nature and is called 'pākṛtika'. When man realizes his essential identity with the supreme spirit, then, for that individual soul, it is the final, 'ātyantika' destruction. The natural holocaust usually takes the form of drought for a hundred years, the oceans getting dried, the rise of seven suns, the entire creation—heaven, earth and hell—become the vessel of the 'tarpaṇa' rite (ambarīṣa). The earth dissolves itself in the 'maharloka' which again loses itself in the heavenly world 'svarloka' and finally everything is subsumed in 'janaloka'. Then comes the cosmic conflagration creating massive storm-clouds. Viṣṇu goes to the illusory deep slumber and then awakens as a mendicant when he creates afresh,[36] where one by one are described the 'Sārociṣa Manvantara followed by the 'Uttama', 'Tāmasa', 'Raivata', 'Cākṣuṣa', 'Vaivasvata', Sāvarṇika' and 'Sarvasāvarṇa manvantaras. Above and superior to the stations of the Manus are the regions of the 'Vaikuṇṭha' and the 'Vaikuṇṭha' region merging with Śiva's becomes the 'goloka', the region of the cow at the time of the cosmic destruction.[37] This excessively worshipful attitude to the cow, more tangibly useful than either Viṣṇu or Śiva, has notionally created a region as nebulous and as unattractive as it can be, because, its only stated superiority is its altitude: above the regions of the two most important and mythologically more significant than the two most prominent Gods. A future existence in that region, unless it is a spiritual replica of the earthly Vṛndāvana, has scant appeal to the imagination and therefore, theoretically, it remains an abstract abode of the pious.

This group eschatology is narrower in its options because it is essentially bound up with the fate of the remnant of the population at the end of an aeon. The only logical difficulty is the assumption that just these few peoples' karman was so similar as to justify the cosmic holocaust, the common fruition of their work as the final annihilation. This can theoretically be bypassed by the law of probability but that needs stretching our credibility too far. Hence group eschatology is theoretically untenable; it defies the theory of karman and allows too wide a lee-way for fate.

Grief or unpalatable experience is the result of sinful karman. Sin can have two connotations (i) that which is ethically wrong and (ii) that which is ritually defective. The last also can be of two kinds (a) a rite not performed

[36] *Mārkaṇḍeym* P. ch. 53, 67, and 72, 74, 76, 78, 80 and 98.

[37] *Brahmavaivarta* P. Brahmakhaṇḍa II: 2–14.

correctly and (b) not done at all.[38] In general almost all religions look upon other religionists as misguided i.e. walking on the wrong path. Zoroastrianism looked upon other religions as evil and Buddhism, Islam and Christianity regarded other religions as fallacious. But each theology defines evil as that which goes against their own basic tenets. In Zoroastrianism evil was personified as an independent power, a cosmic entity, viz. Angra Mainyu (later, Ahriman). Although evil could not be attributed to Ahura Mazdah, its existence had to be accounted for and Zoroaster explained it in terms of free will.[39] Through the exercise of free will man could choose evil which, according to Zoroaster's theology, had a separate and independent entity. Thus within this frame of ideas, free will and not fate had a predominant role. But Angra Mainyu was superhuman and his role was to tempt man into evil ways. Manichaeianism also regarded evil as a separate and equally strong force. In both the old and New Testament of the Bible, Satan is a real and powerful entity, although ultimately subordinate to God. Buddhism knows Māra, also powerful, but he exhausts his energy in tempting the good people and has been definitively defeated by Buddha after which he remained stigmatized as the defeated defier.

Apart from Satan, Angra Mainyu and Māra, sin or evil remains an abstraction. "Sin understood as transgression is usually not concretized."[40] The abstract sin or evil has many synonyms—*pāpa,*[41] *pāpmnn, enas, āgas, durita,*[42] *hedana,*[43] *duṣkṛta kilbiṣn, anṛta, ṛṇa, drudgha, samala* (=pollution) *abhiśasti* and in the Ṛgveda, *brahmapaḍvīśa.* This multiplicity of synonyms for evil clearly signify that (i) the idea was familiar and had a wide currency and that (ii) there were subtle shades of difference between them; in other words, there were contextual variations; because in ancient languages there are no synonyms as such. According to some, evil was a negative concept, it is unreal, the absence of goodness. John Fergusson in 'The Achievement of Clement of Alexandria' says, "Evil is in fact the absence of good, more

[38] RVI: 22, 23, 85 anticipate the concept of moral sin. The God Varuṇa who watches over mens' actions and catches the evil-doer in his noose also bears this notion out.

[39] Whitrow, 1988, p. 33.

[40] Rodhe, S., 1946, p. 147.

[41] Usually used adjectivally or in the sense of a sinful man.

[42] Also in the sense of disaster.

[43] In the sense of offending the Gods.

precisely, the absence of God. Its origin lies in human freedom."[44] It is true that without freedom of will man could not have chosen to be evil, but then, without a free will he could not have chosen to be good either. God could have forcibly kept him on the straight and narrow path, but that would have implied compulsion; man would then be reduced to an automaton. But, "If evil is wholly unreal then a concern for or interest in release or mokṣa is a waste of time... there is a sense in which evil is real, and a sense in which karma and rebirth are real aswell. The dogma of unreality is betrayed by the activity and concern of the faithful."[45]

In ancient India, in the Ṛgveda, sin was regarded as alienation from the Gods.[46] As in Christianity, there is a concept of mortal sins, so India also defined certain actions as irredeemable, ultimate sins. The lists vary from text to text with some common elements. The *Bṛhaddharma* Purāṇa has the more common definition: Killing a brahmin, drinking alcohol, theft, intercourse with the preceptor's wife—these are the four great sins, and the fifth is keeping company with those who commit these.[47] A slight variation is noticed in the definition of the *Devībhagavata* Purāṇa: the killer of a brahmin, stealer of gold, drinker of alcohol, the polluter of the precepter's bed—these are the great sinners; the fifth is he who keeps these sinners' company.[48]

Of the six canonical books of the Hadith, the texts of tradi-tional Islamic rules and practices, each has a chapter on predestination, although the Koran has no place for it. Presumably this was a legacy from the pre-Islamic tribal beliefs and practices. The dictates of scriptures and the beliefs and rituals never tally; the first is prescriptive, the second descriptive. Predestination, once accepted, explained many anomalies, just as karman and rebirth do.

In Brahminism the two major destinations of the departed soul are heaven and hell. Neither place is in general a permanent abode of the soul, one may enjoy heaven for a brief spell, then go to hell to work off his evil deeds and *vice versa.* But whether for a short stay or for a long one, heaven is reward for good works, or it may be attained through devotion, meditation or a boon. In the *Kauṣītaki* Brāhmaṇa we read that at the end of a sacrifice

---

[44] Religious Studies, Vol. 12, no. 1, p. 73.

[45] A L Herman, 1976, p. 247.

[46] VII: 86: 6; 88: 6.

[47] uttara 20: 2.

[48] I: II: 15.

the father blessed the son with "may you gain heaven."[49] The *Brahmavaivarta* Purāṇa gives a catalogue of meritorious deeds which lead to heaven;[50] other Puranic texts also give similar lists. Most of these deeds can be classified into three groups—charity, acts done for the Gods or saints or brahmins, and devotion. Negatively, we are told that the miser who eats alone (i.e. without sharing his food) is demoted from heaven.[51] The hero who does not retreat in battle goes to heaven.[52] The *Mahābhārata* has a long list of the meritorious people who earned heaven.[53] Again we frequently hear that only those who live a clean life go to heaven.[54] Draupadī is told that righteousness is the boat that takes one across to heaven; there is none other... There are only three states for the departed soul: being reborn as man, living in heaven or birth as subhuman creatures.[55] Yet this is not at all an exhaustive list, for, one may go to heaven or hell, be liberated, assume an astral shape, be born again, become a ghost, etc. There is a long description of the three regions, earth, the Bhuva region and heaven.[56]

This region of bliss, heaven, was not for the sonless people. Having a daughter is of no avail, only the man with a son gains heaven; "indeed there is no other way by which a man can go to heaven."[57]

In many mythologies and theologies heroes who do not flinch at the prospect of dying in battle go to heaven. The *Edda,* the Sagas, the *Iliad, Odyssey,* the *Kalevala,* the *Mahābhārata* and *Rāmāyaṇa* the *Popol Vuh* all agree to this. The *Florentine Codex,* too says that heaven is the home of the sun and those slain in battle go there.[58]

The Jātakas are replete with tales of righteous men gaining heaven. Mātaṅga, though innocent was killed at the king's orders and was immediately

---

49 I: II: 15.

50 Prakṛti ch 32; also Goloka ch. 54.

51 *Mbh* V: 12: 20.

52 *Mbh* VII: 48: 34.

53 *Mbh* VIII: 105, 17-30.

54 *Mbh* XIII: pp. 112, 132, 133.

55 *Mbh* III: 178: 8, 9.

56 *Brahma P., ch. 15.*

57 *Devībhāgavata* Purāṇa 1: 4: 15; the sins of a man who has a son arc remitted I: 4: 17.

58 Bk III and XIV.

born in Brahman's heaven.[59] Kosiya chose Honour from amongst Sakka's daughters and because he shared the ambrosia brought to him by Mātali with his bride, he was reborn in heaven.[60] Instances can be multiplied *ad infinitum,* but it is quite unnecessary because it is common knowledge that good works earn heaven. Even ancient Egyptians subscribed to this view: "The ordinary man, if innocent of sin and a follower of Osiris could now cling to a hope of individual immortality. The Osirian realm to which even the humblest could aspire, entry not being dependent upon the ability to furnish and equip the elaborate tomb, was envisaged as a place below the western horizon or on a group of islands, referred to as the Field of Reeds. This paradise experienced eternal springtime and unfailing harvests and here the dead enjoyed the pleasures of their former earthly existence, without any pain or suffering. The world of Osiris was also essentially democratic in structure and rich and poor alike were given plots of land which they were expected to cultivate... The Eleusinian type of initiation rather provided the initiate with good hope of life after death by establishing a relationship with the Gods of the underworld by means of the ritual."[61]

"There is a very old account of Dilmun, written on a tablet from Nippur. It describes how, when the world was young and the work of creation had only just begun, Dilmun was a place where 'the croak of the raven was not heard, the bird of death did not utter the cry of death, the lion did not devour, the wolfdid not rend the lamb, the dove did not mourn, there was no widow, no sickness, no old age, no lamentation.'"[62] We notice that Dilmun is described through negations, negations of the sorrows of mortals. It is like Keats's "what thou amongst the leaves / hast never known." There is no positive description of heaven in the Old Testament, indeed, although the New Testament offers a description of heaven through St. John's apocalyptic vision in the Revelation it is a description which is mystic but not really imaginatively inspiring. The Koranic heaven is a place of earthly enjoyments transferred to a land of bliss, while the Brahminical heaven is heavily compartmentalized with separate realms of the several Gods—again not a moving or imaginatively glowing picture except that there men enjoy all earthly bliss in the company of the Gods.

---

[59] No. 479.

[60] No. 535.

[61] David, 198, pp. 111, 197.

[62] Introduction: *The Epic of Gilgamesh,* p. 39.

The Greek "Elysium which first appears in the Odyssey is said to be a survival from Minoan religion. It is a death-free comfortable retreat for heroes in a place that is neither Olympus nor Hades ... The common folk of the fifth century Athens had wish-fantasy of a sensuous paradise that was far closer to the Orphic poets than to Plato's philosophical heaven of the soul ... In *The Miners* of the poet Pherecrates a character who may be Persephone paints a sensuous Paradise in the nether world ... Emphasis is upon the consumption, sexual desires are but light-ly alluded to... epic literature of the third and second millennia before Christ... both are related to the older culture stratum of Mesopotamian Dilmun ... The word paradise was not used by the Jews in the canonical writings, Persian Paraiddiza, Hebrew pardes (garden) also of Persian origin, the first use of the Greek 'paradeisos.'"[63] Judaic paradise is hardly a very tempting place, the souls enjoy their bliss there from the constant study of the Torah.

In China "The older locus classicus for the fate of the dead is a story in *Tso Chuan* (dated about 721 B.C.). There the home of the dead are the Yellow Springs, a shadowy subterranean abode not too far beneath the earth ... (later) the realm where the dead exist is limited to a house and to their clan i.e., the tomb and those of their family already buried there."[64]

Although the descriptive accounts of heaven in the several old cultures vary in detail, they all agree in two points: that heaven is a place of pleasurable experiences and that it can be gained through good acts. Since not every dead soul has access to heaven (except to a hazy afterlife in a nondescript place in some mythologies) heaven has to be earned through karman. Since this category of heaven-worthy karman is nowhere defined properly there remains an element of chance or fate about it.

"Whereas Coptic texts as well as many Iranian documents are marked by a distinct theology of suffering, the Turkic texts often enough give expression to the joy of victory ... Being protected by a Manichaean King, the community of scribes and elect could assess the world as a place where the blessing of the Gods was experienced already. Certainly ultimate salvation could only be found in the other world, but the light of that other world already shone into this world."[65]

---

63 To translate Gau (Garden of) Eden in the Septuagint of the third century B. C. Manuch, F. E and F. P., 1971, pp. 87–90, 92.

64 Seidel, Numen XXIX, 1981, pp. 108–9.

65 Klimkeit, Numen XXIX, 1982, p. 28.

In Mithraism the cult of Sol Invictus "showed a tendency to reduction to the deification of Time."[66] This, in a sense annihilates eschatology but in practice it was not so; heaven and hell were awarded to men after death in accordance with their work, their loyalty to Mithra and their spiritual progress ... the "Orphic view anticipated an ultimate escape into an Elysium of heavenly light."[67] Some other early mythologies, too, like the Ṛgvedic and Homeric saw the soul in a realm of bliss.[68] Hell came later, possibly with oppression of one social section by another.

In India the earliest reference to heaven-worthy acts was of a ritual kind, "by means of this (rite) the Gods went to the world of heaven."[69] "Both these kinds of Gods (i.e., Gods and brahmins) when pleased, please him in a condition of well-being."[70] The well-being referred to here can be applied to a passage to heaven but it can also refer to mundane well-being. "He passes from the world of men to the world of the Gods."[71] This clearly is heaven. The last book of the Ṛgveda may contain a veiled reference to heaven in its description of the well-being of the departed souls in the next world.[72] The *Chhāndogya* Upaniṣad mentions scents, garlands, food, drink, song and music in heaven.[73] We are given a map of ontological hierarchy of the upper worlds and their inhabitants.[74] "His good action rises (in the scales in the next world), not his bad action."[75] "The good that man does during his life passes into his breaths, the wrongs into his body. When one who knows thus departs from this world, his good deeds rise up together with his breath and the wrong deeds are left with his body."[76] The breath ascends to the world of the Gods and announces to the Gods the quantity: so much good, so much

66 Halbsberghe, 1972, p. 41.

67 *Op. Cit.*, p. 261.

68 Even before that, the idea was that the dead keenly missed being alive and dwelt in a shadowy obscurity in the underworld.

69 *Pañcaviṇiśa Brāhmaṇna* II: 6: 2; III: 2; XV: 2, 3.

70 *Śatapatha* Br. II: 2: 2: 6.

71 ŚBI: 1: 1: 4.

72 X: 1.

73 VIII: 2.

74 Br. Ār. Up. IV: 3: 30; tait Up. II: 8.

75 ŚB XI: 2: 7: 33.

76 *Jaiminīya* Br I: 15.

evil has been done by him."[77] "The sacrifice becomes the sacrificer's self in yonder world. And truly the sacrificer who knowing (this) performs that (sacrifice) comes into existence with a whole body."[78] Clearly such passages have the effect of moral exhortation and the spiritual upliftment of the readers or listeners. The sacrificer "is united in the other world with what he has sacrificed."[79] At death the soul of the dead is addressed thus, "Unite with the fathers with Yama, with the treasury of your sacrifice (iṣṭāpūrta) in the highest heaven. Abandoning defects return home; unite with a splended body."[80] Here heaven or wherever the soul is supposed to pass to is referred to as 'home'; we recall later Upanisadic passages stating that "creatures are born of bliss, live in bliss, and attaining bliss return there." "Truly, some one after having left this world knows (this) self saying, 'This I am'. Another one does not recognize his own world. Bewildered by fire, choked with smoke, he does not recognize his own world. But he who knows the self saying, 'This I am', he recognizes his own world. And then the Sāvitra fire carries him to the heavenly world."[81] Whatever oblation he sacrifices here that becomes his self in the other world, the offering that follows him calls out to him, 'Come here. Here I am your (divine) self.'[82] "He who sacrifices with the desire that he may obtain a place in the world of the Gods, that sacrifice of his then goes forth toward the world of the Gods. After it follows the sacrificial fee that he gives and holding on to the sacrificial fee (follows) the sacrifices."[83] There are also heaven-worthy sacrifices.[84] Such passages tend to lower the moral tone of piety by reducing it to the mere catering to the priests' avarice.

In all these passages the good works which earn heaven or a region of bliss are sacrifices. Karman is ritual and also the fees given to the priests. The notion of good works thus does not ascend above the ritual into something ethical or spiritual. The emphasis on the fees given to the officiating priests is stated firmly and for the first time, its gains increased significance with time.

---

77 *Op. Cit.*, I: 18.

78 ŚB XI: 1: 8: 6.

79 *Taittirīya Saṃhitā* III: 3: 8: 5.

80 *RV X:* 14: 8.

81 *Tait.* Br. Ill: 10: 11: 1, 2.

82 *ŚB* XI: 2: 2: 5.

83 *ŚB* I: 9: 3: 1.

84 *ŚB* X: 1: 5: 4.

As heaven is but a replica of the good life lived by the high-born affluent on earth—plenty, food, garlands, perfumes etc.—similarly hell is but a reflection of the punishments meted out to the unfortunate down-trodden section of the population; it is the masters' punishment of servants, debtors or underlings.

The *Atharva* veda which was the latest of the Saṃhitās to be compiled has a definition of hell-worthy deeds. 'The *Vaśā* cow will yield the milk of all desires in the realm of Yama. When refused to a supplicant, she (will take him to) hell."[85] Such excessive emphasis on gifts makes piety cheap and wholly mundane.

"A man who reviles, strikes and draws blood from a brahmin goes to hell for he will not see the world of the ancestors for as many years as are the grains of dust on which the blood falls."[86] Those who spit on a brahmin or flick on him nose-mucus, spend their after-life sitting in a stream of blood, devouring hair for food.[87] "Whatever food one eats in this world, by the very same is he eaten again in the other (world).[88] The *KausZlaki* Brahmana narrates Bhrgu's long itinerary in the different hells.[89]

It is clear that the Saṃhitās and even the Brāhmaṇas are quite vague about hell and about eschatology in general. Somehow these imprecations and injunctions presuppose an atmosphere of demotion of the social status of respect and reverence for the brahmins. Perhaps real degradation had set in at least among a section of the brahmins, so that an effort to artificially preserve a hierarchy that was showing signs of disintegration. Hence hell-worthy acts are listed and offences against brahmins and later, in the epics, against preceptors, against the scriptural injunctions constituted heinous crimes worthy of hell. With time hells become more clearly delineated and crimes leading to hell can be seen as caste-offences, offences against preceptors, Icings and other powers that be. These, then are offences against the social hierarchy of power and privilege. Hell is prescribed for all non-conformists, in ritual or in belief (cf: the post-mortal punitive prescriptions against atheists and Buddhists). Thus with the transformation of power-relations, with the

---

85 XII: 4: 36.

86 *Taittirīya* Saṃhita.

87 *AV*: V: 19: 3.

88 *ŚB* XII: 9: 1: 1.

89 XI: 3; this is repeated in *Jaitninīya* Br. 1: 4244 and in *ŚB* XI: 6: 1: 13.

codification of scriptural injunctions and with the increasingly rigid stratification of cast, offences could be enunciated with greater clarity, and corresponding punishments could be laid down more precisely. The process goes on from the Vedic to the Buddhist then to the epic and Puranic ages with stricter regulations being laid down at each successive stage.

As hells are earned by evil karman and the connotation of the evil karman undergoes a change from offences strictly ritual through offences of belief—to those against caste and power hierarchy, we notice an increasing lack of correspondence between the moral bearing of the offence and the hell—and— torment that retribution prescribed. This discrepancy can be spelt out as fate because the logic of commensurability fails and yet retributive directives multiply.

The *Rāmāyaṇa* allots hell for the regicide, brahmanicide, cowslayer, thief and those who slay animals, the atheist, those who marry before their elders, informers (or traitors), the miserly, he who kills a friend or pollutes a teacher's bed.[90] We are told that Rāvaṇa fought the forces of hell and won, but left at Brahman's order. The *Mahābhārata* condemns miscegenation of castes and says that the fathers of those who intermarry fall, with their obsequial oblations and libations all spoilt.[91] Again, those who do not perform prescribed religious duties, atheists, disrespectful, wicked men whose sole concern is their sensual pleasures—these have Yama's torments inflicted upon them.[92] The *Harivaṃśa* sends suicides to hell.[93] The Mahābhārata, however, has an ennobling thought in this context; one descends to hell through a deed of ill-repute.[94]

The Buddhist attitude to hell and karman is brought out through some Jātaka episodes. "A fish was about to die in an unhealthy and unrighteous frame of mind when Buddha interfered, lest it should be born in hell."[95] "The Vārāṇasī king heard four voices from four creatures in hell and wished to perform an expiatory sacrifice. Buddha explained the mystery of the voices to the king: when souls in hell raise their heads from iron cauldrons of

90 IV: 17: 36–37.

91 VI: 3: 42.

92 XIII: 105: 15; XVIII: 2: 16–26.

93 Bhaviṣya parvan 129: 13. 93 III: 191: 22.

94 III: 191: 22.

95 No. 34, *Maccn.*

torment, they emit such noises."[96] "A perfidious king was telling lies and with each lie his body sank deeper and deeper in hell."[97] "Kokāliya disregarded Tudu Brahmā's warnings and did not repent; he died and went to hell."[98] "Saṃkicca's son had gone astray, so Saṃkicca appeared to him and described the torments of hell; the son, in terror mended his ways."[99] "A Bodhisattva had suffered for 80,000 years in hell after eighty years of reign. He shuddered when in his next life, his father the king was meting out harsh punishments to a robber (fearing that his father, too, would suffer in hell like him)."[100] The King of Mithila was a wicked man; Buddha appeared to him in the shape of an ascetic and preached to him, but to no avail. Buddha, then described the hells to him; this worked, and the king was converted and left his evil ways.[101]

In these episodes the description of hell has a salutary effect on the listeners and hell is presented as punitive measure for some ethical or theological offence. The ritual or social offence plays no part in them, hence there is a direct correspondence between evil karman and hell. Fate thus has no scope in these tales; karman obtains its legitimate results.

Scholars say that while Mesopotamia gave us the first description of heaven, in Babylon originated the concept of hell and then Mandaeans took it over from whom the Manichaeans adopted it. Whatever the origin, all mythologies have agreed that (a) bad works lead the departed soul to hell and that (b) it is a place of torments. Unlike the Semitic religions, in Indian mythology neither heaven nor hell is eternal. Virtually the Indian hell resembles the catholic idea of purgatory where the soul works off his earlier evil deeds and then is either reborn in a better station or goes to heaven, etc. Since the Indian hell is temporary, it is a place where Yama's minions torment the soul so that it pays off its debts of piety to Yama, Dharmarāja. The Vāmana purāṇa has a whole chapter on which sinful acts are repaid with which torments in hell. The correspondence is wholly disproportionate and arbitrary, but it reflects codes of social conduct.

[96] No. 314, Lohakumbhī.

[97] No. 422, *Cetiya.*

[98] No. 481, *Takkāriya.*

[99] No. 530, *Saṃkicca.*

[100] No. 538, Mūgapakkha.

[101] No. 544, *Mūhānāradakassapā.*

The Garuḍapurāṇa, the special text on eschatology mentions twenty one hells —Tāmisra, Lohaśaṅku, Mahābhairava, śalmalī, Raurava, Kundalī, Preti Mṛtyu, Kālasūtra, Saṃyāta Lohatāḍa Saviṣa, Saṃprayātana, Mahānaraka, Karāla Saṃjīvatia, Avīci, Andhatāmisra, Kumbhīpāka, Asipatravaṇa and Tāpana.[102] *In a general statement it says that altogether there are 8400000 hells.*[103] *The list in the Vāmana Purāṇa varies somewhat; it mentions Raurava, Mahāraurava, Andhatāmisraka, Kālasūtra, Apratiṣṭha, Ghatiyantra, Asipatravaṇa, Taptakumbha, Kūṭaśālmalī, Karapatra, Śvāndhojana* and Saṃśoṣaṇa.[104] Most Purāṇas have their individual lists of hell. The *Bṛhannāradīya* list with slight variations reads:*Tāpana, Vālukākumbha, Raurava, Mahāraurava, Kumbhīpāka, Nirucchvāsa, Kālasūtra, Pramardana, Asipatravaṇa, Lalabhakṣa, Himokaṭa, Mṛṣāvasthā, Vasākūpa*; thirteen altogether.[105] The *Bhāgavata* Purāṇa has its own catalogue of twenty one hells: *Tāmista, Andhatāmisra, Raurava, Mahāraurava, Kumbhīpāka, Kālasūtra, Asipatravaṇa, Śūkaramukha, Andhakūpa, Kṛmibhojana, Sandaṃśa Taptasūrmi, Vajrakaṇṭaka, Śālmah, Vaitaraṇī, Pūyoda, Prānarodha, Viśasana, Lālābhakṣa, Sārameyādana, Avīci, Ayahpāna.*[106] The *Bhāgavata,* a late Purāṇa introduces several new and horrendous concepts of hell. One can almost visualize the torments of early medieval India reserved for social offenders and the helpless poor. The different torments in the different hells are gloatingly described in detail. The*Vāmana* Purāṇa elsewhere gives another list of sixteen hells with a list of sins leading to each. Hell torments and horrors are described in detail.[107] The essence of hell is suffering which the scriptures attempt to present as proportionate to the sinful acts committed but this correspondence is wholly disproportionate, and, therefore, entirely unconvincing. Besides, the element of sadism is evident in the details. The *Mārkaṇḍeya* Purana describes hell in two whole chapters (chapters 12 and 15) and the various torments in another (chapter 14). The *Brahmavaivarta* Purāṇa enumerates the different hells (chapter 29) and the hell-torments of sinners in another chapter (chapter 30). The *Bhāgavata* vividly describes

---

[102] 14: 21–23.

[103] *Ibid.*, verse 20.

[104] 11: 51–58.

[105] 14: 3, 4; The whole chapter is on hell and its different torments.

[106] V: 26: 4–40. 106 61: 1–16.

[107] In *Vāmana* Purāṇa, I: 14: 3–12.

hell-torments: the body encircled by flaming torches, eating one's flesh cut off from the body by his own self or by another, the entrails taken out from the living body by dogs and hawks, being bitten by serpents and scorpions, being severed limb from limb, being crushed underfoot by elephants, pushed down from mountain cliffs, water-sources closed up, etc.[108] A rather unexpected statement of great depth of perception is: "Both heaven and hell are on this earth alone; those hell-tor-ments are suffered here."[109] This indirectly indicates the origin of the concepts of heaven from enjoyments of the affluent coveted by the less fortunate therefore easily used as baits and hell suffering reflecting those inflicted by the powers that be on the less fortunate, criminals or offenders of any description. Hells may be the destination of quite minor offences just as heaven may be gained through quite insignificant acts of piety; both these conceptually reinforce fatalism, based on irrationality.

The Buddhist *Aṅguttara Nikāya* says, "Monks, following six things one is duly cast in hell... One takes life, takes what is not given, lives carnally, lies, has evil desires and wrong views."[110] One who commits suicide or encourages others to do so or approves of taking life goes to hell.[111]

The *Bṛhannāradīya* Purāṇa makes it very easy to go to hell: "the sinner who interrupts a pious conversation goes to hell and stays there as long as the sun and moon exist."[112] This is one of the many instances in late Purāṇas where both heaven and hell become eternal or semi-eternal. It tempting to heaven and put-ting the fear of horrendous hell-torments is the objective of these passages then with the credulous masses they must have been eminently successful, but they fail to ennoble people spiritually.

The *Bhāgavata* Purāṇa mentions the different torments allotted to criminals in the special hells allocated to them. He who steals others' property, children and wives, is sent to the Tāmisra hell. He who deprives another man and enjoys his wife goes to the Andhatāmisra. He who feeds only his own family and not others finds himself in Raurava. The *Vāmana* Purāṇa says that those who eat good food without proper ritual are tormented in hell.[113]

---

[108] HI: 30: 25–28.

[109] *Op. Cit.*, III: 30: 29.

[110] PTS, Vol. VII, p. 81.

[111] *Op. Cit.*, Vol. I, pp. 212, 306–307.

[112] 2: 75.

[113] 12: 20.

In the Mahāraurava a man suffers the torments he caused animals to suffer. The cruel killer of birds and beasts is fated to go to Kumbhīpaka. Kālasūtra is the place for one who hates his father, brothers and brahmins; there he is fried in a hot pan. Asipatravaṇa is specially reserved for the atheist (or Buddhist), pākhaṇḍa where he is scourged and runs to and fro between sword-blades on both sides. His body is badly slashed and multilated but the wounds heal up so that fresh cuts can grow weals again. The unrighteous king who punishes those who should not be punished and orders corporal punishment for brahmins ends up in the Śūkaramukha where powerful demons crush him. Andhakūpa is the destination for those who cannot feel the sufferings of others, there animals bite and gnaw at their bodies and sharp rough insects sting them. By neglecting the five obligatory sacrifices, *(pañcayajña)* and eating selfishly one's own meals alone, one is eaten up by worms in the Krmibhojana. He who lakes forcibly or by stealth a brahmin's wealth is scourged with flaming iron pliers which sing and pluck his flesh out at Saṅdaṃśa. At Surmya the man who had slept with a woman (whose company is) forbidden by law has to embrace heated iron bodies of women. Those who flout the laws of piety go to Vaitaraṇī full of faeces, urine, pus, blood, hair, nail and bones. There also go the paramours of Caṇdāla women who neglect rules of cleanliness. Those haughty men who slay animals in a sacrifice they perform, out of boastfulness, go to Viśasana. At Avīci dogs devour the flesh of the incendiary and poisoner. Brāhmins, Kṣatriyas and Vaiśyas who drink soma and enjoy others' wives are sprinkled with molten iron in Karṣṇāyasa. Kṣārakardama, corrosive mud, is reserved for those who neglect to honour their superiors. Murderers and women who 'consume' men are tormented by Yama's servants. Those sadists who torment others for their own pleasure are similarly tormented in Dandaśūka. The miserly end up at Sūcīmukha... And so the sadist descriptions go on and on.

The *Brahmavaivarta* Purāṇa has whole chapters on hells and diverse torments.[114] The man who refuses a wife's sexual overtures surely lives in Kumbhīpāka for as many years as there are hairs on his body.[115] The *Devībhāgavata* says that those who torment others become 'ruru' deer and go to Raurava hell and to Mahāraurava, according to the gravity of their offence. The Yāmya hell is for those who imprison others. The Kravyāda hell is for

[114] *Prakṛtikhaṇḍia 29,* 30, 31, 33 and 34.

[115] *Op. Cit.*, Kṛṣṇajanma, 30: 77.

those who spoil offerings to the ancestors; and Kumbīpāka is for those who torture others, for as many years as there are hairs on the bodies of animals. Those who are hostile to parents, brahmins and animals are destined for Kālasūtra. People who leave the Vedic path and adopt views of pākhaṇḍas (atheists, Buddhists) are doomed to Asipatravaṇa where they are scourged. Kings or courtiers ordering corporal punishments to brahmins are destined for Śūkaramukha. Stealers of gold and jewellery go to Sandaṃśa. Those who cohabit with women forbidden by the scriptures have to embrace hot iron figures shaped like women. People who cohabit with beasts go to Śālmalī, they live on and suffer.[116] Brahmi who officiate as priests for śūdras and eat the śūdra's śrāddha meal or assist in cremating a śūdra's corpse will surely live in tanks of pus in hell. To accept food from a thief, a caṇḍala, vaiśya or a kṣatriya is an extremely heinous offence. A śūdra's food, association with him, sharing a seat with him—those who do these go to fearful hells for as long as the sun and the moon persist.[117] Hells and the sins that send one there occupy a long catalogue in the *Padma* Purāṇa.[118] Hells mentioned there have some uncommon names. Thus besides the commoner ones we hear of *Nikṛntana, Taptakumbha, Rodha, Tātā, Taptakhalva, Mahājvāla, Śālā, Vimohana, Kimañjana Adhahiśiras, Rudhirāndha, Viḍbhuja, Mūtrakuṇḍa, Lohatāpī* and *Bhedana.*

Such catalogues are strewn in many Purāṇas in the context of karman, death and post-mortal reprisals. The length and details of such lists vary, but the general tone is that of an eye for an eye; only the process of plucking it out is extremely cruel and one detects not only the concern for public ethics but also a note of sadist gloating.

In many tales and prescriptions one common and steady effect of evil deeds is birth in an undesirable condition, but rebirth itself is a necessary concomitant of bad karman. "... retributive birth of an individual after death with reference to the quality of his action in a previous existence. Rebirth in purgatory for a short time for destruction of life... The Jains also believed that the duration or the time for ripening or fruition and the period for which the karmas remain dormant are different for different class of karma ..."[119] Heaven

---

[116] 8: 22–50; also chapters 28 and 32, 37, 1–118.

[117] *Op. Cit.*, 11: 21, 22.

[118] Pātālakhaṇḍa 18: 97–226.

[119] *Numen*, XXX, fasc 2, Dec., 1983, pp. 199, 202.

or hell are two termini of the fruition of karman; a third is rebirth. Of the Sumerian beliefs in this area we read, "When he died, his emasculated spirit descended to the dark, dreary nether world where life was but a dismal wretched reflection of its earthly counterpart."[120] Similarly, the *Pcrpol Vuh* saw a cheerless after-life, "The House of Gloom, many punishments, darkness, cold, jaguars, bats and knives."[121] In both these mythologies karman is totally unrelated to the life-after-death. In both, the post-mortal existence is uniformly dark and dismal for all men, irrespective of their karman before death. The early Vedic men also thought of existence in the next life as dreary and dark; their intense glowing love for this life must have been responsible for this negative outlook. In all three, karman plays no part and after-life is cheerless. When karman assumed a real significance, it had to have some correlation with man's existence after death. An inherent moral judgment became operative: and the irrefutable corollary of this is that those whose karman was good deserved a better station in the next life than the evil doers who came to be deposited in a place of darkness first, which gradually took dearer shape and became a purgatory where evil karman was worked off through suffering. Hence hell-suffering actually helped the soul's spiritual expiation and ascent in still later lives. Now because of the multiplication of hells and their torments, quite naturally an endeavour was made to find at least a veneer of justice in the proportion, quality and duration in hell and the evil acts that led to them. Needless to say, this balanced, proportionate justice was never found—we shall explore the reason later—but an eye-wash was invented: bewildering details of sins, hells and torments. Quite frequently, the same effect derives from multiple causes and the same cause led to multiple results. People were never given tidy paradigms without overlapping or without loose ends hanging. The masses were so conditioned that except very occasionally they never questioned the basic relevance of karman and heaven or hell. Besides, vaguely and nebulously karman pointed to the mirage of a better life in the future; hence people clung to it desperately. Very vaguely they also sensed that going against the strictures of the power-wielders was risky, it may land them in jail on earth and in hell after death. Hence, basically the purpose of this elaborate schemata succeeded.

Heaven and hell are nothing but a form of reward and punishment. But reward and punishments have a few presup-positions. One: that there is a

[120] Kramer, 1963, p. 123.

[121] Pt. II, ch. 2.

stated and universally accepted ethical norm, deviation from which is punishable and conformation to which earns reward. Second: that there is an arbiter who is the final determining authority about certain karmans being evil, therefore hell-worthy, while others are good, therefore heaven-worthy. Third: that this verdict is just and uniform in all cases and therefore dependable.

The crux of the matter lies in this that no scripture mentions an ultimate arbiter. Providence is too vague and is wholly apathetic and not involved in any way. Gods are many and various and their past conduct in no mythology is above reproach, for, evidently they are partisans and fight with each other over the fate of their devotees. Thirdly, if karman by itself generated its effect then it would be uniform and not found different in most cases. Lastly, even with karman, fruition and result is a mystery to man. It, therefore, is fate.

The concept of heaven and hell rest on the two basic concepts: reward and punishment. Even these two concepts presuppose an impartial judge whose verdict determines reward and punishment. The scriptures offer no single judge; different Gods in different contexts are presented as judges or arbiters, and, for that matter sages and sometimes injured mortals who, take upon themselves the task of the judge pronounce verdicts for or against individuals. In Christianity the matter is easy and comparatively linear, "God appropriately rewards and punishes for obedience and disobedience. When this was seen not to be the case in this world, the experience of God's justice was postponed to the next."[122] One remembers Browning's "On the earth the broken arcs; in the heaven a perfect round."[123] So the next world, not the next birth is a place where God compensates what remained uncompensated here. In Islam, too, after death there are only heaven and hell for experiencing the rewards and punishments for deeds done in this life. Zoroastrianism also does not subscribe to rebirth as compensation for acts in this life; after death these acts are weighed and according to the result, the soul's destination is determined. Buddhism and Jainism both have hell as a place to pay off the debts of evils done on earth and heaven for being rewarded for the good deeds. But to neither as also to Brahmanism, heaven or hell is eternal.

Hells in all mythologies are full of evil spirits: these are either Yama's servants who inflict hell-torments on the souls of the wicked, or they are such

---

[122] Sanders 1986, p. 126.

[123] Abt Vogler, stanza 9.

evildoers who are to spend a spell in hell until their evil deeds are paid off with these torments, or they are just demons without name or habitat, unless they are permanent denizens of hell. Such spirits can be of many kinds: ghosts, gnomes, goblins, demons, evil spirits, or monsters. It is difficult to define, describe, categorize or even rationalize such demonic spirits "the demonic is... not only irrational, but also anti-rational".[124] But this position is hardly tenable in theology; all theologies invent, accept and accomodate demons and evil spirits. These instil fear, abhorrence and some awe in men; the concept of evil spirit is ubiquitous and of very long standing. They are there in great number in the *Atharvaveda*, Jātakas, Nikāyas, *Garuḍa* Purāṇa,[125] the *Bible, Talmud, Torah, Avesta* and the entire Medieval Western theology teems with them. Scholiasts have burnt midnight oil over their nature and careers, commentators have sought to classify and define them allotting specific functions to different categories. Demonhood is one of the many potential positions of the departed souls and this is one of the reasons why they provoke fear in men's imagination. It is not the fear of any concrete Rightfulness, but the indefinite fear of the ghastly, of the incomprehensible, which is outwardly projected in the belief of demons ... he represents the frightfulness of the world, the incalculable might which weaves itself around us and threatens to seize us.[126] Witches, wizards, witch hunts and shamanism are all connected with demons, which oblige their masters and mistresses, the wizards and witches, just as mantras and well-performed rites oblige the sacrificer.

In the *Mahābhārata* we are told that demons performed a nefarious rite and created the upper half of Duryodhana's body which was invulnerable.[127] Demons are allotted various functions usually detrimental to men's interest. But then, being harmed by a demon generally presupposes evil acts done by the agent to invite such harm. "For pagan and Christian alike, misfortune was unambiguously the work of superhuman agents, the demons."[128]

We hear of spirits and seizures and of thirty-eight names of evil spirits given in the *Agni* Purāṇa.[129] To the Vedic, epic and Puranic imagination the

[124] Menching, 1976, p. 132.

[125] Also in almost every other Purāṇa.

[126] Mensching. 1976, p. 141ff.

[127] III: 240: 1–8.

[128] Douglas, 1970, p. 28.

[129] 299: 38.

mid-air and the nether world were thick with evil spirits of various descriptions. But in no religion perhaps is demonology so specified as in Mazdeism. "The demons are. conceived of as spirits (Mainyava, daeva) and their number is beyond computerization."[130] The impact of demons becomes formidable from the fear that through evil deeds a man may, after death, become a demon. He and his departed relatives, too. This dreadful prospect explains the ever-present fear. Also, the elements of incalculability associated with spirits, especiaslly because laws of the human world were not applicable to the spirits. And no one knew which karman will result in which kind of demon existence after death.

The *Chhāndogya* Upaniṣad says: "Those who are of pleasant conduct here; the prospect is that they will enter the pleasant womb of a brahmin or the womb of a Kṣatriya...Vaiśya. But those who are of a stinking conduct here, chances are that they will enter a stinking womb, either the womb of a dog or the womb of a swine or the womb of an outcast."[131] The Jātaka stories bear out the dogmas of reward and punishment in subsequent births. Thus a brahmin versed in the Vedas who had killed a goat had his own head cut in four hundred and ninety-nine births.[132] "A rich man who had buried treasure on the bank (of a river) was reborn as a snake there. Another who had buried thirty crores was reborn as a rat there."[133] Evidently, these two were punished for their miserliness, for, instead of sharing wealth with others who needed it, they hid it and paid for this foolish self-centred gesture. "As a lay Bodhisattva lay dying, people asked him: 'what excellences have you won?' 'None', said he and died and was reborn in the realm of theradiant Gods".[134] This is an instance of how humility was rewarded. Śibi was sorely tempted, tested and tormented by Sakka, but with great forbearance and genuine altruism passed all the tests. Sakka offered him a boon. He wanted to regain his eyes not as a boon but as a reward for a virtuous life. A king had a wicked chaplain who took bribes, wrongfully extorted money from the subjects and was given to backbiting. This wicked man saw a fasting woman one day and gave her a mango to eat. After death the chaplain became a monster with one long nail

[130] Winston, *History of Religions,* 1966, Vol. 5, no. 2, p. 192.

[131] V: 10: 7–8.

[132] No. 18, *Matakabhatta.*

[133] No.73, Saccamkira.

[134] No. 99, *Parasahassa.*

on each finger with which he scooped his own flesh out and ate it, but because of that single act of kindness he became a nymph every night.[135] This tale emphasizes the merit of one good deed which earned the otherwise villainous man a demi-God existence every night in his next birth. A monkey, moved to compassion at the plight of a fatigued and hungry hunter, fed him with 'tinduka' fruit. Then, the monkey went to sleep and asked the man to keep watch under the tree. The hunter, however, suddenly had a craving for monkey-meat and struck at the monkey's head. Awake, the monkey knew everything and offered to take the hunter across the forest. The man contracted leprosy and was later swallowed by the earth.[136]A serpent king acted treacherously to his friend, divulged a fatal secret which greatly harmed the friend's interest. They both went to an ascetic for arbitration who said that enemies should not be trusted. Pāṇḍava the serpent king was accused of treachery; his head split into seven bits and the earth Opened and took these in; Pāṇḍava went straight to the Avīci hell.[137] A poor young girl craved for a red garment, but her parents were too poor to buy her one. So she worked as a maid-servant and saved up enough to buy the dress. Before putting it on, she went for a bath; on coming up she saw a Paccekabuddha whose clothes were in tatters. She first gave him half of the dress, but seeing the dress shine on him, she gave it away to him. Through this act of kindness she became a non-pareil in beauty in her next life.[138] The instances of reward and punishment are a cardinal theme in Pali Buddhism and runs through most of the tales.

The Purāṇas are replete with another version of reward and punishment: Although most anecdotes deal with good works being amply rewarded and evil deeds duly punished, the desideratum of goodness is generally caste-oriented or power-hierarchy-oriented. Thus serving a brahmin, giving him gifts, sacrificing self-interest for him or for a king or a rich and powerful magnate earns merit. Neglecting to do this leads to disaster. In a later chapter we shall see that other ritual acts also earn merit, remit sins and lead to a better birth in a higher station in the next life. The criterion of goodness is not so much ethical as ritual or serving the nobly born, wealthy and powerful

---

[135] No. 511, *Kiṃchanda.*

[136] No. 516, *Mahākopi.*

[137] No. 518, *Pāṇḍava.*

[138] No. 527, *Unmādanti.*

persons, higher castes, social or familial seniors. The *Brahmavaivarta* Purāṇa gives a catalogue of the effects of meritorious deeds.[139]

Another chapter catalogues deeds which lead to heaven. The *Bhāgavata* Purāṇa categorically states that the soul exhausts its (accumulated) merits through enjoyment and then works off the evil deeds through non-enjoyment.[140] Clearly, enjoyment is the goal and one attains it as a reward of merits and when one is deprived of enjoyment, it signifies that he lacks merit and non-enjoyment is a punishment for evil deeds.

The way out of this noose of karman—good or bad, leading to heaven and hell, reward and punishment in which man finds himself enmeshed, is liberation. Liberation from what? The unanimous reply is rebirth, saṃsāra, repeated returns to this complex of existence. It may be salvation or spiritual regeneration which ensures heaven after death. Or it may be total extinction of the essential self in Nirvāṇa. Or it may even mean merger in Brahman. In other words, complete annihilation of the individual self as such but existing as Brahman consciously and blissfully. "But Saṃsara and mokṣa are combined already in the *Śvetāśvatara* and since these ancient times they have belonged to one another through the whole history of India."[141] Not only in the late Śaiva *Śvetāśvatara* Upaniṣad but in the Viśiṣṭādvaita and Dvaitadvaita systems of Vedanta and in aveiled way, in some later developments of Mahāyāna i.e., in Sahajayāna and Tantrayāna, such a subtle merger can be sensed. "Great Vehicle Buddhism ... and the Śaiva system constitute, then, a soteriology in which salvation is aimed at, that is to say, the reintegration in us of that luminous Consciousness present as Bodhicitta, as logos, as Śiva. And this salvation is reached by means of an experience which involves all the life of the spirit and therefore, produces a complete revulsion, or if one wishes, reintegration."[142] Of the Mandaeans the *Hasting's Encyclopaedia of Religion and Ethics* writes "It is they (evil spirited deities of other people and other creeds) and their servants who make lire a torment for the Mandaeans. Hence the believer waits with earnest longing for his salvation i.e., his deliverance from this earthly existence."[143]

[139] Brahmakhaṇḍa: ch. 27.

[140] 1: 12: 13.

[141] Rodhe; 1946, p. 133.

[142] Tucci, 1981, pp. 15–16.

[143] Vol. VII, p. 387.

It is in the Upaniṣads that we hear for the first time of liberation, As a continuation of the Saṃhita-Brāhmaṇa karmakāṇḍa (dispensation of the religious action), the Āraṇyaka and Upaniṣads introduce a qualitatively different jñānakāṇḍa (dispensation of gnosis). Here the very goal of life is changed from the earlier happy, long, healthy and prosperous life to release from the chain of rebirth. Needless to say, life for the masses had come to mean poverty, crushing burdens of labour and of debts, starvation, disease and oppression from higher caste and wealthier overlords. If for the masses life meant endless repetition of this state of affairs, if the acts were separated from their fruition by an indefinite time gap and if when the fruition occurs the agent is quite in the dark as to which karman bears which fruit so that the whole business appears as unknown and unknowable, adṛṣḍa, fate, then man could hardly be expected to be tempted to continue this process. He would seek to snap the chain. Another relevant question is that of the continuity of consciousness from this life to the next. True, a few cases are cited to prove this continuity in persons who 'claim' to remember their past lives. But for one thing their memory has not always been vindicated by facts; secondly, other factors can explain such 'memory', thirdly and most importantly, their number is so hopelessly small that they cannot 'prove' any tenet. Under such circumstances when the overwhelming majority of the people have no remembrance of any life beyond the present one, all rewards and punishments become irrational and untenable as awards of justice of any kind. It is like rewarding or punishing an infant who is unaware of any act for which he is being rewarded or punished. Hence the professed purpose of such reward or punishment is wholly lost on the agent; he learns nothing, cannot mend his ways and in his innermost soul feels the utter cruel injustice of being undeservedly punished or rewarded. Hence such visitations of 'fate' become merely punitive when the agent suffers in the dark or has a 'windfall', when he enjoys something without deserving it. As the masses suffered unaccountable miseries, how could they have any faith in a just arbiter? Poor, weak and helpless, they realized that protest against the socio-religious authorities would be futile; so they submitted. And this is exactly what was expected of them. They accepted that their suffering stemmed from sins from a previous life and that the only way to improve their prospects in the next life was abject, unquestioning service to the three upper castes. Keeping the masses in the dark regarding the cause of their suffering, yet preaching that there was a cause in a previous life was the height of casuistic dishonesty. The poor victims caught between the Scylla and Charybdis took the path of least resistance and served the upper echelons of society. The only way out, they felt, was to end this misery of recurring births by bowing out of existence to liberation. This was dangled before them, various paths were prescribed, as we shall see in a later chapter, but devotion was presented as a viable option to this misery; and no wonder that for the last two millennia devotional cults and sects are multiplying. Even now new spiritual 'father' and 'mother' figures are growing like mushrooms. In other countries too, new self-styled 'saviours' are rising quick succession and exploiting the suffering man's dream of respite and happiness.

With the inception of the theory of rebirth in the late Brāhmaṇs and early Upaniṣads, an alternative path was sought. The Upaniṣads prescribe remedies for rebirth. "The man who sheds sense experiences in order to realize the experiencing self behind them becomes immortal after death."[144] "Immortality is obtained through wisdom."[145] "Ultimate peace also comes through gnosis."[146] "By knowing this ātman, which is beyond sense-perception, is without a beginning or end and is the highest principle, man is released from the jaws of death."[147] Clearly this release has reference to repeated deaths, i.e. mokṣa. "Knowing the Puruṣa (=ātman) creatures are released and attain immortality."[148] 'True knowledge regarding the function, condition, power and station of Prāṇa (life-breath) leads to immor-tality."[149] "When the wise man visualizes Brahman, his sin and righteousness are both cast off."[150] Evidently this height of gnosis lifts man above karman—good or bad, he thus moves beyond reward and punishment and attains liberation. "The state of liberation in which name and form are drowned in the supreme Puruṣa, just as rivers lose their individual identity in the ocean."[151] "That which is beyond that (universe) is without form, without suffering: those who know this become immortal."[152] "He who knows 'I am Brahman' becomes all this, even

[144] *Kenu Up.* 1: 2.

[145] *Kaṭha Up.* II: 4: 5.

[146] *Kaṭha Up.* II: 17.

[147] *Kaṭha* I: 3: 13, 15. 149.

[148] *Kaṭha* II: 3: 8–10.

[149] *Praśna Up.* III: 3: 12.

[150] *Muṇḍaka Up.* III: 1: 3.

[151] Muṇḍaka III: 2: 8.

[152] *Śvetāśvatara Up.* 3: 10.

the Gods cannot prevent his becoming thus."[153] (Of the *horse*-sacrificers) "those who know it conquer recurring deaths."[154] One notices the reference to 'recurring deaths' instead of rebirth. Obviously the death-pangs caused a trauma which terrified man with the prospect of its repetition. The disaffection with life, repeated lives, was augmented to this fear later, "The life of a detached man, free from desires, or of one whose desires are fulfilled does not depart (like an ordinary mortal's); becoming Brahman he attains Brahman."[155]

This series of prescriptions for attaining liberation has some common denominators (a) knowing oneself to be identical in essence with Brahman, (b) being free from desire, (c) the name and form are drowned in the Supreme Puruṣa. Basically, these prerequisites are intellectional and ethical, not karmic, later scriptures lay down prescriptions for liberation in different terms: (i) emotional (devotion, bhakti) and (ii) actional (visiting pilgrimages, image-worship, vows, dips in sacred rivers, seas, etc.). This transmogrification presupposes (a) the floruit of Buddhism, Jainism and other non-conformist doctrines and (b) the post-epic transformation of the code of worship, viz. the widespread practice of pūjā which was iconic, temple-based, performed with different oblations and libations, along different lines by different priests. In these changed circumstances the connotation of pious karman underwent a radical transmutation. The karmic part and the devotional part will be treated in a separate section. Here let us give samples of the connotation of liberation.

"If a person, even without wishing it, dies in Purī, he is released from suffering and attains a covetable station."[156] "A man's sins accumulated over millions of lives are remitted, his, and of tens of millions in his (family) line if he bathes in the Yamunā."[157] Slowly and steadily with the upsurge of devotion as a valid path to liberation, liberation is rendered increasingly easier. We thus hear. "He who worships the lotus feet of Hari with the tender leaves of tulasī, is never again reborn."[158] "Whoever gives his most favourite articles to

---

[153] *Bṛhadāraṇyaka Up.* I: 4: 10.

[154] *Bṛhadāraṇyaka, Up.* III: 3: 2.

[155] *Bṛhadāraṇyaka Up.* IV: 4: 6.

[156] Brahma Purāṇa II: 31: 16.

[157] *Nārada* P. I: 1: 43.

[158] *Nārada* P. 13: 33.

brahmins goes to Viṣṇu's realm and is never reborn."[159] He who, on seeing Viṣṇu or Śiva being worshipped, bows to the God, attains Viṣṇu's regions and lives happily for millions of aeons.[160] Thus with the passage of time liberation is increasingly devalued: "He attained supreme liberation on arriving in the city of Vārāṇasī."[161] "He who sweeps a Viṣṇu temple daily and places lamps there also attains salvation."[162] "He who lives on the banks of the Gaṅgā and drinks Gaṅgā water is cleansed of all accumulated sins. He who offers the complete oblation to the fire, this yogin is not smeared with piety or impiety, (but) having attained liberation reaches that supreme station from which none returns."[163] The *Bhāgavata* Purāṇa, however, refuses to offer mokṣa so easily; it says: "Of thousands craving for liberation only one succeeds in attaining it."[164] However, in the *Bhagawidgītā* Kṛṣṇa makes mokṣa easy; he promises to cleanse from all sins whoever takes spiritual shelter in him.[165] "He who tells his high secret to my devotees, will indeed come to me with great devotion towards me."[166] The *Bhāgavata* Purāṇa, an essentially Viṣṇuite text, however, says of Śiva that Śiva alone is the lord of bondage and of liberation for the whole world."[167] Kṛṣṇa's call to devotees to forsake all other religious paths and to take recourse to him, for, he will save the sinner from all his sins reads like Christ's claim "I am the way and the truth and the life, no man cometh unto the father but by me."[168] This claim to exclusive soteriological assurance, totally dissociated from man's karman begins with the emergence of bhakti (devotion) which becomes a substitute of karman, presumably because prescribed religious practice had, by then, not only become too complicated and too expensive but also somewhat confusing for a man who wished to find a coherent pattern for karman, devotion, knowledge—and fate. For, none of these rules out fate.

---

[159] *Op. cit.*, I: 131: 69.

[160] *Op. cit.*, I: 13: 135.

[161] *Op. cit.*, II: 7: 72.

[162] *Op. cit.*, I: 13: 135.

[163] *Agni* P. 211: 23–24.

[164] VIII: 7: 22.

[165] *Mbh* VI: 40: 66.

[166] *Mbh* VI: 40: 68.

[167] VIII: 7: 22.

[168] *John* 4: 14.

Vedic worship was ritualistic, complicated entailing expense, liturgic knowledge and manual labour. Mokṣa in the Upanisadic literature was to be attained through the liberating knowledge of the essential unity of man and the Supreme Spirit. Later, after the non-conformist Buddhist and Jain systems declined, pūjā as the accepted mode of worship combined the emotive element of bhakti and a new mode of ritual. With the advent of bhakti, pious action, intellectional realization, manual ritual labour were steadily devalued until the minimal expression of bhakti became an adequate surrogate for all previous modes of worship. Actually such a tendency is first noticed in the Jātakas, but brahminical bhakti far surpasses all earlier manners of worship.

In the schemata of devotion and deities fate took the form of grace. Of the thousands craving for liberation only one finds it because he enjoys divine grace. (The Manichaean God) "in his grace saves the soul from the course of continual rebirth."[169]And as Robinson says, saviours were always from the other world, never from this. Because of the superhuman, divine na-ture of the saviour, grace is quite easily associated with them and for innumerable seekers for liberation divine grace becomes the desideratum. And to man it becomes another connotation of fate, because, as unmerited favour, it cannot be earned and therefore, cannot be anticipated, predicted or even calculated.

According to the Gnostics "Revelation through a call from a messenger from the world of light who penetrates the barriers of the spheres, outwits the archons, awakens the spirit, imparts saving knowledge. Mission of the transcendent saviour begins even before creation of the world... For this redemption the eternal messenger must himself assume the lot of incarnation and cosmic exile."[170] This salvation bears close resemblance to the Christian concept of the saviour who becomes incarnated after descending from heaven in order to save mankind. It also faintly resembles the Viṣṇuite concept of the series of incarnation of Viṣṇu with the same purpose. In both, karman plays an insignificant part; divine grace is the supremely important factor. Again, as grace is selective and not universal, even karman cannot account for the salvation, an element of predeterminism prevails.

In Buddhism the accumulated merits are more significant, although in Mahāyāna divine grace is an important factor for liberation. ... on accede aux

[169] Bleeker, 1963, p. 261.

[170] *Macmillan Encyclopaedia of Religion: "Gnosticism."*

deux étages supérieurs doit pus la voie d'une renaissance, proportionelle en dignité aux mérites acquis, soi par l' exercise des hautes disciplines qui constituent le yoga bouddhique."[171] The area of uncertainty, incalculability is, theoretically at least, much less in Buddhism and the Semitic religions. But a religion codified in the scriptures is quite different from a religion practised by the masses. And in the religion of the masses whether the ultimate deliverance comes through the soteriological grace of a divine saviour, or through gnosis, or strictly through the agent's actions or through the meritorious deeds or the emotional self-surrender in devotion, bhakti, there still lurks an element of determinism. And since everything about the determinator is shrouded in mystery, predetermination is fate.

What fate is in relation to karman and rebirth, grace is in relation to devotion. From the human recipient's point of view grace is equally capricious, unpredictable and wholly unaccountable. The element that baffles prior calculation, correspondence between action and reaction, correlation between the degree of the cause and effect, between the donor and the donné, this element predominates and puzzles the human mind. For the proponents of the theory of devotion and of the saviour showering the saving grace, it was essential to maintain a degree or an area of irrationality so that without knowing, all would strive for it and few would 'receive' it. During the floruit of devotion and pūjā in the Puranic and post-Puranic age, a different group of priests were active superintending temple worship, cultic practices, vows, pilgrimages, prophecies, dreams and oracles and astrological forecasts. It was to their direct interest to withhold a measure of arcane knowledge regarding the recipient of divine grace. The multitude would strive and clamour, would perform all that the priests laid down for their quotidian life and for the special occasions of worship—but very few would be declared 'elect' on whom divine grace descended. The rest would eagerly perform and lavishly spend, knowing that only the favoured few were predestined for grace. So an equivalence was achieved whereby even when other ethical karman was substituted by devotional acts, some unaccountable destiny was operative in determining the chosen few.

We have already seen that although there is no room for fate in the Koran, both Arabic and Persian literature subscribe to fatalism. In Christianity Fate is theologically ruled out; Providence is God, omniscient, omnipotent

---

[171] Lacombe, O., 1978, p. 46.

and omnipresent, yet the literature slowly veered towards Calvin's theory of predestination, and although this is just one of several schools of thought, yet it is a major and formative thought around which raged a fierce ideological battle for a long time.

Calvin's predestination is not the fate of Indian fatalism, primarily because Calvin ascribed prescience to God, while there is no single apotheosis of Indian fate. Secondly, man enjoyed an apparent measure of 'free will' even in Calvinism although in many cases his illusion of 'free will' guided him irresistibly and irrevocably to his damnation, unless he happened to be predestined to be 'saved'. But there was no way to determine his ultimate destination until it was too late. Indian fatalism, strictly speaking, has no such doom in store, for here there is rebirth. But in the most vital aspects viz, the trait of inscrutability, unintelligibility and immutability, Indian fatalism compares with Calvin's predestination. Especially, where divine grace of the devotional tradition is concerned, they have much in common. The major theological premise in both is: man should be kept in the dark regarding what awaits him in life. And after death. One of the reasons is that the concept had been ingrained in the European mind from its Greek heritage of a many faceted fate. In India also the concept of liberation, mokṣa or nirvāṇa, had to come to terms with fatalism before it could be posited conclusively in metaphysics.

CHAPTER 6

Premonitions and Presages

BOETHIUSIN of the fifth century wrote his *De Consolations Philosophiae* in prison under a death sentence. He wrote a fictitious dialogue between himself and dame Philosophia. The philosophy taught him that "the transient affairs of our life stem from the stability of divine nature and its lasting simplicity. Providence is at the centre of all events. But when we seek to realize God's will in the changing scheme of things we are pushed to the concept of fate, for, fate it is which controls these. Fate allocates to every individual thing its special time and place."[1] God has an infallible foreknowledge of everything which frustrates man's freedom of action. Divine prescience is determined by eternity as an inherent quality.[2] His philosophy consoles him in a manner which reconciles providence with fate. But ultimately this reconciliation is not achieved in theology or metaphysics. Yet man yearns for prescience about his future.

Fatalism stems from man's total ignorance and apprehension regarding what befalls him. Man would give much to 'know' his course of life in this and the subsequent ones. Since there is no solution to this, since the veil falls not only between the present and the future but also between the past and the present, man has at all times and in all climes sought for signs which would warn him and teach him to anticipate and prepare for what is coming. There are ways which man has invented to have foreknowledge of coming events. One of these is dreams. And their interpretation.

In the *Brahmasūtrabhāṣya* Śankara "refers to fortune-tellers as *anvaya-vyatirekakuśala* (those who can make causal connections and also detect logical discontinuance) since they know how certain dream-phenomena are accompanied or followed by actual events."[3] So there was a group of men

[1] IV: pr 6: 1

[2] IV: pr 3: 26.

[3] Halbfass, 1991. *Brahmasūtrabhāṣya* II: 1: 14. Translation by the author.

who made a fortune by interpreting dreams. And they were present in all countries and in all ages. Dreams as such are neither mentioned nor interpreted in the Saṃhitās, Brāhmaṇas, Āraṇyakas and Upaniṣads except in imagery and myths. This does not prove that people did not feel disturbed by evil dreams: Duhsvapna (evil dream) is Nirṛti's son or Yama's son.[4] So, the sinister association of bad dreams was there; only the instances of such dreams and their interpretations are not found. These appear concurrently with the formulation of theories of karman and rebirth and with fatalism. In other words, we hear of dreams and their significance in the epics for the first time; the practice continues through the Purāṇas, Dharmaśāstras, until today.

Coeval with the early sections of the epics are the Jātakas. The Vārāṇasīqueen Khemā dreamed of a golden peacock and managed to bring him (who was none but the Bodhisattva) to the palace, so that she could hear him preach.[5] This theme is repeated in the *Muhāmora* jātaka.[6] The same queen Khemā dreams of a golden goose and she arranges a complicated network to capture the goose,[7] who comes and preaches.[8]

A king dreams at dawn[9] of a tree of wisdom whose brandies are virtues; a black man in red dress, with red flowers tor earrings, comes and cuts the tree down, even from the roots, despite expostulations from the people. The king instinctively knew that his wise counseller Vidhurapaṇḍita's death was imminent. And true enough, the wise man was slain through the wiles of others.[10] A king had a strange dream: he saw a small spark of fire outshining four blazing pillars. Now a wise interpreter of dreams told the king that soon he will have a young man who would outshine his four wise councillors; Buddha was born of a queen and as he grew up he proved to be wiser than the king's councillors.[11] In the famous *Vessontam* Jātaka the innocent prince Vessantara had been banished and led a wretched existence with his wife Māddī, his son and daughter in the forest. One night Māddī dreamt that her

4 *AV* VI: 46: 1, 2; XVI: 5: 1–3.

5 No. 159, *Mora.*

6 No. 491.

7 Also the Bodlisattva in another life.

8 No. 534, *Mahāhaṣmsa.*

9 Dreams of the dawn come true—it is a common superstition.

10 No. 545, *Vidhurapaṇḍita.*

11 No. 546, *Mahaummagga.*

eyes, hands, feet, breasts were cut off and the bleeding heart was squeezed out and taken by a man of extremely inauspidous looks and dress. This came true symbolically because both her children were taken captive and were tortured as slaves; she herself was also taken as a slave woman. Later, her father-in-law saw flowers in a dream and immediately knew that he would see his grand-children. It so transpired that Vessantara's children did come to their grandfather.[12]

In the *Rāmāyaṇa* the men stress Trijaṭā's dream portended an evil fate for Rāvaṇas.[13] The *Brahmavaivarta,* a late Purāṇa tells how the wicked king Kaṃsa had an evil dream portending coming events. It follows an accepted stereotype: A woman in red apparel with a garland of red flowers, carrying a sword and a scimitar was laughing aloud in a horripilating manner. Kaṃsa describes her as of dark complexion "dancing in my city, her hair dishevelled and hanging loose, her nose cut off. Another was a dark śūdra widow in a dark habit, with rough hair and soiled clothes on, who put marks on my forehead and chest. Palm fruits, dark and ripe, fell from trees with a loud thud and got scattered hither and thither. A mleccha fellow with tousled, rough hair in ugly clothes was giving me broken coins towards the morning. He broke full pitchers. A divine lady, very angry with me, gave me a garland of fresh jabā flowers. Every now and then there was a shower of blood on my city. Monkeys, crows, dogs, bears, pigs, asses made loud noises. At dawn, there was a pile of bitten-off nails, a heap of logs, collyrium, skeletons of the frontal lobes of skulls. A woman in a yellow robe, smeared with white sandal paste appeared with a garland of mālālī flowers, with ornaments on her, with a dalliance lotus in her hand; she had a vermillion mark on her forehead. Having cursed me thoroughly she left my house in great anger. I saw men of frightening appearance carrying nooses in their hands, their hair waving loose. Men and women with their hair let down were dancing in every house. A big śūdra widow, noseless and naked, smeared oil on me in a frightening manner. Early in the morning I saw a funeral pyre and heard wedding songs and saw people dancing in every house. I saw red-haired men in red dresses vomiting blood. Even when the eclipse was on I saw the sun and moon. Meteors and comets fell, there were earthquakes, revolutions, storms and

---

[12] No. 547, *Vessantara.*

[13] V: 27; the whole chapter narrates the sinister dream and its import becomes quite clear.

many untoward events like trees along with their trunks rotating in the storm, and mountains falling down on the earth. I saw men with their heads off, dancing naked with pearl chains dangling on their bodies, dancing away in every house. I also heard people lamenting aloud everywhere."[14] Most features of the dream are connected with sodal beliefs and practices: a man under capital punishment was customarily made to put on a red garment and given a chain of red jabā flowers before being taken to his death. A śūdra woman was a bad enough omen, but when she is a widow she is doubly ominous. The divine woman leaving Kaṃsa's house in anger was the patron-goddess of his fortune and her departure signifies the impending doom and total annihilation of his power and prosperity. Men, especially women with rough and tousled hair were regarded as particularly inauspicious, Mlecchas were untouchable outcastes; their presence boded great disaster. Ripe palm fruits falling from trees and getting scattered hither and thither symbolized young soldiers' heads rolling. There is another account of Kaṃsa's fateful dream. He saw dogs, crocodiles, jackals, heaps of ashes, of bones, palm fruits, hair, raw cotton, extinguished fire-brands, corpses on funeral pyres, the potter's wheel, the oil-press, twisted shell-coins, cremation grounds, burnt out faggots, dry wood, kuśagrass, moving spirits, talking skulls, ashes of the creamalion ground, dry water-tanks, burnt fish, iron, gardens consumed by fire, lepers with oozing sores on their limbs, naked śūdras with hair let down, very irate brahmins, cursing preceptors, angry beggars, mendicants and Vaiṣṇavas.[15]

Before Śiva's wrath at Satīs death played havoc at Dakṣa's sacrifice, Dakṣa's queen Prasūti had a dream of what was coming; this she repeated to Satī.[16] Dreams which forebode coming evils are plentiful in the *Mahābhārata* and in many Purāṇas; all of them are dark and sinister. The *Iailitavistāra* and other Buddhist texts tell us of Māyādevī's dream of the white elephant entering her—this is an auspicious dream, anticipating the birth of Buddha. The Kāsī princess Śaśīkalā was assured in a dream of her union with Sudarśana.[17] Bāṇa, the king of demons had a daughter Uṣa who saw Kṛṣṇa's grandson Aniruddha in a dream and she him; they also knew that they would

---

[14] Kṛṣṇajanma Khaṇḍa 63: 3–30.

[15] *Brahmamivarta* Kṛṣṇajanma 72: 70–79.

[16] *Bṛhaddharma* P. Madhya, 7: 6–15.

[17] *Devībhāgvata* III: 17: 14.

be united.[18] Evil dreams in the abstract is the theme of a whole chapter;[19] it also explains the effects of such dreams in terms of loss, diseases, disasters and deaths.

Interpretation of dreams became a special vocation of a section of 'wise' men all over world. "The Mediterranean world knew Egypt as the home of thaumaturgy, theology and esoteric wisdom. Isis worship was attended by a functionary, specifically called aretalogos, an interpreter of dreams, who may have functioned as a proclaimer of miraculous events."[20] In *Iliad* I: 43ff we read "dreams come, too, from Zeus who may tell why Phoebus Apollo is so wroth" ... Dreams, therefore, are sent by the Gods who control human destiny and sometimes it may please them to let mortals know beforehand the manner in which the Gods' minds work.

In the Sibylline Books — a collection of prophecies in verse which the Sibyl of Cumae is said to have sold to Tarquin the Proud, there is a section which says: "First, the soul, because it is akin to the Gods, possesses in itself the power to foresee the future, second, the air is crowded with immortal souls which bear, as it were the marks of truth, third, *when men sleep the Gods themselves speak to them* ... to human minds the clearest vision of the future is vouchsafed when death hovers near. [21] Here we have a clue to man's faith in dreams: in dreams the Gods spoke to men, so dreams are a sort of divine revelation of fate, because they are messages from the Gods. The vision or clairvoyance when death draws near is another form of waking communication with supernatural powers and as such, an awareness of fate. "The knowledge of the art of procuring dreams and the skill to interpret them were greatly prized in Egypt as elsewhere in the East.[22] Papyrus No. 122, 64ff and 359ff describe the methods "To obtain a vision. To procure Dreams...."[23]

Even in this late period of the twentieth century, about a century after Freud's *Interpretation of Dreams* followed by Karl Jung and many others'

---

18 *Op. Cit.*, 72: 114.

19 *Op. Cit.*, ch. 82.

20 *Maamillan Encyclopaedia of Religion*, Vol. 9, Micronesian Religions: 'Divination', p. 544.

21 1: 30, italics added.

22 cf Joseph interpreting the Pharaoh's dreams, Geneisi X1, X1i.

23 Budge, 1972, pp. 214, 216.

works on the subject, this ingrained superstition in the human mind is so strong that an evil dream is taken by most as a fair warning by fate which has a direct bearing on coming events. Karman is only indirectly related to dreams, by our evil deeds we earn an ill fate and this is communicated to us through various supernatural agencies, one of which is dreams. What is interesting is that everywhere, at any time, there are so-called specialists, wise - acres who claim to be able to interpret dreams. When Māyādcvī saw the white elephant coming to her in a dream, King Śuddhodana immediately sent for professional interpreters of dreams who came, fulfilled their obligations and were duly rewarded. In life we forget most dreams, espesially those which according to dream-lore ought to have borne some specific fruit and did not. We remember or think we do — because after an event the imagination very actively fits the dream to the event. The millennia-old beliefs in dreams carrying significance dies hard. And there is always a loophole found or invented if the dreamfails to tally with its supposed effect. Sometimes the interpreters are blamed for misinterpreting the dream, sometimes the dreamer is blamed for misreporting the dream. And we all know how on waking up most dreams fail 'like the champak odour'. It is precisely because fate is a totally dark area of man's life that any inkling of its contents conveyed by howsoever fragile a medium in whatever context—since these can be twisted to suit our needs of wishful thinking—any such inkling is so welcome. That is why dreams are still regarded as significant even though we have umpteen instances of the lack of corroboration between the dream and its meaning.

Of other such supernatural messages another universal belief is that of prophecy, oracle or divination. What is communicated through these is part of destiny or fate. Destiny presupposes a being who destines, governs man's fate, orders his life and decrees the events, experiences and happenings. Where oracle is usually concerned with collective fate, divination is about an individual's fate. Divination literally means assuming divine foreknowledge, i.e., at least in one respect, acting as God.

"Divination through which the cause of divine displeasure was ascertained was of three kinds; augury (divination by flight of birds) haruspicy (divination by examining entrails of sacred animals) and dice-throwing".... In this way by a lengthy process of elimination, it was possible to determine the precise offence that required expiation. Divination was a science inherited by the Hittites from the Babylonian seers. Signs of people's fate were thought to be sent by the Gods, manifested in unusual occurences. Haruspicy was one of the most popular practices of divination."[24] An ordeal was used in primitive societies (or in societies of limited legal or scientific experience) to establish the innocence or guilt of an accused person. The aim of divination is knowing, knowing the offence so that it can be remedied. It is this area of ignorance which makes disasters, dangers, diseases, etc. appear as divine visitations, a surprise is sprung on him and he is quite perplexed as to its cause. Hence, "Divination aims to circumvent man's inability to see beyond the present by a circuitous appeal to supernatural sources of otherwise hidden information." Divination, as we have seen is for an individual, who wishes to know what is in store for him so that he can take adequate measures for preventing disasters. Since, he feels, that things are ordained elsewhere beyond his knowledge and guess, his anxiety prompts him to somehow remove the veil that hides his future from him. "Divination is the art or practice of discovering the personal, human significance of future or, more commonly, present or past events.... Dreams (oneiromancy) involuntary body actions.... inediumistic possessions, consulting the dead (necromancy) observing animal behaviour.... All kinds of possession and divination assume a mysterious, arbitrary world governed by personal powers who are involved with vulnerable humanity.... It is perhaps inevitable that at the centre of social power, attempts are made in such cultures to master all that can be known of the arbitrary will of the Gods... I earned priests who interpreted the will of the Gods in elaborate augury ceremonials, while among the lower classes mediumism and a much more random and confused use of omens indicated the insecurity of ego control."[25]

In ancient Greece, possibly in all other ancient cultures, people took recourses to various methods in order to know what fate kept obscure from them. We perhaps have a fuller account of these efforts in Greece than in many other countries. Prophecy, oracle, divination, haruspicy, necromancy, augury, omens, portents—all had the aim of ripping the veil of ignorance. Besides Tiresias the blind prophet, in the *Iliad,* Patrodus's ghost prophesies, in the *Odyssey* seers' descendants are endowed with the power to prophesy. We hear of prophesy 'from the laurel' of the Dodona oak.

---

[24] *Encyclopaedia Britatnica Macropattlia*, Vol. 21, P. 191.

[25] Macmillan *Encyclopaedia of Religion,* 1987, 'Divination', pp. 375, 377, 378.

In the Sibylline Books a whole section[26] seeks to present a logical case for divination being real, that what is revealed by the diviner really happens because he is divinely inspired. In the Islamic tradition current among the common people there was a recognized method of divination by an arrow.

The Ājīvikas developed a complex system of divination and oracular prophecies through interpreting dreams, portents and omens. This kind of prescience fortified their basic tenet that everything is preordained and human effort cannot alter anything. This was the only consistent fatalism in India and in the world. Like the Lokāyatas or Cārvākins they also repudiated causation, but unlike them, they were resigned to fate and divination only strengthened their complete surrender to fate. Records of divination come from ancient China, Egypt, Sumer, Assyria, Babylonia and Greece. Ancient India also must have had its own method of divination current among the common people, but since we only have records of the later Great Tradition, what obtained among the people has not found mention in this literature. The Upaniṣads record instances of spirit possession.[27] Bhujyu, the son of Lāhya, told that wandering about in Madra he went to Kāpya Patañcala's house whose daughter was possessed by a Gandharva. Him Bhujyu had addressed: who he was and he had replied that he was Sudhanvan of the Angiras clan. Then followed a religious dialogue regarding ritual and metaphysical matters.This is not divination proper but this is the closest we come to divination in the early records. It can be legitimately surmised that people in doubt and perplexity took recourse to 'Supernatural' means of ascertaining their fate, past, present and future. The proper procedure of divination, however, bearing similarity to Egyptian, Middle Eastern, Greek or Chinese is not met with in Indian texts. But the common man whose voice is not recorded had his methods, frequently in other forms, like dreams, prophecy, divine messages, sages' interpretation of events, etc. "In ancient Egypt we hear about magical stones, amulets, figures, pictures, formulaic spells, secret names and mystery rites with the aim of harming enemies, gaining power over them or killing them as also of gaining one's own interests. Demonical possessions, dreams and ghosts, lucky and unlucky days, horoscopes, prognostications were quite widespread beliefs."[28]

---

[26] II. 38.

[27] Cf *Bṛhudāmyyaka* Up. III: 3: 1. 2.

[28] Budge, 1972, pp. 206–34.

Prophecy is one form of the knowledge of fate which was universally recognized. Who are the prophets? Usually when a country, a people or a tribe passed through trouble or crises, from among them arose a person claiming divine, or superior knowledge, prevision, or clairvoyance by virtue of which he could penetrate the veil which obscured others' vision. Thus he could detect causes of good or ill fortune, predict them and reprimand the people and their misdeeds responsible for the trouble that befell the group. The prophet thus diagnosed the collective ill, indirectly pointing a way of escape from calamities and miseries. He was the spiritual therapeutist for his people. In China have been found "Inscriptions on oracle bones and in bronze sacrificial vessels... Divination and sacrificial ritual (i.e. reading cracks in turtle plastrons or animal bones)."[29]

According to Arlistotle, Epimenedes (sixth centrury B.C.) was a 'sophos' i.e. a poet or prophet with supernatural power. The *Principium Sapientuie* mentions a shamanistic wise man from whom came mentis, poets and sophists-philosophers. Together these constitute the function of Apollo at the Delphi oracle, "...the shaman rendtirs the supernatural immediately available to the cult, acquiring It of Him or I Ier through spell, ritual and charismatic experience. Whether simple or complex, the religions of mankind regard direct revelation as primary, and intuition and theology as secondary. The shaman is concerned with the primary vision; trance, ecstasy; the shaman is 'possessed' of the divinity. He mediates the core of primitive religion."[30] Although Indian religion had no shaman as such, it had priests, prophets, medicine men and wizards of various brands, who together performed the offices of the diviner, prophet, shaman and oracle. These are charismatic personalities, held to be in direct communication with the supernatural powers which controlled the affairs of the world.

(In ancient China) "These men were the Spokesman of God. Their message did not come by the suspension of their personality as the Hebrew prophets' message is thought by some to have come, and they did not disdain the use of the mind which God had given them. But they acknowledged that they were raised up to do their work and that they were the Spokesmen of the Unseen."[31] Many times such prophets became a plaything in the hands

---

[29] *Maemillan Eneyclopaedia of Religion*, p. 258.

[30] Menshing (ed.), 1976, p. 87.

[31] Rowley, 1956, p. 26.

of those who wielded political power or they consciously assumed political power. Knowledge is power whether proved or unproved. This kind of arcane sagacity carried an aura of transcendental mystery and generated awe. The self-styled prophets enjoyed social prestige and frequently political power also. In a very real sense they acted as God's deputies on earth with a direct supernatural link with God — who was supposed to speak through these prophets. It is also true that at the prospect of impending calamity some men took upon themselves the task of moral chastisement of the people to turn them from their evil ways — most of the Old Testament prophets were initially inspired by philanthropy and later "established communication with God"... revolution in the neighbouring kingdom of Damascus was fostered by a prophet All of this abundantly illustrates the political and usually revolutionary interest of many of the earlier prophets.[32]

In China the ancient historical classic Shu Ching[33] declared the political mission of leaders in times of decadence. Then the true patriot, the prophet should not try to maintain the status quo, but should make efforts, any effort, to change history in favour of the people. "The classics repeatedly declare that to take up arms against a tyrannical rule is not a rebellion but a deed carrying out the will of God. All deplored the decay of society in their day and the naked selfishness that reigned. All deplored oppressive and unprincipled government and desired to see the principle of justice and benevolence put into practice."[34] Prophets regarded themselves as mouthpieces of God and in their manner of address they assumed the mode of God addressing men. In this capacity they impersonated Providence and what they said became imbued with the aura of divine message and authority. This brought the divine dispensation, the hidden role of fate a little closer to men. Prophecy thus became linked with the supernatural manifestations of fate.

The connection of prophecy with divine inspiration is clear in Gnosticism. "Something like fear of this creature (man) fell upon the angels, for he made utterances greater than were suitable for his creation, because of the one who had invisibly put in him the seed of the substance from above — the one who expresses himself freely".[35]

[32] Kowley, 1956, p. 28.

[33] IV: BK3: 11: 3ff.

[34] Hsil, 1932, p. 72.

[35] Grant, 1961, p. 143

We hear of Marduk gaining the power of prophecy "Gods... gave him (Marduk) the power *for his word to cotne true...* In gratitude Marduk lightened their labour by creating man."[36] The role of the priest was sometimes partially distributed; the prophet quite frequently worked as a liason officer between the Gods and men *"For conveying human wishes and needs to the Gods and asking for help,* a ritual of seeking audience to present petition. This in Gudea was used as a check on the message obtained when he was dreaming ... An extensive and highly detailed literature serving as a textbook for these and many other manners of prognostication developed during the second and first millennia. Originally meant as guides for rulers and war leaders, this literature soon broadened its scope to take in the fortunes or ordinary citizen."[37] Prophets thus fulfilled one part of the priest's function, he supplied assurance, knowledge and foreknowledge for the common man groping for some light. And thus the prophet became an epiphany of fate and Providence.

The *Popol Vuh* frequently mentions soothsayers with magic powers to create and destroy.[38] The Oracle as an institution stands very close to prophecy. Oracles are "often regarded as verbal responses by a supernatural being, in contrast to prophecy which is thought of as unsolicited verbal revelations given through human mediums and often directed toward instigating socialchange."[39] There is one essential difference between prophecy and oracle. While the prophet is the self-appointed messenger of God speaking on His behalf to people in need of the message, the oracle is approached by men needing divine guidance in vitally important socio-political issues. The oracle temporarily becomes God's mouthpiece at the solicitation of the community. At the famous oracle in Delphi the Goddess Gaia was the earlier divinity associated with the oracle; later Apollo usurped her position. The snake Python which Apollo slew was actually a surrogate for the Pythoness, the oracle, when it was connected with Gaia. This is very significant: Gaia, the earth, was symbolized by the Python, a chthonic creature. The oracle prophetess (who in later literature became the Pythoness) of Dodona around the eighth century B.C. had selloi, interpreters, who were of "unwashen feet,

---

36 *Macmillan Encyclopaedia of Religion,* 1981, 'Babylonian Religion.' 463; italics added.

37 *Op. Cit.,* p. 465; italics added.

38 *Florentine Codex,* Bks. IV & V; these deal with soothsayers and omens and the prophets who mediated between the Gods and man.

39 *Macmillan Encyclopaedia of Religion,* Vol. XI, 'Oracles'.

sleeping *on the ground.*"[40] Now even today in the numerous village chapels recognized as temples where oracles are still current, the practice of the oracle-seekers is to *lie on the ground,* fasting patiently and indefinitely until the 'living God's' deputy, the temple priest or priestess declares the oracle message to the seekers. Unlike in Greece where whether at Dodona or at Delphi the beneficiary was the country — it was the national fate which was at stake and the devotees approached the oracle, reverentially waited until the message came, often as a *double entendre* which again was interpreted by wise, holy men, in India the temples famous for oracles are visited mainly by men and women who want children, wealth, jobs, recovery from some deadly disease or even victory in property suits. In a word, the benefits go to the individual seekers or couples; the issues at stake are smaller, much less comprehensive in scope than in ancient Greece. In Greece although originally the oracles were only on the seventh day of one particular month, (later one day each month) yet lots were cast on other days, too. The lots were black and white beans signifying 'yes' and 'no'. Pythia, the priestess picked up one and she symbolized the God's assent or dissent. Besides Gaia and Apollo, Athena, too, was regarded as a goddess associated with oracles, "Athena's ornithic relationships also confirm her originally oracular quality, for all three birds[41] were rumoured to be prophetic."[42]

In China "the oracle texts.... express uncertainty, appeal, perplexity, risk .... oracular methods to gain knowledge of fate."[43] Mencius, however, was against such practices; he said, "to contrive what men cannot contrive, that rests with Heaven." Oracular methods in some form or other is widespread; even the modern practice of casually opening a book and reading the text as if it held certain hidden message is part of this knock at the closed gates of the future. "Fate according to the Lepchas, is, the multitude of future events which supernatural beings have in store for human beings and that the character of these events is constantly being created or recreated according to the favourable or unfavourable response of the supernatural beings. Consequently, man is not absolutely without any influence on his own fate, for its character depends on, two factors, and although man constitutes

---

40 cf. *Iliad,* XVI; 234; italics added.

41 owl, crow and gull.

42 Jesi, *History of Religions,* Vol. 2, no. 2, p. 154.

43 Ringgern, 1967, p. 127.

always the inferior factor, he is not left in a state without any hope at all."[44] This is clcarly an attempt at reconciling two obviously opposed principles, fate and freedom of will. As we have seen earlier, this has remained a major preoccupation of theologians throughout the ages.

The Orphic hymn to Themis says of the Goddess "who taught the oracles to lord Apollo."[45] Here, too, we know that before Apollo took over the oracle, a goddess was in charge, a goddess of fate. In the hymn to Hermes regarding the Thriae, Apollo says, "Three virgins.... these are the teachers of divination apart from me, the art which 1 practised while yet a boy following herds.... And when they are inspired through eating yellow honey, they are *willing to speak truth;* but if they be deprived of the Gods' sweet food, then they, *speak falsely*.... Zeus.... commanded that glorious Hermes should be lord over all birds of omen, and grim-eyed lions, and bears with gleaming tusks and over dogs and all flocks that the wide earth nourishes, over all sheep, also that he only should be *the appointed messenger to Hades,* who though he takes no gifts shall give him no mean prize".[46] So Apollo and the three fates[47] were the Gods in charge of human destiny. The Gods, properly entertained, "speak truth" through oracles, but if man fails to feed and honour them then they speak falsely. Here a loophole is left for false oracles and divinations. Hermes, the psychopompos was the divinely appointed messenger to the lord of the communication between man and the agents of fate. In other religions, the beliefs are based on the Gods not keeping man completely in the dark regarding their fate; they were willing to concede and reveal destiny through proper channels and after proper approach. At least occasionally and also partially. Often the message was so unclear that it remained a mystery.

"Living saints were credited... with special powers, of healing, of clairvoyance, of protection. Some were consulted almost like oracles."[48] So human agencies were also raised to the pedestal of oracles if they were believed to be divinely inspired. In Islam Lhe oracles were vocal arbiters, they used rhymed prose in a lofty style; the oracular diction however was cryptic.

---

44 Ringgern, 1967, p. 157.

45 No. 79, 6.

46 Homeric Hymn NO. IV 550–65ff; italics added.

47 Clotho, Lachesis and Atropos.

48 Wilson, 1983, p. 9.

They also believed in geomancy i.e. drawing on sand.[49] Latin has different words to express different procedures of unveiling fate: *ostenta* (to make clear), *portenta* (foreshadow) *monstra* (point out) and *prodigia* (predict).

The Jātaka tales have many instances of these; we furnish a few examples. A brahmin prognosticated from a piece of cloth, Buddha denounced him: no man should believe in luck, no man should practise prophecy for those curious to know the future.[50] When Buddha as Dhamma was wrangling wilh Devadata, Adhamma, they decided to fight. But even as Dhamma was speaking, there was an earthquake to prove Buddha's superior right. This closed the issue.[51] Where vindication of Buddha's supremacy was concerned, earthquakes and other omens are frequently introduced to clinch the issue. We also hear about fortune-tellers who prophesy about the future of two princes of Kalinga; they also foretell a woman's future.[52] In the *Sādhīna* jātaka[53] we find fortune-telling as a distinct profession. Mahārakṣita, through divine vision granted to him, knew that that very night Buddha would be conceived by his queen.[54]

In the *Mahābhārata* Sañjaya received divine vision which enabled him to see the entire battlefield at one glance and so he could describe events happening simultaneously at different parts of the battlefield to the blind king Dhrtarāṣtra. Nārada, Sāvitrī's counsellor-friend foretold Satyavat's span of life.[55] When Arjuna was reluctant to fight against kinsmen and Kṛṣṇa failed to convince him with words, he, Kṛṣṇa was transfigured before Arjuna and spoke like an oracle, Arjuna obeyed Kṛṣṇa's command and fought. Gāndhārī, shocked beyond endurance at the terrible massacre at the end of the war, prophesied a horrible manner of death for Kṛṣṇa and the total annihilation of all his tribesmen;[56] it came true, proving that at that point she was divinely inspired as a prophetess, like Cassandra. When some clansmen of the Yadus sought to playfully deceive sages the latter foretold a terrible doom which was fulfilled; so the sages acted as prophets. In the *Rāmāyaṇa,*

---

49 Cf Serjeant, 1981, pp. 74–75.

50 No. 87, *Maṅgala.*

51 No. 457, Dhamma.

52 No. 479, *Kālingabodhi.*

53 No. 493.

54 No. 505, *Samranassa.*

55 Mbh III: 29.

56 XI: 23: 40–41.

too, Daśratha's curse to Kaikeyī came true.[57] Jaṭāyus's forecast about Rāvaṇa's death and defeat were also proved true.[58] Instances may be multiplied indefinitely of holy men and women acting as divinely inspired prophets and prophetesses who, at critical junctures act as agents of fate. In the epics it is such men and women rather than the Gods themselves who forecast future events. Most of the divinations, oracular utterances and prophecies occur in the late interpolated sections, at a time when fatalism was gaining ground steadily though surreptitiously. In Kālidasā's *Raghuvṃśa,*[59] King Dilīpa's family priest Vaśisṣṭha diagnosed the cause of the king's sonlessness through clairvoyance and prescribed a remedy which worked, thus proving the divine inspiration which had prompted the sage to prophesy and act oracularly. "The oracle gives access by the implicit sign language... a freedom from the formal conditions of knowledge. The oracle gives access to a form of reality which is free from the restrictive frame of time."[60]

It is not true to say that in prophecy, divination and oracle the inspiration is always divine. Let us remember that in the spiritual world there is a battle on, a relentless tug-of-war between the powers of good and evil. In the epic-Puranic mythology this is symbolized by the churning of the ocean where both the Gods and demons pulled in opposite directions and out of the ocean arose many auspicious items along with poison. Similarly, these prophetic, diagnostic and remedial directions are sometimes inspired by evil forces. When Duryodhana in mortal depression after suffering great humiliation decides to fast to death, it was not Gods but the demons who came and succoured him until he agreed to fight again. Thus in these supernatural messages there is a distinct link with the chthonic world. "It was early in mankind's history that prophecy and divination were associated with underworldpowers and the dead... The mantic properties of water are one long phase of the polemy with which men have endowed it... It was used in all sorts of ways for magical divinations and real purposes."[61] It is not accidental that those who crave for an oracle lie on the ground, cover themselves in dust and in India they almost walk on their knees long

---

[57] II: 12: 21.

[58] III: 51: 125.

[59] Cnto II.

[60] Douglas, 1975, p. 130.

[61] Fontenrose, 1980, p. 548.

distances to reach their destination. Once there, they lie on the ground and do not leave the spot until their desires are fulfilled. The closeness to earth, to dust remind us of the first Goddess of the oracle viz. Gaia, Mother Earth. Even when Apollo had! taken over the Delphic oracle, the chthonic creature, the python, symbolizes the priestess who was later called the Pythoness. Thus a lurking belief that arcane knowledge came from the bottom of the earth is there. And this power after Gaia was no longer chthonic, was vested in Apollo, although the Pythoness even then carried distinctly chthonic associations. But in Athena the chthonic associations of her birds—the crow, the owl and the gull—connected with prophecy and divination bring back the chthonic traits. In India too, though not in the scriptures so much, yet very much, in folk practice it is to the predominantly chthonic God Siva in his various epiphanies that simple villagers come to unburden themselves, to pray for the apparently unattainable. The fundamental belief in Mother Earth's power and the chthonic God's power to assist them in their crises keep them on the ground, smeared with dust not only to signify abjectness but also close contiguity with the earth and the subterranean forces which guide human destiny.

"Foreknowledge of coming events is claimed, not only by the priests who scan *omens in the sky*, clouds, birds and interpret events as eclipses ....but as a natural gift of clairvoyance peculiar to some priestly families .... In cases of illness, cures and herbs fall under the influence of certain *planets and certain signs of the zodiac* and a man should take only the medicament or cure which belongs to the sign under which he fell ill."[62] The author here talks of the Mandaeans of Iraq and Iran, but what he says holds good of all ancient cultures. Here we are between two kinds of effort of unveiling the unknown—astrology and omenology, of these astrology grew into a separate and self-contained 'science' and omenology into another.

The Canaanile Mari texts are of the nature of oracular utterances. They apparently carried divine massages through ordinary people. Such is the basic pattern of the oracle. Even the priestess at Dodona or Delphi, however holy, was a mere mortal through whom Gaia, Apollo or Athena transmitted their voice to the seekers. Today the Indian village priests at temples famous for oracular messages are also ordinary mortals. Sometimes they are supposed to be possessed by the temple God or Goddess who delivers the required message

[62] Drowor, 1962, pp. 82–83.

to the supplicant. This shamanistic belief or practice is widely current not only in India but all over the world for ages. It endows the mortal medium with the necessary charisma.

It was believed that God chose his own media for speaking to man. He also sends signs to warn, encourage or assure his people. All scriptures are full of such instances. In Egypt, " ....the protent, when it occurred, was at once interpreted as a gesture of good will by the 'God of the highlands' to Pharaoh."[63]

The discipline which began with the observation of stars in ancient Babylonia, India and many other ancient civilizations everywhere ended with the deduction of human fate from the position and movements of the asterisms. So what started as a pure science, viz. astronomy, developed into an applied 'science' viz. astrology. "The macrocosmic-microcosmic correspondence that seems to occur with the structure of human religious symbolization everywhere ....The first full-blown astrological systems appeared in Babylon in the Greek language of Hellenistic period." "Now it became possible to calculate the relation of a person to the course of the heavenly bodies on the basis of the time of that person's birth and the sign under which the birth had taken place. Hence, in principle, it became possible also to alter destiny."[64] In so far as the events of a man's life can be calculated from the constellar position at his birth, the interpreters undertook to influence the stars to prevent any untoward situation indicated by the stars. Through both these, the astrologers acted as accomplices of fate and to some extent, the controller, diverts or deflectors also.

Late Babylonian texts present many beliefs allied to astrology. There was hemerology according to which only certain days are propitious for offering to particular Gods, also for ritual acts directed towards certain stars. Trees, plants, stars, and stones correlated with zodiacal signs—they contain some magic and healing properties. Catarchic astrology provided rules selecting the precise moment that is the most auspicious time for a significant undertaking.

"Chance is simply a name for undiscovered causes. All future events are theoretically predictable, and astrology and divination were appealed to as

---

[63] Grant, 1959, p. 57.

[64] *Macmillan Encyclopaedia of Religion* 'Fate', p. 291.

evidence for the validity of the causal nexus. Possibility exists to the extent, but only to the extent that men are ignorant of the causal connection between events."[65] "In other words, to an omniscient being, like a God, all the causal relations and the consequences of actions are immediately clear; since man lacks omniscience, he appeals to astrology to throw light on a particular dark area of his life, the knowledge of which is expedient for him. An astral determinism, independent of God's will, he (St. Augustine) rejects as paramount to atheism. A determinism coming from autonomous stars acting under God's control, he likewise condemns as bringing dishonour to the heavens."[66] St. Augustine clearly sees that reading God's decree from his creation viz. the stars, whether they are independent of God's will or dependent on him, is not compatible with the Christian dogma. As a matter of fact such a position regarding astrology is not compatible with any theistic religion. But scriptural prescriptions have never prevented the common people from clinging to their age-old beliefs. Strictly speaking, fatalism cannot be entertained by believers in God, karman and many associated beliefs. Celestial omens began to be used as portents on a considerable scale in the first Babylonian dynasty (the eighteenth to the fifteenth centuries B.C.) although lunar eclipses may have been regarded as ominous previously. The prediction of this so-called 'judicial' astrology referred to the royal court and the state and not to ordinary individuals. In Greece astrology the stars were looked upon as the tools of Heimarmene. The stars, eternal, ever bright and high above the human world were regarded as being in close contact with divinities who control human destiny. "Horoscopic asttology according to which the position of the planets at the time of birth determines the fate of the individual, did not develop until much later when Babylon was part of the Persian empire... The oldest known horoscope goes back to 410 B.C. ... Both the older 'judicial' astrology and the later horoscopic astrology were based on a fundamentally deterministic or fatalistic view of time."[67] "People who believe that history and the destinies of men are controlled by the stars are not likely to entertain the idea of historical progress. Instead they are more likely to adopt a cyclical view of time."[68] The late Babylonian priest

---

[65] Long, 1986, p. 164.

[66] Wilson, 1983, p. 78.

[67] Whitrow, 1988, p. 31.

[68] *Op. Cit.*, p. 53.

Berussus (c 300 B.C.) believed in the periodic destruction and recreation of the universe. Indirectly, the author shows that the concept of historical progress does not go with fatalism which favours a cyclical view of time—so that there are periodic annihilation and recreation of the cosmos. This is quite true of India where from the epic-Puranic times the notion of a Kalpa i.e. creation, continuity and destruction, is followed by another kalpa which repeats the same pattern. Time moves cyclically, beginning at the same point of each creation. Theoretically, such a view precludes progress because from one Kalpa to the other the only thing that is carried over is the Vedas, the eternal texts. This theory was elaborated in later texts and possibly partially explains the absence of historical literature which presupposes a faith in progress through time. However that may be, it is clearly an extremely favourable view which accommodates fatalism.

Macmillan's Encyclopaedia of Region gives us several names of omens, portents and divination: Greek *mantike techne, semion,* Latin *divinatio, signum.* These indirectly cover auspicious birds, augurs from Latin *Libri auguralis, haruspicy* study of entrails, *prodigy* means a sudden disturbance of *paxdeum* (divine peace). Then there are *ornithomancy* (bird-augury) *hepatoscopy* (study of animals' liver) *oneiromancy* (dream divination) *sortilege* (casting lots) *physiognomy* (study of body signs) and *palmistry* (study of lines on the palm).[69] Most of these were practised in most ancient civilizations. In India we have oneiromancy, astrology,[70] physiognomy, bird-augury[71] (Śākunaśāstra), divination and sortilege. However, the earliest reference to omenology (Nimittanidāna) is not found in India but comes from the cylinder of Gudea which contains terrestrial omens and the ritual procedure for the exorcism for the sick.

"Since astrology is only an approximate reflection of unknowable head-writing, there is always a chance that a prediction is inaccurate. Or he may begin to prepare himself for the disaster adopting an attitude of resignation to a fate beyond his understanding or control... The individual who has suffered the disaster generally seeks refuge in the deterministic perspective which offers him solace by depicting him as the helpless victim of an

69 "Portents and Prodigies", Vol. II, pp. 454–457.

70 Sāmudrika Jyotiṣa.

71 Sāmudrika Sāstra.

unalterable fate."[72] When the blow has already fallen and remedy impossible, the only consolation the sufferer can be given is that (i) nothing he did brought on the fate and (ii) nothing he could have done would have thwarted the blow. This function of the modern psychopath was fulfilled by the astrologer and/or diviner. The chance of a prediction going wrong was always there, because it was not a perfect science.[73] Because it was a two-way traffic[74] which like "mercy is twice blesst. It blesseth him that gives and him that takes,"[75] it has flourished for all these millennia.[76] "On the whole (it) enable(s) one to make predictions which although they may have practical use, do not suggest any action other than evasion. They predict the motions of the heavenly bodies or the weather but there is nothing that we can do to change them."[77] Then comes in the village shaman who directs the enquirer about what steps he may take to evade untoward events. There is thus a neat division of labour among the astrologers, sooth-sayers, dream-interpreters, sign-interpreters and 'holy men' who prescribe for the emerging eventualities. "In most ancient societies there were those spiritual helmsmen who studied the supernatural phenomena 'read' them and collected their lore in tablets or parchments. The Canaanites possessed three omen texts that describe the predictive value of unusual human and animal births."[78]

The notions of fate and its various manifestations, once invented, remain with the society. They do not disappear but change their contour or assume new accretions. In the Mediterranean world in late antiquity old views of fate do not disappear; but new views come to prevail.

The Akkadian goddess "Inanna hangs the *mes* (destinies) on her head like jewels." In Babylon "the highly developed art of divination was a central item in a world of magic. In Mesopotamia Fate was Ananke which denoted necessity. This is a very important and significant aspect of fate: whatever

---

[72] Kayes and Daniel, 1983, pp. 44, 45.

[73] In the real sense it is no science at all, but a pseudo-science the practiser of which (a) gained money in return of his prediction or interpretation and (b) offered badly needed consolation and mental peace to the enquirer, the function a psychopath performs loday.

[74] Leaving an escape route for wrong divination.

[75] *Merchant of Venice,* Act IV. II 181–182.

[76] Astronomy and metereology.

[77] Popper, 1980, p. 43.

[78] *Macmillan Encyclopaedia of Religion,* Vol. II, p. 43.

happens to man which does not have a primary and obvious causal explanation was fate. And this fate was 'necessity' to the spiritual powers that be. Israel, along with its other occult practices practised necromancy. King Saul, in an hour of crisis goes stealthily to the Witch of Endor who conjures up the ghost of the dead Samuel,[79] Samuel imparts the necessary instructions."[80]

In Babylon celestial omens in the first millennium B.C. were arranged according to topics and subdivided into tablets and sections according to some phenomenon affecting several of these. The diviner resorted to handbooks for the affairs of the state. The objective was to draw from heavenly bodies warnings for impending dangers. In Mesopotamia there are seventy tablets of the omen series. They derived from heavenly bodies, weather phenomena and also evolved from observation of the two eclipses. 'Shooting stars' and their direction had significance and a 'yes'-or-'no' answer to queries. Stars and planets were believed to influence men's fortune and his undertakings and are, therefore invoked to thwart crisis-situations and grant success and plenty. There was no direct revelation of the future but through observation of conjunctions of constellations and other abnormal terrestrial phenomena men's fate was predicted. Extispicy was a practice where the diviner asks for reliable signs in the exta of the sheep. Certain apodoses of the celestial omen collections predict that the query of the haruspex will be answered, others that it will not. The genuineness of the portent was tested by extispicy. Astral connections with the parts of the liver also make part of the diviners' corpus. Hepato-mathematics developed the micro-zodiac. Besides these, there was hemerology, the 'science' of certain days which were propitious for sacred acts, offerings and ritual directed to certain Gods and stars. There was also another pseudo-science of minerals with a faint possibility of pharmaceutical base for some instances. Human mediums were used for getting messages from the spirits of the dead. Before undertaking a voyage, the navigator or ship-owner sought messages from catarchic astrology so that they could choose the auspicious hour. Amulets which contained auspicious articles for countering the ills of life were made and worn all over the world and in all ages. People prayed while they exposed the medicine under the stars, so that

[79] Sam. 128: 8–25.

[80] An echo is found in *Macbeth* Act IV. Scene 1, where the witches showing Macbeth the eight future kings is clearly an indirect instance of necromancy. This is mentioned just as an illustration of the power of such beliefs and practices, their hold on the peoples' mind over millennia.

beneficent influence of the stars could be stored along with the medicinal properties. Illness was believed to come in drops from the stars and even from the bowels of the earth.[81] It becomes dear that man devised different complicated and time-consuming methods for approaching the supernatural with the express intent of knowing his fate in advance and of pre-empting the inauspicious. All of these methods are indirectly linked with fatalism, since the foreknowledge was of fate' and the pre-emption also. It is difficult to agree with Ringgern when he says, The practice of divination does not necessarily involve fatalism.[82] If not directly, divination surely is an attempt at knowing what fate holds in store; behind it is the belief that somehow the diviner has an access to fate's workings which are hidden from the mortal eye. If we assume that in divination contact is made with the underworld where ghosts, evil spirits bear the message, even in that case such spirits are the agents of fate.

The Torah... forbids all appeals to local nature-spirits or to the dead. While the efficacy of such appeals is not necessarily denied, such acts were thought to suggest that God*is not the one source of all events and of all truly reliable knowledge...* This prophetic inspiration was directly from God ... certain kinds of omens and even dream divination... were certainly acceptable[83]. If omens and dream divination were acceptable, then extra-divine sources of knowledge are tacitly acknowledged. This is a concession to popular beliefs and practices current among the people for over many centuries. Such compromises are abundantly noticeable in societies where monotheism precludes fatalism at the apex but people at the base cling to it.

"Chance is simply a name for undiscovered causes: all future events are theoretically predictable and astrology and divination were appealed to as evidence for the validity of the causal nexus. Possibility exists to the extent, but only to the extent that men are ignorant of the causal connection between events."[84] What man does not know and yet what happens is given the apellate 'chance' which, in other words, designates the area for which causality is as not yet applicable. Chance is thus another name for fate. What is interesting is man's underlying belief in causality, rational explanation of

---

81 Summarized from *Macmillan Encyclopaedia of Religion* on Fate, pp. 291–298.

82 Ringgern, 1955, p. 52.

83 *Macmillan Encyclopaedia of Religion*, 'Fate', P. 292–293.

84 Long, 1986 (1974), p. 164.

phenomena. The area where causality explains things is daily expanding through man's increasing discoveries regarding nature and human life. Hence as Long says, today's ignorance about things whose causes are not known ascribes them to chance, when tomorrow will discover the causal link which is beyond today's horizon of knowledge.

In ancient Greece, mortals are doomed by fate. At the same time Zeus can do as he pleases. Zeus remains supreme; yet in perfect harmony with his supremacy fate is accepted. In Old Norse mythology Ur&r (Urd) is a personification of fate, a female figure seated at a source under the world free, determining destiny.[85] The association of Urdr with the world tree has a bearing on the chthonic aspect of her personality. We remember the Delphi cave where dwelt the chthonic python. This is the nether world connection of fate.

In late antiquity, gnosticism's doctrine of salvation shows patterns with very striking resemblance to a *Fate beyond God.* This is an extreme position seldom taken in any other mythology. It makes Fate independent of God, a self-sufficient power judging and allotting by itself, not inhibited by divine justice or divine interference. "In late Zoroastrian orthodoxy many identified fate with time; a system approaching determinism developed. This in later period is commonly referred to as Zurvanism. Manichaeism was strongly affected by Zoroastrian thought in its ideas about time, fate, good and evil."[86] The identification of Time and Fate is very significant. What man cannot decipher although he is dying to, is what lies in store for him in future. And the future is that aspect of time which most closely symbolizes fate.

Among the Aztecs "witchcraft, omens, portents dominated everyday life." "Pessimistic outlook co-exists with the wonderful dynamism of Aztec, civilisation."[87] There was a clear concept of fate dominating human affairs and omens, portents, etc. were but its objective expression in man's life. "Merchants made offerings before setting out, finding out auspicious days."[88]

In India although the theory of rebirth possibly goes back to the seventh century B.C. and the theory of karman followed soon after or was coeval with it, the concept of fate emerges somewhat later, around the third–second centuries B.C., the time when the final interpolated sections of the epics began to be

---

[85] *Macmillan Encyclopaedia of Religion,* 'Fate', P. 292–293.

[86] *Op. Cit.,* 'Fate', pp. 296–7.

[87] *Encyclopaedia Britannica Macropaedia,* Vol. 2, p. 551.

[88] *Florentine Codex* Bk X: 9.

added to the bulk. The accessories of fate, divination, prophecy, omens and portents, dreams and oracles all make themselves felt in a very clear fashion around the same time although their full fruition takes a few more centuries.

In the Jātakas we can trace these with some degree of clarity. For a wedding, the family astrologer was asked for an auspicious day. He told a lie from a selfish motive; he was piqued because the townsmen wanted a village bride. The marriage took place despite the astrologer's predictions.[89] In the unique *Śatapatta* jātaka Bodhisattva was born as a leader of robbers. This is explained as: "Now, the Bodhisattvas, even though they are great beings, sometimes take goods of others by being born as wicked men; this they say *comes from a fault in the horoscope?*"[90] This is a ridiculous explanation because the horoscope is a calculation of future events as decreed by fate or the stars, but here the actual life takes the course of what is predicted in the horoscope! In another tale Buddha, at the Kalinga king's request asked Sakka regarding the outcome of the battle. Sakka read celestial signs and prophesied correctly.[91]A banished prince was told by an astronomer that the king, his father, was dead; he then returned to the capital and became king.[92] Another time a jackal prophesied the death of the king and destruction of the kingdom; it came true, partly because king Farantapa, after hearing of the prophecy and seeing ill omens gave up fighting.[93] It remains a question whether human assistance made the prophecy come true. In a rather curious incident Buddha gave instructions regarding omens—possibly to demonstrate his erudition in that area. He, however, concluded the session with, "in omens there is no truth at all."[94]An astrologer desired king Śibi's daughter Unmādantī of exquisite beauty; the astrologer vetoed a proposed good match, but the princess was given to the commander-in-chief. So the false prophecy did not eventually benefit the astrologer at all.[95]A chaplain praises Mahosadha saying that he is clever and knows all omens.[96]

---

89 another atthassa nakkhattam kim kariṣyati, what can stars do if the matter is evil? No. 59, *Nakkhatta*.

90 No. 279, italics mine.

91 No. 301, Cullakalinga.

92 No. 320, *Succaja*.

93 No. 416, Parantapa.

94 No. 453, *Mahāmaṇgala*.

95 No. 527, Unmādantī.

96 No. 546, *Mahāmmagga*.

The *Rāmājṇa* has a catalogue of good omens signifying Rāma's victory over Khara and Dūṣaṇaand the fourteen thousand monsters accompanying them; all of it came true.[97] Evil omens are all around when Rāma and Lakṣmaṇa return to the empty cottage; even before they discover the abduction, they are forewarned by these.[98] The monstress Trijatā's dream shows her good omens regarding Sītā's fate.[99] Rāvaṇa and his minions see evil omens in nature even before Rāma has crossed the ocean.[100] Rāma himself sees ill omens signifying the massive massacre immediately after he has crossed the ocean.[101] Again they see omens that boded evil at the start of the battle esp. Rāvaṇa and the monsters see them.[102] The *Mahābhārata* too is full of supernatural foreboding before the beginning of each day's battle and before each great hero's death.[103] In the *Harivaṃśa* we are given a list of good omens of Kṛṣṇa's birth.[104]

The *Mahābhārata,* especially its later interpolated sections, are full of omens and portents. The magnitude of the issue at stake viz. the destruction of the eighteen akṣauhiṇīs of soldiers, fratricide and reaping the fruits of some evil deed on both sides,[105] all this had shaken the bottom-board of self-confidence which comes only from a clean conscience. Such a state of mind lends itself very easily to superstitions. The sense of guilt had sapped the moral strength hence they waited for fate to take its course and to manifest its motives and workings through omens and portents. At Arjuna's birth a disembodied voice proclaimed that someone like Indra is born.[106] When Kṛṣṇa goes to the Kurus with a peace proposal there were ill omens all around.[107] Karṇa admitted that

---

97 III: 24.

98 III: 57.

99 V: 29.

100 VI: 10: 14–21.

101 VI: 23: 3

102 VI: 35: 20–35

103 cf before Droṇa's death VII: 163: 10–13; after Duryodhana's death IX: 57: 46–57.

104 *Viṣṇuparvan* 4: 15–20.

105 The cruel insult and humiliation of Draupadī at the hands of Kauravas and agreeing to the game of dice, twice, by Yudhiṣṭhira, the eldest Pāṇḍava.

106 *Op. Cit.,* V: 135: 2.

107 *Mbh* V: 82: 5–10.

there were evil omens even before the battle was joined.[108] Omens are visible when Bhūma almost succeeds in killing Paraśurāma in a single combat.[109] Before the battle begins, everyone saw ill omens in nature.[110] When Bhīsma, the first general who led the Kuru army for ten days, was about to die all nature broke forth in inauspicious signs.[111] Also, before the death of Droṇa, the second general of the Kurus, such dark omens became visible.[112] In the *Mauṣala* Parvan where a curse is fulfilled, we find, men and beasts behaving in an unnatural way.[113] This is by no means an exhaustive list but one that will give us the idea of the spiritual climate of the times, fate had been provoked by both sides, an unnatural massacre was taking place where avarice, the desire for self-aggrandisement, malice and hostility had prompted both sides to engage in the fratricidal war witnessing the death of a vast number of innocent people including venerable old men. Hence people saw fate expressing its disapproval and vengeful extermination of noted heroes on both sides. And fate expressed its moods through these omens at all critical junctures of the course of action.

Coming to a much later culture, in the *Florentine Codex* we are told that there were "Omens regarding the advent of the Spaniards."[114] Also one remembers the word 'wyrd' (from which came the word 'weird'; cf the 'weird sisters' in *Macbeth*) in Old English meaning 'one's appointed lot or fortune, destiny, an evil fate inflicted by supernatural power esp. by way of retribution'. In Middle English it meant 'predetermined events' collectively, but in Old English it is personified.

Apart from omens and portents in the epics, the Purāṇas are chockful of the planets, the effects of constellations, the sun and moon and their influence on men's lives. Also, the appeasement of the heavenly bodies. Thus we have directions for the worship of planets.[115] Influence of planets[116] and omens

---

108 *Op. Cit.,* V: 141: 2–30.

109 *Op. Cit.,* V: 183: 21–23.

110 *Op. Cit.,* VI: 2: 16–3.

111 *Op. Cit.,* VI: 108ff.

112 *Op. Cit.,* VII: 15: 11–14.

113 *Op. Cit.,* XVI: 4: 5–46.

114 Bk. IX: 112.

115 *Viṣṇu* P., 1: *2, Kūrma* P., ch. 42; *Bhāgfrvuta* P., 5: 2.

116 *Agni* P., 51: 121, 126, 136, 164, 196; *Matsya* P., 54–70, 125, 126; *Kūrma* P., ch. 41.

are treated at great length in the *Matsya* Purāṇa.[117] Auspicious and inauspicious signs in men and women are dealt with."[118]... since astrology is only an approximate reflection of unknowable head-writing, there is always a chance that a prediction is inaccurate or he may begin to prepare himself for the disaster, adopting an attitude of resignation to a fate beyond his understanding or control.... The Deterministic perspective which offers him solace by depicting him as the helpless victim of an unalterable fate."[119]

True, Buddha discouraged the cultivation of astrology and omenology, yet these persisted very effectively among the people. This is what happened in all religions which advocated God or Providence or a supreme spirit as the sole dispenser of man's destiny and teaches the people not to try to tear the veil that hides their fate. But the common people who chafe under distress, want, diseases and disasters can hardly be expected to accept their fate without a murmur and not to be anxious to know if they may look forward to a brighter future. And not only the common people but the privileged few who are ever scared lest their privileges and wealth—either inherited or frequently amassed dishonestly—are snatched away from them. In their heart of hearts they are aware that morally they are not the rightful heirs to the wealth and their enjoyment is tinged with the guilt of usurpation, especially when there is so much of unrelieved misery all around. Hence their fear of losing. In order to keep the wealth in their possession forever, they take every measure to coax and cajole the forces of destiny. This privileged section is one of the strong plinths on which stands the edifice of superstitions regarding destiny and its various supernatural manifestations. Avarice of this section and real unmitigated suffering of the masses uphold this superstructure of these superstitions.

'Tithi' or the auspicious and inauspicious calendrical days is one major preoccupation for any serious undertaking, marriage or obsequial rites. The *Bṛharmāradīya* Purāṇa devotes an entire chapter (27) to the determination of the proper tithis. The *Matsya* Purāṇa has a chapter on auspicious times for departure,[120] another for building a house.[121] A pseudo-philosophical

---

[117] Chs. 229–36 and the relevant expiations in ch. 239; catalogue of portents, ch. 241, *Vāyu,* P., 19: 16; *Mārkaṇḍcya* P., ch. *34; Agni* P. ch. 229, *Garuḍa* P., chs. 230–231.

[118] *Agni* P., chs. 230–33, Omenss, ch. 263 and procedures for averting omen in chs. 243–14.

[119] Kayes and Daniel, 1983, pp. 44–15.

[120] Ch. 239.

[121] Ch. 242.

discussion starting from different kinds of years and their characteristics and results; names of different seasons, months, planets, stars, auspicious days and hours, names and descriptions of karanas, their presiding deities, descriptions of 'horā', 'kulika-velā's and 'Magna'—suitable hours for specific activities, the nature of the influence of planets and stars on different countries, under different circumstances; long and detailed descriptions of the method of performing 'grahayajñas' (sacrifices to planets), relative positions of the planets and stars — all these constitute the content of the lengthy section in the *Viṣṇudharmottara* Purāṇa.[122] Astronomy and astrology proper with special emphasis on the position of planets and stars and their influence on the king's life occupies another long section.[123]

Mithraism also had some dogmas connected with astrology; the Mithraists believed that planets and the sun and the moon exercised significant influence on the course of human life and guided human destiny. In all countries where theories of planetary influences on human destiny originated, this happened because science had not yet calculated the astronomical figures for the light-years which the planets, the sun and moon would require before the rays reached their earth. Hence the extremely hollow base of astrology was not comprehended. Time or Zervan Akarana of the later Zoroastrianism controlled the unchanging order of the heavenly process. From this as a necessary concomitant arose fatalism. Where Mithraism differed from other fatalistic theories, however, is that its theoretical fatalism did not smother the incentive to action. In principle Mithraism was an activist discipline. Its belief in astrology and the consequent fatalism did not constitute a logical structure which would necessarily have militated against the activism. In other words, its different formative elements were not mutually reconcilable or strictly coherent. This is true of most religions. With Zurvan, Time, as the ruling deity and the special reverence for the sun, moon and the planets, it is quite natural to expect that auspicious and inauspicious hours would be determined by the heavenly bodies' position and movements. And these were believed to have significant impact on the course of human life.

Astronomy, astrology and the worship of the planets, the sun and the moon constitute large chunks of many Purāṇas. A bird's-eye view will have to suffice. An entire chapter (80) of the *Vāmana* Purāṇa deals with the

122 Chs. 82–105.

123 Ibid., chs. 166–174.

heavenly bodies. Sections of the *Nārada* Purāṇa[124] are largely occupied with astronomical and astrological material. A special 'science' called 'Sāmudrika Lakṣaṇa'[125] i.e. determining fortune and character from body signs, where the specialist tells whether a boy will be a success in life or not.[126]

But the subject that was elaborately cultivated was omenology. Omens and portents bode evil or good for men and men everywhere in the world are ever curious to know what will befall them. That is how this pseudo-science thrives so well. The *Brahmavaivarta* Purāṇa gives a list of articles which, if a man about to depart sees, his journey will succeed: "a full pitcher, a brahmin, a prostitute, white paddy, a mirror, curd, clarified butter, puffed rice, flowers, dūrvā grass, *white puffed rice,* a bull, an elephant, a horse, burning fire, gold, leaves, ripe fruit, a woman with husband and sons alive, a lamp, precious jewels, pearls, garland of flowers, fresh meat, sandalwood, a jackal, a mongoose, a jar, a corpse on the left, swan, pigeon, white kite, cakravāka bird, parrot, cuckoo, peacock, wagtail, spotted black deer, cow, yak, a white feather-fan, cow-and-calf and a white flag on the right."[127] The same Purāṇa offers a slightly different list of auspicious signs at departure from home: spotted deer, elephant, lion, horse, rhinoceros, yak, swan, parrot, cuckoo, peacock, wagtail, white kite, the cakravāka, Creek partridge, pigeon, crane, the kāraṇḍa duck, swallow, lightning, rainbow, the sun and its halo, fresh meat, live fish, conch shell, gold, precious stone, silver, pearl, diamond, coral, curd, puffed corn, white paddy, white flower, red pigment, leaves, flag, umbrella, mirror, white yak-tail fan, cow-with-calf, a king on a chariot, milk, clarified butter, areca nut, nectar, honey, milk-porridge, the śālgrāma stone, ripe fruit, the svastikā sign, sugar, honey, cat, a mighty bull, sheep, rock-mouse, the sun rising in a cloudy sky, the moon, musk, fan, water, turmeric, pilgrimage-soil, white mustard, black mustard, dūrvā grass, a brahmin boy, girl, deer, a prostitute, a bee, camphor, yellow garment, cow-urine,cow-dung, dust raised by a cow, soil marked with cows' feet, cow-pen, cow's path, a pretty woman, a manger, the auspicious gait of cows, ornaments, icons, burning fire, a great festival, copper, crystal, a doctor, vermillion, garland and sandal-paste, perfume, diamond, jewel — all seen on the right and also sweet

---

[124] 2: 18–20, *interalia.*

[125] from Sa (with) *mudrā* (physical traits, auspicious or inauspicious).

[126] *Agni* P., 33: 1–9 Man ch. 243, Woman ch. 244.

[127] Gaṇeśakhanda, 16: 23–29.

redolence borne by the wind.[128] The same text has a third catalogue of auspicious things: a corpse on the left, a she-jackal, a full pitcher, a mongoose, black jay, a good woman decked out in fine ornaments whose husband and sons are alive, white flowers, paddy, wagtail, cow-with-calf, a white horse, swan, a prostitute, a garland of flowers, a banner, curd, rice porridge, jewels, gold, silver, pearl and precious stones, fresh meat, sandalwood paste, mead, good clarified butter, spotted deer, fruit, puffed corn, white mustard, a mirror, a decorated chariot, white kite, cakora bird, cat, hill, sheep, peacock, parrot, crane and the blowing of a conch-shell.[129]

Similarly inauspicious signs or ill omens also play a very significant role in man's life. The villainous Kaṃsa before his death saw a dream; the sun on the earth split into four, the moon into ten, deformed naked men with ropes, naked śūdra widows with their noses pecked off, laughing with curls of their hair around their faces, with black and white hair done up high, with swords and scimitars in hand, tongues hanging out, with head-gears of skulls, ass, buffalo, bull, pig, bear, crow, vulture, crane, dogs, crocodiles, jackals, heaps of ashes of bones, palm fruits, hair, raw cotton, extinguished fire-brands, etc.[130]

"Omens also can portend death: the victim sees the sun's periphery as without light, in reality or in dreams sees urine, faces, silver being spewed out (by a person); the victim (of these hallucinations) dies within ten months. If he sees a golden tree, a gandharvacity, he dies within nine months. If he grows lean or fat suddenly—eight months. He whose footsteps grow heavy or light in sand or mud—in seven months. He on whose head a crow, a pigeon, a vulture, or a carnivorous bird settles — in six months. He who moves surrounded by crows or a shower of sand or sees deformity in dean places — five or four months. He who sees lightning in the sky or rainbow in water—three months. He who does not see his reflection in water or a mirror or sees it truncated—one. He who smells of corpse or fat — a fortnight. He whose heart feels dry immediately after a bath, or from whose head smoke rises— in ten days. He whose insides feel cut up at the touch of water is near death. He who sees in a dream a bear or monkey-drawn chariot in which he himself is being carried singing, is very close to his end."[131]

---

[128] Gaṇeśakhaṇḍa 33: 11–28.

[129] Kṛṣṇajanmakhaṇḍa 70: 23–29.

[130] See section on dreams, *Brahmavaivarta* P., Kṛṣṇajanmakhaṇḍa 72: 70–79.

[131] *Linga* P. Pūrvabhāga ch. 91.

As is evident from the catalogues, the articles deemed auspicious are either connected with fertility, plenty, beauty, valour or purity. The inauspicious signs are the opposites—associated with ill-luck, a humble social position, infertility, ugliness, wildness and darkness. Those signs which forebode imminent death are either medical signs of a fatal disease i.e. diagnostic or symbolic or semiotic. In all of these cases, messages of success, failure or death are transmitted from a superhuman transcendental sphere and are couched in a veiled language signifying approaching fate.

It is remarkable how although the basic pattern of these symbol- system had already been firmly established by the third or second century B.C. that is, the latest interpolated portions of the epics and are therefore proto-Puranic in nature, the real floruit happens during the Gupta and post-Gupta revival of brahmanism which today is known as Hinduism. As maritime trade with the West dwindled, there arose a close insularity as far as receptivity, complacence and self-sufficiency are concerned. Openness to new ideas so declined in such a climate that these signs of fate assumed an all-important role. Sanskrit literature teems with the use of augury, divination, dreams and their interpretation by a specialized section of people, omens and portents and their interpretation by another group of specialists. Things came to such a ridiculous pass that works of literary criticism, rhetoric and dramaturgy laid down that a man and a woman can fall in love with each other in dreams in which they see each other. Now such dreams are not merely romantic but are clearly of supernatural origin. Some superhuman agency lends a hand in bringing a couple together by sending photo-like dreams to each other. Opportunities of meeting partners of the other sex, especially in the upper echelons of society were getting limited, hence falling in love with a vision of each other's portrait or of seeing each other in dreams became an accepted ground of primary courtship. Similarly, physical signs of a good or bad man or woman by which to judge their character or future lives was another channel of supernatural pointer. Prophecies have almost always been there but in post-Gupta texts their role dwindles perceptively although they persist throughout history.

Man's anxiety before any weighty event or undertaking— especially at birth, marriage and death—swamps his common sense as is bound to happen when the sense of insecurity and uncertainty are real. Hence, before these events, birth, marriage and death, as also before business deals, mercantile or ordinary voyages, military expeditions and long journeys, in the face of apparently incurable diseases, the 'expert' is called in who calculates and pontificates. Much of the death predictions are really sinister, they crush the will to live in the patient, the will to cure in the physician and lead to dejection. None of the predictions is medically quite valid. But people wait impatiently for some indications before such ponderous, sometimes onerous endeavours and anything that even symbolically penetrates the veil of fate, any whisper of guidance, of forewarning or reassurance is something the groping spirit of man clings to. Hence the survival and ever increasing bulk of *Śākuna śāstras,* texts for birdaugury and *Nimitta-nidāna* texts of omens and portents. They grow in direct correlation to the increasingly firm hold of fatalism in society. As in other ancient cultures fatalism militates with karman and rebirth, with the dogma of a providential godhead, against the theory of Nirvāṇaor mokṣa which gnosis leads to with temporary stays in heaven and hell, without a universally accepted judge or jurors whose verdict legalizes such stays.

Fatalism presupposes ignorance, a sense of insecurity, a stake in knowing and a desire for altering fate in one's favour. In dreams, prophecies, oracles, astrology, omens, portents, omithomancy, haruspicy, necromancy and such other practices the insecure man seeks to reach out to a fate beyond his grasp and, if possible, to incline it in his own favour. Knowledge, they say, is power and all these transcendental sign-language is interpreted by 'experts' appointed and/or acknowledged by society. What the interpretations bring to the anxiety-ridden individuals is 'knowledge' of a sort, under the given state of 'knowledge' in society. With this knowledge man either makes a venture, prepares himself for an impending joy or doom, chooses the right partner or discards the wrong one, banishes the ill-omened son, fights a rival or surrenders to him, undertakes or does not undertake a military or a mercantile expedition, accepts imminent death as inevitable, disburses his property and performs last rites dictated by the priests, or accepts a disaster as an immutable verdict of fate. Whatever else he is impelled to do, such messages do not ask him to fight what the supernatural messages reveal to him, because they come from powers that control human destiny, powers which man cannot dictate to or combat. At best he can placate an irate Providence, seek to appease some God's wrath and so avert unpleasant experiences, if such are what the messages reveal. These agencies of the supernatural have something unalterable about them, they come as *fait accompli,* at least notionally, of aspects of human destiny. Man, at most gains the knowledge, but not the formative or deflective power over his destiny.

In a sense, therefore, such knowledge is morally debilitating and paralysing; even the theologians were obscurely aware of it. A section of the populace also dimly felt the weakness generated by entertaining or anxiously groping for glimpses of things to come, as we shall see in the last chapter. Meanwhile, these agencies held a powerful sway over the consciousness of the masses that is ubiquitous and at least apparently, unending. Man craves for these premonitions and presages, clings to them even though like the witches' forecast in *Macbeth* they land the enquirer into a greater doom than he could anticipate. But according to the law of probability, a certain percentage of these forecasts are bound to prove true and these guarantee longevity to such queries through the ages. People seldom keep a full record of the presages and tally them with the actual events, so their blind helpless faith remains intact despite many evidences to the contrary.

CHAPTER 7

Deflection: Remedial Measures

A ritual act which aims at establishment or exoneration of imputed guilt is the ordeal, 'satyakriyā', the act of truth. It is an indirect appeal to fate or the invisible agencies which act and control human destiny. When falsely accused, a person sometimes appealed to the elements in nature and to supernatural powers to bear witness to his or her innocence. "Forms of ordeal and the whole theory of the oath as well as its practice up to the latest stages of civilization depend on the principle of the conditional curse often embodied in symbolic action. An oath may be regarded as essentially a conditional self-imprecation, a curse by which a person calls down upon himself some evil in the event of what he says being untrue. All the resources of symbolic magic are drawn upon in the multitudinous examples of this principle... The oath carries with it the punishment for perjury. In ancient states all laws were accompanied by a curse upon the transgressor... Law gradually takes over the function of the curse, as a form of retribution."[1] In India the ordeal is first met with in the Ṛgveda[2] where a person calls death upon himself if he is a monster as his enemy apparently accuses him of being. Now he calls upon the supernatural agencies which are in charge of life and death to prove his innocence (i.e. he is a man and not a monster) and if he truly is a monster as the accuser says, may death be visited on him that same day. How does he expect this to happen? He has an innate faith in some sort of cosmic justice operative in the world, in a fate whose visitations are morally balanced. Hence this oath.

Law as an institution came late to India; we have no means of finding out how the Indus Valley kings and potentates governed their kingdom; nothing resembling a jurisprudence has come down to us. The nomadic tribal Aryans were most probably under the sole control of their leader and

---

1 *Encyclopaedia of Religion and Ethics*, Vol. IV, pp. 373, 374.

2 VII: 104: 15.

in eases of dispute this leader would adjudicate. How? In the absence of written documents, we can surmise that the Ṛgvedic 'sabhā', the assembly of elders was summoned and they deliberated on the pros and cons of a case and then gave a verdict which was wholly binding on the plaintiff and the defendant. It is significant that one concomitant of the break-up of the tribal system was the emergence of a code of law first formulated by Kauṭilya, presumably before the rise of the Maurya dynasty. As in Rome, the earliest law is not based on 'equality of all in the eye of the law'; the Roman citizen enjoyed privileges which slaves, foreigners and offenders did not; yet by and large, it was a uniform code with some balance between offence and punishment, although with distinct codes for each section. But within the section there was an equitability. In India Kauṭilya's *Arthaśāstra* is distinctly a caste-based law book. But within that framework there was a correspondence between offence and punishment. This long preamble is an attempt to depict imaginatively a situation when the tribal composition has disintegrated and the real rule of law has not yet arisen. The social lawgivers, the opposite numbers of the Vedic 'sabhā' functioned as judge, jury and magistrate. In the absence of a code, there was an area where suspicion could not be formally dispelled, innocence indisputably established and unjust punishment and stigma effectively averted. It was during this legal vacuum, this interregnum or transition that we have accounts of ordeals and 'satyakriyās'. Later lawgivers also accomodated ordeals as valid modes of judgment-ordeal by fire, water, poison and scales. However cruel, these modes presuppose a firm conviction that the unseen power which controls human affairs viz. fate, would not let an innocent person suffer; miraculously the Gods or the elements would come to vindicate the innocence of one unjustly accused. Faith in fate is thus at the back of ordeals.

Kauṭilya's *Arthaśāstra* is an early Gupta text Although in a rudimentary form its antecedents could be pushed to a more remote antiquity. But even before then a nebulous code of judgement and punishment was current, presumably from the time of the sixteen Mahājanapadas. But rulers of these kingdoms judged cases according to the codes of each king, chaplain and/or minister-judges separately. Before Kauṭilya there was no common law over the whole of northern India that was followed uniformly. Even before and after Kauṭilya, the common fourfold practice of proving guilt or innocence of a person was by (i) drowning (the innocent would not drown), (ii) fire (the innocent would not be hurt), (iii) poison (same) and (iv) balance (the innocent would not sink or weigh more). These were time-worn practices, later legalized in the law-codes. The oath of the Satyakriyā was another legally accepted method of proving one's innocence. What is commonly known as Sītā's trial by fire was not initially such a trial; Sītā, on learning that Rāma suspected her chastity, had decided to put an end to her life by being cremated on a pyre which she commanded Lakṣmaṇa to build for her. Eventually, it was transformed into an ordeal by fire when the Gods came and asserted her innocence. Numerous such cases occur, usually for proving a woman's chastity, but occasionally also to prove mens' innocence. In Mesopotamia we have the record of a woman being put to the ordeal of the river current in the twenty-fourth century B.C.; she was accused of witchcraft and adultery, the two main accusations which have taken the lives of billions of woman all over the world throughout the ages. At last in the eighteenth century B.C.[3] King Hammurabi, formed a law-code, the first in the world. "The appearance of ordeal in European culture can be directly attributed to Roman and Christian adaptation of a Germanic custom in the tribal laws of the various Germanic populations because it had also come to be regarded as manifestation of divine justice."[4] The idea was that the divine High Court, when appealed to could not issue a false verdict; their prestige for justice would be rudely shaken if they did. So an 'act of truth' forcibly inclined the forces of justice to manifest the truth regarding the appellant. This is another way of appealing to fate to speak out so that false accusations could not lead to wrong judgment.

Among the steps one takes to deflect the verdicts of fate is to expiate for sins. Sins are bound to be punished by fate or the principle of justice operative behind the universe, call it Ṛta, Providence, God, Dharma or the Gods would be totally falsified. Ṛta is the Ṛgvedic concept of the cosmic law and order which upholds the universe and whose supreme custodian Varuṇa punishes man for his sins, crimes and remissnesses. The belief in the existence of Ṛta as the inherent morality and truth which controls the universe persisted and the 'act of truth' is one indirect form of invoking this Ṛta. Since sins will irrevocably carry their punishment, man expiates either in anticipation or in retrospection. Almost all ancient civilizations betrayed their awareness of sin or guilt and their expectation of supernatural visitations of punishment. Expiation or exculpation is the human step to prevent the blow from falling.

---

3 1790–1750 B.C.

4 *Macmillan Encyclopaedia of Religion*, 'Ordeal', Vol. XI.

"It is believed, however, that a person's karman may be altered in three ways. First, by repenting of previous misdeeds, of making a habit of leading a good life.[5] Second, if an individual's dose relative, a monk or a nun chants sacred verses or holds religious services for him, then such assistance—*in addition to his own good deeds*—heightens or destroys his own bad karman. Third, if a relative or religious specialist *chants sacred verses after a person's death,* such actions, themselves meritorious, will help alleviate the dead person's accumulated karman."[6] Expiation thus can be vicarious, in some theologies, but in India, although it can be vicarious it is, primarily the individual's action for removing his past guilt; and in some cases, as we shall later see, it can be anticipatory i.e., some expiatory acts have a far-reaching effect. But the chants of holy men also add to the individual's good deeds.

In India expiation is prāyaścitta, and "in some (less typical) passages, the locus of concern shifts from sustaining relationship with the Lord through right ritual responses to the maintenance of an open attitude of love and trust, or to the exhibition of responsible ethical action. In such cases the atoning acts are appropriate to the offences—if the sins are of the 'heart' and adversely affect the relationship of love and trust, then it is the heart also that one attempts to make amends for by repentance and minor renewal; if the sins are those of irresponsible or unethical behaviour in response to divine dictates, then it is the penitential actions and reformed ways that one attempts to make amends for wrongs done."[7] Expiation or prāyaścitta raises some fundamental questions; sin against whom? God? Man? Some universal code of ethics? How does expiation affect the sin and the sinner? Does it expunge the guilt or destroy its effect and/or punishment? Who lays down the rules for what precise measures should be taken for which specific sins or offences? How does expiation affect the man sinned against or the ethical code transgressed? How does sin and expiation affect God or Ṛta or the universal ethical code?

Different theologies have answered the questions differently, the simplest and linear replies come from monotheistic religions. Man sins against God by flouting his laws and he has laid down an emotional repentance and an ethical/volitional course of action for atonement. After the sinner fulfils

5 Good karman red nesses or exterminates the power of bad karman.

6 *Macmillan Encyclopaedia of Religion*, Vol. 8, p. 26; italics added.

7 Smith, *The Adyar Library Bulletin*, Vol. XXX, 1966, p. 27.

these conditions he is released from the sense and effect of guilt. Even Varuṇa, the punishing agent in the *Ṛgveda,* does not hold the sinner guilty after the punishment is meted out to him; the Vedic literature does not know irremediable deadly sins. Buddhism and Jainism vary expiatory measures according to the gravity of the sin, but presumably that is the end of it. Although in Buddhist tales sometimes the earth opens up and swallows the sinner into the 'avīci' hell where, presumably he is doomed to remain eternally if he has committed one of those deadly sins.

It seems that with the growth of the legal literature, the ideas of transgression, sins of commission and omission, amendments and punishments became increasingly firmly entrenched in the popular mind and theologians set down to the task of framing a code of law, ethical rules of expiation. "While in the legal literature prāyaścitta may refer to the removal of sin or guilt due to evils done in a context where an impersonal dharma dominates, in the theistic texts... prāyaścitta refers to the ritual removal of separation and alienation between devotee and his adored deity due to deeds done defectively or simply deeds undone in a universe ruled over by a personal Lord."[8] This ritual removal of the distance and alienation was a grave psychological necessity, it could be obtained ritually and otherwise. For example, with the Mexicans, "If they had committed a sin... and wished to atone for it, they went to the priests of the goddess Tlacoltcotl and made confession and the priests after having heard the confession imposed some penance... By performing the penance, they were believed not only to have got rid of the sin committed but also of the punishment for it enjoined by law."[9] This humane procedure bears resemblance to the Catholic one and may have been influenced by it. But in most primitive religions or those modern religions which carry strong vestigial characteristics of their primitive origins, expiation consists of a rite. The physical performance of a rite, involving effort, some discomfort, expense and occasionally some form of self-deprivation or self-flagellation generated a mental relief of having 'paid' for the guilt. And the guilty person hankers for the sense of a balance of debit and credit. This act of expiation symbolically ties the hands of wrathful fate by clearing the ethical debt.

---

8 Smith, *Ibid.,* p. 24.

9 Hasting's, *Encyclopaedia of Religion and Ethics,* Vol. VIII, p. 614.

"Constituent elements of prāyaścitta practices: confession of guilt, repentance of the deed and the damage it caused, exercise of breath-control for inner purification, practice of expiatory austerities, institution of local fire offerings, utterance of verbal formulas, an offering in gifts, the endurance of a fast and completion of a pilgrimage."[10] This catalogue almost exhausts the ritual expiation. In later and/or monotheistic religions, the rituals are dropped and expiation becomes more and more internalized and spiritual repentance, confession and a mental vow to turn a new page.

Confession of guilt is obligatory also in Jainism, but confession is not adequate as expiation, it is just the primary step towards expiation. "Punishment is the consequence of guilt, and guilt is... something leaving the path of truth, hence called māyā, māī, he who has made himself guilty... A sin is not confessed in a salla... What lies between the confession of guilt and the acceptance of the penalty inflicted upon the confessor... (of the six rules about this) the first two say the delinquent reproves himself and his teacher, the second pair expresses the process of the inner purge from ill-doing, and the last two, the will to amendment... The atonement frequently is coordinated with inward asceticism, vivega, the reuniciation of the corpus dilecti and viusagga, standing motionless with one's arms hanging down (for a measured time),... tava is the food either reduced, dropped or changed."[11]

Jainism has, on the one hand, internalized the guilt as a contaminating, polluting element which envelops the pure glory of the soul; on the other hand, it has concretized the punishment by physical penalties inflicted by the order (or self-inflicted) and thus materially expunging the dark blot of the sin. However, it does believe that unexpiated sins lead to births in lower stations. Hence although "there is an option of expiation for the sins one may commit during a life-time, failure to do so, or doing so inadequately or committing more inadvertantly or bearing the backlog of sins from a previous existence may be carried over to the next life." There being no clear-cut chart of correlation between sins and their penalties, as is also the case in Brahmanism, Jainism does indirectly admit fate as the unforeseen and unforeseeable part of karman and their effects.

When the guilt is externalized and the theologians detect spirit possession, it is a peculiar manifestation of the workings of fate and has a peculiar

---

[10] Smith, *Ibid.*, p. 30.

[11] Schubring, 1962, pp. 278, 280, 281, 282.

remedy prescribed which, exorcism, is the same everywhere with difference in the ritual details. Of a shamanistic nature of origin the cure is also shamanistic in character. "The evil spirit which possesses a member of the community is an extraneous evil which threatens the community through possessing one member. Then the shaman, witch or wizard is summoned and he performs the exorcistic rites. Evil as represented by the demon is not eliminated. It is brought under control and subordinated to the higher values of society."[12] In India, however, the exorcist performs his prescribed rite with mustard seeds and/or some obnoxious articles, beats the victim with a broomstick, humiliates him/her with slaps and insulting words; then when the victim in exhaustion says on behalf of the spirit that it is ready to leave, the shaman commands it to leave (even directing the place where it should go). There are also seasonal exorcisms which the shaman performs for the community; special disasters and crises overtaking the community call for the witch-doctors' special rituals. In all this, fate functions from behind and the shaman or witch-doctor merely acts as an agent of fate or some supernatural cosmic agent proceeding according to pre-formulated rules and rituals to strike a balance between two sets of supernatural powers and to rid the individual or the community of the sudden flaring up of the wrath of the unseen fatalistic powers. When that is achieved, harmony between nature and the supernatural is re-established and there is smooth-sailing for the community. Until the next disaster.

Communal and individual expiation constitute the theme of many episodes in the epics and Purāṇas. But expiation begins in the Vedic period—any ritual transgression had to be expiated with suitable rites prescribed in the texts. The specific task of the Brahman, the Atharvavedic priest was to detect all ritual remissnesses and to prescribe expiatory rites. The Brāhmaṇa literature contains many such rites. The *Taittirīya* raṇyaka has a set of Suparṇa spells which should be muttered to preclude a sudden termination of the life-span.[13] The *Mahābhārata* lists sins and their appropriate expiations. The tendency to multiply these increased because, on the one hand, they afforded peace to the person who offends the Gods or the powers that are in the high spiritual places and, on the other, it was lucrative for the officiating priest whose avarice was growing with time.

---

[12] Alverson, *History of Religions*, Vol. 10, no. 4, 1976, p. 355.

[13] X: pp. 48–50.

The *Matsya* Purāṇa lays down ritual acts for expiating for the various natural calamities.[14] When Brahman asks Śiva for expiatory rites the latter prescribes only one way, to take shelter with Viṣṇu.[15] The *Kūrma* Purāṇa has a long section on the various sins of commission and omission and the proper rites of atonement for these.[16] A rather curious stanza says "neither the Vedas nor devotion to Hari or to Maheśvara can purify the fool who slips from the conventional code of conduct."[17] Chapter 28 of the same text, however, is a long catalogue of expiations for exactly the same kind of ritual slips.

The common refrain of most of these passages of expiation is: a person who has bathed in a river (or lake) at a pilgrimage, given gifts, praised the Gods, sung hymns, kept vows, done worship, served the king, husband (if it is a woman) especially the brahmins—is immediately cleansed of all his sins, there is not a shade of doubt in this. In the *Agni* Purāṇa separate sections are devoted to the expiatory prescriptions for ritual impurity from death or contact with corpses;[18] from haemorrhage, or menstruation, expiation of the cardinal sins and special expiation rites.[19] The *Devībhāgavata* Purāṇa says: "If a man fasts on the Janmāṣṭamī day he obtains the fruits of performing a horse sacrifice even without a vow or keeping the 'wake'. This cleanses a man from sins committed in childhood, for seven successive lives."[20]"If one drinks water with which a brahmin's feet have been washed in an attitude of devotion, he is freed from sins of seven lives. Having committed five kinds of sins, if a person bows to a brahmin, he attains the merits of bathing in all pilgrimages and is redeemed of his sins."[21] "The merit that accrues to a man from all the sacrifices and at initiation, the same merit is gained from giving fodder to cows."[22]

---

14 Chs. 227–237.

15 *Vāmana* P. 76: 9–10.

16 Chapters 30–33.

17 *Bṛhannāradṣya* 4: 25.

18 cf. the sin of the contact with the corpse, nassu in the *Avesta*.

19 Chs. 157, 158, 169, 172 and 173–74.

20 Kṛṣṇajanmakhaṇḍa 8: 74, 75.

21 *Ibid*., 93.

22 *Ibid*., 129.

Even the mendicant has special rites for expiation catalogued in a whole chapter (90) of the *Liṅga* Purāṇa. The late *Devībhāgnvata* Purāṇa suddenly comes out in support of muttering the Vedic gāyatrī spell because the Vedas do not recommend the worship of Viṣṇu or Śiva or the initiation rite; Gāyatrī worship is postulated by all the Vedas, without which a brahmin really falls from the path.[23] For various kinds of sins the *Padma* Purāṇa lays down appropriate expiations in a whole chapter (56). The second half of the *Garuḍa* Purāṇa has a verse which says, "After committing heinous crimes in large numbers a man makes atonement by giving gifts of land and cowhide"(40:6). In the first half of the same Purāṇa an entire chapter (52) recommends expiations of many kinds: "he who sleeps with his preceptor's wife shall make the same atonement as one who has killed a brahmin or (he should keep) five or four cāndrāyaṇa vows."(65: ll). One notices how although the severity of the crime remains the same, the expiatory measures get toned down considerably. The Cāndrāyaṇa vow requires one to eat one mouthful less everyday in the dark fortnight, fast on the new-moon night, then increase one mouthful each day of the bright fortnight to fifteen on the full-moon night. This is an astonishingly light punishment for one who sleeps with the preceptor's wife, which is one of the five deadly sins, or for killing a brahmin. Another verse says: he who feeds brahmins is cleansed from all sins.[24] A similar inexplicable mildness is noticed in the *Padma* Purāṇa verses which say: the Brahmin-killer, the ungrateful wretch, the alcoholic—these can make adequate amends with self-deprivation, cāndrāyaṇa, charity and vows observed properly; all their sins vanish and are remitted.[25] The disparity between the so-called irremediable offences and these unexpectedly light expiatory recommendations strikes one as absurd. But possibly two items of the prescription throw some light on the possible explanation of the discrepancy: charity and vows. In both, the recipient of the material offerings is the brahmin priest. Thus what fate and social lawgivers had earlier pronounced as too heinous for expiation is now expiable and the expiation is rather cheaply bought to the benefit of the brahmin priests. We should also notice a subtle devaluation in the social rank of the brahmin, for the brahmin-killer tops the list which signifies that the offence was becoming somewhat

23 XII: 88, 89.

24 *Op. Cit.,* 56: 15.

25 Pāeāla Khaṇḍa, 19: 31, 32.

more common; also alcoholism was possibly coming into vogue more and more. Thus what fate would have decreed earlier as sins without a remedy, the later lawgivers decided to look at with greater lenience. This was a dominant tendency of the time. As we shall see later on, some social changes were introducing this tolerance and greater indulgence for the moral offenders.

As sins are on the debit side of the ethico-religious balance-sheet, so merits were on the credit side. Merits could be earned through various means and could be spent, laid by, used, lent, borrowed or destroyed. It is a spiritual asset and is treated very much as mundane assets by the authors of scriptures. As with the advance of civilization, cash or currency came to play an increasingly significant role in society, on the spiritual level merit played a similar part. It could be earned through observing vows, offering sacrifices and pūjās, giving gifts, serving the husband, one's superiors, kings and sages, through visiting pilgrimages, taking baths at appropriate spots, meditation, fasts, other self-abnegatory rites, offering obsequial rites for ancestors and parents and through devotion to the Gods. Merit could be used to counter or neutralize some adverse decrees of fate.

Many other—actually most other—ancient civilizations had no notion of this kind of merit as a theological asset. Mesopotamia, for example had no idea of such merit, "where notions of existence had no post-mortal goal. Hebrew She'ol —a silent forgotten abode beneath the earth, related at least in type to the Babylonian hell. In both the teachings of Koran and of the New Testament, the concept of calculable merit is entirely lacking."

The Rabbinic doctrine of merit, though articulated in detail in the first four centuries of the common era, is based on two fundamental ideas which reach much further back in Jewish tradition: (1) keeping the mosaic covenant with God (i.e., observing the Torah) will lead to blessing and welfare (2) the responsibility and benefit of this covenant are essentially corporate and pass from generation to generation. Stated negatively, disobedience leads to punishment in the form of social or political suffering but the punishment can be moderated by credit accumulated by previous generations."[26] We see that although Mesopotamia, with its rather primitive kind of eschatology did not form a concept or merit, Judaism had one. And analysing the association of such merit we find that the rise of private property which could be earned

---

[26] *Macmillan Encyclopaedia of Religion*, 'Merits', p. 381.

by an individual, accumulated through several generations and which could be used as wealth uses is at the back of the concept of religious merit. Merit counters verdicts of fate and is earned by individual effort and stored against calamities or untoward situations ordered by fate.

An extremely popular, widely recognized act of merit, publicized in the scriptures is: visits to pilgrimages. With the spread of the Aryan culture from north-west to south-eastern areas of India, sages spotted out naturally beautiful and pleasant resorts, near the sea or some river, lake, fountain of fall, initially away from the crowded villages and towns; but as pilgrimages became popular these spots drew crowds, temples were erected, sages clustered there and business in articles used in vows or pūjā, or appeasement of Gods and sages began to thrive, so that, with time, separate holy townships grew in these spots. The proximity of the sea or river helped sea and river-trade. All these were the mundane factors helping the pilgrimages to grow into flourishing business centres. There are, however a few exceptions which are still located in places difficult or dangerous to reach, few visit them and of those who do, some are attracted by the natural beauty of the spot, while others are tempted by the prospect of earning extra merits, (because life there was more difficult) promised in the scriptures. Throughout India there are millions of pilgrimages of different communities, sects and cults and billions visit them all round the year. Most of them are drawn through the desire to earn merit.

"The term pilgrimage covers a wide variety of phenomena, most of which involve visits over a greater or lesser distance to shrines or holy places. Pilgrimages may also be distinguished by the type of site visited."[27] These shrines can be of many different categories and vary from large stone or brick-built structures with bathing facilities and other allied constructions to the simplest small shrine under a tree in a village. They belong to alt the major and many minor faiths. With many of them are associated some anecdotes which endowed the structures with their initial glory and sanctity. For brahmanical temples most of these anecdotes are recorded in the Purāṇas; some are current orally in folk tradition, in floating ballads, songs, hero-legends and all pilgrimages are of the 'omphalos' type, they are the epicentre of the earth and therefore, in close touch with the chthonic powers or cosmic forces which control the universe as well as human lives. It is this subterranean belief current through the ages which sanctifies a spot, sets it apart from areas

[27] Wilson, 1983, pp. 12–13.

contiguous to it because here the 'hagios', holy, is present; it is charged with the power to bless the pilgrim, to fulfil his desires to endow him with merit which he can lay by.

Most pilgrimages are deemed to be charged with extra holiness on some specially stipulated days, seasons, occasions. Baths at holy places on eclipses of the sun or moon and at special conjuncture of some planets according to special ritual directions earn the pilgrim some extra merit.[28] Similarly, he who places one 'tulasī' leaf in a temple in the month of Kārtika attains the same merit as of giving away a thousand cows as gifts.[29] He who places a 'tulsī' leaf on a dear elevated spot enjoys eternal heaven.[30] Pilgrimages are strewn all over India. The *Mahābhārata* has many catalogues, even whole chapters devoted to their names, degrees of holiness and merits which accrue from visits to these places.[31] The *Harivaṃśa* a late supplement to the *Mahābhrāta* mentions sacred spots, rivers, mountains and even sacred groves.[32]

The idea of pilgrimage is indissolubly connected with absolution of sins. Special pilgrimages have special powers to absolve specific types of sins. But there are some universally acclaimed pilgrimages such as the Gaṅgā, Vārāṇasī, Prayāga and Gayā which contain concentrated holiness and can remit all kinds of sins. Even though a man has committed sins elsewhere ablution in the Gaṅgā washes all sins away. But sins committed near the Gaṅgā immediately multiply by a million.[33] A man who has committed sins in India but has bathed in the Sarasvatī is immediately cleansed of all sins and lives in Viṣṇu's realm forever.[34] The Gaṅgā has been specially venerated in all the Purāṇas.[35] Directly associated with the sanctity of the Gaṅgā are Prayāga, Vārṇāṇasī and Gaṅgāsāgara; the first is the place of the confluence of the Gaṅgā with another holy river, the Yamunā and the second, a city on

---

28 *Matsya* P., ch. 66.

29 *Bṛhannāradīya* P., Adys, 8: 23.

30 *Op. Cit.*, 8: 53.

31 III: 30–81: 96; 114–178; II: 82, the whole chapter; 83: 1–101; 85: 4–23; 86–88 there whole chapters; 93, the whole chapter.

32 Balarāma, the noted wanderer describes these in the Viṣṇuparvan ch. 109: 22–42.

33 *Brahmavaivarta* P., Brahmakhaṇḍa 10: 83.

34 *Brahmavaivarta* P., Prakṛtikhaṇḍa 6: 4.

35 Thus *Agni* P. ch. 110 *Bṛahannāradīya* P., Aya ch. 5; Madhya ch. 25; *Devībhāgavata* IX: 12: 37 *et al.*

the Gaṅgā deemed specially holy from times immemorial. A bath in the Gaṅgā wipes away sins, like slaying a brahmin, committed in billions of lives.[36] Vārāṇasī is holy in most Purāṇas and subsequent texts.[37] He who sweeps the banks of the Gaṅgā, mornings and evenings, is released from sins committed over billions of lives. Prayāga is also a very holy spot.[38] The Yamunā itself is a holy river from olden times, but is particularly sanctified by Kṛṣṇa's activities connected with it.[39] Kurukṣetra, where the epic battle is supposed to have taken place is another sanctified place, presumably because of its 'historic' gravity; it is also a major pilgrimage. A man bathing at Kurukṣetra is freed from his sins.[40] The Purāṇas mention other rivers as holy, like the Kāverī and Narmadā[41] and the Revā,[42] Gayā's holiness is associated with obsequial rites performed there by people from all over India, hence as a pilgrimage it ranks in the first category.[43] Many other minor pilgrimages are strewn all over the Purāṇas.[44]

Apart from the vicinity of seas, rivers and lakes the Śiva liṅga (iconic reproduction of Śiva's phallus worshipped as extremely sacred), established at various places makes them extra holy. The *Vāmana* Purāṇa explains its sanctity and the spiritual benefits attained from visits to such pilgrimages;[45] one obtains the merits of the *Agnihotra* sacrifice from seeing the Śiva liṅga.[46] Now, visits to pilgrimages often meant long trips, which, before the railway was introduced in the last two centuries, was quite strenous, quite risky and pretty expensive, hence, with the best intention in the world, the sick, the elderly and the impecunious could not afford to undertake such journeys. So

---

36 *Devībhāgavata* P. IX: 12: 37.

37 *Padma* P., Sṛṣṭi Khaṇḍa ch. 19, *Matsya* chs 179–184, *Kūrma* ch. 30; *Nṣrrada* ch. 112.

38 *Nārada ch.* 111; *Padma* svargakhaṇḍa chs. 21–23; Kūrma 35–37; *Matsya* 105–111; 28: 19 *et at.*

39 *Brahmāṇḍa* P. 6: 31, *Kūrma* P. ch. 38; *Pudma*, svarga chs. 17, 18; *Brahmavaivarta*, Brahma. 11: 25; Bṛahannardṣya, Madhya ch. 28.

40 *Vāmana* P. 41: 21; Padma Svargakhaṇḍa ch. 13.

41 Padma, Svarga chs. 6, 8–10; *Matsya* P. ch. 185–193; *Agni* 113.

42 *Op. Cit.*, ch. 113.

43 Agni chs. 114–116.

44 *Brahma* 2: 15; chs. 16–32; *Matsya* P., ch. 115; *Vāmana* 2, 36–42; chs. 36, 37, 42; *Brahma*, 1: 17: 1–86, chs. 24, 40–46; II: 15–32.

45 ch. 46.

46 46: 33.

surrogates were found: he who greets brahmins reverentially every morning after getting up has bathed in all pilgrimages and has performed all sacrifices.[47] At one place Kṛṣṇa says, 'where my devotees wash others' feet there is a pilgrimage which eradicates the sins of slaying a woman, a cow, a brahmin, a benefactor and the sin of sleeping with the preceptor's wife.' These become liberated even in this life.[48] Thus one attains the merits of pilgrimage without actually visiting any. In the first of these two prescriptions the brahmin arrogates to himself the powers of a God, the power of remitting sins; and in the second, acts prompted by devotion to Kṛṣṇa obliterate even heinous sins.

Many pilgrimages derive their aura and sanctity from Puranic legends. However, it is difficult to determine whether the legends were composed to raise particular spots to pilgrimages or vice versa. Mythical characters are reported to have lived, moved and performed some mythical feats, at some special areas which later became pilgrimages. Each pilgrimage needs the mystique of a myth and the major pilgrimages have more than one myth attached to them which hallow those particular spots. Why visit pilgrimages? For the same reason that one gives gifts, worships Gods, fulfils vows or performs other expiatory acts. The burden of a backlog of sins pursues men like the Erinyes and each of these acts bring them to the altar of brahmin should be versed in the scriptures and bear an unimpeachable character, later texts do not make these stipulations, so that any brahmin, needy or not, learned or not, of good character or not, qualified. The concept of 'jātyā brāhmaṇah', a brahmin by birth, came in vogue in the late antiquity Purāṇas. What the donor received in return for his gifts had thus no bearing to the moral fibre or intellectual equipment of the recepient. The scriptures were extremely lenient in holding the donor as cleansed of all his sins, his and his ancestors' and successors' for several generations. Fate thus operated or was supposed to operate, through the abstract directions for gifts and was prepared to shower merits mechanically.

Gifts given for collective or public good as is evidenced in the Buddhist texts, by a rich merchant Anāthapiṇḍada who fed thousands at the time of a famine or of the rich courtesan Ambapālī who acted similarly and gave gardens and tanks for the monks, obviously earned greater merits; they rose

---

[47] *Brahmavaivarta*, Brahma, 11: 25.

[48] *Devībhāgavata* IX: 5: 26, 27.

to the highest altitude of spiritual power, came nearer to nirvana. But in Brahmanism the prize offered to the donor is happiness in heaven, birth in a rich and aristocratic family and remission of a multitude of sins of many births before and after, together with those of ancestors and successors. Clearly, this last has a spiritual overtone, but it really makes atonement for sins unbelievably cheap and easy. It does not say that doing good for the public by building houses, tanks, gardens, etc. fetches greater merit as it should, because the number of beneficiaries is much greater and the gifts are much more lasting than gifts given to an individual brahmin, who could bear an immoral character and be devoid of learning, but who qualified through the accident of his birth in a brahmin family. Repeated mention of merit earned by charity to brahmins, irrespective of their character, conduct or condition signified a degeneration of the brahmin as a caste. Later Purāṇas vaunt the birth in a brahmin family as a merit in itself; this looks like a pointer to increase of the ratio of brahmins who, bereft of merit, rectitude or qualification had nothing to recommend them except the accident of their birth. Giving to such worthless men just because of their brahminhood degrades the donor to a large extent.

When the scriptures make the verdicts of fate subservient to such mechanical considerations there seems to be a degeneration in the moral timbre of the society itself. Ironically enough it also betrays a devaluation in the concept of fate; man could now ensure that the heinous, unpardonable sins that he himself and his ancestors had committed and that his successors are likely to commit, could be eradicated in retrospection as also in anticipation. If the verdict of the erstwhile grim forces of fate could be simply abrogated by giving suitable gifts to brahmins, the ethical structure behind society becomes ridiculously mechanical and feeble.

Vows appeared somewhat later than charity, which is of Vedic origin. Both must have been practised simultaneously from very olden times. Stated in very simple terms, a vow is an inner resolution to temporarily forego certain articles of necessity or pleasure in return for which the person supplicates for something he desires. There is always a time-limit for such self-abnegation, at the expiry of which the person performs the concluding rite with the assistance of a family or community priest and offers certain stipulated articles to this brahmin priest as his official fees. By observing such vows the supplicant expects to alter the verdict of fate in his/her favour.

The spiritual forerunner of the vow is the oath or 'the act of truth' (satyakriyā). Here if a person is under suspicion by one or more members of the community he or she undertakes a vow which is immediately performed by calling upon the Gods and/or the elements of nature (like the sun and the moon, air, fire, etc.) to bear witness to his or her innocence. Usually those forces, natural or supernatural appear and exonerate the supplicant whose innocence is then accepted by the community.

Apollo where they are assured of the grace of the Eumenides, so to speak. Pilgrimages serve as confession-and-expiation and offer a sense of release or moral cleansing. The presiding deities of the pilgrimages are just the overt excuses, the actual cleansing is achieved through the complete act of pilgrimage—beginning from the arduous journey, the self-deprivation in some form or other, the dip in the holy water, the worship and the charity. Pilgrimage thus is a composite act which, on the one hand, remits sins and on the other, earns merits. The moral debit is first balanced and then is turned into credit. Actually, all deflective measures are aimed at scoring over fate and pilgrimage does this in a ritually complex manner.

Pilgrimages thus had a mystique about them. Topologically it could not always be satisfactorily explained. Historically, except for Kurukṣetra[49] the others do not justify the degree of sanctity attributed to them. The Purāṇas supplied the demand for myths to explain the sanctity of the pilgrimages; but these myths may have been an after-thought, invented to explain the 'hagios', sanctity, of the place. As in present day India when a person feels, thinks or dreams that a spot is God-inhabited, that itself endows it with sacrality. What does this sacrality do? For most pilgrimages the scriptures have a formula of 'absolution from sins committed over many births', repeated *ad infinitum.* In other words, they act as agents of fate *in situ.* Visits undertaken with the right reverential attitude, rites performed there—bath, worship and charity—according to scriptural prescriptions take away the punishments otherwise due to the sinner. And the punishments could be extremely severe because of the nature of the sins and the duration of time, the number of lives over which these have been committed. Normally long stays in hell or birth in extremely loathsome stations, existence as gnomes or despicable creatures, for lengthy periods—these the sinners had deserved. And when we are told that pilgrimages wash the slate clean, then it is clear that they act as mysterious

---

49 If the battle was really a historic one, which is doubtful.

and exceptionally powerful agents of fate, representing the forgiving, remitting, saving face of a supremely benign Providence. The fact that the innumerable pilgrimages situated throughout the length and breadth of India—east, west, north and south—besides indicating the place where the particular Purāṇas were composed also signify the intention of the composers to make it easy for the inhabitants of the different quarters of the country to undertake a trip to the pilgrimage nearest to their residence. Psychologically, the sense of absolution—which follows the cathartic confession and the priest's absolution—is a very real benefit. It not only takes away the burden of past sins, known and unknown, over the millions of lives over which he has no control in the present life, but this very relief, this feeling of freedom from guilt instils in him a courage to live better and to face life with a greater sense of assurance. At least for those who take pilgrimage seriously and seek to derive this sense of moral cleansing from them.

Pilgrimages had also an educative function, bringing pilgrims from distant areas in touch with not only different landscapes but with unfamiliar ethos and socio-cultural values, thus enlarging the pilgrims' horizons of awareness. This generated a sense of release and emancipation, which brought them peace and spiritual tranquillity. This indirectly mitigates some of the fear of fate.

One important, even absolutely bounden duty of the pilgrim is to give gifts to brahmins. On that depends the successful completion of the pilgrimage and its propitiatory potency. "Giving a living to the twice-born is said to be highly meritorious. And if (the recipient) happens to be one with spiritual knowledge the (fruit of the) gift becomes everlasting. A virtuous person with a wife, versed in the scriptures and the Vedas, to such a one if a man gives an established living—listen to the fruit of his merits: (this giver) lives in Viṣṇu's realm together with two crores of families from his mother's and father's lines freed from sin."[50] A whole chapter of two hundred and twelve verses is composed on the merits of charity. "The man who sweeps a temple (a gift of labour) lives for those many thousand kalpas in Viṣṇu's realm as the specks of dust he sweeps"[51] "There is no higher gift than of food in the three worlds."[52] "Gifts to a twice-born on an ordinary day is meritorious, but those

---

50 *Bṛhamāradṣya* 13: 27–29.

51 *Op. Cit.*, 13: 178–79; A Kalpa consists of creation, duration and destruction of an acon.

52 *Bṛhaddharma*, Uttara 15: 26.

on a new-moon or full-moon day fetch a hundredfold merit."[53] Charity is sought to be made obligatory with strictures like "after a religious ceremony if the performer fails to give gifts to brahmins through accident or ignorance, the evil or sin doubles after a 'muhūrta', multiplies by six after a night, by ten after three nights, by twenty after a week, by a hundred thousand after a month and by three crores after a year."[54] On the gifts depend whether the performer is to have many sons or be cursed with the extinction of his line, many wives or no wife, whether he will be poor or rich, handsome or ugly, have dead sons or long-lived ones, of many merits or deficient of limbs,[55] the text harps on defaulters in giving gifts to brahmins, increasing the magnitude of his crime until he is sent to hell and lives in a pool of urine for a thousand years.[56]

With the passage of time articles for gifts got specified. Beginning from food, sesame seeds (for oil), a cow, a thousand bulls, a golden horse, a mound of sesame seeds, a lower mound of sesame seeds, a Lakṣmī (icon, presumably), a maiden, a cow (for the sacrificial milk), it ran to the giver not refusing anything to any supplicant.[57] Brahmins symbolized the lokapālas, and hence rich and varied gifts were given to them on all occasions. Land, cows, gold, food and maidens figure in most catalogues, sesame seeds and ghee (clarified butter) figured next as cooking media. The *Mahābhārata* has lists of gifts of articles with the corresponding merits to the giver.[58] Charity could be offered individually or to groups. Thus constructing tanks, gardens, wells etc. are public works benefitting many and correspondingly earns greater merit for the donor. Similar are the merits of planting trees and parks.[59] But the commoner gifts to brahmins are gifts of a cow made of molasses, of mounds of rice, salt, gold, sesame seeds, cotton, clarified butter, gems, silver, sugar, cows, skins of spotted deer. These items grow and multiply until we hear of

[53] *Brahmarvaivarla* Prakṛti 9: 1–3; the chapter continues in the same vein up to verse 29.

[54] *Brahmavaiarla* P., Prakṛtikhaṇḍa, 42: 54–58.

[55] *Op. Cit.,* 43: 29–32.

[56] *Op. Cit.*, Kṛṣṇajanma, 87: 72–74.

[57] 'Kalpapādapa' *Liṅga P.*, Uttarabhāga, chs. 30–43.

[58] XIII: 65/24–63, 66; merits earned in the next world III: 184: 8–11; XIII: 67: 15–33; gifts of land, etc XIII: 68–4–21, of cows, of milkand milk products XM: 70: 27–35; 45–55, of umbrellas and shoes XIII: 97, the whole chapter.

[59] *Matsya* P., chs. 58–59.

'sixteen great gifts', 'the great gift called Hiraṇyagarbha', 'the great gift of Brahmāṇḍa', the gift of the wish-fulfilling tree, the wish-fulfilling cow, the great gift known as horse-and-chariot, the golden elephant, five ploughshares, the cow made of gems etc.[60] At the end of many sections of charity we are treated to a 'māhātmya' glorification section, in which charity is praised as the best form of righteousness and the donor is praised to the highest heaven.

Now, it is clear that gifts to brahmins placate the powers above so that fate is appeased and rescinds its adverse decrees. Thus charity is a power which is indirectly operative in affecting the verdicts of fate. Brahmins or sometimes the twice-born which technically means brahmins, kṣatriyas and vaiśyas but which due to the many changes in society by the Puranic times connoted only the brahmins had been singled out as the fittest recipients of gifts. Although some Purāṇas say that the recipient

This is analogous to oath. The foetus in the widowed Uttarā's womb was killed by Aśvatthāmān; Kṛṣṇa performed a satyakriyā and revived it and thus ensured the continuity of the Pāṇḍava line.[61] "In a society where public authority is weak and legal institutions rudimentary, the oath assumes a special importance as a means of making such contracts binding and of enforcing group responsibility for the behaviour of individuals and it requires supernatural sanctions in order to be effective."[62] When Śītā called upon the Gods to testify to her innocence and in her utter agony attempted to commit suicide by self-immolation on a pyre, the whole affair took upon the appearance of a 'satyakriyā' after she was vindicated by the Gods. The simpler and earlier form of satyakriyā was performed, when exasperated at Māra's repeated offers of power and dominion as the latter was tempting him, Buddha touched the earth saying that the overlordship of the earth belonged to him. And the earth vindicated his claim, there was an earthquake.

In Buddhist literature there are several instances of the satyakriyā. In one jātaka an act of truth freed Polajanaka.[63] In another the dead boy Sāma's guardian angel Vahuśodarī made an act of truth, is parents, too, did the same,

---

[60] *Matsya* chs. 81–91, 204, 205, 273–288, Kūrma ch. 26, *Agni*, ch. 206–213.

[61] *Mbh* XIV: 68: 20–24.

[62] Wilson, 1983, p. 36.

[63] No. 539, *Mahājanaka*.

at the end of which the dead boy came back to life.[64] In a third instance when Caṇḍa was taken to the sacrificial enclosure and Khaṇḍa was about to cut his head off, Caṇḍa's wife made a satyakriyā and her husband was saved.[65] These satyakriyās not only counter false charges but compel nature to act in the performer's favour. Thus in two instances, the dead came back to life. This is the domain of fate and these very instances clearly prove that a man's or woman's clear conscience can put pressure on fate itself and compel it to oblige them. These tales, contemporaneous with the *Rāmāyaṇa* have the same purpose; vindication of the innocent with the supernatural testimony. This is the earliest type of oath, as we have seen earlier, the Vedic literature has a parallel to it.

'The vow' on the other hand, "is a promise to the saint to perform certain actions... a utilization of idioms taken from gift exchange and notions of transactions and reciprocity among equals or from quite inegalitarian debt relationships or from a variety of forms of patronage somewhere between... a sacralization of such secular lies and structures to which they belong, or... an invasion of the sacred sphere before wholly inappropriate consideration."[66] The saint in the Indian background is often the officiating priest, who is supposed to implore a God to grant the supplicant's wishes. Technically, the vow is 'vrata' which literally means *Lebensmittel,* what a man lives on. In practice, for most vratas there is a period of fast enjoined and food, its nature, quantity and frequency forms one of the constituent elements by which the officiating priest, and through him the God-head, is placated.

All the days of the two lunar fortnights have special vows attached to them, some with special names or associations attached to them. Thus besides the 'pratipada' (second day of either fortnight), second, third, etc., we have Jayantyaṣṭamī, Akhaṇḍa Dvādaśī, etc.[67] Beside these, there is a short homily on the vow itself,[68] on the night of Śiva,[69] the season vows,[70] etc. More special

---

[64] No., 540, *Sāma.*

[65] No., 542. *Khaṇḍhala.*

[66] Wilson, 1983, p. 16,

[67] *Agni* P., ch. 175–194

[68] Ch. 175.

[69] Ch. 193.

[70] Ch. 198.

occasions like offerings to Agastya[71] or the fifth of Bhīṣma,[72] the full-moon[73] Rukmiṇī, (Kṛṣṇa's wife, the fortunatelady has a vow to her name),[74] there are vows for the days of the week, for seasons for gift of lamps.[75] Even the prostitute has a vow for 'the bed never to be vacant'[76] The *Brhānnaradīya* has the best part of six whole chapters on vows.[77] As the heavenly bodies were gaining ritual predominance we have special vows for them. Nakṣatrapuruṣa or the man in the star is the subject of a vow,[78] there is one for the sun,[79] one for the moon with his favourite wife Rohṇī,[80] for a happy bed.[81] There is even a vow which ensures, the overlordship of the seven worlds;[82] another for attaining the good conduct of holy women.[83] Then the days of the fortnight with special names like Śuklātṛītiyā, Viśokasaptamī, phalasaptamī, Śarkarā-saptamī, Kamalāsaptamī, Mandārasaptamī and so on. The same theme is treated in many Purāṇas. The eleventh day of the lunar fortnight is specially observed with different rites; this has been treated at great length[84] to emphasize its special significance. Similarly, certain vows are based on myths; Sāvitrī managed to thwart Yama's claim over her husband's life and reclaim him from death; hence a special Sāvitrī vrata was instituted.[85] The Navarātra vrata remits all the sins of a great sinner.[86] Special vows are directed to

---

71 Ch. 206.

72 Ch. 205.

73 Ch. 207

74 *Kalki* P., 3: 17; the whole chapter.

75 *Angi* P., chs. 195, 197–199.

76 Aśūnyaśayana. Ch. 16.

77 Ch. 16–21.

78 *Matsya* P., Ch. 54.

79 Ch. 55.

80 Ch. 57.

81 Saubhagyaśayana, Ch. 60.

82 Ch. 61.

83 Ch. 69.

84 *Padma sṛṣṭi*. Chs. 22–26, 29.

85 *Brahmavaivarta*, prakṛti, 23: 14–39.

86 *Devībhāgavata*, III: 27: 29.

special Gods, like the Pāśupata to Śiva.[87] Miscellaneous vows are treated in different sections of the various Purāṇas.[88]

Two characteristics of the vratas demand special attention. The first we have had occasion to mention before, viz. that vratas appear rather late in the religious scene and they rapidly multiply with time, i.e., the later Purāṇas have a greater number of vratas. Second, most vratas are confined to the womens' world. Women were generally neglected in the earlier phases of religion. Deprived of the right to investiture of the sacred thread[89] they could not perform the sacrifice except with silent presence and incidental manual assistance. In the Puranic pūjā, also, the officiating priest who performed the actual ritual was a man and in his absence any brahmin male versed in the scriptures could substitute; but never a woman. So debarred from other avenues of actively earning religious merit the women clung to the vrata. Together with the husband or other male members of the family, she could visit a pilgrimage, but not having any individual income or wealth[90] she had no access to a fund which would enable her to give gifts; so by and large, charity, too, was beyond her means. But she had her own anxieties, her worries about her near and dear ones, her fear of widowhood, of having co-wives, of penury, of the well-being of her husband and children, of the wrath of some constellation of divinity. In order to allay these fears and assuage her anxieties the priests kept inventing vrata after vrata. The husband and in-laws saw that they would be the ultimate beneficiaries, so they sanctioned her undertaking the vows which kept her engaged in pious activities and whose benefits came to them.[91] She also lost her sense of guilt, as feeding a brahmin and giving gifts to him have ever been described as redemptive acts. Moreover, she had the satisfaction of moulding her and her in-laws' fate in a favourable direction. She who was ritually neglected and was virtually a social non-entity, assumed a sort of identity and the assurance of a smooth sailing of the family's fortune through the vrata, for, by observing the various occasional,

---

87 *Liṅga Purāṇa.*, Chs. 81–86; on different aspects and functions ascribed to Śiva.

88 cf padma, ch. 80–81; Bṛhannāradṣya, Chs. 19–21; Matsya, chs. 55–100; Agni, chs. 176–207 et al.

89 and incidentally, therefore, from institutional education, for 'upanayana' was the pre-requisite of education.

90 with a few exceptions.

91 for there Is no 'vrata' that a married woman could perform for the well-being of her parents and siblings.

seasonal and temporary vows for which she fasted, took upon herself some self-abnegation, eventually earned a proportionate merit to overrule the adverse verdicts of fate. Few of the vratas have any direct promise for the well-being of the woman herself,[92] yet she so merged her identity with those of her marital family that she indirectly sensed this identity as the performer of the vratas.

The absence of anything resembling vows[93] in the Vedic religion and its abrupt and conspicuous efflorescence during the Puranic period leads us to the conjecture that 'vrata' had been a mode of religious practice among the pre-Aryans. After the racial miscegenation and cultural amalgamation between the indigenous Austria Dravidian and other pre-Aryans, their religious practices resurged and with these the vrata also surfaced in the Puranic society in a very big and significant way. But then, the Vedas do not record personal or familial rites, so, presumably, there were counterparts of vratas in the Little Tradition even in the Vedic age.

An acknowledged method of earning spiritual merit from very olden times is meditation. Quite possibly, there were pre-Aryan indigenous people who practised meditation as a religious activity. In the first stage of miscegenation of the Aryan and the indigenous population there are clear traces of Aryan sneer for these 'munis' or 'yatis'—this latter Indra delivered over to wolf-hounds. However, with time a section of the mixed people took more kindly to meditation. By the time of the Upaniṣads, Brahman or Puruṣa himself engaged in meditation, in order to create. So meditation was invested with creative potentiality. It somehow raised the person above the mundane sphere and vested him with some supernatural power and glory.

Meditation is concentration on a God, a symbol or a concept for a length of time with the objective of gaining some material or spiritual benefits. It presupposes austerity and austerity in all climes and times denotes self-abnegation whereby a God feels indebted and obliged to fulfil the meditator's wishes. In Brahmanism, Buddhism and Jainism austerity is a value in itself; meditation raises it to a higher spiritual level and augments it with extra piety and charisma. Time and again, Indra was alarmed at a mortal's meditation

---

[92] except those directed at preventing widowhood, which however, directly assured a longer life for the husband.

[93] except short periods of self-deprivation for the sacrificer before engaging in a sacrifice.

and hurriedly sent a nymph to distract him so that the meditator should not compel the Gods to grant his desire which could be embarassing or inconvenient for the Gods. Not only men but demons and monsters also meditate for astronomical number of years and unless thwarted by the wiles of the Gods, wrested their desires from the Gods. There are instances of objectless meditation undertaken usually by the Gods for their spiritual uplift.[94] But most frequently the non-attached meditation of Gods preceded creation. Sometimes they simply meditated gratuitously. But the association of meditation with creation[95] raised it to a cosmic power with which man or God could dictate terms to fate, avert the verdicts of fate, deflect them and achieve what they, not fate, wished.

In the epics, meditation had become a multi-faceted process of approaching the supernatural. In the face of an impending calamity the threatened person began to meditate. To avert a curse, death, disease and misfortunes, meditation was prescribed. When Diti's son Vṛtra was killed by Indra, she sat and meditated, her husband Mārīca granted her the boon of a son who would slay Indra.[96] This, however, was counteracted by Indra's wiles.[97] When Viśvāmitra's military force was rendered futile, he meditated and attained brahminhood.[98] Viśvāmitra had fallen for the charms of the nymph Menakā, he repented and was directed by Brahman to meditate as atonement. With upraised hand, without leaning against any prop, subsisting on air alone, he meditated penitently for ten thousand years and suffered various hardships.[99] As an irate kṣatriya, Viśvāmitra had cursed Rambhā and was repentant, practised penance to conquer such evil propensities and finally attained brahminhood.[100] At the very beginning of the *Rāmāyaṇa*, Vālmikī, the author of the epic meditated before undertaking this epos of stupendous significance. Meditation enhanced his spiritual and creative power and equipped him with divine blessing so that he could accomplish the task. Rāvaṇa, the ambitious

---

94 One wonders if any kind of imperfection lurked in these Gods so that they engaged in meditation for spiritual improvement.

95 from the time of the Upaniṣads.

96 Rāmāyaṇa I: 46: 1–5.

97 *Op. Cit.*, I: 47: 1–8.

98 *Op. Cit.*, I: 47: 63.

99 *Op. Cit.*, I: 63: 23–75.

100 *Op. Cit.*, I: 65: 20.

monster king, practised meditation for thousands of years and extorted boons from Brahman that he would be invulnerable to almost all creatures. He wrested Kuvera's chariot and reigned with great aplomb. But somewhere the meditation leaked and in the ultimate reckoning he lost all through lust for a mortal woman.

We have various instances of meditation in the *Mahābhārata,* even a short section on meditation in the abstract and the merits which it generates.[101] Fasting is almost the invariable prerequisite of meditation. Various austerities associated with meditation and merits accruing from them are discussed.[102] In the Buddhist *Mahāvagga, I.alitavistāra, Mahāuastu* we have detailed descriptions of the various stages of Buddha's own meditation. This was prompted by the desire to solve the basic problem of existence, rebirth, karman, desire and finding out the way to terminate the chain of repeated existences. The Jātakas and other Buddhist texts have many persons engaged in meditation. The power of meditation is such that whenever a man engages in austerities Indra's seat in heaven becomes hot and he descends to find out the reason. In the epics the Gods adopt various means to prevent a man from becoming so pious as to challenge Indra's station. Through meditation Triśanku was going to heaven but half-way up he realized that his store of merit acquired through meditation fell short of the required amount and he hung in midair because the Gods pushed him down.[103] In the *Mahābhārata* we have many sages who meditate piously for long stretches and in the intervals brag and curse others; Viśvāmitra is one such, Durvāsas is another. Still another is the sage Cyavana who practised such a stiff penance for such a long time that an ant hill grew up around his body. But almost at the first provocation, when a very young girl pricked the two eyes visible through the ant-hill, the sage flew into a rage and cursed her father and all who had come with him. When the king, her father, sought to placate and mollify him with gifts and promises, he refused to thaw until the king offered him his very young daughter. Apparently the long meditation had not given him victory over the first two passions: wrath and desire.[104] Thus some meditations remain spiritually barren although they entail great physical hardships for a

[101] XIII: 106: 3ff.

[102] XIII: 110: 5–137.

[103] *Bhāgavata* P., 9: 7.

[104] *Mbh.* III: 122.

long period. In such cases fate conquers and demolishes whatever merit was earned through the meditation. Yayāti who, unable to meet the financial demands of Gālava, a brahmin scholar, offered her young unmarried daughter Mādhavī and asked the young student Gālava to hire her out to kings and demand money on her giving birth to a son to each of them. In this way Gālava hired her out to three kings and collected enough money to pay his preceptor's fees. Mādhavī, the princess, then began to meditate and kept acquiring merit. Yayāti wanted to ascend to heaven, but half-way through, discovered the shortage of his fund of merits, came down and begged Mādhavī to lend him some she had laid by. With this merit borrowed from a daughter (whom he had cruelly humiliated by hiring her out to strangers to make up for the dearth of his treasury) he now ascended heaven by the spiritual wealth she had acquired.[105] This, however, is one of the rare instances where a woman meditates. Normally, she is forbidden to meditate without her husband's permission. The exceptions are found plentifully in the later Purāṇas like the *Devībhāgavata, Bṛhannāradīya, Bṛhmavaivarta,* etc. where goddesses when piqued at something leave the home and/or husband in a huff and engage in an austere meditation and gain their objective, usually to teach the husband or co-wife a lesson, or even to improve her complexion!

In the *Harivaṃśa* Vajranābha the demon practised stiff meditation, Brahman was pleased and made him invincible and the lord of the city Vajrapura.[106] The *Brahmavaivarta* Purāṇa gives a cardinal truth about meditation: when a righteous man meditates in a holy land for a long time, the Gods themselves recompense his penance; this indeed is beyond doubt.

Meditation, we have seen, can be of various kinds with different objectives: it can be (a) penitential for the removal of some sin, (b) for gaining a mundane object like obtaining a kingdom, a suitable partner or a heroic or pious son, (c) for minor immediate issuses, like improving the complexion or teaching the husband or co-wife or an enemy a lesson; but it can also be, (d) for accumulating merit, (e) it can give a man or God creative power as is frequently the case in the *Mahābhārata,* there at Brahman's command Śiva meditates for long aeons to accumulate sufficient spiritual and creative power. Even in the Upaniṣads Brahman meditates before creation; Vālmīki meditates before composing the *Rāmāyaṇa*. In all its aspects it counters fate, in

[105] *Mbh* V: 118–22.

[106] II: 91: 7.

anticipation or in retrospection. But the merit accumulated is treated by the scripture as worldly asset: it can be enjoyed in the form the earner covets, it can be given away, it can be destroyed by counterproductive acts or passions like lust or wrath.

Meditation, the scriptures tell us, is open to all; only for women it is severely restricted. But Gods, men, yakṣas, demons and monsters all meditate and unless thwarted by jealous Gods, attain their objectives. Since 'munis' and 'yatis' figure early in *Ṛgveda,* and since Indra looks upon them spitefully, it seems that it was a pre-Aryan practice which won followers steadily down the ages. People took resort to it as yet another path along which they could avert fate.

Meditation is treated like currency notes which can be encashed at will, deposited in safe custody for any length of time without increasing or diminishing; it can be lent or donated. But like money it is power and as power it can be used in an invisible spiritual bargaining with fate.

Where fate decrees punishment in this life or in subsequent ones, one emotional attitude was proclaimed as to be able to counter it: devotion to one's favourite God (iṣṭa devatā). Of the five sects: Śaiva, Vaiṣṇava, Śākta, Saura and Gāṇapatya; the first three hold the position of greater popularity where devotion to the cardinal deity is held to be potent. Potent against fate. In other words, if a man is devoted to his God, through this devotion he helps achieve his objective. Needless to say, the God concerned acts on his devotee's behalf, but theoretically the devotion itself serves its end. The *Bhāgavata* Purāṇa which, is regarded as the supreme scripture of bhakti, says: Even a caṇḍāla (the lowest rung in the caste hierarchy) (if he is) devoted to me (i.e. Kṛṣṇa), his devotion will prevent future births.[107] In other words, his devotion liberates him from the chain of rebirths—the spiritual *summum bonum* is thus attained through devotion. The syntax is of special significance: it is not Kṛṣṇa who is the direct agent of liberation, but the devotion itself acts and achieves the ultimate goal.

In the *Bhagavadgītā* Kṛṣṇa speaks about "being devoted to the Lord with utter surrender in everything and through his grace he (Arjuna) will attain supreme peace and the highest eternal spiritual station."[108] Kṛṣṇa gives out an unequivocal and unambiguous call to a prospective devotee: "Give up all

[107] XI: 14: 21 cd.

[108] XVIII: 62.

other laws of piety and take shelter in me alone, I shall deliver thee from all sins; do not grieve."[109] We are reminded of Christ's claim, "I am the way, the truth and the life, no man cometh unto the father but by me."[110]

What is devotion, bhakti? The late text *Haribhaktivilāsa* defines it as: " "the determination to be on (the God's) side, the repudiation of all hostility, the faith that 'I shall keep it', the acceptance of (the God) as the preserver, throwing oneself into his work—these are the six-characteristics of taking recourse to a God."[111] These can be summed up by "total self-surrender to one's God'. Bhakti is equivalent to works. Thus 'the fruit one gets by observing the cāndrāyaṇa vow, the same fruit is obtained by seeing Kṛṣṇa on an altar."[112]

What are the physical manifestations of bhakti? If one's preceptor is graciously inclined, Hari himself is pleased and he who is immersed in his God, dances, shouts like a braggart, laughs and moves about, falls on the ground utterly unselfconscious and loses all sense of distance.[113] The same text says that bhakti is the eternal nature which reveals the treasure of Brahman, the (nature) of Śiva, Viṣṇu and Brahmaṇ, the best of the Vedas and other (scriptures).[114] The yogin (mendicant) who has settled his mind through devotion, who, praising His name leaves his body is released from desire and action.[115] How is this devotion generated? Most texts say it is uncaused; such devotion is superior to success.[116] Another text says that devotion to Bhagavat comes from good fortune.[117] Vyāsa says to Janamejaya: "you are indeed fortunate that you have this sincere devotion to the Goddess. Even if a caṇḍāla serves Viṣṇu he redeems hundreds of thousands of ancestors and successors."[118]

---

[109] XVIII: 66.

[110] John XIV: 6.

[111] Vilāsa 11: 417.

[112] Brahma P., 32: 72; the whole chapter lists such equations nullifying the significance of sacrifice and glorifying devotion, positing it as a valid and adequate substitute.

[113] *Kalki* P., III: 11: 34, 42.

[114] *Ibid.*, verse 44.

[115] *Bhāgavata* P., I: 9: 23.

[116] *Op. Cit.*, III: 25: 33.

[117] *Devībhāgavata,* VII: 31: 3.

[118] *Op. Cit.*, IX: 24: 3.

We must remember that even after devotion took over as a valid mode of approach to divinity, there co-existed other modes— karman and jñāna, work and gnosis and to some extent devotion ran counter to these. Hence there were those who sought to stem this tide of devotion and opposed it (a) as not adequate, and saying that (b) it cheapens the piety of the devotee by insidiously comparing it with other strenuous modes of approach. The *Bṛhannāradīya* Purāṇa says, "he who gives up karman and lives on devotion alone, Viṣṇu is not pleased with him as Viṣṇu has to be worshipped according to the ritual tradition. Therefore, one's devotion to Hari should not run counter to his own action."[119] On the other hand, repudiation of all pious action on the excuse that devotion is the be-all and end-all of the righteous person is ridiculed by the *Mārkaṇḍeya* Purāṇa: "Those devotees of Viṣṇu who have the cinder-mark on their forehead are the best of the Bhāgavatas,"[120] or "those who observe the vow of the eleventh day of the lunar fortnights are the best of the Bhāgavatas."[121] Or "the name of the Gāṅgā destroys all worldly griefs."[122]

Bhakti, devotion appears late in the religious scene. It is the only wholly emotive approach to the sacred. Faith, another emotive path was implicitly present in ritual and some other late Puranic approaches, but its emotive content is not so powerful and it is not a complete approach by itself. In a sense it is the easiest of the paths which does not entail ritual action, strenuous intellectual effort to attain liberating knowledge or expensive gifts, vows or pilgrimages. It is open to all and through the force of emotive power it controls fate.

Devotion swept over India for over two centuries; the Nayanars[123] and the Alwars[124] in the south, the Vaiṣṇavas, Śaivas and Śāktas in the north clung to bhakti as an adequate substitute for all karman, all knowledge. In a way, this attitude devalued bhakti itself as the mere muttering of the name, a dip in the Gaṅgā, the daily songs, etc. became admissible substitutes of the

119 As laid down by the scriptures, according to his caste and āśrama i.e., stage of life; 15: 8, 10.

120 i.e., Viṣṇu-devotees, I: 5: 68.

121 *Op. Cit.*, I: 5: 74.

122 *Op. Cit.*, I: 6: 26.

123 Nayanars, Śiva-worshippeis.

124 Viṣṇu-worshippers.

more active, arduous worship or the long and probing search for theological knowledge. As if striking a bargain with fate, the scriptures endow meditation with a unique power, because compared to vows, charity or pilgrimages it is much more spiritual, abstract, in a direct line with the Gods and the supernatural and therefore has a greater charisma and is closer in contact with the powers which control a man's destiny. And throughout literature this role of meditation has been magnified. Those who meditate immediately transcend the mundane sphere, presumably because Brahman meditated before creating, other Gods meditated and gained their objectives, Viśvāmitra meditated and became a brahmin, sages meditate and draw closer to the Gods. And the Gods meditate on Brahman — not for any gain but to get spiritually closer to the cosmic power-complex. He who meditates is symbolically at pār with these hierophanies and fate will no doubt be malleable and obedient to them.

Just as meditation supplies a link with the powers that be, there are other channels to approach the hierophany of which fate is an experiential evidence. Magic and sorcery are two such channels. To the supernatural powers belong the practices of sorcery and magic rites. Sorcery is usually associated with evil. There is a person who officiates in a rite; this person is appointed by one who has direct stakes and on his or on the community's behalf this sorcerer performs some rites in which he is in touch with the supernatural and succeeds in baffling fate.

Sorcery is essentially bound up with the belief in witchcraft; wizards and witches wield destructive power either through a direct access to die nether world or through ghosts or spirits who obey the wizards or shamans, do their bidding and manipulate supernatural power to do some harm to the person the enchanter signifies. From the earliest times man has believed that the nether world holds a different kind of potency from the upper world, that it can do real harm to man and beast.

"Essentially witch-belief can be reduced to the fact that some people put the blame for some of their sufferings on a peculiar power which is usually regarded as evil. This power is either seen as someting which can be manipulated or served by individuals."[125] Witches, wizards, shamans, soothsayers, sorcerers and magicians are a broad group with some shades of distinction in their functions but they work as a team and have been doing

[125] Carlton, 1972, Vol. II, p. 100.

so from primitive societies. Broadly again, soothsayers are the opposite numbers of prophets and oracles; wizards, witch-doctors and sorcerers of priests, while magicians can be of both hues. "There has never been any time in India, when personal enemies, diseases, curses have not been the subject of prayers for deliverance." (Before) "There were diseases which were sent by human sorcerers, demons or Gods or which were themselves demons."[126]

We remember the content and some peculiar characteristics of the *Atharvaveda.* There are many hymns with the express intent of doing harm to one's enemies or to a woman's co-wives. Diseases were frequently looked upon as demon-inspired and just as some hymns are truly therapeutic in content, others are for the witch-doctor, shaman, wizard or sorcerer's use. They invoke spirits, presumably from the nether world and summon them to accomplish specific tasks. For fever, worms, dropsy, consumption, jaundice, haemorrhage, falling hair and miscarriage, spirits from the underworld are commissioned in an arcane language, with definite names given to the spirits. The tradition is very old. The shaman renders the supernatural immediately available to the cult, acquiring It or Him or Her through spell, ritual or charismatic experience. Whether simple or complex, the religions of mankind regard direct revelation as primary, while institution and theology are secondary. The shaman is concerned with the primary vision, trance, ecstasy. The shaman is 'possessed' of the divinity. He mediates the cure of primitive religion."[127] The shaman in early Russia, China, Mexico and some other countries have their tasks less finely demarcated than the witches, wizards and soothsayers of medieval Europe and ancient India. Here the different agents had their appointed tasks more clearly defined. Frequently they were not 'possessed' (as in oracles) by the divinity, but had spirits from the nether world as their minions who accomplished the tasks they were commanded to carry out—be it by slaying the hostile person (enemy, rival or co-wife), or by harming them physically, or by curing specific ailments by driving out the avil spirits which caused them or by preventing the evil foetus-devouring monstresses and spirits who infested the upper and nether air. Sorcery is 'black magic' from the hostile force's or being's point of view; it was quite white from the performer's point of view. But if we consider the means—i.e., driving an evil spirit out by another evil spirit, it was black. But

[126] Rodhe, 1946, p. 78.

[127] Presler, 1976, p. 87.

from either angle it was the sorcerer fighting against fate. The enemy, rival, co-wife, the disease, barrenness, possible miscarriage were one's fated experience, the sorcerer's effort was to thwart it and thus challenge and fight fate. According to Arabian belief, however: "Sorcerers cannot protect from fate."[128] Arabian theology may have precluded the belief, but elsewhere, it was precisely with the aim of protection from the onslaughts of an adverse fate that sorcery was undertaken.

In Buddhist literature sorcerers and wizards play a significant role. In the *Mahlāvagga* Buddha performs many miracles with his magic power,[129] it is a long account of a series of miracles performed to convince the doubters, to edify believers and to establish his indisputable supremacy over the rival orders and sects.

In the same text we read of diseases arising from a philtre which, when administered brings the desired person under one's control. We read, "he was bewitched, was suffering from the results of sorcery."[130] Buddha also healed with his miraculous power[131] and even filled a granary by merely wishing so.[132] We shall first present a few instances from the Pāli jātakas where in certain texts sorcery proper is found. Thus we hear of a charm called Vedabbha which at certain conjunction of planets had to be repeated and the person had to gaze upwards to the skies and seven precious articles dropped, viz.; gold, silver, pearl, coral, cat's-eye, ruby and diamond.[133] Now this charm, given to a poor man was aimed at making him rich, thus defying fate's orders. In another tale Buddha was challenged, went to Taxila, learnt Vedic texts and elephant-lore in one night, returned and the next day discomfited his rival.[134] Buddha born as a very rich and prosperous man's son went to Taxila; there his syllabus included magic lore.[135] A wild boar picked up a magic gem.[136] A king set impossible tasks to Dhammadhvaja who accomplished them through

[128] Ringgern, 1955, p. 51.

[129] I: 15–21.

[130] VI: 14.

[131] *Op. Cit.*, VI: 23: 7.

[132] *Op. Cit.*, VI: 34: 1.

[133] No. 48, Vedabbha.

[134] No. 163, *Susṣma.*

[135] No. 185, Anabhirati.

[136] No. 186, Dadhivāhana.

magic power.[137] For a horse Buddha performed a number of miracles.[138] King Māndhātā also displayed magic power.[139] Priests advised the Vārāṇasī king to perform extremely cruel rites for gaining supremacy over other kings.[140] Some of the instances, however, are simply magical. Udaya who was renowned for his supernatural power could levitate and sit in the air.[141] On many occasions Buddha, some Bodhisattvas and other saints, too, demonstrated the power of levitation; in yoga it is reckoned as one of the minor siddhis which is not held in high respect.[142] A good spirit warned the mariners whose vessel was about to be sunk by an evil spirit; the mariners heeded the warning regarding the impending disaster and were saved.[143] What differentiates it from real sorcery is the absence of the human agent; here the good and evil spirits are in open and independent hostility. Another instance of divine magic was when Sakka found that a kinnara had died and his wife was lamenting woefully, he came and revived the dead kinnara.[144] Here, too the verdict of fate was altered by a God's compassion; the human agent is missing. Another tale tells how a poor childless woman got seven children by worshipping the indwelling spirit of a banyan tree.[145] This primitive belief in fertility cults associated with vegetation was so powerful that here the supernatural power acted directly without a huṃpan medium. A goblin had swallowed the first two princes of a Vārāṇasī king; the third prince, Buddha, was kept within an iron chamber. Eventually the goblin died and Buddha was saved.[146] The ghost is very much present as a reality in many tales. A jealous, childless queen became a monstress and gobbled up her co-wife's children at birth. The third child, mistaking her for his mother suckled her and she felt tender towards the babe, brought him up as her own son. She gave him a charm which made him invisible. He became an ogre and lost the charm.

---

137 No. 220, Dhammadhvaja.

138 No. 254, kuṇḍakakucchisindhava.

139 No. 258, Māndhātā.

140 No. 353, Dhonśakha.

141 No. 421, Gaṅgāmātā.

142 Yogasūtra, Ch. III.

143 No. 466, Samuddavānijja.

144 No. 485, Candakinnaraka.

145 No. 509, Hatthipāta.

146 No. 510, Ayoghara.

When he was about to eat king Jayaddisa the latter begged leave for a while to pay a debt. When the kim; returned, the ogre was so impressed that he was converted.[147] Here, too, there is an open battle between the forces of good and evil; but the tale begins with a caprice of fate: the infant mistaking the ogress for his mother. In the final tussle the power of goodness wins, for the prince was never fated to become an ogre and when he saw real goodness in king Jayaddisa keeping his word and coming back to die, the initial mistake of fate through which the prince had become an ogre was rectified. The absence of the sorcerer is here made up for by the ogress-ogre theme. In one jātaka we have a guardian angel who saves a man's life.[148] In a strange tale Buddha assumed an ascetic form, so did Sakka, some Gods, goblins and also some evil spirits, too.[149] This changing of forms, however, is pure magic, without the intervention of a sorcerer. Another instance of magic is found in the episode of Mahoṣadha who made plants grow tall overnight *et al*; he told the king, "wise men in this world learn magic."[150] So knowledge of magic was part of a wise man's lore, the sorcerer thus becomes redundant since magic power could be openly practised. Similarly, we hear of prince Vessantara's elephant which could bring rain and it was an elephant of good omen.[151] Tales of magic power abound in Buddhist literature possibly because what a sorcerer could do is done openly by monsters, ogress and evil spirits, hence the sorcerer is left out.

A biblical instance of sorcery comes to mind. Daniel approached the witch of Endor; at Daniel's bidding she conjured up the ghost or spirit of Samuel who forecast the future for Daniel.[152]

A much later reference to sorcery is found in the *Florentine Codex* which says that the "sorcerer is a wise man, a counsellor, a person of trust, serious, respected, revered, dignified, unreviled, not subject to insults ... He bewitches women ... deranges ... deludes, he causes them to be possessed. He deceives people, he confounds them."[153] Apparently, there is a contradiction between

---

[147] No. 513, Jayaddisa.

[148] No. 540, Sāma.

[149] No. 544, Mahānārdakassapa.

[150] No. 546, *Mahāummagga.*

[151] No. 547, Vessantara.

[152] I Samuel 28: 8–25.

[153] Bk X: 9.

the character of the sorcerer and his activities; this is resolved if we bear in mind that the sorcerer was (i) in direct contact with the divine powers and that he acted (ii) in the larger interests of the community which were not obvious to the uninitiated and appeared evil, although, in the ultimate analysis, it was for the well-being of the community.

From the Atharvaveda onwards we have various types of sorcery: Māraṇa (killing), stambhana (making a person inert), ucāṭana (making one mad with love), vasīkaraṇa (bringing someone under one's power) and śānti (bringing peace). Of these the first four are provoked by ill-will and fall in the domain of sorcery. What the sorcerer uses along with his charm or spells is the prescription for amulets, sheets of metal, inscriptions, symbols, drawings and paintings, figurines, sculpture, tools, medicine, effigy, alchemy and astrology.

Much of the sorcerer's trappings and equipment is semiotic and ritually imitative of the desired effect. Paintings, symbols, effigies are types for the actual prototypes who are the real objects of the sorcerer's rite. The underlying belief is that by imitating reality up to a point the sorcerer transforms it for the benefit of the person on whose behalf he seeks to deflect the unfavourable movements of fate.

We hear of magic beasts and birds in all mythologies. Vaśiṣṭha's cow which yielded whatever one wished, the Kāmadhenu, is mentioned in the *Rāmāyann.*[154] Among other magic objects the Puṣpaka plane, the Vāḍava fire, the wishful-filling tree (kalpadruma) and many similar things may be mentioned. Viśvāmitra gives divine weapons to Rāma and Lakṣmaṇa[155] and also the spells valā and ativalā[156] which he taught Rāma and Lakṣmaṇa for conquering hunger and thirst; Śarabhaṅga shed the dross of mortality by entering fire;[157] Rāma revived Ahalyā;[158] he countered monsters' spikes with arows.[159] Mārīca assumed the shape of a golden deer.[160] Kabandha slain by

[154] I: 52: 70, 117, et al.

[155] I: 27: 4–20.

[156] *Op. Cit.,* I: 22.

[157] III: 5: 39–42.

[158] 1: 49: 19.

[159] III: 20: 17.

[160] III: 42–43.

Rāma went to heaven.[161] Sabarīs self-immolation helped her obtain a divine shape.[162] Hanumat jumped across the sea, killing Siṃhikā and defeating Surasā.[163] By magic Rāvaṇa showed the severed head of Rāma to Sītā,[164] Rāma and Lakṣmaṇa were caught in the weapon (serpent-noose, nāgapāśa) and were released by Garuda,[165] the Brahmāstra of Indrajit was rendered impotent by the Viśalyakaraṇībrought by Hanumat for the hero-brothers' release.[166] Rāvaṇa's killing the illusory Sītā to scare Rāma with the sight;[167] the śakti spear was hurled and thwarted by magic,[168] Agastya instructing Rāma to recite the ditya-hṛdava spell for the final victory[169]—all these and many more constitute the magic strand in the *Rāmāyaṇa*.

The *Mahābhārata*, being four times in bulk as the *Rāmāyaṇa* has many more similar incidents of magical nature. Vegetable juice dripping from sage Maṅkaṇaka's body as a proof of the severity of his asceticism and his final dismay at finding cinder dropping from Śiva's body; this is one of the earliest such instances.[170] Agastya drinks up the ocean;[171] Mt. Vindhya bends down to let Agastya pass;[172] sage Kaśyapa's semen spilled on the ground, drunk by a doe made her pregnant.[173] The monstrous tale of the childless king Somaka who was advised by his sorcerer-like priest to sacrifice the son Jantu in order to obtain a hundred sons; it came to pass exactly as the priest had prescribed. The king and the priest, however, went to hell for this unnatural deed.[174] Kuntī conceived from Sūrya and the latter confirmed Kuntī's claim that Karṇa

---

161 *Op. Cit.*, III: 69–70.

162 *Op. Cit.*, III: 74.

163 VI; 19: 2.

164 VI; 31.

165 VI: 50: 36–48.

166 VI: 73, 74.

167 VI: 81.

168 VI: 101: 31–45.

169 VI: 105.

170 ID: 81: 97–107.

171 III: 101: 7–102.

172 This was stop to humiliate Vindhya who had wanted the Sun to circumambulate it as the latter did Mt. Meru.

173 III: 110: 11–17.

174 III: 127–28.

was his son.[175] Śikhaṇḍī changed sex in order to take vengeance on Bhīṣma who had unwittingly humiliated her before.[176]

The *Harivnṃśa,* a sequel to the *Māhabhārata,* has quite a few magical incidents, most of which are boyhood feats of Kṛṣṇa. Thus the breaking of Śakaṭa, the killing of Putanā, the uprooting of the twin Arjuna trees are described.[177] Wolves came out from the pores of his body, destroyed the cattle and frightened their owners who then accepted Kṛṣṇa's decision about something.[178] Kṛṣṇa defeated the mighty serpent king Kāliya.[179] The Dhenuka demon was killed by Balarāma[180] who also killed the fearful demon Pralamba in a prolonged fight.[181] Indra caused a tumultuous shower, the cowherd community was endangered; Kṛṣṇa bodily uplifted the Govardhana hill to give them a shelter.[182] The Ariṣṭa demon, too, was killed by Kṛṣṇa[183] and as an infant Kṛṣṇa sucked the venomous monstress Putanā so hard that she perished; she had secretly poisoned her own milk to kill Kṛṣṇa.[184] The horse-shaped demon Keśin also fell at Kṛṣṇa's hands[185] as did the violent demon wrestlers Cāṇūra and Muṣṭika at Balarāma's and the elephant demon Kuvalayāpīḍa.[186]

Such displays of magic power are common to all religions. One remembers Buddha and Jesus walking on water and feeding the multitude with very scanty food, or Buddha's fire-sermon and many similar feats. "Magic, witchcraft and sorcery are rooted in traditional customary ideas whereby cultures categorize and order the universe around them. As such they not only are intertwined with every aspect of culture, thought and language but also provide coherent and systematic means to influence the world in which man lives."[187]

---

[175] V: 144: 1-3.

[176] V: 144: 1-3.

[177] Viṣṇuparvan: 6: 1-21, 22-29; 7; 13-22.

[178] 9: 1-35.

[179] Ch. 12.

[180] Ch. 13.

[181] Ch. 14.

[182] Chs. 17, 18.

[183] Ch. 21.

[184] Ch. 22.

[185] Ch. 24.

[186] Chs. 28-29.

[187] Yalman, 'Magic' *International Encyclopaedia,* 1969, p. 527.

Magic, sorcery, witchcraft are thus ubiquitous and international. They are the stuff of which folk lore is fashioned and folk lore has everywhere shaped and modified religion. They are a special attempt at gaining control over nature and human destiny. In the Vedic and post-Vedic literature the word 'abhicāra' denotes magic rites calculated to do harm to one's enemies. By semantic expansion of meaning the word covers "rites which a sorcerer or wizard performs not only to harm a person but also to create evil forces." When Duryodhana, *in extremis,* had been rescued by the Pāṇḍavas and felt so deeply mortified that he sat moping, contemplating suicide. Kṛtyā, the evil sorcery-power, took him to the nether world, morally upheld and succoured him, told him that he, Duryodhana had been created by kṛtyā.[188] Again, we hear that Raibhya summoned a kṛtyā through which he killed Yavakrīta.[189] Yātudhānī, a demon power was created by Vṛṣādarbhi and commissioned to kill the seven sages, the saptarṣi.[190] When sages or Gods create a destructive force they do so either to defeat some evil or to take a just vengeance. In other words their action preserves the balance and harmony in creation and therefore, cannot be categorized as sorcery. Similarly when they perform a magical act it aims at convincing the doubters, to retrieve backsliders and generally to demonstrate their divinity.

The *Viṣṇudharmottara* Purṇ̄na has three whole chapters on sorcery and magic covering 'abhicāra' and 'kṛtyā' which are directed against or give rise to different diseases.[191] In a later chapter Buddha is clearly identified with Mahāmoha the cosmic illusion, the arch-enemy according to late Vedanta theology; Mahāmoha means the great delusion. Here Mahāmoha was born of a malevolent kṛtyā rite performed by the demons Ṣaṇḍa and Marka for the destruction of the Gods. Buddha's followers and devotees have been denounced at every step.[192] Evidently, this late Purāṇa draws upon the *Mahābhārata* account of the creation of the epic antagonist Duryodhana and also on the eleventh century drama *Prabodhacandrodaya* which aims at establishing the theology of bhakti for Viṣṇu; there the antagonist is Mahāmoha. However, the concept of the creation of an evil personality through sorcery rites performed

---

[188] Mbh III: 239: 22.

[189] Mbh III: 124: 39.

[190] Mbh III: 94: 40.

[191] Chs. 28, 31, 32.

[192] Ch. 66.

by demons is an accepted one which runs through Indian literature for over a millennium and a half. It is obvious that sorcery was a widely practised and generally accepted mode of controlling nature and fate in favour of the practitioner who wishes to destroy whatever seems to obstruct his desires or well-being. Thus sorcery challenged fate as a powerful adversary, it sometimes performed propitiatory rites also to achieve the good intended for the supplicant.

In the *Popol Vuh* the first and second creations by the Gods are said to have been unsuccessful. 'Then they said to the soothsayers: 'Cast the lot with your grains of corn.' They went down at once to make their divination and cast their lots..." 'Fate, Creatures,' said an old woman and an old man ...' creation.'[193] 'This is an extremely significant account of creation. It tells of the two futile attempts by the Gods to create; so the creation is not divine in its origin. These same Gods then summon and commision the soothsayers to create, by casting the lot with their grain—a time-honoured practice of sorcery. The soothsayers obeyed and presumably cast lots with their grains and then uttered the creative words, 'fate, creatures, creation'. The first thing to be created was fate, then living beings and then the inanimate creation. And who are these soothsayers? And old woman mentioned first—and then an old man, a typical pair of a witch-cum-wizard sorcerer team.

It is rather striking that the *Popol Vuh* views the witch-and-wizard pair as cosmokrators; they invoke creation into being with their creatively charged logos. Here the grains and the words are together potent enough to create; later sorcerers use some accoutrements and articles, but what really is regarded as potent are the charms and spells they mutter. Another interesting point is that the Gods ask the creative team to cast their lots. Lot is fate and fate is the prime creator in this myth, the Gods themselves are here subservient, *manqué,* before the sorcerers and to their first creation fate. Not all mythologies are as candid as this. But even in the ancient heroic poem the Gods take sides, but what finally decides the outcome of the battle or the course of the protagonist's life is Destiny or Fate. Here sorcery alone is creative, done with the primitive method by the primitive types of persons who practise the myth-and-ritual paradigm: ritual in casting lots with grains and myth with the creative logos. And in the catalogue fate comes first, so successive sorcery rites are inherently connected with fate, directed to manipulate it. The domain

[193] Racinos, G and Morley, S.C. (ed.), 1947, p. 87.

of the sorcerer or soothsayer is fate and the universe comprising the animate and the inanimate. This is a prototype of sorcery and each sorcery rite is a minor etiological or a major cosmic creative act exerting power over fate and nature—animate and inanimate.

"Early man, frustrated by the absence or inaccessibility of the object which he desired to control instinctively went through the motions of the desired action in mimicry using a substitute for the object concerned. Out of this experience grew the belief in the efficacy of the 'analogical' methods which we call magic."[194] This explains the *Popol Vuh* version of the prototypical creation which actually places a familiar practice at a mythological distance of primordial time.

Like the other modes of coming to terms with fate, sorcery and magic, too, are the blind, helpless human's effort to somehow tap the supernatural sources and incline these powers favourably to his interest. While the shaman, soothsayer or sorcerer was looked upon with awe and expectant humility by supplicants, society has ever looked down upon witches whose services were never coveted or used, but who stood for the unmixed evil personality, bringing catastrophes on the community and death, disease and disaster on the individual's life. This explains the social persecution associated with witch-hunting.[195] And witches are always women, one of the persecuted sections of society, society which has been putting them to torture and death for many centuries. The attitude and practice still persists in India and elsewhere. This undeserved persecution possibly explains rites like the witches, sabbath, myths of flying on a broom-stick, the get-together of women who chose to identify themselves as witches perhaps as a self-assumed stigma, a kind of a social stamp—even though of the injurious kind—on their own identity. They also wished to wield some dialogue with the supernatural, with fate, which male chauvinism armed with theology branded as originating from the nether region which, therefore, needed to be eradicated, extirpated totally for the sake of preserving social health. Hence the witch-hunts everywhere in the world. It is still practised overtly in the third world and covertly in some areas of the 'developed' countries. It is the most socially detested form of attempting to modify fate.

---

[194] Gurney, 1954, p. 160.

[195] The medieval witch-hunt in Europe had an overtone of righteous punishment of heretics and thereby of heresy, through torture and the death penalty. We are, however, talking here of the specific persecution and killing of female witches whom society looks upon as the embodiment of the forces of evil.

CHAPTER 8

Vicarious Deflection

AS the person concerned can himself attempt to deflect the verdicts of fate through vows, charity, meditation, pilgrimage etc. similarly others also can act on his behalf with the same end in view. Sacrifices in Vedic times were sometimes performed by an officiating priest on behalf of his client who wanted a son (putreṣṭi) or overlordship (aśvamedha or rājasūya) or the destruction of his enemies (various abhicāra performances). This trend continued even when sacrifices gradually went out of vogue and in their place came the pūjās. The Little Tradition which had occupied itself with such mundane needs of the society, resorted to sympathetic magic and sought to deflect the adverse moves of fate.

Among such vicarious or indirect deflective measures the ones of first importance were curse and boons. Boons could be awarded (1) by a God to a God, (2) by a God to men and by (3) men to men while curses belong to these three categories as also to a fourth (4) by a man to a God. Boons or blessings can be deserved and undeserved. In the *Rāmāyaṇa*, Vaiśravaṇa received the boon of overlordship from Brahman.[1] Rāvaṇa, the ten-headed monster received a boon, from the reluctant Brahman only after he had severed his ten heads one by one and offered them to the God; he was blessed with being invincible to birds, serpents, daityas, demons and monsters. When Dakṣa cursed his son-in-law Çandra with consumption (for partiality to one of his twenty seven wives), Çandra or his wives, to be more precise, (as all twenty seven faced widowhood) took recourse to Śiva who countered the curse through a boon.[2] The stiff penance of the sonless gandharva Pañcaśikha pleased Śiva who granted him the boon of a son, Nārada.[3] Viṣṇu grants a boon to Śiva.[4]

---

1 VII: 3: 9–18.

2 *Brahmavaivarta* P. Prakṛti 9: 57, 58.

3 *Op. Cit., Gaṇapati,* 12: 42.

4 *Op. Cit., Gaṇapati,* ch. 6.

The later Purāṇas, esp. the *Brahmavaivarta, Devībhāgavata* and *Bṛhannāradīya* have many instances of Gods blessing each other, granting special boons when pleased with another God's conduct or simply for victory over formidable demons threatening Lhe safety of heaven — generally for the well-being of the universe. The *Brahmavaivarta* Purāṇa however, cuts at the root of any theological justification of curses and boons and says that 'curses and boons depend solely on fate.'

The optative mood[5] used in pronouncing boons reflects the community's belief and practice regarding boons. One superior, older, greater, better, mightier or nobler could grant boons to one inferior to him. There are literally innumerable instances of boons in Indian literature some even lead to real complications, as when the demon Andhaka who was blessed by Śiva began to plague the heavenly community, finally, Śiva was obliged to release Andhaka from demonhood.[6] Most frequently, Brahman feels helpless at long and strenuous penances of mortals and the God grants the boon of immortality or invincibility to quite undeserving candidates who turn out to be oppressive dictators and then the Gods go to Śiva or Viṣṇu who devise a solution.

Ancient Greek mythology is full of instances of Gods and Goddesses blessing and granting boons to each other. There also, some boons caused jealousy and mischief, which posed difficult entanglements and the divinities often look tortuous paths before these were solved. In ancient Israel, the Old Testament offers numerous instances of the significance of blessing (cf brk = 'barakha' = blessing) which were carried out by Jehovah, his angels and men. Boons bestowed by the Gods is quite common in many ancient cultures, sometimes they had to be solicited humbly, sometimes earned with rigorous penance or some prescribed discipline and sometimes they were gratuitously bestowed by the Gods. In ancient Phoenicia the *pater families* alone could supplicate God to call down blessings on the family.

In the *Kaṭha* Upaniṣad when Naciketas went to Yama's place and fasted for three days there, because Yama was out, the onus of placating a brahmin fasting at his door was on Yama. Since Naciketas had fasted for three nights Yama offered him three boons;[7] on these grew the structure of the entire

---

5 āśīrliṅ.

6 *Vāmana* P., 70: 58.

7 *Kaṭha Up.* I: 1: 9.

Kaṭha Upaniṣad. The Brāhmaṇas and Upaniṣads offer many anecdotes where Gods bestow boons on men, because the latter practise penance, forego comforts or meditate. Many times it transpires that the boons are bestowed unjudiciously, often leading to tangles which the Gods find difficult to solve.

In the *Rāmāyaṇa* the demon Suketu practises stiff penance for obtaining a son; but Brahman, instead of granting him a son sanctioned a daughter, Tāḍakā, who was just as strong as a man because her father had desired a son and had, for this reason, gone through a period of painful penance.[8] Drupada had solicited Siva for a son and was granted a daughter who later turned into a man.[9] On the subject of Draupadī's polyandry Vyāsa told the story of the girl, who could not find a suitable husband and did very stiff 'tapas', pleased Śiva with her penance who granted her a husband, but since she had prayed to Śiva five times, Śiva gave her a boon of five husbands.[10] Clearly, Vyāsa is explaining polyandry which had either become extinct or was no longer common[11] in the society which would therefore look askance at this polyandry. This boon offers a mythical justification for an isolated revival of an obsolete practice.

The *Brahmavaivarta* Purāṇa mentions Yama's boons to Sāvitrī.[12] The demon Vṛka had become a great nuisance and growing increasingly ambitious, obtained a boon from Śiva:[13] "May he on whose head I place my hand turn to ashes." The demon was so pleased with his good fortune that he became careless of his gestures, placed his hand on his own head and the boon came true; he was reduced to ashes.[14] Rādhā offered a boon to none less than Brahman himself: Brahman's desire was, "May 1 be ever devoted to you both (i.e. Rādhā and Kṛṣṇa)" and Rādhā granted it.[15]

---

8 I: 25: 5–6.

9 *Mbh* V: 188; the whole chapter.

10 *Mbh* I: 189: 41–46.

11 Although the *Mbh* itself mentions Jaṭilā with seven husbands and also Bārksī as polyandrous in this context and there are one or two other stray references of such cases.

12 *Prakṛtikhaṇḍa* ch. 34.

13 Who is notorious for being pleased too easily, hence his name Āṣutoṣa, easily pleased.

14 *Op. Cit.*, Kṛṣṇajanma 36: 31–39. Tills tale recurs at many place with minor variations and with different names.

15 *Kṛṣṇajanma* 15: 120–21.

The Vṛka episode is very significant; like many, another anecdote in the epics and Purāṇas it shows that fundamentally, boons, when granted, are amoral in character. The undeserving, wicked and ill-intentioned supplicants get their wish from Gods just as soon and just as easily as the good and the pious. But these are hoist with their own petard. So, finally even though granting a boon to a Rāvaṇa, a Vṛka or Andhaka, or a Tāḍakā or Vṛtra, the boon is initially a very wrong act, the Gods see Lo it that the evil recipients of boons do not do great or lasting harm. They devise some plan whereby these boons become just; they give them a long rope with which recipients eventually hang themselves, so that cosmic harmony or balance is not disturbed. Rādhā's boon to Brahman is a transparent authorial device to magnify the cult of devotion in Rādhā and Kṛṣṇa. In the *Devībhāgavata* Purāṇa we have a strange anecdote: Kṛṣṇa had a brief affair with Tulasī in heaven; Rādhā, the beloved wife cursed her to being born as a mortal woman. Her long penance brought Nārāyaṇa down whom she desired as a husband but was told that she had to be Sudāman's wife first and would be united with Kṛṣṇa only when she had been unfaithful to her husband. Sudāman was cursed into being born as demon Śaṅkhacūḍa who provoked the Gods and harassed them. So it was decided in heaven that while Śiva would fight the demon, Nārāyaṇa in the latter's guise would enjoy Tulasī. She grew somewhat suspicious despite his disguise, so that Nārāyaṇa divulged the divine ploy and asked her to die and be united with him in heaven.[16] Even this tale has coils within the coils; in the social code of morality, Tulasī had at one level betrayed her own husband, Śaṅkhacūḍa whom she loved; but at a still deeper and more real level she had not done any wrong because her penance and deep, long desire was for Nārāyaṇa himself with whom in reality she had been united. And all the social morality and religious morality are comprehended in the broader tangle of the pattern of curses and boons. Therefore, even though the Gods bestow boons, there is no ethical validity about the boons although, in the final analysis. They work out for the general well-being and no serious or lasting injury is inflicted to anyone.

The commonest type of boons, however, are those granted by men to men. Boons bestowed by the Gods are easily understood: Gods possess and wield supernatural power and they can exert on behalf of whomsoever they please. But what is the source of similar authority for men? "The intermediary

---

[16] 9: 17ff.

who uses both ritual and symbols, may be a king, or a priest, a saint, a prophet or the head of the family. By ritual means he animates the forces that make communication with the transcendent power possible and thereby creates a special relationship with the divinity ... The (spoken) word is also the instrument of divine power which may be invoked by the civilizing word, the prophetic word or the evocation of the holy names. Among peoples without writing, blessing is intimately linked to myth. Indeed, in the life of these peoples, myth constitutes a sacred history that puts man in contact with the supernatural world joining present and primordial time and linking present action to the initial acts of creation."[17] The authority of a priest derives from his direct professional contact with the divine, the saint's from his holiness which allows him the same kind of contact, the prophet's from God being the source of his inspiration, the king's from the 'divine right' theory or its equivalent in most cultures.[18] The spoken word in India in the Vedic context was 'brahman', word charged with power, Logos, which derived its sanctity from its creative power which myths endow it with. When these men of authority curse or bless, their words become charged with creative power. The Upaniṣads have many myths in which Brahman desires something, utters his desire and it is immediately translated into reality. It is like God saying 'Let there be light' and the reification of the utterance in light coming into existence. These men listed above, act the divine role so that what they say come to pass.

In most cases of boons, the worthiness, merits and morally just cause for which a supplicant approaches a God are not taken into consideration. Rather, like the Old Testament Jehovah picking up a candidate for starting a line of 'the chosen people' or for kingship, here, too, Gods frequently choose the recipients gratuitously, presumably to emphasize their own power and majesty. And frequently, they land the entire pantheon in a morass because the recipient is the wrong one. Sometimes long penance and arduous meditation earn the boon which even then can be equally wrong morally, yet the Gods display their power and generosity by granting the boons; to show that even if the grantee is wrong the giver is kind. Boons in the later Purāṇas are earned

---

[17] 'Blessing', *Macmillan Encyclopaedia of Religion*, Vol. 2, p. 248.

[18] In India, the ancient texts say that the king is made of portions of the eight divine overlords of peoples, the lokapālas. The fact that the Goddess Lakṣmī is the king's bride also establishes the divine essence of the king.

cheaply, unethically and often used harmfully. But no God has the strength to say 'no' to a supplicant. Boons complicate the course of events and in the hands of the inferior authors of the Purāṇas, with little creative imagination, the tale moves tortuously just to square the events. Boons are thus bad anecdotal devices, mainly introduced to emphasize the Gods' generosity and the merits of unqualified devotion and to bring the tale somehow to a rounding off. What emerges from such tales of boons is that any supplicant—God, man, demon, monster, gandharva, nāga, kinnara—can wrest a boon from any God after going through some hardships and often without it. It is a theological device to deflect the course of fate to suit the candidate. Thus Gods and holy men, acting as subordinate agents of fate affect its course to suit the supplicant's needs, whims or interest. Since there is no moral accountability to a supreme overlord of destiny as such, and since karman complicates the issue further, many times the boons granted appear irresponsible, even capricious, a mere display of the Gods' or holy mens' power to do as they—or their supplicants—please. Worth, character, spiritual altitude, impeccable conduct, a righteous cause, a philanthropical need—all that could have justified such boons seldom figure in these anecdotes. The donor-recipient relation is the core of the tale with ethical justice for the boon often wholly absent. Sometimes the boon justifies a social situation (as Draupadī's five husbands) or is self-frustrating, containing, a comic element as is the case of the demon Vṛka's boon, sometimes even the fulfilment of the boon entails immoral conduct[19] as in the case of Tulasī. What is really absent in many of these boons is any religious solemnity and ethical justification.

Curses, the opposite of blessing, however, function in the same manner: people wielding supernatural authority or placed in special predicament come in contact with the 'hieros' and their curses come true. As we have seen, Gods and Goddesses grant each other boons, so they also curse each other. As Yāska has said in the sixth century B.C., Gods are made in the image of men;[20] so they behave exactly as men. This explains their very human tempers and tantrums. A king ruled unjustly; his subjects were disgruntled. The chaplain found their complaints just and uttered an imprecation against the king which took effect.[21] In the *Rāmāyaṇa* we hear that Pārvatī, because

[19] Although care is later taken to give a pious veneer to it.

[20] Nirukta VII: 2, 8.

[21] Jātaka No. 520, Gandatindu.

she was prevented by the Gods from conceiving from Śiva, cursed the Gods that they would not beget offspring in their lawful spouses but only in others.[22] She also cursed the earth into becoming a consort of many.[23] Here a Goddess cursed all other Gods and goddesses.[24] The same epic narrates how the semi-divine nymph Puñjikasthalā (= Añjanā) was cursed into becoming a monkey and to marry the monkey Keśarin, because the God Vāyu had wooed her but she had repulsed his advances. Yet Vāyu blessed her with a mighty son, Hanumat.[25] Ravana who also was above the ordinary mortal was cursed by Brahman,—because Rāvaṇa had raped Puñjikasthalā—that he would die at the next attempt at rape.[26] This is inserted to explain why Rāvaṇa had not tried to rape Sītā although he had her within his power; it also incidentally confirms that it vindicates Sītā's claim to fidelity and chastity. In some minor episodes of the *Mahabharata* there are instances of Gods cursing Gods. The Purāṇas have many such stories.

The *Devībhāgavata* narrates Sarasvatī cursing Lakṣmī into becoming a plant (Tulasī) and a river.[27] Gaṅga also cursed Sarasvatī [28] into becoming a river.[29] Tvaṣṭṛ cursed Indra because the latter had killed Tvaṣṭṛ's son.[30] When Viṣṇu found Lakṣmī looking intently at the horse Revanta, he suspected her of being in love with Revanta and cursed her into becoming a mare.[31]

Dakṣa, enraged at his son-in-law Candra's partiality to Rohinī, one of his twenty seven wives, cursed the latter with consumption.[32] Viśvakarman desired Ghṛtācī who refused to entertain him, they cursed each other. She was born as the cowherd Madana's daughter, practised penance and returned to

---

22 Which gives us food for thought, because no Purāṇa corroborates it; in them all divine children are legitimate.

23 cf mythically all kings are husbands, lords of the earth.

24 I: 36: 21–24.

25 IV: 66: 8–20.

26 VI: 13: 10–14.

27 IX: 6: 32.

28 IX: 66: 39.

29 The river Sarasvatī and Sarasvatī retaliated by cursing Gaṅga into descending to the earth and carrying sinners' sins. IX: 6: 41.

30 VI: 7: 14.

31 VI: 17: 53–61.

32 *Brahmavaivarta* P., 9: 55–56.

heaven. At her curse Viśvakarman was born as a human artist.[33] When Prakṛti delivered an egg after a thousand years of pregnancy, in shame and anger she dropped it in water, Kṛṣṇa then cursed her with childlessness.[34] Pārvatī cursed the Gods who had interrupted her and Śiva's dalliance, with barrenness.[35] The nymph Mohinī cursed Brahman who had expressed sneer to her; she said: "May you never enjoy a cult (worship) of your own."[36] Once Pārvatī in a moment of wrath cursed Śiva, "From now on he who worships you will be born and live one life as a cat."[37] Tārā was desired by Candra, she cursed him with: "you shall be consumed by Rāhu, overshadowed by clouds, be inauspicious only at specific times; you shall be tarnished with calumny and will suffer from consumption."[38] She next cursed Madana, "you shall be reduced to ashes by some mighty one". Kṛṣṇa cursed Rādhā with childlessness.[39] "Barrenness among women and infertility among men may be produced by disease, *sorcery* or *curse* of people endowed with supernatural powers. But ultimately whether a couple will or will not be blessed with children, the much-sought-after sons in particular, is a question of *fate* (Prārabdha) or karmalekha (the written/pre-ordained results of one's actions in the previous life). In the normal course of events, there is no escape for the consequence of one's actions, only divine grace (anugraha) can come to one's rescue; but this is hard to obtain."[40] Now, in the case of goddesses this theory is seldom applicable. We do not hear of Rādhā's previous existence, hence, that she should suffer from barrenness due to her evil actions in a previous birth is unthinkable. But let us not forget that Pārvatī was so in her second incarnation, in the earlier life She had been Satī, the daughter not of Himālaya, but of Dakṣa. Similarly, the later interpolated part of the *Rāmāyaṇa* says that Sītā was none other than Lakṣmī, Viṣṇu's spouse in Vaikuṇṭha, heaven. And she committed no sins in that birth for which she should pay so dearly in her incarnation as Sītā. Neither did Rāma reincarnated as Viṣṇu

[33] *Op. Cit.*, Brahmakhaṇḍa 10: 42ff.

[34] *Op. Cit.*, Prakṛti 2: 52.

[35] *Op. Cit.*, Gaṇeśakhaṇḍa 2: 4 But the purāṇas amply disprove her curse: they all had children.

[36] *Op. Cit.*, Kṛṣṇajanma 33: 37.

[37] *Ibid.*, 37: 32.

[38] *Op. Cit.*, Kṛṣṇajanma: 80: 17, 18.

[39] *Op. Cit.*, Kṛṣṇajanma 84: 90.

[40] Madan, 1987, p. 25; italics mine.

deserve such deep griefs. Similarly, Draupadī was Padmā, i.e. Lakṣmī as the angel tells Yudhiṣṭhira when the latter reaches heaven. Once again, her public insult and humiliation at the hands of Duryodhana and his brothers, her long exile with her husbands, the loss of all of her sons in the epic battle are such cruel blows of fate that nothing in her career prepares us for these. There are quite a few of such instances where a person is stated to be a God or Goddess and it makes us pause because the fate they suffer on earth can hardly be called due recompense for a sinless heavenly being.

Rādhā, a romantic heroine, the beloved of Kṛṣṇa cannot be visualized as a mother of children. If she had them by her lawful husband that would tarnish her image as Kṛṣṇa's lover and if she conceived from Kṛṣṇa, the child would be illegitimate and society would be up in arms against all three. Yet fertility is an attribute of good and auspicious women, hence the motif of the curse is introduced. The real reason, however, is motherhood would aesthetically ruin her appeal as the eternal lover. The curse motif helps her retain this aesthetic charm, it was specifically invented for this purpose. The gandharva Upavarhan desired Rambhā, she felt humiliated, Brahman cursed the gandharva to be born as a śūdra.[41]

Gods have always cursed men on what they regarded as sin or remissness. The *Atharvaveda* has various terms for curse, grāhi (siezure), avadya (curse), abhiśasti (calumny), śāpa (curse) and durita (disaster).[42] In the *Rāmāyaṇa* Kuvera had cursed Tumburu into a monster-form.[43] In heaven Śvetaketu felt hungry, disgusted at this, Brahman cursed him with eating his own corpse, later, however he took pity and released him.[44] Gaṅgā cursed Ambā into becoming a river infested with wild aquatic animals, if the latter vowed to kill Bhīṣma.[45] Hariścandra had promised his son to Varuṇa, but when the latter came to claim him, the king lied, "I do not know where he has gone," at this Varuṇa cursed Hariśçandra with dropsy.[46] Pārvatī cursed Śuka to be

---

[41] Brahmakhaṇḍa 13: 10.

[42] *A V* II: 10: 6. Also found in the *Ṛgveda* X: 3: 7; 164: 9. Let us not note that they occur in the latest portion of the *Ṛgveda*, the tenth book which is distanced from the previous bulk of the *Ṛgveda* by about a couple of centuries.

[43] *Rāmāyaṇa* III: 3: 16–18.

[44] *Rāmāyaṇa* VII: 7–78.

[45] *Mbh* V: 187. Bhīṣma was Gaṅgā's son by Śāntanu.

[46] Devībhāgvata VI: 12: 67.

born in the hateful demon line, "so that you can do no more harm here."[47] King Citralekha was born as Vṛtra through Pārvatī's curse.[48] Brahman cursed Nārada to be born as a maid servant's son, but, later, through Kṛṣṇa's grace Nārada could again be born as Brahman's son.[49] When Rādhā had cursed Sudāman, Brahman promised to see that the curse did not touch Sudāman.[50] Rambhā cursed Durvāsas with a harsh fate: "go and assume an extremely deformed-shape, be maligned in the three worlds, all your old merits will disappear immediately."[51] Dakṣa and Śiva, hostile to each other cursed each other and the curses came true.[52] King Pṛṣadhra had mistaken a sage's cow[53] for another animal and had killed it; the sage cursed him into becoming a śūdra.[54] The Yadu dynasty was destroyed through a sage's curse.[55]

The *Epigraphia Indica* is full of imprecations against usurpers: "He who steals property gifted by a brahmin or property given to a brahmin becomes a dung-worm for six thousand years." In other similar texts we find such usurpers cursed to becoming a vulture for sixty thousand lives, a pig for a hundred lives, a ferocious animal for a hundred, a rhinoceros for seven, a horse for seven, a crocodile for five, a vagina-worm of prostitutes for a hundred, worms in prostitutes' pimples for seven, an iguana for seven, an ass for seven, a cat for seven, a mongoose for three, Uccaihśravas for a hundred, a mule for a hundred, a creel serpent, tiger, buffalo for seven, a frog for a hundred, a goat for seven, a bear for a hundred, a jackal for a hundred thousand, a leech for a hundred—and at the end of his horrendous itinerary he remains in Kumbhīpāka hell for a hundred life-times of Brahman.[56] Such epigraphic imprecations are found in many epigraphical records. Dhruvasena's Valabhī grant[57] reads, after some laudatory verses on gifts of land and

---

[47] Bhāgavata P., VI: 17: 15.

[48] *Op. Cit.*, 61: 7.

[49] *Brahmavaivarta* Brahma. 8: 43ff.

[50] *Ibid.*, 17: 13.

[51] *Op. Cit.*, kṛṣṇajanma, 30: 100–102.

[52] *Bhāgavata* P. 4: 2.

[53] Which supplied him with the necessary sacrificial butter.

[54] *Mārkaṇḍeya P.* 112.

[55] *Bhāgavata* P., 11: 1; *viṣṇu* P., 5: 37.

[56] This last comes to an astronomical figure in terms of years; *Op. Cit.*, Kṛṣṇajanma 75: 31–37.

[57] II 47–49

temples, "one who grants land lives for sixty thousand years in heaven and he who destroys or harms it or approves of such harm lives for that number of years' in hell." The Cālukya King Karṇa I in his Sanaka grant (1091 A.D.) repeated these imprecations.[58] Kṛṣṇa Devarāya, in the Sanskrit portion of his Hampi inscription blesses those "who protected brahmins and subdued Sultans."[59] In 595–596 A.D. the land-grants of Saṃkheda has the time-worn imprecations of sending the usurper to hell for sixty thousand years and continues: "the stealer of what is given to a brahmin is born as a black serpent living in the dry hollow of the waterless forests of the Vindhya region." This is repeated in the Saṃkheda grant of Dadda between 249 and 640 A.D. In the ninth and tenth centuries A.D. the Badal pillar inscription has blessings for "The pious one who explains the Vedas in the wondrous sections of law and history marked by the birth of the Vālmīki of the Kali age."[60] The cardinal formulaic imprecation[61] occurs in many Purāṇas.[62] The fifth-sixth century copper plate of Mahārājā Lakṣmaṇa repeats the familiar imprecatory phrase of dooming the stealer of property to sixty thousand years in hell. Lines 9–10 say, "He who steals land given by oneself or by others becomes a dung-worm and sinks (to hell) together with his ancestors." King Mādhava Varman's Bugunda plate has: "The king enjoys eternal bliss if he himself donates (land) and for sixty thousand years if he maintains land given by others."(48). King Jayasiṃha of Dhārā issued the Māndhātā plate which says, "Men should not destroy others' significant acts." (L 28), Again King Janukeśvar of Balaka in his Kamaya plate writes, "If there be any person who does any harm to this object of charity (viz.land-grant), he shall incur the sin of killing a cow on the bank of the Gaṅgā." (L 8) King Dhruvasena I in his Gaṇeśagarh plates repeats the formula, "If one steals land donated by himself or by others, he incurs the sin of killing a hundred thousand cows", the rest of the text is corrupt, evidently through dialectal confusion or scribal errors, but the basic sense is clear, "Kings have erected temples, given gifts and constructed images; no good men usurps such gifts given before' to brahmins. Protection, preservation and donation are meritorious acts."[63] The Pīthāpura

[58] In II 20–21.

[59] Verse 29.

[60] L. 25.

[61] Svadattām paradattām vā etc.

[62] cf *Garuḍa* uttara. 40: 1; *Brahmavarvaria,* Prakṛti, 9: 8.

[63] II 24ff.

inscription of King Prithvīśvara says, "If any, one causes obstruction to this charitable land-grant, he shall incur the sin of those who have killed one thousand cows and one thousand brahmins on the banks of the Gaṅgā."[64] King Ravi Varman's Raṅganātha inscription says, "For kings who follow Rāma, it is not a crime to kill the wife, but you are killing poverty, the close attendant of good men."[65] King Veṅkaṭa in his Vilpaka grant writes: "Between donation and preservation the latter is better. One ascends to heaven through charity, but reaches the eternal station (or Viṣṇu's realm) through preservation of the gift. The merit of protecting what is given by another is twice as much as donating- oneself, by usurping another's gift, one's own gift becomes fruitless." Then follows the formulaic statement.[66] It continues, "Land donated to a brahmin (or by a brahmin) should not be enjoyed by anyone or even taxed; this common bridge to piety should be protected through the ages by you all."[67]

The psychological source of these imprecations is the anxiety lest a donation of land given to brahmins be usurped by others after the donor's or the donnas death. It was a genuine anxiety born of real instances of usurpation, hence the curse had to be made equivalent of that for the most heinous crimes.

There is a peculiar characteristic about the epigraphical imprecations. Who is cursing? And whom? Quite clearly, the one who curses is distanced by a considerable span of time from his intended victim, he is thus cursing unseen and unknown persons. His objective is to prevent some land and/ or landed property being usurped by avaricious person(s) in the near or distant future. The only weapon he can possibly use is to instil the fear of God in a prospective usurper. This fear he generates by calling upon agents of fate to regard the usurper as a killer of brahmins and cows — the most heinous crimes in the early and medieval periods. Hence, donation is made lesser than protection because no donation is safe unless some powerful person undertakes its protection. If the donated land is not usurped then the donor enjoys the fruits of his piety — land-grant to brahmins was near the top of the catalogue of acts of charity. How does the donor make sure that the supernatural agents will stand by his proclaimation? Charity is an

---

[64] Line 159

[65] Line 20.

[66] Svadattām parpdattām vā etc line 149.

[67] Line 155.

acknowledged act of piety which generates merit. This merit brings him in contact with the supernatural agents of fate. If these agents do not honour his imprecations then the spectacular piety of granting land to brahmins is debased, even nullified and does not inspire future generations to follow the Dharmaśāstra injunctions. Brahmins cannot be assured of continued enjoyment of the gift and a sanctified plot of land and the constructions on it become polluted through sacrilege from change of hands. Surely, the divine powers that be would not tolerate such impiety; they will honour the imprecations in their own interest or people will not stand in awe of the unknown horrors fate holds for such usurpers.

This curse is a long distance one, a weapon hurled at a yet unknown, unseen enemy but since the weapon is divinely charged, it cannot fail to reach its target. Conceivably, such threats and imprecations did prevent prospective usurpers for a few generations, but after the memory of the donor and the donné faded, the granted land changed hands, became taxed and/or cultivated or built upon a fresh after time had demolished the dilapidated remains of the earlier structure. The fear was very real, as long as the living memory persisted, it worked and had the desired effect for a time, simply because fate was appealed to by the donor, a dire fate was called upon the criminally inclined person who dreamt of desecrating it by enjoying it personally. But no imprecation can indefinitely hold back avarice. So fate was regarded as losing interest in protecting old property and people took the risk of usurping with impunity. The epigraphic imprecations are echoed in the later Purāṇas,[68] but what strikes one is the new note: the inclusion of hundreds of generations under the curse; the ancestors and successors of the usurper of a granted land, would go to hell for a hundred, even a thousand generations. Now this runs contrary to the theory of karman. If the progenitors had been pious and are in heaven, they in such vast numbers will descend to hell because of the sin of one progeny. What about the effect of their karman? Even more horrible is the idea of the unborn generations, again, hundreds, even thousands of them. In their case it becomes a case of unfathomable cruelty, of blind, irrational, undeserved, unprovoked malignity on the part of the imprecator and according to the popular belief, on a supremely callous and unjust fate. Imprecations as organs of fate, if they reach beyond the present malefactor, are a contradiction of divine kindness

---

[68] Either of them may have been the borrower.

and justice. Yet not only in epigraphy but also in hundreds of Puranic passages such imprecations abound; they throw even the vestige of justice overboard and indulge in the bitter, unrelenting, revengeful curse.

The epigraphic imprecations are nothing but the reflection of social ethos and attitudes to property and these are but measures taken by donors and donnés for the preservation of the property in their absence. One notices that the harshness of the punishment increases with time. Except for Uccaihśravas who enters the list unaccountably most of the rest are obnoxious creatures in the *Brahmavaivrtia* Purāṇa which and a few other Purāṇas have palpably influenced the epigraphic imprecations. Kṛṣṇa Devarāya's venomous attitude to Sultans is possibly understandable if we remember that the Bahmani kingdom was contiguous to his Vijayanagara.

> Religious cursing is an activity closely related to blessing: the people are usually empowered to do both and the forms given to curses and blessings are frequently parallel. Deities and holy persons and others with a temporary aura gained through such conditions as great suffering or advanced age, in short, those who have earned the power to invoke blessings—are the ones who can legitimately call down misfortune, including death and destruction upon people or things.
>
> The sages of the ancient Vedic tradition were store-houses of verbal power, greatly to be feared by enemies and even by those who interrupted them in prayer. Some sages were a necessary component in the entourage of any political of military leader.[69]

There is sometimes an attempt to make the curse proportionate to the sins but quite evidently these were exceptions; in most cases the curse is proportionate to the degree of the ire invoked, not so much by the intrinsic impiety involved, as by the occasion, circumstances, temperament and the indignation aroused just then. Quite frequently, we find that the sages and 'holy men' feel slighted, or neglected by 'innocent victims' very natural pre-occupations or inability to please the irate sages. At such times the deeply offended sages pronounce vindictive curses not so much to punish the victim for the remissness as to give vent to their unbecoming and uncontrolled wrath.

As to how and why curses and boons are deemed effective, we read that curses and boons may be self-executing or a God is invoked to bring about

---

69 *Macmillan Encyclopaedia of Religion,* Vol. 4, 'Cursing', p. 182.

the desired effect. "Irish folk lore has it that a curse once uttered must alight on something; it will float up in the air for seven years and may descend any moment on the party it was aimed at."[70] In India there is no such time-limit (seven years) but actually the span of the curse is longer because it can cover several generations before or after the person aimed at. We remember the imprecations which envelop many generations. The fate of the yet unborn, unconceived people who may exist centuries later are thus determined beforehand; they are doomed to sinners' fate and torment, to loathsome births and long sojourns through many such despicable births to reach the terrible dungeons of hell where they live indefinitely. In such curses the victims of later generations are completely guiltless, yet they are consigned to humiliation, torment and hell. If for the sake of argument it is assumed that the sins committed by the later generations will justify their own doom then it first renders the curse futile and secondly, it becomes a case of double causes (their own sins and the imprecations) producing a single effect, which is logically untenable. Yet like imprecations, many curses, as we have seen, cover yet unbegotten generations and they are logically fallacious and deny any scope for the free will to act piously to counter dooms. This is completely predeterministic.

As vehicles charged with supernatural power the sages and 'holy men' for the time being i.e. while they curse or bless become awesome and formidable. "The Talmud warned against looking at the priest while he is pronouncing the blessing, for the glory of God is on him. It is a natural process of suggestion working through strength of emotion, fear of ill-will and enmity and reinforced by a complex of associated ideas relating to the essence of words and the energy of souls that gives the curse or blessing its independent power... Obviously the wishes of one who is professionally in touch with the magical or the supernatural are more efficacious than those of ordinary men ... The curse is particularly the weapon of the wronged and oppressed against their more powerful enemies and of zealots against their bigoted opponents ... Throughout their history private cursing and blessing preponderate over public and unofficial over official ... The enormous collection of private *dirae* or imprecations which have survived from Greek and Roman times chiefly in the form of leaden tablets or symbolic nails, inscribed with curses consigning an enemy to the infernal powers, testify to the hold retained by

[70] *Hasting' Encyclopaedia of Religion and Ethics*, Vol. IV, 'Cursing and Blessing', p. 367.

the primitive theory of curse... The mutual conditional curse... allows the curse proper to be more or less lost in the material symbolism of union."[71] The morally wronged persons and the oppressed in society frequently curse the wrong-doers. Since society or a section of it has deprived them of their right to justice, fate becomes their debtor, from the point of view of a cosmic justice: for the time at least they have the upper hand morally. By cursing the wrong-doer they oblige fate to repay the debt of justice to them; they retaliate spiritually by calling down doom on the evil-doer. In other words, words of curse are uttered not merely with a personal vendetta but also in order to restore the balance of cosmic justice: they do what fate should have done and did not and they thus become direct agents of fate. One remembers the raped Vedavatī cursing Rāvaṇa, or Gāndhārī cursing Kṛṣṇa. Such instances of righteous indignation create dramatic situations, momentous in their depth and significance and we hear fate's own voice and its attempt at redressing the evil meted out to the helpless victims, the very wrongs done give the victims a moral and spiritual right to curse with truth, so to speak. "The heavier the load of sins which alone could make the curses pronounced by others effective, the greater the chances of suffering as retribution."[72]

The sage Kapila was so angry at the wicked intention of the sixty thousand sons of Sagara that his wrath, expressed in a curse turned the entire horde into ashes.[73] Gautama was so indignant at his wife Ahalyā's infidelity and her relation with Indra in the husband's disguise, that he cursed her to live on air, become invisible, doing penance on a bed of ashes for many thousands of years.[74] Viśvāmitra, born a kṣatriya, had attained brahminhood through stiff penance. When he was about to act as the officiating priest of Triśanku's sacrifice, he invited other brahmins but they would not acknowledge his caste promotion and declined to participate. In great mortification Viśvāmitra destroyed them with a curse.[75] The blind sage, whose son Daśaratha had inadvertently killed, cursed the king to die of grief over the separation from a son.[76] Although most curses take effect instantly, some have a delayed

---

71 *Hasting's Encyclopaedia of Religion and Ethics,* Vol. IV, 'Cursing', pp. 367, 369– 373.

72 Madan, 1987, p. 36.

73 *Rāmāyaṇa* I: 34: 30.

74 *Op. Cit.,* I: 48: 29, 30.

75 I: 69: 17, 18.

76 II: 54: 54.

effect. At that point Daśaratha was sonless, so at first he rejoiced at the prospect of having a son, although later the full import of the curse came home with its brutal reality. Kabandha was born handsome but he perversely enjoyed frightening sages by assuming fearsome or loathsome forms. Sthūlaśiras, frightened, cursed him to a permanent ugly shape. Many times the man under curse begs for a remission or asks for a terminus to the curse, Kabandha placated Sthūlaśiras who relented saying "when Rāma lops off your arms you shall be freed from the curse."[77] The young Vedavatī had chosen Viṣṇu as her husband, but Rāvaṇa molested her and she cursed him: "The next attempt at rape will kill you."[78] Rāvaṇa had forced Rambhā against her will when she was going to meet her lover Nala-Kūvara, she had also cursed him like Vedavatī.[79] Viśvāmitra cursed the nymph Rambhā into a block of stone when she sought to seduce him.[80]

In the *Mahābhārata* Maitreya, a sage had not been properly honoured by Duryodhana. Piffed, he cursed Duryodhana with defeat in the battle.[81] Clearly, the disproportion between the sin and curse is glaring; not honouring a sage properly may betray Duryodhana's impious, haughty and generally disrespectful nature but does that justify the death of millions of men and ultimate defeat in battle? Yavskrī raped Raibhya's daughter-in-law. Flying into a terrible rage, Raibhya pulled two hairs from his head, created two Kṛtyās (demonic beings) who killed Yavakrī. Later, Raibhya relented and the victim revived through Raibhya's boon.[82] Curses, if divinely inspired, are often mitigated, a term is set to its duration and not infrequently, he who curses later relents and revokes the curse. This episode ends in an unusual manner: Raibhya permitted the two Kṛtyās, male and female to live together. So Kṛtyās are evil forces not only properly reified but here acquired a life of their own and lived on. The famous episode of the righteous hunter (dharmavyādha) who was a vipra with a kṣatriya friend, a hunter whom he had killed unwittingly and was cursed into becoming a hunter.[83] Pāṇḍu killed a deer

---

77 *Op. Cit.*, III: 71: 1–7.

78 *Op. Cit.*, VII: 17: 8–42.

79 *Op. Cit.*, VII: 25–26.

80 *Op. Cit.*, I: 64: 12.

81 III: 11: 28–34.

82 II: 137; the whole chapter.

83 III: 205–206: 5.

engaged in dalliance and was cursed by the deer "you, too, shall die while you are united with your wife."[84] Although there is parity between the sin and the punishment in the first instance, there is hardly any justification between these in the one before, one incident of unwitting killing should not doom a man to a life-long vocation of killing. Vaśiṣṭha's son Śakti was cursed by Kalmāṣapāda into a monster; the latter had kicked the king for right of way.[85] A brahmin who was just going to be united with his wife was eaten by Kalmāṣapāda, he was cursed by the wife that the monster would similarly die at union with wife.[86] Paraśurāma cursed Karṇa for falsely pretending to be a brahmin and receiving lessons in weaponry from him: Parasurama said that Karṇa would not be able to use his knowledge, when he needed it.[87] King Yayāti was cursed by Śukra into premature senility,[88] he also cursed Daṇḍa for raping sage Bhārgava's daughter, the latter cursed Daṇḍa with death within seven days.[89] We see that the same offence, rape, is punished with curses of different degrees of severity. Once again, we are faced with the result of there being no arbiter, no accepted code of uniform law which explains the diversity of punishments and the discrepancy between the offence and the curse.

When the pious Prahlāda's grandson Vali became wayward and began oppressing subjects, Prahlāda cursed him and his retinue with utter destruction.[90] Vaśiṣṭha was about to curse Saudāsa but desisted, some of the water he was going to curse with dropped on Saudāsa's feet, turned them black and he came to be known as Kalmāṣapāda, 'black-speckled feet.'[91] A second version of the Kalmāṣapāda tale reads: As a monster Kalmāṣapāda ate a brahmin whose wife entreated him for her husband's life, but the monster paid no heed to her; she cursed him to die when he approached his wife. Angry, the monster cursed her into a goblin.[92] A brahmin, neglected by

84 I: 109–29.

85 I: 166: 9.

86 I: 192: 12.

87 VIII: 29: 6.

88 VII: 58.

89 VII: 81.

90 *Vāmana* P., 29: 33.

91 *Nārada* P., I: 9: 1–42.

92 *Op. Cit.*, 9: 50–70.

King Suyajña cursed him into exile, loss of kingdom and all glory.[93] King Kārtavīrya was cursed by Paraśurāma in the same manner with the addition that the latter would be a leper with running sores, bereft of intellect and pestered badly.[94] Durvāsas found the nymph Tilottamā and Sāhasika at dalliance and cursed Tilottamā into becoming an ass, because only asses are such shameless creatures.[95] A Kaliṅga prince who failed to greet a brahmin was cursed into becoming a beast.[96] After a prolonged fight Vaśiṣṭha cursed Viśvāmitra into becoming a crane and in his turn was cursed into a bird.[97] A long episode narrates that the sages Parvata and Narada had pledged to keeping no secrets from each other, when, they were guests at king Sanjaya's palace. Princess Damayantī tended both until she fell in love with Nārada who reciprocated. For keeping this love a secret from him, Parvata cursed Nārada into a monkey, who in his turn cursed Parvata and prevented his going to heaven. The princess refused to marry any other. Suddenly Parvata came and the sages released each other from the curses. Parvata went to heaven and Nārada regaining his human shape married the princess.[98] Trisanku had stolen Vaśiṣṭha's cow, so the latter cursed him into becoming a goblin with stakes on his head. He had been prince Satyavrata before, but now with three stakes on head was called Trisanku. Satyavrata's father Mandhatr dismissed his priest Vaśiṣṭha who then cursed the king into becoming a candala.[99]

To curse one needs some authority, which can be of three kinds: (i) holiness earned through austerity and (ii) moral superiority earned through suffering undeserved injury or wrong. In the above instances we have both categories of curses. A third category is that of a vindictive or self-vindicative counter- curse. A Purāṇic text says, "he who is grieved through inner agony curses; indeed, even fate (or God) is not able to counter that curse."[100] The aggrieved person acquires a moral right to curse. And all such curses come to take effect. There are two exceptions: (i) a counter-curse sometimes scares

---

93 *Brahmavaivarta* Prakṛti, 51: 29.

94 *Op. Cit.*, Prakṛti 50: 28–29.

95 *Op. Cit.*, Kṛṣṇa 23: 136.

96 *Op. Cit.*, Kṛṣṇa 122: 18.

97 *Op. Cit.*, VI: 26, 27. two whole chapters.

98 *Op. Cit.*, VII: 10: 54-12: 29.

99 *Brahmavaivarta* P. Kṛṣṇa, 30: 99.

100 As in the instance of *Pārvata* and *Nārada.*

and mollifies the curser to revoke his curse[101] and (ii) quite frequently the person under curse pleads and placates the God or the 'holy man' and he either revokes the curse but much more frequently modifies or lessens it or sets a term after which the person is released from the curse.

The last section of the curse is those uttered by man to Gods. Before we go into that, there are just a few instances of men granting boons to Gods; thus a brahmin granted a boon to the Goddess Parvati,[102] Visvakarman the God cursed by a sage became a monkey[103] and impelled by fate fell from a mountain top to the earth. Saraswatī, a Goddess was cursed by Visvamitra.[104] The sage Mankagana's seed fell at the sight of a nymph, she cursed him.[105] Through Nārada's curse Brahman lost cultic worship on earth.[106] King Janamejaya cursed Indra who thus lost cultic worship on earth.[107] Evidently, this myth and that of Brahman losing worship are late mythical justification of the fact that these Gods,[108] though powerful earlier, were deprived of cultic worship.[109] Besides mythical justification, these incidents of curse incidentally glorify brahmins as formidable persons who can even curse Gods, not to speak of mere mortals. Society thus indirectly generated an awe towards brahmins.[110] The sage Sutapas cursed the Gods Asvins never to have a share in the sacrificial oblation.[111] The Sun-God fell sick and pleaded with a sage who granted him cure. Durvasas cursed Indra so that the latter lost his kingdom, power and glory. Sage Jamadagni was in the habit of being united in the daytime with his wife Renuka, the all-seeing Sun-God was disgusted. Jamadagni cursed him with periodic eclipses.[112] Sūrya also cursed jamadagni

---

[101] As in the instance of Parvata and Nārada.

[102] *Brahmavaivarta* P. Ganapati, ch. 8.

[103] Vamana P., 64: 2.

[104] *Ibid.*, 40: 20–21.

[105] *Op. Cit.*, 72: 73.

[106] *Brahmavaivarta* Brahma 8: 63.

[107] Harivamsha bhavisua 5: 18-18.

[108] *Op. Cit.*, 11: 8.

[109] *Op. Cit.*, Prakṛti, ch. 36.

[110] *Op. Cit.*, 36: 27–30.

[111] *Op. Cit.*, Kṛṣṇa 79: 30.

[112] *Ibid.*, 79: 40.

with death and defeat at the hands of a kṣatriya.[113] Vaśiṣṭha cursed the divine Vasus who had[114] stolen his cow into being born as mortals. Because Hari had cut off the sage Bhṛgu's wife, the sage cursed him into being born as a monkey.[115] Tulasī cursed Kṛṣṇa into assuming a stone form (the śālgrāma śila).[116] When the loving wife Mālāvatī's husband died, she threatened to curse Nārāyaṇa if he did not revive her husband.[117] Curses are sometimes terminated immediately at the prayer of the victim, sometimes pre-empted by granting the victim's wish, the duration of the curse is lessened or the curse is modified substantially or remitted conditionally. Sri Lankān Buddhists have a convention of singing 'poison songs' which are complementary rites for counteracting and de-activising curses. Buddhist theology has no room for curses; strict adherence to the theory of karman and of pratītya-samutpāda, conditional generation, precludes the curse or counter-curse which moulds or undoes the course of fate. But we have seen that popular religion contains much that runs counter to official theology. The 'poison songs' belong to the primitive shamanistic tradition lingering in the subterranean streams of popular convention. Vedic curses are directed against "he who hates us and him whom we hate."[118] The hostility and hate of the enemy is regarded as a formidable force and all primitive theologies took cognizance of it.

In Nigeria when there is a dispute, people 'blow out a curse' at its conclusion i.e. by common consent render the curse ineffectual which presumably was at the root of the dispute. A curse unremedied disturbs the mental peace of the victim and sometimes of the entire community, precisely because it then remains an active agent of fate.

'Cursing' ranges from spontaneous explosive rage to carefully considered rendering of an adverse judgement.[119] Two incidents of human beings cursing Gods deserve special attention. The first is Gāndhārī's curse to Kṛṣṇa in the Strīparvan of the *Mahābhārata.* Walking around in the battlefield strewn with hundreds of corpses, including those of her own hundred sons,

---

[113] *Devībhāgavata* P. 1: 3: 35.

[114] *et al.*, II., *Op. Cit.*, VI; 7: 34.

[115] *Op. Cit.*, IX: 24: 14.

[116] *Brahmavaivarta* P., Brahma 13: 60.

[117] 'Yo'smān dveṣṭi yaṃ ca vayam dviṣmah, ' a most common and familiar phrase.

[118] *Macmillan Encyclopaedia of Religion:* 'Cursing'.

[119] This came true in Dharma's incarnation as Vidura. *Mbh* I: 57: 77–62.

she, in the company of a hundred young widowed daughters-in-law, felt so fiercely indignant and so deeply aggrieved that she turned to Kṛṣṇa and cursed him, because he was the one whose personal interests were not involved in the battle and who alone, therefore, could have effectively averted this terrible massacre, because both the belligerent sides would have listened to him. In failing to do this he had incurred the righteous indignation of the aged queen. She cursed him with an obnoxious manner of death, with the total annihilation of his line and the destruction of his kingdom. Now, Gāndhārī, a mere mortal summoned the courage to curse Kṛṣṇa, the God of Gods in the epic through her intense agony at the avoidable massacre, which she had interpreted as the result of Kṛṣṇa's heartless apathy to the horrendous outcome— devastation, deaths and inconsolable lamentations. This grief and rage turned her temporarily into a Cassandra and the powers of fate were mobilized in her favour; every single word she had uttered came true. This was an inspired prophet's curse and it gained in significance when we think of the image of Kṛṣṇa in the epic. It is a short curse, but truly horripilating. And it assumes supreme significance because it was effective.

The second curse by man to God occurs in the very first book of the *Mahābhārata.* The sage *Aṇīmāṇḍavya* (or simply Māṇḍavya) had taken the vow of silence and was lost in meditation in his own hut. A band of burglars, chased by guards entered the hut, deposited their plunder in the cottage and ran away. The policemen following them entered the cottage, found the plunder and asked the sage whether the burglars had fled. But his vow of silence prevented him from replying; so imagining him to be an accomplice, they at the king's command placed him on a stake to die. When the sage knew the charge against him, he enquired of Dharma why he was punished thus and was told that as a small boy he had pushed a sharp blade of grass inside an insect's body—that karman had brought about this effect. Then, overpowered with righteous indignation at the utterly disproportionate enormity of the punishment, the sage cursed Dharma: "be born as a śūdra."[120] It also came true, Dharma was born as Vidura, a śudra.

This conception of a man cursing not just 'a God' but the upholder of cosmic ethics, Dharma himself, for behaving in a manner completely incompatible with man's idea of Dharma is wholly revolutionary. First, because Dharma had meted out a totally unjust verdict on a righteous man. Secondly,

120 XIII: 69.

because it shakes the bottom-board of man's conviction; Dharma is not really justice, it can make horrible mistakes. And, therefore, thirdly, there is a sinister loophole in the thoery of karman and retribution. Hate, therefore, is not just, steady, uniform and dependable, but erratic, capricious and fallible. We remember that another name of Dharma is Yama and he, too, can make mistakes: an anecdote in the *Mahābhārata* tells us that once a brahmin named Śarmin was fetched from the world of the living to Yama's realm. At his entry Yama rose courteously and apologized to him saying that it was a case of error; his messengers had brought the wrong man of the same name.[121] Neither as Yama (Death, Kāla, Antaka) nor as Dharma was this divinity of fate, Destiny or Providence infallible. Hence Aṇīmāṇḍavya's curse is a palpable evidence of man's inherent scepticism about the way the universe is governed, i.e. if it is governed at all. Justice is not the red thread of honour running through its cord.

"Belief in the power of saints to punish their offenders reflects a more fundamental belief in an immanent justice that also underlies the contemporary institution of trial by ordeal and all that is related to other social or political factors, most obviously the availability of other kinds of sanction. Belief in the punishing saint is also another example of the religious cult using the idiom of its social context... Saints are also overwhelmingly male."[122] Saints through their curses and prophesies play the part of social judges. But most curses are attempts at rectification of rewards or punishments fate has awarded wrongly. Hence the respect these cursing saints or prophets enjoy in society: they assist fate, lend a hand where fate has been feeble in its retributive function. But in effect, such anecdotes raise human beings, their sense of justice and expectation from Gods above the justice-dispensing Gods themselves.

The objective of curses, when individual, is harassment of enemies, and when communal or social, it is an attempt to enforce justice, to establish doctrinal discipline and proper reward and punishment. It thus is an assistant of the fatalistic powers inherent in the cosmos which the human imagination has ever associated with justice.

Another mode of influencing fate indirectly or vicariously is to offer sacrifices or other forms of placatory, expiatory or ameliorative worship to

---

[121] Wilson, 1983, pp. 27, 30.

[122] *Garuḍa* P. Pūrvakhaṇḍa 56: 23.

allay or divert the verdict of fate. All individual sacrifices in Vedic times aimed at manipulating fate in man's favour. The childless man offered the 'putreṣṭi' sacrifice to obtain a son. A mighty monarch performed the 'aśvamedha' (horse-sacrifice) to attain overlordship over monarchs all around and in these attempts he forced the hands of fate. During a pūjā the priest does 'saṃkalpa' (devotional decision) for the good and on behalf of those near and dear to the performer. All this is vicarious i.e. for the person on whose behalf people plead in different ritual language to the Gods. When "a woman enters the funeral pyre to lift up her brahmin-slayer or ingrate husband polluted with the cardinal sins,"[123] she vicariously expiates her husband's deadly sin by self-immolation. After his victory the Babylonian God Marduk slew Kingu and said, "I will make him bear his punishment in order that you may sit in peace."[124] All prayers, atonements, pleadings for others fall in this category of transference of fate's verdict from one person to another.

One recognized mode of vicarious efforts to manipulate other's fate is the performance of obsequial rites, 'śrāddha'. The earliest attempt at moulding the destiny of the departed souls is found in the grave-goods even in pre-historic periods all over the world. Survivors were anxious for the well-being of their dear departed and wished to do something to mitigate the evils that could befall them in the next world. We do not know what else the primitive survivors did—besides providing grave-goods, food, clothes, servants, sometimes useful beasts and women. Presumably, they periodically visited the burial site and supplied what they deemed the departed spirits would need for a comfortable existence. Śrāddha is in India exists under various names and forms among most peoples. It is solely an attempt to make the dead man's life in the next world free from torments they would otherwise deserve normally through their own acts. Śrāddha aimed at diverting fate, to allay suffering and to afford and ensure a comfortable after-life for the departed, was performed to modify an otherwise adverse fate. The *Rāmāyaṇa* describes crematory rites but the *Mahābhārata,* especially in the later interpolated portions dilates greatly upon this subject. This proves that postmortal rites were gaining in social importance with time. During the composition of the Vedāṅgas and afterwards, especially, from the early Gupta period manuals on

[123] *Enuma Elish* VI: 26 in *Babylonian Genesis*, tr. Heidel, p. 35.

[124] XIII: 90–91; and on 'tarpaṇa' in ch. p. 2.

śrāddha multiplied. One reason was regional variation of the rite, another was assimilation of the indigenous rituals along with miscegenation of Aryans and pre-and non-Aryans, The *Mahābhārata* deals with the different varieties of śrāddha and their effects on the dead at great length.[125]

The *Matsya* Purana devotes a whole chapter to sraddha;[126] its main theme is the śrāddha for the ancestors. Another chapter deals with the auspiciousness of the rites, their effect on the dead as also on the survivor, the invitees and the feast itself, etc[127] Evidently, the purpose behind such lengthy and detailed treatment of the subject is not merely the well-being of the departed souls, but also to provide adequate incentive to the survivors so that, when their own turn comes, they may be ensured of similar honorific service from their progeny. Another possible aim may have been to motivate brahmins to bear suitable conduct which will justify their being invited as guests to the feast. And last of all, the feast and sumptuous gifts to brahmin recipients is no less an incentive for this elaborate ritual. True, birth, marriage and death everywhere receive extravagant rites and Śrāddha is the last of these rites. Here death imposes a terminus: The dead cannot anymore rectify their evil deeds and may suffer for them;[128] so the survivors feel called upon to placate the fate reserved for the departed souls on the basis of their own karman and offer tempting gifts to brahmins in articles of daily necessity, land, gold, etc., so that pleased with this generosity to brahmins–itself a pious gesture, fate will relent and make the after-life of the dead one somewhat easier in the next world. Almost every attempt to control, deter or deflect fate, however, involves direct or indirect payment to priests.

The *Kūrma* Purana, too, has a very long text on the details of procedure and merits, accruing from them to the dead and the survivors from observing these rites.[129] The *Mārkaṇḍeya* concentrates on the 'Naimittika śrāddha', 'pārvaṇa śrāddha', 'tithikalpa' and 'kāmyaśrāddha' i.e. rites on special occasions, with other festive days and 'specially desired' śrāddha rites.[130] In the *Matsya*

---

125 chs. 13.

126 chs. 17, 18.

127 The *Garuḍa* Purāṇa paints horripilating scenes of hell torments and the long and arduous journey to hell.

128 Uparibhāga, chs. 20–23.

129 ch. 30–33.

130 19: 8, 9.

Purāṇa there is a separate section on gifts given to ancestors which get transformed into good or bad elements according to the character and mood of the giver.[131] The *Bṛhannāradīya* stipulates articles which should not figure in the catalogue of gifts of goods.[132] The *Padma* Purāṇa has two entire chapters on śrāddha;[133] so have all other Puranic and Smṛti texts. The growing importance of the śrāddha with ever longer catalogues of 'do's and 'dont's is in direct proportion to the landlords' and kings' invention of various types of tortures for debtors, defaulters and the defiant. As the horror of these gripped the people and kept them in perpetual awe and alarm, they automatically got transferred to hell-torments and people realized that the remissnesses of their ancestors had to be set atright somehow. Hence the elaboration of śrāddha which silently told the next generation how to conduct themselves with regard to their own fathers. With time not only did the number of the śrāddha texts multiply but also the directives for the elaborate rituals. Hence śrāddha increasingly became a matter of life and death with the dying, the survivors, their children and the community as a whole. Most texts on Sraddhakalpa dwell on how the rites modify and occasionally nullify the effects of karmans performed by the deceased, free them from just punishments which otherwise would have been their portion. And all this depends on alms—giving, the pomp and splendour of the ceremony and the gifts given to brahmin recipients. In other words, a well-performed śrāddha interferes with the course of fate and turns it favourably towards the well-being of the deceased in the next life.

Śrāddha has a vicarious element in it: the survivors' actions modify the fate of the deceased. But there is a more direct way of transference of merit and sin. "Man may attempt to stop it (karman) by transference of merit, but that is a late idea and more a Mahāyāna Buddhist rather than Hindu."[134] This is one of the points of departure between Hīnayāna and Mahayana, in the latter the Bodhisattvas chose to defer their Nibbāṇa in the interest of fellow-creatures for whose enlightenment and edification the Bodhisattvas voluntarily opted for rebirth so that they could be spiritually useful to the laymen. The Epigraphia Indica gives us a few instances. In the Paja inscription it says, "for

[131] Madhya, 28: 10–12.

[132] Chs. 10 & 11.

[133] *East and West,* Vol., 38, nos. 1–4, Dec. 1988, Smith, p. 102.

[134] Vol. II: p. 63.

the spiritual happiness of all creatures the patron was willing to share merits"[135] or "for the happiness and merits of all creatures."[136] and "for the merit of all creatures."[137] Merit, as we have seen, could like wealth be earned with care and austere painstaking, had to be preserved cautiously, could be donated to a supplicant; of course, it can also be destroyed through foolish squandering or be shared with another. It was a spiritual property and authors treat it in this manner. "The doctrine of transfer of merit in the Great Vehicle implied that through faith rather than works of self-discipline, etc. the devotee could gain paradise and thereby propitious circumstances for the attainment of nibbāṇa."[138] This faith also consisted of an attitude of compassion which prompted the Bodhisattvas to forego immediate nibbāṇa when with the extinction of their karman and desire they were ripe for it, for the sake of struggling brothers with whom they shared their merits. One could also transfer one's merit to loved ones, to members of the family and friends. "Transfer of merit with members of the family (but the owner does not lose his own fund of merit, in fact he gains more) or for the larger social group."[139]

Buddhist literature also presents several instances of this kind of sharing. Although this is more clearly a mark of the Mahāyāna literature, it emerged conceptually some time before the schism became apparent and it will not probably be wrong to surmise that a section of the Sarvāstivādins was veering steadily towards what later came to be known as Mahāyāna. The Jātakas thus clearly exemplify compassion as their main incentive.

A rescue ship was sailing with only those who had the required degree of piety, a merchant who lacked them was dejected at being left back, when a lay Buddhist disciple donated to him the fruit of his own virtues, merits and spiritual power, only then the merchant was eligible for rescue; he thanked the disciple profusely.[140] At one time ten brahmins lay under water so that when the king bathed, the bath water would fall on them and with it the king's sin and moral pollution which these generous brahmins would wash

---

[135] *Jamalgarhi inscription, Ibid.,* p. 114.

[136] *Kurram inscription, Ibid.,* p. 115.

[137] Smart, 1967, p. 164.

[138] *Macmillan Encyelopaedia of Religion,* Vol. 9, p. 382.

[139] No. 190, Sīlānaśaṃsa.

[140] No. 495, Daśabrāhmaṇa.

away with their own merits.[141] One notices that here physical uncleanliness symbolizes spiritual dross and can be cleansed in a similar fashion. A courtesan saw the saint Kisabaccha and selfishly decided to shed her accumulated sin on this holy man and be wholly cleansed by bathing. He allowed her to do so. A deposed family priest also dropped his sins on another, became purified and was reinstated.[142]

In the *Mahāvagga*[143] such universal grace or karuṇā to all creatures finds expression. We also remember Jesus saying in a prophetic discourse, "Verily I say unto you, in as much as ye have done it unto one of the least of these my brethren ye have done it unto me."[144] This is a lofty instance of transference of merit; by serving human beings one serves God and earns merit through vicarious acts of philanthropy. In all these instances— and there are others in the vast bulk of Buddhist literature—the compassion which moves the donors to share their merits with the less fortunate and less pious, to uplift them spiritually is clear. In Brahmanism, however, the motivation is less altruistic. Even in the Ruru and Pramadvarā incident, the motivation was partly selfish, Ruru's life had lost all meaning after he lost Pramadvarā. Somaka was stung by compunction at finding his priest suffering in hell, but we remember that the priest had earned his hell by instructing the king in an inhumanly cruel remedy. However, the king's remorse made him plead with Dharma. Dharma saw the truth in the king's argument and allowed the priest to borrow part of Somaka's merits and then he sent both to heaven. By and large, the Buddhist texts portray great compassion which prompted sharing of merits. Although Christianity also is based on compassion there is a tone of finality about sins and righteousness, specially in the post-mortal stage. The leper who used to sit at the rich man Lazarus' gate begging went to heaven and rested on Abraham's breast. The rich man in hell begged Abraham to let the beggar dip his toe in water and cool his parched tongue in hell; Abraham categorically denied the possibility: there was no communication between heaven and hell.[145]

---

[141] No. 522, *Sarabhaṅga.*

[142] VIII: 26.

[143] *Matthew,* 25: 40.

[144] *Luke* 16: 19–31.

[145] Kayes and Daniel, 1983, p. 35.

One reason why inspite of sharing merit with others the owner, instead of losing on his own fund gains on it is because the very impulse of sharing merit is such a righteous one that it adds to his store of merits so that he does not lose by sharing. Another reason seems to be that: "This karma consists not only of a person's own past deeds but the deeds of others from whom the person has received karma through shared blood, food and so forth. Thus a person's head-writing insures punishments and rewards for the deeds of others over whom he has no control."[146] The clear insinuation is that man is a creature of his environment, his familial background, members with whom he has shared the daily necessities and from whom he has inherited a spiritual legacy and therefore, to them he has an obligation. The vulgate Bengali edition of the *Rāmāyaṇa* makes the author Vālmṇki a brigand to begin with. One day he felt guilty for the crimes he had committed and tried to console himself that those who shared the ill-gotten money and food had a deep spiritual obligation to share part of his sins. But when he asked them one by one they all replied that they had eaten his food, but how he had procured it was entirely his business, they would not share his sins; it was all his own. Somehow this view seems to be a more natural view of sins and their effects: the burden of privately incurred sins was to be borne by the perpetrator of the sins although as familial dependants they felt no qualms about sharing his profits. It almost tells us that although it is easy to share merits it is very difficult to coax others to bear the burden of their sins. In sins, in departure from the straight and narrow path, man becomes isolated and spiritually lonely.

But sometimes even sins could be shared although under exceptional circumstances. The *Florentine Codex* says that "the illtreated slave could transfer his sins on to the miscreant i.e. oppressor."[147] Here in India sharing of sins is rare, unless where ancestral sins devolve on successors, much more common is the transference of merit. We have already seen how the shameless king Yayāti, Mādhavī's father, after exploiting his daughter's beauty and tender years came begging to her door where she sat meditating and asked for a share of her merit to make up for his deficiency in merits in order to go to heaven and felt no qualms when she made this ultimate sacrifice for a heartless father.[148] Sins can contaminate generations beyond the present.

---

[146] Bk. VI: 36.

[147] *Mbh* V: 119: 23–27.

[148] *Mbh* VI: 38: 7.

"One commits crime, under the delusion of Kāla, that low one through his own acts sinks the entire line to annihilation."[149]

Pramadvarā, whom her loving fiancé could not live without, had been bitten by a serpent and died. Ruru was distracted, demented and lamenting heart-breakingly he managed to make the Gods allow him to share half of his span of life with this deceased sweet-heart. The authorities moved by his utter agony granted him permission to do so.[150] A late Puranic account of this uncommon anecdote has a new dimension added to it. When Ruru was mourning his wife's death in a demented heartbroken manner, to him came two sages by the name of Yajñamālin and Sumālin and they said something very significant to the bereaved Ruru: "O Brahmin, listen to the way out — *which the Gods have recommended from of old*; with half of your life, revive Pramadvarā."[151] What strikes us is that the Gods have approved of such sharing of life-span 'from of old.' A very telling incident in the *Atharvaveda* says that the Gods had sinned and were on the look-out for a scapegoat. They found one in Trita on whom they wiped their sins. But Trita was too clever to carry the dark stigma of the Gods' sins, so he promptly went and wiped it on men.[152] The tale being inherited from the *Ṛgveda* and continued to the *Śatapatha* Brāhmaṇa makes it rather significant. It is etiological in nature: on the one hand it tells us that the Gods are not above sinning, it also explains how the sinful Gods became sinless by transferring their sins on to men and it also incidentally explains how men became sinful by transference.

In the *Brahma* Purāṇa Pārvatī transfers her merit earned by tapas to her spouse Śiva and Śiva accepted it without a demur.[153] It is mostly a woman[154] who shares the merit and in male-dominated society the man accepts it as his due. The childless king Somaka was advised by the family priest to sacrifice the son which the king had had after an interminably long wait. Somaka was deeply perturbed by (1) the prospect of finally losing the only child he had after such a long time and (2) by the totally unnatural step the

149 *Mbh* 1: 9: 15.

150 *Devībhāgavata* II: 9: 32, italics added.

151 *AV* VI: 113: 1–3; also *RVII*: II: 28; VI: 51: 7; VIII: 52: 2. *Vājasaneyī Saṃhitā* III: 48. *Śatapatha* Brāhmaṇa IV: 4: 5: 22.

152 XXXV: 31–60.

153 Except is Ruru's case of emotion *in extremis*.

154 *Mbh* III: 127: 1–10.

priest had prescribed viz. the father sacrificing his only son. But the king, greedy for a hundred sons followed the priest's instruction and quartered Jantu in the sacrifice, burned the child and made his hundred agonized queens inhale the smoke. Eventually, the queens did give birth to a hundred sons. The king and the priest after their death found themselves in hell and the king requested Dharma to allow him to substitute the priest. To this, Dharma replied: "No one ever experiences the fruit of another's karman." But the king took the onus of the heinous crime on himself and begged Dharma for the priest's release. Moved by the king's long and persistent pleas, at last Dharma relented and said: "Share your merits equally with him and then both of you can go to heaven for a shorter stay." King Somaka very happily did so.[155]

As has been clear by now, man is not born with merit, except what he had earned in his previous births. With merits earned by pious works, vows, pilgrimages, almsgiving, performing sacrifices and pūjās, making donations to worthy brahmins, spending on works of public utility, fasting, meditating and being devoted to the Gods, he can add to the store of merit and lay by a stock. With this he can go to heaven, be born as a high, noble, rich, handsome and learned person, or be born into one of the higher Gods' realms. If his stock is truly adequate, it will bring him the liberating realization and he will attain mokṣa or nirvāṇa. But since the stock of merits is his own property, he can share it gratuitously, or at another's request with other deserving candidates, if he so chooses. And in this way he transforms the other person's fate and by the same token his own fate, too, is modified. Yayāti's own merits would not have taken him to heaven, so when Mādhavī lent him part of her merits, Yayāti's ascent to heaven was through vicarious means, through transference of merit. Fate in this case was not predestined in the sense that Mādhavī was free to decline to share her merit or to donate it. Her generostiy altered the course of her father's fate and this became possible because merit was conceptually reified, it was looked upon as a material possession which could be loaned or donated. Life-span and spiritual merits are like assets which can be shared at the owner's will. This concept of looking upon these as material objects is Indo-European, strewn over many anecdotes in Indo-European literature.

---

[155] This reminds us of the story of Kastor and Polydeukes who shared their span of life. on the earth and in the firmament.

These vicarious, deviationary measures are all various forms of karman. Even devotion prompts different kinds of devotional services i.e. acts. Śrāddha involves karman, as do vows, pilgrimages, charity, etc. Only curses and boons are words charged with supernatural power, but their objective is the same: to deflect or modify the course of fate. Fate thus can be manipulated by human and divine agencies. In one aspect, then, fate is not as immutable or irrevocable as we are given to understand. These loopholes are invented to reassure men of a way out of adverse verdicts of fate and at the same time, for priests and 'holy men' to come forward to assist men in distress. And to line their own nests in the process. In most cases the assistance defies proof, as no one knows what was intended by fate; therefore, whether the deflectionary measures have been effective will never be known for sure. For example, no one can predict what a dead man's lot in the other world is going to be. Therefore, that a well-performed 'śrāddha' with rich donations given to brahmins improves the soul's destiny is also beyond proof. And, for that matter, the existence of the soul beyond death itself cannot be proved. Similarly, pilgrimages, vows, charity etc. are cited as measures through which sins committed in previous lives are remitted, but since rebirth itself is merely conjectural, the efficacy of these deflective measures are little more than fictitious. But all myth, ritual, theology are built on conjecture, hence these measures, at best offer the kind of service a psychiatrist offers his patients: placidity and a sense of relief. But people everywhere all through the ages have hankered for this sense of relief. Priests first create an elaborate structure of various types of guilt, some real, ethical, anti-human acts, others, ritual, mythical, anti-god, anti-priest, anti-brahmin acts. Then the same priests construct an edifice of beliefs in fate, its inscrutability, the laws of karman and rebirth and measures to counter the intentions of fate. Since neither the malady nor the remedy can be proved, men are given the assurance that the prescribed measures will thwart the evil designs of fate and improve their chances of happiness, longevity, success and heaven. When once the sense of guilt is established firmly as it has been in most religions, men become only too eager to wash away the guilt. Redemption is thus the keyword in religions. Theologians and priests exploit mens' willing suspension of disbelief because redemption is dangled before the poor guilt-ridden souls. Once the guilt-redemption syndrome is firmly entrenched in the human consciousness, this vast complex structure for assuaging the wrath of an adverse fate is readily accepted by men. Heaven, hell, purgatory, the astral state, rebirth as

Gods, demi-gods, men and beasts—all fall in their places in this structure. With time, the variety of intentional and unwitting offences multiplies and with it multiplies the many and various preventive, expiatory and deflective measures. All of these presuppose fate. In India, to fate have been added karman and rebirth, complicating matters further. An intricate pattern is woven which only the tribe of priests and god-men claim to be able to disentangle. When they prescribe measures against the imaginary wrath of fate provoked by imaginary sins committed in imaginary previous (and/or successive) births potentially, the clientele feels nothing but gratitude and abject submission which prompts them to surrender rationality and free-thinking. Freedom of will is presented as ultimately illusory since fate predestines the course of human affairs. Then what is a man left with, but the will to improve his luck by obeying the prescriptions laid down in scriptures?

Yet, as we shall see in the next chapter, human rationality is very difficult to count without. Man is inherently aware that he can, to a large extent, organize his affairs with his own effort. In this he scores over fate. Instead of fighting an adverse fate along the path dictated by the scriptures, down the ages some men have chosen to fight it with their own endeavour.

CHAPTER 9

Fate and Human Endeavour

BEFORE plunging into the main theme of this chapter viz. the relative positions of fate and human endeavour as presented in the scriptures, we shall once again probe into the nature of fate itself. Life for the toiling masses in anciént India, as everywhere else, was hard and bitter. The Aryans came as a nomadic pastoral people; cattle was their base of subsistence, roots and fruits supplemented their food, as did hunting. When they had virtually subjugated an urban agricultural and trading people their ethos first clashed with, then was overwhelmed by it and finally it assimilated some part of the subjugated people. What was this ethos? We have no records of the indigenous non-or pre-Aryan peoples. Our sole source is first the *Ṛgveda* Saṃhitā and then the slow and steady changes ushered in the *Yajurveda,* the Brāhmaṇas and finally the *Atharva* Saṃhitā. These changes can to some extent be ascribed to the miscegenation and the cultural amalgamation of the two peoples. Whatever other differences they may have had, the fact that life was difficult and fraught with many dangers persists throughout. Even when the invaders had learned to cultivate and to make houses with kiln-burnt bricks,[1] nature posed many problems for them—there were floods, droughts, locusts, bad feuds, harvests, plagues, epidemics among men and cattle, earthquakes, forestfires, tempests, etc. Many were the threats to life and property for these early settlers here. Chance, the unapprehended, was thus taken for fate which was behind such insecurity and was responsible for such accidents.

> Conditions of unresolved wretchedness are fertile soil for the fatalistic attitude. In many cases the anaesthesia of fatalism combines with the rigidity of long established patterns of social behaviour and the interest of the privileged classes to produce the quietistic resignation which results in toleration of social wrongs and incapacity for experimental change... Fate is blind, it gives solace, not guidance. The same fatalism that may serve to entrench autocracy in the privileged position of a caste will justify successful

[1] Instead of shacks of sun-baked bricks of the first phase.

> revolution... so long as tools and technology for the mastery of nature are lacking, so long as there is no effective solution for the social problems of poverty, sex injustice, insanity, crime and war the attitude of resignation—be it to fate or to the will of God— is there.[2]

Where monotheism predominates as in the Semitic religions, it theoretically precludes fate or chance, because God is the ultimate arbiter, without his approval or permission nothing can take place. If the definition of fatalism is a belief in man's destiny as determined by an impersonal agent called Fate, then fatalism excludes belief in God as the dispenser of destiny.

In India, as we have said earlier, there is no trace of fatalism in the earliest literature—Saṃhitās, Brāhmaṇas and Upaniṣads. Society had advanced, the Aryan, non-Aryan composite culture spread farther towards south-east. The forests were utilized, some were burnt to expand the area of arable land, the iron ploughshare was gradually employed to facilitate cultivation which together with trade enhanced surplus wealth, townships sprang up and communities changed their social contour. Tribes disintegrated, joint families 'kulas' arose governed by the *pater familias.* All this had a direct influence on the conceptual world of the country.

> The process of accelerated food production must have received impetus from the availability of slaves in. large numbers recruited from the vanquished aboriginals... in the pre-Mauryan society rural raw materials and the finished urban products had gone into the hands of the same class... The vanquished tribes working as slaves on the estates of the Aryans were deprived of their resources and wealth. A large resourceless population came to depend for its subsistence upon a comparatively smaller section of victors. Thus within the Aryan society purchasing capacity was absent from a substantial section of the population. Consequently, the economic factor for the development of markets and towns remained for centuries conspicuously non-existent... the disintegration of the tribal or communal structure and the emergence of the family as the unit of production became marked features of the age... A drastic change in the social competence of the priestly class was brought about in the post-Mauryan period as a result of the development of new ideologies and institutions, a change in the social competence of both the donné and the members of the donated villages effected by the policy of donation.[3]

---

2 *Encyclopaedia of Social Sciences, pp. 147, 148.*

3 Rai, 1974, pp. 105, 127, 152, 165, 394.

In the land grants sometimes entire villages were given away to brahmins and priests. This change of ownership affected the inhabitants, too. The predominance of the priestly class after the revival of Brahminism, as an aftermath of the decline of Buddhism, ushered in conspicuous changes in people's attitude to life, the new modifications all helped to entrench fate as an ineluctable and formidable force. One natural factor led to the rise of fatalism viz. observation of the inexorability of death. "Among the Orphics fate was viewed as the law which controls the conditions of our birth, death and successive reincarnations. The belief in process of a constant, monotonous and unavoidable return to the point of departure came to be symbolically represented in the revolutions of a wheel."[4] This statement about the Orphics is true also about ancient India where recurring births meant recurring submission to the repetition of cheerless lives, especially for the downtrodden masses in an oppressive class-divided society. For such people this existence was governed not so much by a compassionate God but by the blind machine-like fate. And the notion of fate was fostered by the discrepancy between the classes and the apathy of the ruling classes to the depressed sections of society.

The quality of life for the vast majority of people must have been deplorably poor. This contrasted sharply with the rise of a class of *nouveau riche* with conspicuous consumption as some late Brāhmaṇa texts testify. The consequent spiritual upheaval can be easily surmised. Even during the Vedic age the quality of life had been spare and meagre, but then the community was tribal with no sharp class distinction which upheld some kind of balance and cohesion. "It was apparently a fairly marginal existence which was possible under the given circumstances: survival was precious and threatened by famine, disease, enemy and wild animals. Every catastrophe was necessarily attributed to a break in the power-circuit that connected the devas with the world of men; Vedic Indians did assume that the Gods were capricious, but they considered them to be almost mechanically acting elements in a power-circuit (Dravya-Deva-Mantra-Yajamāna)[5] which was kept charged by the sacrifices performed by the competent members of the community (the brahmins). If the power-circuit failed, the point where it had to be ended was the sacrificial karma."[6]

---

[4] *Dictionary of the History of Ideas,* 1973, p. 226.

[5] i.e., oblations–God spells and the sacrificer.

[6] Jash (ed.), 1984, p. 351.

With improvement in agriculture and resumption of Western maritime trade, surplus was generated rapidly which was controlled by the upper echelons of society. This section was numerically insignificant compared to the vast majority of the masses under grinding poverty. The natural and almost immediate result of this was that there was a stiffer stratification of classes which cut across caste. As the second century A.D. text *Aṅgavijjā* says "there are only two classes ajja and pessa,"[7] the nobility and the serving masses. With this transformation in society the earlier simple tribal equitable distribution of wealth disappeared. Sharp inequality between social security, consumption and the quality of life between the primary producer and the consumer of goods led to greater disaffection not only towards the social norms but also to the religion which sanctioned such wide hiatus in people's life. If religion sanctioned this gross unseemly discrepancy, then it did not stand for any kind of equality, justice or fairness. Along with the economic changes, caste, caste-rules and practices sharply divided a handful in the upper caste from the majority of the lower, primary producer castes. The communication and relationship between these two sections shrunk increasingly, putting manual labour at a disadvantage and endowing the intellectual elite and the priestly caste with an aura and charisma which facilitated the suppression of the majority by the minority.

The picture had changed radically through the Upanisadic thought, dissident religious trends like Buddhism, Jainism and Ājīvikism and many other nameless sects with independent sets of beliefs and practices, until in the century or two before the Guptas, we have clear pronouncement of fate. There must have been considerable ideological turmoil for quite sometime raging in the community's inner life before this could happen. Such turmoil touched the common man as well as the religious thinker and social law giver. "The development of rival religious trends reflected not only the increased contradictions within the ruling classes, some of these trends also found a response among the broad masses which was a sign of unconscious protest against oppression of the caste system."[8] Without doubt by the time of the epics, caste had become a tool of social oppression. The majority of the common people were non-brahmins, therefore, less privileged in caste consideration, they were the poverty-stricken tillers and artisans who worked

[7] i.e. 'arya' and 'preṣya'.

[8] Tokarey, 1989, p. 173.

under and for the rich. Thus under this double oppression, good, harmless and innocent people chafed inwardly. They could not blame their acts in this life and the scriptures told them that their acts in previous lives were responsible for their present suffering. That part of their life was completely unseen and dark to them: it was, therefore, adṛṣṭa, a preordained scheme which allocated suffering to them blindly. Did not the people recognize the same blind irrationality in fate as they saw in the state machinery? Could they fail to see that fate was but another name for the hidden acts of a power which was nothing but a replica of the powers which ruled on earth, meting out unjust, cruel lots to the poor whose murmurs of protest went unheard and unheeded?

"The situation on the land had deteriorated because *taxes and liturgies* were too high: burdens were too great... A vicious circle of evils was in full swing. The ancient world was hastened to its end by its social and political structure, its deeply embedded and institutionalized value system and underpinning the whole, the organization and exploitation of its productive forces. There, if one wishes is an explanation of its productive forces. There, if one wishes is an explanation of the end of the ancient world."[9] In India also although the burden of liturgies was not so obvious to the common people in the Vedic sacrificial era, the Puranic religion introduced personal Gods (iṣṭadevatā), familial Gods (gṛha-devatā or kula devatā) who had to be propitiated on specific days, together with vows, almsgiving, pilgrimages—all of which was optional but if fate looms large in a man's horizon, he will spend his last savings to manipulate it. By one or more of the deflective measures. It is the awe, the fear of the unknown that impelled him irresistibly.

In ancient China also "Social change and widespread civil turmoil and suffering led some in this era (eighth C.B.C.) to question the power of the Gods ... many Gods charged with protection were deemed to have failed while their desecrators flourished. In the Shih Ching (600c. B.C.) were verses that question the justice of heaven itself."[10]

The sense of the Gods failing men was felt here in India also, if only subconsciously and not as overtly as in China. Before fatalism became a factor in the Indian religious life there was a period of multifarious troubles.

---

9 Finley, 1973, pp. 172, 176.

10 *Macmillan Encyclopaedia of Religion*, 'Chinese Religion', p. 260.

Beginning with a series of foreign invasions, the contour of the economic life changing considerably with the resumption of maritime trade with the West via the Middle East, the introduction of coinage, writing, the calendar, disintegration of the tribal organization of society, wealth accumulating in the hands of a minority who wielded disproportionate power over those below, all this rendered life for the vast majority of the poor and miserable appear like a curse which they would fain escape. Release from this chain of rebirths became a tempting dream. Belief in the efficacy of the sacrifice had already been shaken to its very roots.[11] In such an atmosphere the theory of karman would naturally thrive. But since sacrifices did not deliver the goods, men naturally looked elsewhere in the hope of finding a logical explanation of what happened to him, a causal basis for his experiences. The very first premise about the Gods effectively negated the possibility of cruelty, oppression, penury, diseases, undeserved suffering and disasters; no kind and almighty God would allow these to happen to men. With the theory of karman experiences would have been explained adequately if there was an infallible correspondence between acts and results, or, if there were an acceptable arbiter whose judgements people could admit as just and therefore, could rely on. In the absence of these there remained the sole possibility of an unknown and unknowable capricious power which governed human affairs. This man called fate.

The legacy of Vedic exegesis and the corollary of its metaphysics, Mīmāṃsā, which "deals with Dharma, not with Mokṣa... Mīmāṃsā carries the heritage of the pre-karmic past of the Indian tradition, into an epoch for which karma and saṃsāra have become basic premises."[12] It is interesting to note that while the Saṃhitās consistently express the desire for a long life, because life was good, because it did one good to see the rising sun every day, the later Vedic Upaniṣads propound the theory of rebirth and look upon it as an evil to escape from. "Here would be a gradual passing from an initial naturistic harmonistic attitude where the human soul is not yet violently opposed to the world, to a final anti-cosmic and anti-somatic position and as such dualistic and pessimistic, which is peculiar to gnosis."[13]

---

[11] cf. the *Muṇḍaka* Up. passage about the sacrifices being mere shaky boats, unstable 1: 2: 7.

[12] Halbfass, 1991, p. 301.

[13] Bianchi, Blecker & Bausani (ed.), 1972, p. 107.

We thus see that fatalism had multiple causes. On the material plane there was turmoil, invasion and political insecurity leading to social unrest; innovations which led to long-term changes in the mode of production, cultivation of new areas of knowledge which forced men to make an effort for assimilating these and which, to that extent, revolutionized the basis of the known world. These, together with improved techniques in production and resumption of overseas trade brought in surplus in wealth which gradually but steadily shook the foundations of tribal organization ushering in the joint family as the social unit. On the economic plane the surplus sharply divided the population into the affluent and the destitutes; in other words, besides the existing evil of caste, the newer evil of class made its appearance, further complicating social relationships. Foreign invasions disturbed the ecological and sociological balance by posing the problem of ethnic, social and cultural assimilation of the new-comers. A new post-epic pantheon now dominated the religious scene, pūjā replaced yajña, sacrifice and this was a radical change, the entire paraphernalia was new. The attitude to life changed drastically, escape was the motto. During the Upaniṣads this escape was through gnosis,[14] now it was primarily through allegiance and devotion to one's chosen God, for the mundane bliss and bounty as well as for the final release. Karman inevitably generated its fruit and left a residue of desire which bound one in the chain of rebirth. Hence the effort was for attaining mokṣa, release from rebirth, from karman and desire. Yet the equivalence of karman and its fruit was shaky, some karmans visibly produced the effect: you put your fingers to the flame and it is singed. But what if you do so and it is not singed? Or you do not put your finger even near the flame and it still gets singed? Then one is pushed to the conclusion that in karman and retribution, there is more than meets the eye. But this is not adequately explained by theology or the Gods, unless we assume that they normally behave erratically or capriciously. Then man ordered his moral universe differently by inventing fate to which he could ascribe whatever did not fit it in the paradigm. Fatalism came as a complement to the theory of karman and rebirth. The veil that separated the known, visible, rational, expected, calculable from what could not be explained save through fate was attributed to it. It is to the credit of man that he invented fate *in extremist* in his

[14] Earlier, during the Saṃhitā-Brāhmaṇa period it was through karman sacrifice.

innermost drive for knowledge of reality, his desire to understand why things happened to him as they did. When rationality failed to explain, irrationality was called in an attempt to fill the vacuum in his knowledge. The idea that life itself is wholly irrational was unacceptable to him, hence he preferred to think that there is an unknown area beyond his karman and their results, beyond the benign Gods who are basically philanthropic if propitiated correctly, beyond all that is known about life. Here is the domain of almighty fate, it is fate which governs this area, fate is dark to man—the area of those karmans done unwittingly or in one of his previous lives. How is man to penetrate that supernatural umbrage? He can only submit to the unlimited might of fate - the supreme. And this he did elaborately inventing rituals to gain some prognosis or presage, also inventing what he regarded as remedial measures undertaken by himself or vicariously. But nothing, nothing at all, gave an adequate account of what caused human experiences and yet was rooted beyond human knowledge.

Very early in human history, the Babylonians felt perplexed by the many facets of the problem of human suffering and human destiny. "No real answer to the problem of why he had to suffer is attempted. The text[15] merely holds out the consideration that the Gods can have a change of heart and take pity. The other composition is known as *Theodicy,* it is in the form of a dialogue between two friends about the fact that evil men appear to prosper where as good men fall on evil days. Here, too, there is no real answer, only a conviction that eventually retribution will come to evil-doers."[16] This visible discrepancy between piety and suffering and between impiety and happiness is one of the reasons which pushed men to the theory of fate and to that of karman in a previous birth attaining fruition in the present. Yet this leaves a large margin of uncertainty: which karman did one perform in which previous birth that will bear fruit in the present? And what kind of fruit? Where is the chart of correspondence between work and its effect? In the pre-legal society this correspondence could have no basis in man's social right. But even after Hammurabi and his code, the concept of an inscrutable fate ingrained in the social consciousness continued to be operative. Partially because first, even in the law-codes there were many loopholes and some

---

15 'Ludlul suffering unjustly'.

16 *Macmillan Encyclopaedia of Religion*, 'Babylon'.

remote local judges passed arbitrary judgements and secondly because there were special prerogatives reserved for the privileged and thus the common people and the powerful affluent section were not the same. This left large loopholes in an otherwise just, civil and criminal code. Thirdly, an agricultural people knew that time must elapse between the sowing and the harvest which fortified the theory of man reaping the fruits of his actions done in a previous birth. Unaccountable suffering, sometimes, unforeseen windfalls of happiness were sure; what was not sure was a just retribution. Hence the belief in fate found a solid foothold. Yet the expectation of eventual just retribution dies hard, hence the apocalyptic myths of a future redeemer who will redress all wrongs. The second coming of Christ or a Kalkin, a Ragnarök or of a Cargo cult are dangled before men, the vision of a New Heaven and a New Earth. '*The Epic of Gilgamesh*' of the third millennium B.C. describes an apocalyptic vision of a land full of the good things of life. "There was the garden of the Gods, all around him stood bushes bearing gems... there was fruit of carnelian with vine hanging from it beautiful to look at; lapis lazuli leaves hung thick with fruit, sweet to see. For thorns there were haematite and rare stone, agates and pearls out of the sea."[17] The *Bible* has a comparable description in the Book of Revelation. "And I saw a new heaven and a new earth... and God shall wipe away all tears from their eyes and there shall be no more death, neither sorrow nor crying, neither shall there be any more pain, for the former things are passed away."[18] Does not all humanity languish and pine for a place where God will wipe away all tears, where all wrongs shall be righted and there shall be no more suffering, lamentation and death? It is theologically necessary to use this bait of apocalyptic hope of a final, total and lasting redressing of all the ills of life.

In India the earliest picture is that of the Soma-drinkers' paradise depicted in the Soma book of the *Ṛgveda:* "Where (the fulfilment) of all desires (is) food (and) satisfaction, make me immortal there. Where there is joy and happiness, pleasures and ultimate delight, where desires have a final fulfilment, make me immortal there."[19] This dream persisted down the ages. The earliest reference to Uttarakuru, the land of all pleasures is in the Brāhmaṇas,

---

[17] Penguin edn. ch. IV.

[18] Ch. XXI: 1, 4.

[19] IX: 114: 10–14.

significantly during the period of the earliest class divisions:[20] the next reference is in the *Mahābhārata* which describes it as "a land which yields harvest without cultivation, where each bud or tender leaf-sprouts holds honey"[21] and one of the latest Puranic references is in the *Bhāgavata* Purāṇa. "Here (in Uttarakuru) was where the Aryans had their first habitat, siddhas (a species of blessed beings) dwell here, trees bear fruits and sweet scented flowers, the wish-fulfilling tree grows here, gold and jewels are strewn on the ground. The heavenly Mandākinī flows here and the Caitraratha bower is also here."[22] Even in the Gupta age, poet Kālidāsa describes such a place once in the last act of his drama *Abhijñānaśakuntakm*[23] in the description of the semi-divine sage Mārīca's hermitage. In his poem the *Kumārasambhava* Kalidāsa describes the Oṣadhiprastha "where age stops at youth, (where there is) no other killer but the God of love."[24] "It is such a happy place that people deem the heavenly happiness as deprivation."[25] And the last time in the description of Alakā in the *Meghadūta*: "Where the only tears are those of joy and not from any other cause, no other suffering except the pangs of love which is allayed through union with the beloved, no other separation except that of a lover's quarrel and the yakṣas (who dwell there) have no other age but youth."[26]

All this was extremely necessary to keep a dream alive, a dream of all retributions men miss on earth, for which he hankers all his life long and which, he is told repeatedly, is either there in Uttarakuru or Alakā or will be ushered in at the final apocalyptic stage. Incidentally, all mythologies place this idyllic realm of perpetual unalloyed happiness at the two poles of time: in the beginning[27] and at the end, after Kalkin has demolished this tarnished and corrupt creation, or a new aeon is ushered in at Ragnarök, a new Heaven and new earth at the apocalypse etc. These mirages at two ends of time are supposed to instil courage in men so that they can bear patiently

---

[20] *Aitareya* VIII: 23.

[21] II: 28: 7–20.

[22] V: 18: 34.

[23] VII: 12.

[24] VI: 44.

[25] VI: 47.

[26] Verse 66.

[27] In the Satya aeon, the *Garden of Eden*, Yama's heaven, etc.

their miserable sojourn here. Meanwhile, these are remote in time and place but keeps any possible revolt in check, any effective protest against innumerable social anomalies.

The Nippur inscription of the second millennium B.C. describes Dilmun, the land of Heart's Desire as "(Where) the croak of the raven was not heard, the bird of death did not shriek the cry of death, the wolf did not rend the Iamb, the dove did not mourn, there was no widow, no sickness, no old age, no lamentation."

But as long as retribution fails to materialize and is merely a dream kept alive by repeated references by priests and poets, man lives in an essentially unjust world and can hardly accept this non-rational state of things as irremediably final. Till the apocalypse arrives, there is the belief in fate which offers a pseudo-explanation to all mundane anomalies, all social discrepancies, all injustices and undue oppressions. Even before the epics, the Buddhist literature presented instances of belief in fate. In one tale a series of chance incidents decide vital issues.[28] Here chance predominates and decides the course of human life; such chance incidents act as agents of fate. Of some innocent boys remaining calm in the face of adversity, Buddha said that Fate was too strong and had done his utmost with regard to these boys.[29] Here Buddha representing the supreme spiritual authority himself acknowledges the authority of fate and ascribes the boys' misfortune to fate. Accidents are depicted as agents of fate; a series of such accidents were introduced in a tale to fortify the concept of fate.[30] Buddha in one of his incarnations was born as a golden goose. Caught, he did not flee because, he said, "when life is coming to an end and death's hour draws nigh / tho' you may close upon it come, nor trap nor snare you spy."[31] A king was chased by ill-luck for a long time, to Temiyakumāra he said, "I know wherever I go, fate watching never slumbereth."[32]

The *Rāmāyaṇa* defines fate succinctly, "that which cannot be grasped by thought is fate, it is not destroyed in creatures."[33] This epic is full of unforseen

---

[28] No. 257, *Gāmanichanda.*

[29] No. 368, *Tacasāra.*

[30] No. 432, *Padakusalamaṇava.*

[31] No. 502, *Hamsa.* Fausböll's translation.

[32] No. 538, Mūgapakkha.

[33] II: 20: 20.

events and even otherwise heroic characters here often betray a submission to fate; Rāma says to Lakṣmaṇa 'who can afford to fight against fate?'[34] Elsewhere we are treated to a homily on fate, "happiness and grief, fear and anger, gain and loss, being and non-being, whoever undergoes any of these, that is an act of fate. Even saints who have practised rigorous penance, when acted upon by fate, forsake their rigour and fall through passion and wrath. What had not been intended, what occurs abruptly, preventing the thing undertaken by (other) undertakings— that indeed is an act of fate."[35] Kauśalyā laments at Rama's banishment saying, "Kālā, verily is hard to cross."[36] or "the course of fate on this earth, my son, baffles thought."[37] "Prowess succeeds over the drunk, the accused, those struck by fate; this has been decreed by fate after deliberation."[38] "Even the heroic, the strong and the armed when overwhelmed by Fate collapse in battle like bridges of sand."[39] At Rāvaṇa's death his women lament, "fate prevails everywhere, the dead one is slain by fate."[40] The same idea of the supremacy of fate is found in the Mahābhārata also. As a more mature and complex creation of artistry it probes the issue at greater depth. How does fate work on a man? "Fate robs one of his vision, falling like an eye of fire (on hirn)."[41] As an orb of fire descending on a person's eyes dazzles his vision so completely that he cannot see anything clearly, so does Fate suddenly overwhelm a person's discrimination so that he behaves as one morally blind and the resulting misfortune comes to him almost in the shape of retribution for his own acts. The famous statement on Fate's mode of action says, "The man to whom Fate allots defeat, it robs him of his intellect (first) and he begins to see things in a reverse fashion."[42] "Whatever a man gets by chance or by fate is without doubt fate itself."[43] 'There is no reason for dangers, no limit, no reason,

[34] II: 22: 20.

[35] II: 22: 20–24.

[36] II: 24: 33.

[37] II: 24: 35.

[38] VI: 8: 9.

[39] VI: 17: 24.

[40] VI: 110: 23.

[41] II: 52: 18.

[42] II: 72: 8.

[43] III: 33: 15.

Dharma, indeed, divides between sins and merit."[44] "Fate is stronger," says Kuntī to Karṇa after Karṇa turns down Sūrya's order to him to fight alongside the Pāṇḍavas. Kuntī says, 'fate is stronger.' Stronger than what? Human efforts to direct or govern his own course in life. This simple comparative is thus extremely eloquent. The earlier image of fate muddling the intelligence of one whom it wishes to crush reminds us of the saying, 'whom the Gods destroy they first make mad?' So fate does not act directly; it takes the subtler method of clouding its victim's wits. Why? So that the onus of his acts done under such clouded intelligence should be his own and the evils which follow should appear a natural consequences, retribution for his own misdeeds. Yet the initial mischief is clearly fate's work.

When Ambā had been abducted along with her two younger sisters by Bhīṣma, she went against her will because she loved Śālva, ultimately, Bhīṣma let her go, but by then Śālva's ego was hurt; feeling piqued, he jilted her. Then she was in a quandary and in deep anguish of soul she cursed fate.[45] Let us pause for a moment and ponder on Ambā's life. She loved king Śālva which had nothing sinful about it Abducted by Bhīṣma to be given to another, she revealed her love for Śālva to Bhīṣma and Bhīṣma, acting like a gentleman, let her go to Śālva. But Śālva had heard that she had been abducted to be another's bride, so he felt insulted and refused to wed her because she had been intended for another. In Śālva's rejection of Ambā we see the hand of fate. But on the face of it, Śālva's right royal kṣatriya pride was injured – a fair-enough explanation for jilting Ambā. In this episode, as in hundreds of others, fate acts as a living human enemy hurling its weapons on the innocent and unsuspecting human victims from its place of hiding. It is this subtle malignity which presents fate in numerous episodes as an intelligent hostile force, playing his games from concealment—adṛṣṭa—therefore, impossible to combat. His moves are recognized only after the axe falls and then it is too late. During the war soldiers felt that victory was essentially unsure, unstable i.e. unpredictable; fate alone prevails.[46] This is really an insult to kṣatriya soldiers' prowess and chivalry. What is the use of sound military training of clever, heroic fighting of superiority in arms and numerical superiority of a well-trained army fighting bravely and tenaciously if the outcome depends

---

[44] III: 295: 1.

[45] V: 172: 6.

[46] VI: 4: 35.

on fate alone? Human effort is devalued in a rather humiliating fashion in order to glorify fate. And such passages are strewn all over the epics and Purāṇas.

The naturalist explanations of phenomena as we have seen earlier is an attempt to ascribe all responsibility to the working of nature. "The tasks nature with her attributes accomplishes, the man bewitched by pride in himself, thinks that he himself does,"[47] when Dhṛtarāṣṭra repents his misdeeds and laments, he also blames fate as impelling him to act as he did, "what evils 1 did in the past through a mind eclipsed by fate."[48] "Kāla has no favourites or enemies, Kāla is never indifferent, every one is dragged by Kāla."[49] "Kāla in turns takes away the lives of all creatures."[50] "Understand Kāla to have no parents, none is favoured by him, he is witness of mens" actions and his soul has the shape of karman, a witness of the auspicious and the sinful, the result of happiness and grief is kāla (know him as) the bestower of the fruits of actions."[51] "It was fated to happen, so you should not mourn it, who can ever thwart fate by special wisdom?"[52] "So the Pāṇḍavas ever suffer their own fate."[53] "We know that (power) to be fate which cannot be thwarted. It is not possible to overcome fate with human effort."[54] "Fate does not save man full of greed and illusion."[55] And the ultimate consolation is; "fate will never decree any injustice."[56] It seems to echo a line from an Orphic hymn, "for rightful necessity governs all things."[57]

But then, if necessity was "rightful" and never allowed injustice to take place, then men would simply not bother about fate at all. It is precisely because fate sends the good man the wicked man's dessert and vice versa, that fate appears so incalculable, formidable and therefore, so awesome. Under the

---

[47] VI: 25: 27.

[48] IX: 2: 58.

[49] XI: 2: 14.

[50] XII: 34: 4.

[51] XII: 34: 5, 7.

[52] I: 1: 186.

[53] II: 44: 1.

[54] XV: 13: 1, 2.

[55] XIII: 1: 42.

[56] II: 45: 55.

[57] No. 3 *night;* 111.

name of Kāla who merely "witnesses" such mischievous allocation of lots passively, without moving its little finger to redress any evil, fate is exonerated from all responsibility. This detachment of Kāla, this deadly apathy of fate renders it quite amoral and raises it above praise or blame and this face of fate is neither benign nor malevolent. Yet, if fate is 'adṛṣṭa' and all-powerful, if before its majesty all human effort is futile, then call it fate or call it Kāla, the prime undeserved injustices of life should be laid at its door. In most mythologies this apathy of fate is described in such a way that fate is glorified as a force not involved in the affairs of men. Yet all scriptures lay down prescriptions for placating fate, for not provoking it. This alone presupposes the malevolence of fate when provoked; hence the preventive prescriptions. This uninvolved apathy of fate is really founded on the theory of karman in India, it is another name of the unrepaid debt of karman incurred in a previous life. So man himself is made responsible not only for the punishments he deserves for the obvious sins and errors, but also for those he does not have any inkling about, those sins he is supposed to have committed in a previous life. So, by this very clever move, Fate or Kāla becomes an uninvolved witness, supremely detached from human good or evil.

The supremacy of fate had much earlier been declared by Maskarin Gosāla in[58] the *Uvāsagadasāo*[59] the *Saṃyutta Nikāya*[60] and the *Aṅguttara Nikāya.*[61] These were inherited by later Buddhist texts; these and the Upanisadic ideas which, however, did not posit fate but prepared the ground for fatalism by introducing the theories of rebirth.

Some schools of thought seek to enlarge the scope and function of nature so as to include fate and its workings within it. But most systems see nature, God or the Gods and fate as distinct powers... "not God and nature alone are identical but Destiny is identical with both. Fate, and Seneca repeats again and again, is nothing but God himself... *Providence* is the divine will, the Divine Notion or plan in its quality as existing in the divine mind, as the plan for the perpetuation of the Universe, the eternal unfolding of all events as viewed in their units. Fate, on the other hand, is again primarily Law, the law that regulates the unfolding in time a plan which exists eternally

---

58 *Dīgha Nikāya* II: 26; II: 20–22, p. 56.

59 1: 97: 115: II: 111, 132; Appendix II, pp. 17–29.

60 III: 210.

61 Vol. I, p. 286.

before the Divine Mind under the name of Providence. Providence is the residuum which escapes the laws of fate and which must be acted for in some other way; this residuum of free will and chance. Fortune is the incalculable element of successful interference in the process of our purposeful activity."[62] It is not true that Fate and Providence are interchangeable terms: fate can be good or bad or, to be more precise, fate is mostly ill-luck, for, the unexpected windfall of good luck is generally known not as fate but fortune. Even fortune and Providence are not synonymous because Providence has a different nuance, it is more akin to the divine will whereas fortune is merely adventitious.

"Fatalismus meint den Glauben dab die Geschicte des menschen und der Welt von einer unpersön, allbestimmenden Schicksalmacht unentrinnbar versucht werden, wie etwa in der germanische Religion durch >'Legung'< order > die Schickung Die Schicksalmacht Kann aber auch persönlich vorgestellt und uber den etwa vorhandenen anderent Göttern stehend gedacht werden wie die Moiren in Grieshenland, Die dritte moglichkeit findet sich in Islam. Hier ist der will Allahs allbestimmend unbönderlich, aber oft auch undurschsaube... Des Islam Fatalisms ist also Bejahung nicht eines unpersön."[63] Writing on the theme of Islam and fatalism, Ringgern says, "... at the transcendental level the dialectic is concerned with demonic versus divine necessity and at the human level, collective versus individual responsibility and guilt."[64] Since theistic dogmas leave no room for the operation of a third power—apart from God and Satan, Ahura Mazdah and Angra Mainyu, Allah and Shaitan—there is no theological space for fate. Hence the opposition here is more linear, between good and evil or between the community and the individual.

As we have seen earlier, Greece has a whole galaxy of divinities representing different aspects of fate. In Apuleius' *Metamorphosis*[65] "Isis overcomes fate but at the same time adopts the role of fate. Even in Egypt the Gods and Pharaoh seem not only to have appeared as the masters of fate but also identified themselves with fate."[66] In Paris there is an Egyptian Magical

62 Wilson, 1983, pp. 52, 54.

63 *Brockhaus Enzyklopaedie, 'Fatalismus'.*

64 Ringgern, 1967, p. 31.

65 *The Golden Ass* in the Penguin English translation.

66 p. 47.

Papyrus called "fate, the God of Gods." People all over the world have looked upon fate as 'the wheel of fortune' that turns arbitrarily, i.e. it is a force which no other force can control, thwart or modify. Discussing the situation of the early Sumerians, Kramer came to the conclusion that "man's life was beset with uncertainty and haunted by insecurity, since he did not know beforehand the destiny desired by the unpredictable Gods."[67] As Sumer is the seat of one of the world's earliest civilizations, this clear presence of the idea of an ineluctable fate there is very significant. Sumer had a considerably large pantheon and there the Gods acted as fate. The dichotomy between fate and the Gods, found in some mythologies is not found there. As in Homeric and classical Greek mythology, in Indian mythology also some Gods acted as fate. What is different in Indian and Greek mythologies is that they have distinct Gods of Fate apart from a regular pantheon. The two sets of Gods co-exist and interact with each other in both mythologies.

Rational explanation. In Old English poetry, the word 'Wyrd' stands for fate. In *Beowulf,* for example, there are several instances where 'wyrd' the inexplicable power or agency is translated authentically as fate. "Fate (wyrd) will always go as it must."[68] In other words, the course of 'wyrd' is unpredictable, incalculable; it is autonomous and uncontrollable, "at the rampart it shall be for us both as fate (wyrd), the Providence ruling every man, shall decree."[69] Again, "... fate (wyrd) has swept away all my kinsmen, courageous warriors, as destiny decreed."[70] Evidently, fate, 'wyrd' works hand in hand with destiny, of they both stand for the same force. In the last passage the valour of warriors availed nothing, they were slain because destiny had willed it so and so 'wyrd swept them away.' It is this word 'wyrd' which is directly linked with the 'Weird Sisters' in *Macbeth;* local witchcraft prevalent in late medieval England has coloured the conception somewhat, they predict the future of the king, succession in the royal line and the future of the country. Everything happened as they had said or willed. The later, present-day meaning of 'weird' as something dark i.e. unknowable and unexpected is derived with a semantic devaluation; the 'wyrd' of old English is depersonalized and becomes an adjective which means an evil of unknown and unpleasant associations.

67 Kramer, 1963, p. 123.

68 1455.

69 1. 2526.

70 1. 2824.

Fate in all religions is inscrutable as Ringgern says in the context of fatalism in Arabia "Men cannot understand the secrets of Destiny."[71] "Mahammad speaks of books kept in heaven in which the deeds of men are written down to be used in the last judgement."[72] This bears resemblance to the late Indian myth of the divine clerk Citragupta who keeps account of each man's deeds—good and bad. In ancient Egyptian religion as also in Zoroastrianism, the dead soul is weighed to see what kind of a future he is entitled to. Apparently, the Christian God's memory Zoroastrianism, the dead soul is weighed to see what kind of a future he is entitled to. Apparently, the Christian God's memory unaided by any such records performs miracles at the last judgement. Until then a Hindu, Muslim, Christian, Parsi or a man of any other faith is kept in total ignorance of his destiny in the next world. But the Indian scriptures kept the soul in the dark even after it passes into the next world; it is only given to know its immediate future; any long-term vision in the distant future is denied to him. Hence to him destiny is dense and dark. And not only with regard to his fate after death but that awaiting him in the subsequent births. The *Vāyu* Purāṇa categorically states that "It is impossible to know (what happens to man after death), not even philosophers know it, let alone ordinary mortals."[73] Sāvitrī puts the fundamental questions to Yama/Dharma, "What is that Dharma, why should it be (so)? Who is its cause? Who is the soul? What is the body? Who is here the doer of deeds?"[74] "When such basic information is lacking it is idle to probe into a man's destiny."

When Yudhiṣṭhira was playing the disastrous game of dice, he said, "I am under the control of fate."[75] One remembers Kali entering Nala's body and impelling him to bring himself to utter ruin. But for Yudhiṣṭhira even that fig-leaf is not there. Son of Dharma, respected all around for his judicious actions and discrimination, he blames this cardinal vice on fate. But he had not been bewitched or possessed by an evil spirit, he knew the pros and cons of his act; he knew that he should have and could have desisted from the game by an effort of will. By playing this game, at which he was not adept, he sowed

---

71 1955, p. 127.

72 *Hasting's Encyclopaedia of Religion and Ethics, 'Fate',*

73 55: 63.

74 *Devībhāgavata* P., IX: 18: 2.

75 *Mbh* II: 53: 13.

the seeds of the holocaust, the vast destructive epic war. When he blames his decision to play on fate, he is shifting responsibility, trying desperately to exonerate himself. But the readers do not excuse him, he has to take the blame for this massive devastation. We know the saying, "whom the Gods destroy they first make mad." Yudhiṣṭhira's is a similar case, though not quite; because his piety and insight into the rights and wrongs of an issue was sharper than the others'.

Fate being 'adṛṣṭa', unseen, 'niyati', preordained, it is very natural for man to deny that there is any inherent justice in the scheme of the universe. When Rāvaṇa abducted Sītā, people said, "There is no dharma (justice), where is truth, where straightforwardness or compassion? If Rāvaṇa abducts Rāma's Vaidehī (all these do not exist.)."[76]

The *Mahābhārata* has many more statements about the inscrutability of fate. "The creature is ignorant with no power over his joys and griefs, he goes to heaven or hell wherever God sends him."[77] "This body is nothing but an excuse, created by God and called 'a field' by which God himself causes good and evil works to be done."[78] Thus, "the Self-create great grandfather God causes destruction of creatures by creatures through subterfuge, O Yudhiṣṭhira."[79] This attitude shifts all moral responsibility on to God, man thus relinquishes his obligation, moral choice and poses as an automation worked by God's will acting in any way God pleases. It is an Indian version of total determinism. Another passage states, "if an act performed follows the performer, then God gets contaminated by an evil deed done."[80] "Or else if the performed deed does not follow the doer, then the cause is powerful, one pities the feeble man."[81] "Of acts, pious or wicked, the result, the origin and disappearance are all secrets with the Gods, lady."[82] Fate is the working of the unseen power which manifests itself as Time, because it is said to bring to fruition the deeds performed in an unknown and unknowable past, this Time thus is none other than Fate. Gāndhārī says at Duryodhana's death: "See the passage (and

---

76 *Rāmāyaṇa* III: 52: 39.

77 III: 2: 27: Vulgate Edition.

78 III: 31: 30.

79 III: 31: 35.

80 III: 31: 41.

81 *Ibid.*, 42.

82 Or secrets even to the Gods; III: 32: 33

disappearance) of Time."[83] Why then does God let this happen? Why does he let some (people) act piously and suffer, then let others act wickedly and reap a harvest of benefits? The epic answers: "God plays with creatures as a boy plays with toys."[84] Apathy, "As flies to wanton boys are we to the Gods." This is not an atheistic point of view, not even a deistic one, in which God is unconcerned with what happens to creatures after he has finished creation,[85] but it is a theistic one in which God is actively *playing* with the fate and fortune, the griefs and joys of his creatures *for his own pleasure*.

A remarkable passage says, "Whether God himself is the agent or man or Chance that exists in the world, or the fruits of action—everything, good or evil is appointed by God. Man performs his deeds but the fruits are ascribed to God. O Son of Kuntī, it is not desirable that the fruits of one's action should be attached to another, therefore impute it to God. Whether man is the doer of actions, good or bad, there is nothing beyond it, therefore, do only good. O King, no man anywhere can be diverted from fate; sins committed through carrying out a penalty or with weapons does not cling to man."[86] The first verse clearly states that irrespective of the identity of the actor, since God had caused man to act that way by impelling him invisibly but irrevocably, the onus is God's not man's. This exonerates man from the moral responsibility, but by doing so it turns him into an automaton and robs him of his human dignity which is rooted in his moral choice.

There is an interesting and significant dialogue between the sage Brahmadatta and the bird Pūjanī whom he had married. He: "Kāla itself causes various acts to be performed, they (men) are all impelled by Kāla, who should be held responsible to whom?... Kāla burns creatures as fire when it finds fuel... Kāla even allots joy and sorrow to creatures."[87] She questions his statements saying, "if Kāla, indeed is the ultimate reference for you, then none should feel offended... If joys and griefs, being and non-being disappear with Kāla, then, why do patients send for physicians, for medicines? If the ripening is done by Kāla, what is the use of medicines? If you swear by Kāla, how can there be judgement of the authors of works?"[88]

---

[83] XI: 17: 10.

[84] *Ibid.*, 56.

[85] The clockmaker theory.

[86] XII: 32: 11, 12, 14 and 16.

[87] XII: 43, 47 and 48.

[88] XII: 50–53.

Clearly Pūjarī almost echoes the views of Bṛhaspati or Cārvāka denying any authority to Kāla, God, Providence or Fate. In other words, she asks her husband to make up his mind about at whose door the praise of blame of actions should lie — Kāla's or the human agent's. If Kāla was that all-powerful being, then it is immaterial whether a man does right or wrong, since Kāla becomes the ultimate referee. Yet people do go to a doctor for treatment, believing that (i) Kāla will not, cannot or may not cure it, that (ii) with the physician's remedy there is better chance of recovery and that (iii) there are rational human cures for diagnosed human maladies. She stands for strong materialistic common sense as opposed to her husband's passive surrender to fate.

Fate is thus described as totally inscrutable; it was invented to somehow explain what remains inexplicable in life. Not that fate is an explanation in any rational manner. Inscrutability is intentionally attributed to fate to preserve the status quo in society, to prevent any probe and to preclude any protest. It was an effective measure to ensure that the sufferers of social injustice accept their lot.

"Popular accounts of the idea of fate are persistent because it allays anxiety and remorse or excuses indolence and improvidence. Prophecy and fortune-telling, especially astrology encourage fatalism but contravene it when, as is usual, they provide for exploiting or circumventing the destiny they foretell. The confusion of fatalism (that our decisions lack effects) with causal determinism (that they have causes) is unfortunate. However, the rarer, 'intrinsic' determination (that every occurence is logically necessary irrespective of circumstances) does imply a sort of logical fatalism."[89] This logical fatalism is the real fatalism in the Ājīvika sense; it is this brand of fatalism that effectively rules out any effect of human effort. And all religions have and philosophies had to have this at sometime or the other, in some form or other. "Hinduism, Stoicism, Christianity and Islam, each in its own way adjusted the inescapable determinism to the demands of social morality. Even when fatalism was taken logically as by the Ājīvikas in India Yang Chu of the fifth C.B.C. and the Sufis in Islam, it was the interest in action and courageous joy of living... Man sees himself changing purposive organization of desires integral with a complex flowing stream of events endlessly; order in nature, the continuity of heredity, social controls in custom and institution and learned

[89] *Encyclopaedia Americana*, 'Fatalism', p. 46.

patterns of response."[90] Thus man realized that abject acceptance of fatalism destroys the glory of manhood in him. Conditionally accepting fate as an area—an only area in life where unforeseen accidents may and do occur, man proposes to face life courageously, more manfully, and fight against those odds which he can fight, if only to redeem the pride of his manhood.

Clifford Geertz says,

> If man acts unjustly Zeus punishes them sooner or later. To that extent he is a God of justice. It does not, however, modify his *original and enduring malignity and illwill.* Zeus' omnipotence is what really matters. That inspires overwhelming terror and its only value is that this fear is the only restraint effective among iron men. Avoid the anger of the Gods, protect yourself against them by sacrifices and magical devices and work incessantly and ritualistically as a substitute for hope. Such is Hesiod's advice to us... Fatalism in the old sense has small place in this scheme. The new determinations—and they are many—are naturalistic and include man's inherent intelligence as an essential and effective element of the complex.[91]

Hesoid thus sees Zeus, in preclassical Greece, a major divinity of fate, as malevolent towards men. Man's most vital effort was required to placate him with sacrifices. In time other Gods imbibed this element of malevolence, meting out punishment to men and rewards. By then fate has a counterpart, fortune and man reaps the fruits of his good acts. But basically Greek mythology saw a relationship of hostility at worst and apathy at best between man and the Gods. So fate was a force man felt powerless against, yet fought to keep up his human dignity. Literature in classical Greece reflected this attitude, man's fight against adverse forces for preserving his human dignity.

Occasionally, however, society lets out the pressure of its accumulating steam against cosmic injustice and we have the emergence of cathartic religions. "When social life threatens to become seriously disrupted, cathartic religious ceremonies are performed. The religious rituals present a recognition that there must be a basic quantum of agreement and that the quarrels must be contained if social life is to continue within the existing framework."[92] Cargo cults and cathartic religions are expressions both of basic frustration and of the desperate endeavour to rectify social, economic and political

[90] *Encyclopaedia of Social Sciences*, Vol. V, 145.

[91] 1971, p. 135; italics added.

[92] Worseley, I960, pp. 246, 257.

wrongs which society refuses to face and redress. Inherent in such expressions as of Cargo Cults is the awareness that what happens around man is seriously unjust and needs balancing by collective effort. This in individual effort takes the name 'puruṣakāra' the initiative with which man, pitted against the insuperable powers of fate fights manfully to wrest justice from a basically unjust universe.

Religion especially polytheistic religions have everywhere accomodated fate as the special province of some Gods or has invented various Gods and Goddesses who discharge the functions of fate. Priests, prophets, authors of scriptures and law-givers have mostly sought to prove man's burden of guilt which the monotheistic God punishes in this life or the next, while in most ancient polytheistic religions the different aspects of fate as distinct deities weigh, judge and punish or reward accordingly. In Brahmanism the backlog of karman whose quantity and quality is unknown to man, assumes the role of fate shrouded in impenetrable mystery. Quite naturally, scriptural and priestly teaching convinces man of his total inability to penetrate the mystery of fate and, what is worse, his complete helplessness in the face of this mysterious power; he cannot alter the verdicts of fate.

Whatever priests and prophets have preached and forecast for millennia, man's own experience has never been fully deterministic or fatalist. Man has often found his own endeavour crowned with success, sometimes immediately, at other times after a passage of time; so he could not honestly afford to negate the effectiveness of his own endeavour. But, then, this same man observed that some of his efforts did not bear fruit, or that he was subjected to undeserved sufferings—failure, humiliation, poverty, diseases, loss of harvest or trade, diseases, epidemics, death of near ones, disasters of great dimension shaking the very foundation of his self-confidence. What was he to conclude? Is fate stronger than human efforts or vice-versa? This has been a moot question all over the world through the millennia.

The Sanskrit word for human effort is 'puruṣakāra', lit., what a man does. There is a long and varied controversy between the respective superiority of daiva, fate and puruṣakāra. We know the famous jātaka story of how an enterprising man built up a vast fortune by steadfast and patient effort out of the capital of a dead mouse.[93] However, unconvincing or fairy tale-like it may appear, it tries to teach the apparently inconceivable power of human

93 No. 4, *cullakaseṭṭhi.*

endeavour. In the *Rāmāyaṇa* Viśvāmitra was humiliated by his brahmin preceptor's son and said in utter dismay: "To my mind Fate indeed is supreme, human effort is futile. Fate over-rides everything."[94] But let us remember that the kṣatriya Visvāmitra, thwarted and humiliated by this brahmin and others, did not give up. He practised the required tapas for a long time and eventually gained brahminhood, for lack of which his dignity had been socially crushed before. Not that being a brahmin was really anything so grand in itself, but, if not being one means insult and hurt, it is quite natural, that the injured person will make an all-out effort to tell the brahmin world that his 'puruṣakāra' was worth something. Whenever a person fails to receive his due desserts he blames fate. Lakṣmaṇa upbraided Rāma saying, "Why do you praise feeble, pitiful fate?"[95] Continuing in the same vein he said: "He who is handicapped or lacks virility follows fate, heroes with self-respect never worship fate. He who is able to counter fate with personal effort, never grows faint. Today (people) shall see the prowess of fate and of man, the (comparative merits) of fate and man shall be manifest today. Today people will see fate crushed by my valour, those who have watched this coronation held up by fate. Today I shall, with my own prowess obstruct fate which is like a rutting elephant which defied the thongs of the hook and breaks its fetters."[96] Later, when Rāma becomes truly morbid at the false news of Sītā's death, Lakṣmaṇa harangues Rāma on the conflict between fate and effort, "Dharma, feeble and eunuch-like follows might. To my mind, a weakling who has lost his reputation should not be served. If Dharma succumbs to might, then one should forsake Dharma and serve might... That Dharma which takes shelter in unrighteousness is destroyed; in everything man acts justs as he pleases."[97]

Lakṣmaṇa, more than any other character in the *Rāmāyaṇa* stands for human dignity which he calls 'puruṣakara'. lie fails to understand (or refuses to accept) why an able-bodied man with his faculties intact should accept unjust verdicts of fate without a protest. His argument has a subtle point: fate follows the valorous. In other words, when success is achieved through brave deeds, people regard it as an act of fate, this is robbing man of the glory he deserves for his own efforts. To Lakṣmaṇa it is cowardly to submit to fate,

---

94 I: 58: 22–23.

95 II: 30: 16–20.

96 II: 30: 16–20.

97 VI: 83: 26–28, 30.

suffer injustice without the protest he is capable of making and then blame his misery on fate. Beside the submissive Rāma, Lakṣmaṇa thus provides a refreshing contrast. Actually, all through the epics and Purāṇas and in other sections of literature the conflict between fate and human effort persists. Lakṣmaṇa here symbolizes manly endeavour and Rāma fatalism. Here, as also after the abduction of Sītā after the 'Śakti' weapon was hurled on Lakṣmaṇa, and after Rāvaṇa showed a magic image of a dead Sītā. Rāma loses heart at the smallest provocation and tends to blame every misery on fate.

The *Mahābhārata, not* only four times in bulk compared to the *Rāmāyaṇa* it is also infinitely deeper in its spiritual import. In an atmosphere where fatalism was in the air, any exploration of the values of life would entail probling into fate. Therefore, we have many more references to the respective merits of fate and human effort. Duryodhana says, "I deem fate as supreme and human effort as futile."[98] "Some say it is due to human effort, while others hold that all three are responsible."[99] This stand is clearly untenable logically, because if fate is responsible for what happens to man, then karman becomes redundant. And if one's course of life is determined by his own karman; past and present, then the assumption of fate becomes redundant. And finally, if God controls man's affairs then both theories of fate and karman lose viability. It is thus riddled with inherent contradictions. yet most theistic theologies seek to reconcile fate, God and/or karman; but such a paradigm is logically untenable. When human effort is added to this complicated pattern, it either takes the place of rational self-reliant endeavour without a backlog from previous lives and without a residuum for future—which aims at controlling one's own destiny in opposition to fate or divine dispensation and also in opposition to karman and its dispensation.

It can only be understood as 'puruṣakāra' independent of other forces like fate or God. The attempt at reconciling all of them in any paradigm is completely futile. "Whatever a man attempts with an object in view, bears fruit if there is (nothing contrary) done in the past." The oft-repeated formula is 'who can counter fate with effort, fate I deem as supreme, human endeavour, quite futile.'[100] 'Man is the author of actions, good or bad, when it bears fruit

---

98 I: 192: 12.

99 III: 33: 34.

100 III: 176: 27.

he enjoys it, why should God be assumed as the author?'[101] Such contradictory views abound in all scriptures.

Sometimes general statements sound rather naive: "Whenever a man intends doing good, every time all his endeavours succeed."[102] But again sometimes more mature and experienced views are expressed simply as: "The cause of this world is rooted in fate and man. But I shall attempt (to achieve) through human effort (as) I am not able to function through fate."[103] Kṛṣṇa, the speaker does not presume to be a divine agent here. 'All men are restricted (or bound), the pertinacity of the two (sets of) karman (depends) on fate and puruṣakāra, there is nothing above them. Works do not succeed through fate alone... nor through effort alone, success depends on a combination of these two.'[104] 'Of the two, fate recognized (as such) exists under its own power; the wise, through efficiency make use of *puruṣakāra*. Accomplished *puruṣakāra* also succeeds through fate alone, then the fruit of the action follows the author of the action. The rise of efficient men without (the aid of) fate, although (their acts are) accomplished properly, is found to remain fruitless. In the world most works are barren; undone, they bring sorrow: works should bear good fruit. If people without making due efforts achieve something just as they wish, and the man who performs the acts and does not obtain the fruit—both of these are unfortunate. Bereft of (the assistance of) human effort and of fate, of these two reasons, (the attempt to) rise in life becomes futile.'[105] 'An extra attribute of effort is that it should be approved of by the aged.'[106] 'No human effort is superior to fate.[107] 'Therefore, one should act, there, is no success for the idle.'[108] 'Fate and human effort exist in a symbiotic manner.'[109] 'As a seed not planted in a field becomes barren, so fate does not succeed without human effort.'[110] Another such

---

[101] III: 180: 5.

[102] V: 35: 34.

[103] V: 77: 4, 5.

[104] X: 2: *2*, 3.

[105] X: 2: 8, 10, 11, 13, 14, 19.

[106] X: 2: 22, 23.

[107] X: 6: 25.

[108] XII: 137: 75.

[109] XII: 137: 78.

[110] XIII: 6: 7.

saying is, 'Fate without human effort is barren.'[111] In an entirely new vein is the statement, 'what can fate do to a righteous man?'[112]

The diversity of the views regarding the relative merits of karman, fate, divine favour and personal effort is representative of the different anchors of human faith in late antiquity and early medieval times. The lack of unanimity is quite symptomatic: people were probing the significance of life, the meaning of the occurrences—favourable and unfavourable—in different milieus and different spiritual climates. The mental make-up of the seekers were different, hence their conclusions too were different. What, however, emerges only too clearly is the diversity—very healthy sign in a society throbbing with real questions for which they sought answers not only eagerly but also with vital interest as though in a dire necessity.

Dhṛtarāṣṭra says 'Sañjaya, I regard fate as supreme, because my son's armies are countered by the Pāṇḍava army.'[113] 'Whatever work, a man afflicted by fate may do, again and again it is rendered futile by fate. Whatever the enterprising man ever does, he must do it fearlessly, the success, however, depends on fate.'[114] 'In the face of fate, the mind does not suffer.'[115] 'Human effort is never regarded as superior to fate.'[116] Kṛṣṇa says to Karṇa, 'Low men given to indulgence of the passions, blame fate and not their own evil deeds.'[117] As a lamp grows dim when the oil runs out, so fate grows weak when the (fruit of) actions is exhausted.'[118] This passage and many others like it—seeks to conceptually harmonize or find a correlation and balance between fate and action. Fate is only operative as long as the fruit of action' is still there to be suffered or enjoyed. So the unseen remainder of past or present action is equated with fate, because the unseen part is 'adṛṣṭa', another name of fate. "One who cleaves to fate without conducting himself like a man, labours in vain like a woman with an impotent husband."[119] Here clearly

[111] XII: 6: 25.

[112] XIII: 6: 29.

[113] VI: 58: 1.

[114] VII: 127: 16, 17.

[115] VIII: 1: 47.

[116] X: 7: 25.

[117] VIII: 67: 1.

[118] XIII: 6: 44.

[119] XIII: 6: 20.

emphasis is laid on human effort without which even fate is powerless to achieve anything. Here cleaving to fate is not condemned outright but doing so and abandoning personal effort, is. Again, here is the attempt to combine fate and human effort, but if either is stretched to its logical conclusion, the other is ruled out or nullified. Nowhere do the scriptures admit the paradox: but pretend that the square fits perfectly within the circle. Only In Pūjanī's argument does it become clear that these theories are essentially contradictory to each other.

Time and again we hear 'Fate is supreme, fie on human effort which is futile.' In the *Mahābhārata* and in many Purāṇas we hear,' ... There is nothing more powerful than fate.'[120] Kaṃsa in his dejection says after defeat and destruction, "I could not overcome fate with puruṣakāra."[121] "Some wise men call fate powerful, others who believe in human endeavour regard fate as futile."[122] "What the wise call fate is still the hope that the feeble cling to. For the powerful men no fate is ever noticed. The heroic and the feeble take recourse to effort and fate respectively."[123] "Fate and effort are favoured by men. One should not remain devoted exclusively to fate; using one's own intellect, one should find out a way of making effort."[124] A wholly different note is struck in another verse in the same scripture: "this whole universe is governed by fate, so are victory and defeat. Knowing that (all this) is ruled by fate, one should not fight it."[125] A more balanced view is expressed in:" Men should honour both fate and 'puruṣakāra'. How can there be success without effort? Wise men should make efforts, in a proper manner, success will come if effort is made, not otherwise.'[126] "O you versed in the Vedas and the Vedāṅgas, in this world some say it is by one's own works, some by fate, others by nature; these three are recognised in the Vedas. One is the author of one's own actions, (but) that act is (decreed) by fate, mens' past acts done by themselves is made by nature."[127] Clearly, although the passage pretends

[120] *Brahmavaivarta* P., Brahma 11: 17.

[121] *Harivaṃśa* viīṇu 4: 51.

[122] *Devībhāgavata* P., V: 22: 12.

[123] *Ibid.*, V: 12: 28–30.

[124] *Ibid.*, V: 13, 14.

[125] *Ibid.*, VI: 6: 10.

[126] *Ibid.*, VII: 14: 36–37.

[127] *Brahmavaivarta* P., Prakṛti, 60: 25–28.

to distinguish between three causes, nature, 'puruṣakāra' and fate, it does not succeed in doing so. On the other hand, by introducing nature without due definition it makes confusion worse confounded. Metaphysically, it is a jumble. This 'svabhāva' or nature may be attached to a person's nature, to cosmic Nature or to some kind of attribute of fate itself, the nature of fate. Obviously there were three sets of values obtaining in society—(i) absolute reliance on human endeavour, (ii) absolute dependence on fate, (iii) recognition of the limits of both i.e. that, without one the other was powerless, or that where one ends, the other begins.

The *Matsya* Purāṇa introduces Kāla in the place of 'svabhāva' "Know your own acts done in a previous birth to be fate. Hence the wise hold that prowess is best. Even an adverse fate can be overcome by prowess of those of good conduct who are ever active. O, the best of men, those whose past actions are pious, even without human endeavour, some of them can gather fruits of their actions. With actions men also reap the fruit of enterprising moves and dark and low are the fruits of the 'tāmasa' acts whose fruits are reaped with great austerity. O, thou the best of men, the desired fruit is obtained by human effort. People without prowess know fate alone. Human effort, blessed by fate bears fruit in due time i.e. in Kāla. Thus fate, 'puruṣakāra' and 'Kāla', the conglomeration of fate, effort and kāla bears fruit ... therefore, one should always be active *in the prescribed manner of his own status.*" One notices this condition: 'in the prescribed manner of his own status'; the status is the caste, the stage of life (one of the four, student, householder, forest-dweller, roving mendicant) and by insinuation his class status. In other words, in no case should man's endeavour transgress the limitations set by society. The authors of the scriptures are anxious that a man's self-reliance which propels him to show his prowess does not disturb the socio-economic status quo. Within the given limits he should be active and in the final analysis, rely on fate, so that even though he faces danger here he will surely reap fruits in the next world. 'The idle never obtain what they desire, neither does the one who is solely loyal to fate. Therefore, with an all-out effort man should conduct himself in the pious works, "Lakṣmī", the goddess of prosperity forsakes lazy-bones, who cling to fate, she moves over to men of endeavour. Searching carefully one should adopt a course, O mighty king; therefore, one should always be active and ambitious."[128]

[128] *Matsya* P., 220: 2–12; Italics added.

In the *Bhagavadgītā* Kṛṣṇa says to Arjuna, "I am the sweet juice of the waters, I am the light of the sun and moon, the Om of all the Vedas, *the manliness in man.*"[129] In the beginning of the Kurukṣetra battle when Arjuna is dejected at the prospect of the imminent massacre, Kṛṣṇa says, 'Do not be like a eunuch, Arjuna, it does not become you. Shed this small weakness of the heart and arise, O Arjuna.'[130] Kṛṣṇa also explains to Arjuna that "God himself dwells in the heart of all creatures, he rotates all creatures like those on a mechanical wheel."[131] Kṛṣṇa says to Arjuna: "Rise, therefore, acquire fame, by defeating foes enjoy the prosperous kingdom, I myself have killed these beforehand, you Arjuna should merely be the excuse."[132] 'The second half of the stanza robs the message which seeks to instil courage and enterprise in Arjuna; if Kṛṣṇa has already slain the enemies beforehand, how does Arjuna gain any glory through his prowess? This neatly bears out the inherent contradictions in many such passages between fate and 'puruṣakāra'. Here Kṛṣṇa, like fate has predetermined or preordained the issue.

The most moving anecdote is that told by Kuntī when she finds that her sons had lost heart. She then told them of king Sañjaya, who had, like them lost his kingdom and lay moping, when his mother Vidulā upbraided him for this unmanly, unkṣatriya-like attitude, this irrational defeatism. The son pleaded his helplessness, lack of army and weapons; how could he fight? She put him to shame saying, "instead of being like the fire in the husk, you should blaze up like a log of wood even if for a moment. You are a kṣatriya after all and this conduct does not become your glorious tribe. Go and procure the things that you lack." Finally Sañjaya felt the shame, shook off his inertia, procured what he needed, fought and won.[133] This anecdote sums up the controversy between fate and puruṣakāra, she instilled *puruṣakāra* in her son who had become a fatalist and therefore a morbid defeatist. Relying on his own effort he became victorious.

Karṇa, though a kṣatriya by birth did not know his origin because he was reared by a charioteer. When others jeered at him on his low extract he made the famous remark. "A charioteer or a charioteer's son, whoever I may be, my

---

[129] VII: 8; italics added.

[130] II: 3.

[131] 18: 61.

[132] XI: 33.

[133] V: 131.

birth was decreed by fate, but I am the master of my valour." Here we have a true instance of proud self-confidence which undertakes tasks and accomplishes them with his puruṣakāra. The epic battle was in one sense a conflict between fate and human effort as all epic battles are. When the Pāṇḍavas chose the 'superman' Kṛṣṇa instead of the mere numerical military superiority, the outcome of the battle was already a foregone, conclusion. Like the Greek tragedies the Kaurava heroes fought to redeem the pride of their manhood. Undoubtedly, they had been in the wrong, specially, when they had defeated Yudhiṣṭhira in an unfair game of loaded dice and had dragged and humiliated an innocent woman in her woman's course in the open court before many pairs of male eyes. But with Kṛṣṇa on the Pāṇḍava side they never had the ghost of a chance of winning the war. Because it is an extremely mature epic, the issues are more complex, but basically the Kauravas fought a losing battle because they fought against Kṛṣṇa, the supernatural, power personified, as he had claimed repeatedly in the *Bhagavadgītā*.

This conflict between fate and human effort is dealt with at length in the *Yogavāśiṣṭha Rāmāyaṇa*, it seems to be one of its major preoccupations. This is another height of false, games that people talk of Kāla and fate as 'doing': 'eating', etc."[134] 'The third bears the terrible name Kṛtānta; of the shape of a drunk Kāpālika, Fate dances away in the world."[135] "Before him of this shape the eternal feminine. Fate, begins to dance and never ends her blandishments."[136] "Because she is a woman, fate is ever forward."[137] "Fate and human effort fight like two rams, equal and unequal, of oneself or of another, the mightier of the two wins."[138] "I think that my previous effort impels me."[139] The *Yogavāśiṣṭha Rāmāyana* makes fate a dancing girl. The image is eloquent: the motions of a dancer depends on the choreographical needs. From a distance the dancer's movements look unpredictable, as fate's movements are. But the fact that fate is made into a dancing girl, the '*femme eternelle*' makes her attractive. Another verse makes fate a loathsome man, a

[134] Vairāgya 25: 1.

[135] *Ibid.*, 25: 5.

[136] *Ibid.*, 25: 10.

[137] *Ibid.*, 26: 5.

[138] *Mumukṣu* 5: 7.

[139] *Ibid.*, 5: 10.

drunk Kāpālika who also dances under the influence of his drink. Both are indifferent to men who are the dumb, passive spectators with whose fate these two dance their līlā, playful dance. Both are immersed in their own dance and totally apathetic to the spectators, the unfortunate victims of their līlā. Such is the relation between fate and men that the *Yogavāśiṣṭha* visualizes. A late work, it reflects centuries of fatalism in India and depicts the passive acceptance of fate by men and even fate's enjoyment (in the case of the dancing girl) and its motions. Now this is a rather serious position to accept, even human endeavour does not depend on one's will; it is propelled by what one did in a previous life; logically, it is a total denial of free will and therefore of free human endeavour, an unconditional, utmost surrender to fate. "A man should so labour manfully in his endeavours that his previous puruṣakāra itself negates or abolishes all ills."[140] "The hapless maintain that fate impels them, Lakṣmī seeing those who hold fate as supreme, turns away."[141] 'The best of men even though plagued by penury, want and misery attain the station of Indra himself through effort and manliness."[142] 'Thus those who see what is palpably visible, felt, heard and done yet think that it was done by fate are the wretched men of no intelligence."[143]

Lieh-Tzu (third century A.D.) has a dialogue between effort and fate. At the moment when fate seems all-powerful, fate's reply to the question 'whether the way things are, they are indeed under its control' is: "Since I am called Fate, how can I control ... (all things) come naturally and of themselves. How should I know anything about them?"[144] This scepticism regarding the limits of the powers of Fate generates a healthy self-reliance in man. Here fate does not claim, as Indian Purāṇas frequently do, that it is all-powerful; 'all things', says fate 'come naturally and of themselves.' In other words, nature which is equally unpredictable in many cases seems to control human affairs about which fate itself is quite in the dark. This fate shifts the entire onus of human destiny on to nature, in Indian terminology 'svabhāva'. Nature's movements are to a large extent unknown to men, but Lieh-Tzu's fate does not claim to organize even that dark area of nature. Here human endeavour has a much

[140] *Ibid.*, 5: 11.

[141] *Ibid.*, 5: 20.

[142] *Ibid.*, 5: 27.

[143] *Ibid.*, 5: 29.

[144] 6.1a. Blount and Sanches, 1977, p. 294.

freer play than in Indian fatalism. By underplaying the role of fate, by making her appear as subservient to nature, it gives a wider scope to human action.

In ancient Greek mythology there are fixed positions for Tyche the goddess, for the Gods (i.e. the pantheon) and man's own power and skill. Tyche contrasted with consciously purposeful human endeavour over which it exercises extensive sway, being a powerful minister of God. "In this third place, after God and Fortune comes man's own skill."[145] "If this God is equated with Nature or the overlord of Nature, then we have the same neat scheme of the ruling triad; 1. Free Will / 2. God or Gods / Nature- 3. Tyche / Fate / Destiny - Human Effort / Puruṣakāra. In some systems the first two; nature and Fate remain undistinguished but Free will and fate are acknowledged in every system, "(the argument) by which they patched up the logical inconsistency was the definition by Artistotle of Chance as a cause not clear to human understanding... Seneca is very pronounced in assigning a definite place to Fortune in his moral system; it became necessary in order to give a man strength and courage. He tells us that God gave Fortune no power to strike against the mind, therefore, we should scorn the power rather than make ourselves slaves to it. Fortune is a power against which we must offer ourselves so that we may be strengthened by it."[146]

Whether as an invincible enemy or as an enemy which must be fought and crushed, most systems of thought—metaphysical and theological—acknowledged the existence of fate. The only exceptions are the strict theistic systems which have no room for fate. In Christianity there is a constant conflict between the powers of evil (symbolized by Satan) and God. Christ's temptation in the wilderness by Satan was a prototype of what happens to man all through his life; he faces a choice between self-indulgence, self-aggrandisement and self-denial, walking on the path of righteousness. In Buddhism, Buddha was tempted by Māra, his daughters and followers, but prototypically Buddha resisted, won and showed his followers the way to conquer evil. In Zoroastrianism there is constant conflict between the good personified by Ahura Mazda and the evil by Angra Mainyu and it is man's moral duty to be on the side of good and conquer evil. Jainism, too, leaves man an option to resist evil and progressively cleanse himself with the spiritual assistance of the Jinas.

---

[145] Cioffari, 1935, p. 42.

[146] Wilson, 1983, p. 50.

What is of cardinal importance is the moral choice. Ancient Greece had fate with many names and attributes, arrayed against them were the other Gods of the pantheon. Although the theology in its earlier phase did not clearly enunciate the role of human effort of free will, the tragedies quite early emphasized it; in them although the decision about man's action was mostly a foregone conclusion,[147] yet the protagonist did face a choice in most cases, a choice of supreme significance on which depended his/her future happiness or suffering. In India the problem of free will and choice becomes apparent from the epics. Posed against the Gods, Death, Kāla, Antaka, Niyati or Daiva, man could either passively accept what happened to him or 'take up arms against a sea of trouble' and fight manfully against fate. In other words, he could remain inactive and be merely acted upon, or he could act and redeem his manhood even though defeat seemed inevitable.

The Iranian *'Epistle of Tonsar'*[148] condemns absolute believers in fate or in human effort equally. It thereby advocates human effort and admits the subordination of such effort to fate. In India as we have seen in this section there are two equally powerful stands: (1) fatalistic, which acknowledges the superior authority of fate and (2) the upholders of the superiority of puruṣakāra. But while the instances of mandatory, didactive and anecdotal support to fatalism is numerically more overwhelming than the other position; the *puruṣakāra* school seldom categorically advocates defiance of fate. Innumerable tales of successive rebirths bring out how fate plans human life and do what he may, he can seldom alter the decrees of fate. Many of the tales are jejune and without any serious impact[149] on the moral consciousness of the reader. But a Rāvaṇa, a Karṇa or a Viśvāmitra when they defy the social ethos and religious norms in order to vindicate their own prowess and human dignity they do impress us. Unfortunately, most of such characters come from the antagonist side whose effort does, not receive the ultimate sanction of ethics or theology. But the moral conflict is really poignant and impressive.

One reason why the protagonist is not shown as challenging destiny and winning is because most of the epic-Puranic authors felt called upon to

---

[147] *cf Oedipus Rex, Oedipus Tyranus, Alkestis, Antigone, the Agamennon trilogy, et al.*

[148] of the sixth century A.D.

[149] one remembers Indra seducing Ahalya, Nārāyaṇa seducing Tulsi in their respective husbands' disguise.

establish fatalism and thus to quell protests. Countless passages comment on the bafflement and failure of human effort with: 'Fate is supreme, human effort is futile'. The protagonists in the epics are sometimes faced with a choice; Rāma could have defied his father's order for his exile, or could have agreed to return with Bharata to Ayodhyā. In both cases he would have failed as a model of virtue and be condemned as one who seeks his own pleasure. But this same Rāma paid the price of an unheroic gesture when murdering Vālin from a hiding place, just to gain Sugrīva's friendship so that he could find out about his abducted wife—self-interest, pure and simple. Then rejecting an innocent wife on a palpably false suspicion was a morally heinous crime, a second time also he rejected her in Ayodhyā to redeem the Tkṣvāku line's good name—self-interest once again. But the killing of Śambuka was a crime because the scriptures about Śambuka's so-called offence could be countered with other scriptures which could exonerate the latter. Just as the rejection of Sīta in Laṅkā on a baseless suspicion and in Ayodhyā on a trumped-up popular charge could have been effectively avoided on the basis of scriptures which lay down that even a quarrelsome, polluted, abducted and raped wife who has left home should be accepted after a month.[150] The man who forsakes his wife is himself punishable, it is true that the other kinds of misogynistic scriptures are more numerous. But Rāma could, if he so wished, accept Sīta on the basis of scriptures. He acted so as to be in the good books of brahmins, to gain fame as a ruler who respected caste hierarchy and was not loath to murder a person who was meditating and was prepared to banish a wife on a wholly conjectural suspicion. So the moral choices before the protagonist were dear; he could have acted otherwise in a more humane and therefore, in a more righteous manner in all these instances. Yet the epics glorify his wrong choices because they suited the needs of the society's caste and male chauvinistic values.

So there was moral choice, the hero was not acted upon. Yudhiṣṭhira could have desisted (i) from the dice game and (ii) from pawning a wife who did not belong to him alone. After making the wrong choices, he blamed it on fate. Yet this same Yudhiṣṭhira had been willing to prevent the bloody war and accept five villages in lieu of a kingdom, had on the eve of the war fallen at the feet of the elderly Kaurava preceptors and begged them to stop the war. But again at Kṛṣṇa's instigation he had told a blatant lie which cost his old

[150] *Vaśiṣṭha Dharmasūtra* 21: 8–10.

preceptor Droṇa his life, although he sought to cover it up with a muttered half-truth. Tried for piety by the crane, he asked for the lives of his half-brothers' instead of his own brothers'; after the war was over he confessed to Gāndhārī his own guilt. In other words, here is a hero with a split conscience, who makes different kinds of choices in different situations and that makes the epic all the more significant. Also, it gives Yudhiṣṭhira more credibility as a human being. There was scope for free will and he used this freedom not uniformly but from the point of view of exigency, his point of view.

What is of significance is that epic characters—protagonists and antagonists—were no automatons in the hands of a blind irrational fate. And that includes Dhṛtarāṣṭra whose moral blindness was externalized, but who really was not blind morally, not a plaything in the hands of fate. At each step his conscience, queen Gāndhārī, sometimes Vidura, at others Sañjaya presented the other option which Dhṛtarāṣṭra could have adopted. And the other two echoes of his conscience—Sañjaya and Vidura made his personal guilt and onus in the horrible holocaust amply clear to him at every step. Faced with a moral choice he failed and failed miserably and consistently. But fate had no hand in this. It is in the post-epic Puranic literature where anecdotes are invented and discourses are inserted to show that fate is supreme. Like an invisible network of live electric wires it surrounds him so that the smallest slip or defiance spells death. Yet very occasionally people do defy what seems obviously planned by fate and pay a heavy price for the defiance.

Even from the time of the Brāhmaṇa literature, many times what the demons, asuras did was right, yet because they were demons, the Gods deprived them of their rightful shares or cheated them in an underhand manner. Numerous tales narrate quite unashamedly these incidents of the Gods' treachery against the demons. They had a shabby deal at the hands of the Gods. Now if their discomfiture or defeat is blamed on fate, then human endeavour is always at a discount. So through narratives free will and effort are degraded to a subservient position under fate. The overwhelming majority of such tales creates an oppressive weight of 'evidence' so that man loses faith in human effort.

The logical corollary of this loss of faith in puruṣakāra is a passive submission to fate. In concrete terms this is apathy to life. The Ājīvīkas led by Maskarin Gosāla carried the doctrine to its extreme logical conclusion. They preached the total futility of human endeavour, the unquestionable supremacy of fate. Gosāla had many followers and Ājīvīkism had a scattered and sporadic lifespan for about a millennium. Yet what is more significant is that it died out. For two reasons: (i) much of their doctrinal position was assimilated by Brahmanism, (ii) its theory that after 64000 births a man automatically attained liberation; this reduces the scriptures to insignificance. This was modified and assimilated by Jainism which retained the karman and rebirth theory in a different form but did not advocate absolute surrender to fate. In fact fate had an extremely minor role in it. But the most powerful reason was (iii) that succumbing to fate unquestioningly went against human dignity. There was something in the pride of manhood which revolted against merely being acted upon; man was too proud to surrender his free will to choose a course of action and to act on it even though the effort meant sure defeat and death. Finally, (iv) human experience over the centuries made it dear to man that effort is often crowned with success and that with the extension of man's horizon of knowledge, his control over nature is increasing. The scope of what appeared as caprices of fate or decrees of destiny diminished. Hence the will to act had a fillip from human experience in history. Slowly but surely, he realized that some things occur through chance like an earthquake, drought, flood, thunderstorm, road or other accidents, an epidemic, disease, deformity or premature death; over these man truly has no control. But as earthquakes and floods can be predicted through advanced machinery and steps can be taken to prevent a massive havoc, similarly with the progress of science many diseases have been eradicated, more can now be arrested. All this boosted man's self-confidence, so he refused to surrender to fate without putting up a fight. At the same time he is aware that accidents of various kinds will occur and man can neither pre-empt nor fight against them. He, prefers to call these 'accidents', not 'fate'.

The invention of the calendar and the study of the trade winds prevented many shipwrecks, similarly the knowledge of various areas of nature and the mode of its function provided man with adequate means to guard his well-being against unforeseen phenomena. The introduction of increasingly uniform law expanded man's sense of social, economic and political rights and obligations and gave him some protection against the caprices of the powers that be which had hithertofore appeared as his inevitable fate. Social injustices on slaves, women and the poorer sections were recognized and are being remedied to some extent—although not at all adequately. But that it is not the 'fate' of these sections to submit dumbly to oppression because fate metes it, out to them, is now recognized. Effective protests, revolts and successful revolutions have given man the confidence that much of what passed as the decrees of fate were in fact, remediable. This knowledge itself is worth a fortune to mankind. Individuals still do and will in the foreseeable future suffer from many adverse experiences, but the collective struggle is on to challenge destiny and, rectify unjust customs and practices. Each success knocks out one stone from the foundation of fatalism. Finally, men will learn to live with chance accidents over which he has no power because they cannot be diagnosed or preempted, but he will refuse to accept and submit to fate as fate, for those phenomena which he now understands better and is, therefore, able to fight better and overcome. Modern society all over the world is inventing, introducing and promoting new maladies which the concentration of capital in the hands of some multinational companies generate. These new groups of international magnates are wholly apathetic to the interests of the common man. Their worship of Mammon reveals its true nature; red in tooth and claw, it symbolizes fate and with the increasing degradation and impoverishment, the common man turns more to fatalistic and obscurantist cults. This new oppressive international regime wields enormous power.

While natural calamities like earthquakes, floods, droughts, pestilences and epidemics threaten man's well-being, man's own greed causes wars, social and economic oppression of the majority by a powerful minority. Now for nearly half a century man's greed has been posing a global menace. This is a new manmade calamity which appears to the common man as irremediable fate.

For a quick return in a bumper harvest chemical manure is used profusely and repeatedly and the tired soil will soon turn barren and quite unproductive. Stronger chemicals will defer the process for some time longer, but in the foreseeable future the result will be total disaster. Cattle are injected with injurious chemicals for increasing the volume of their meat and milk yield; this endangers the life of the cattle and the consumers of the produce. Deforestation for the sake of paper, etc. is another global ruin facing humanity. Poisonous medicines are passed on to the vast third world market, birth control measures of dubious worth and potential deleterious effects are used recklessly by unscrupulous medical practitioners. The use of 'drug' continues unabated and with secret assistance of 'mafia' kings all over the world. 'AIDS' rages globally.

The environment as polluted with poisonous emissions from modern machines and with blaring noise well over the admissible decibels. Nature which was by and large friendly to man is now being converted into a gas-chamber. Slowly but surely. The helpless common man, the majority of the world's population has to submit to this ruinous process planned by the commercial tycoons who take shelter in their 'bunkers' dooming the world's population to a slow but sure decimation. Sinister experiments in genetics are on; Hitler's unfulfilled dream of creating a progeny of passive submitters is well on the way to a deadful fulfilment, the 'gene of resistance' can be exterminated and moral automatons with crushed volition will submit to 'the powers that be'.

All this comes in the shape of fate to the modern man. Yet, as we have seen, man refuses to submit passively to fate. The 'Green movement' is a case in point. Recycling of used material, afforestation, resistance to brand new medicines marketed by the multinational companies, revival of indigenous systems of medicines, slow almost imperceptible turning away from fast foods and from mechanized, 'synthetic' and fast living—all these are welcome sings of resistance to the most sinister aspects of fate the twenty-first century is faced with. The fight will be protracted, with the right thinking man fighting with his back to the wall, but the irrepressible self-preservative instinct will eventually crown man's efforts with glory. This face of fate which poses a menace to civilization, as also to human existence on this planet has to be fought tooth and nail. This new manmade fate is horrendous in its power and dimension; therefore, the life instinct in man will fight it and however long the battle the ultimate triumph over all aspects of fate will redound to man's glory.

The common man is slowly yet surely seeing through this evil game and when they unite to fight it, they shall surely overcome. In our familiar terminology, 'puruṣakāra' will then be pitted against destiny, but not chance or that aspect of nature which is yet unpredictable and therefore, unpreventable. But he will fight relentlessly to know more about all aspects of life and the powers in society and his knowledge will equip him to fight what previously was regarded as fate. Above all, he will slowly but surely, reject the dogma of karman and rebirth, especially, the idea that previous karmans mould the pattern of his present life. Once he recognizes the vested interests of the guardians of society in maintaining the socio-political and economic *status quo*, with threats of hell and baits of heaven, of forcing him to submit to 'the powers that be' to uphold the existing social relationships and norms, he will refuse to submit, he will seek to mould the course of his life with as much of it as lies within the scope of his own effort. Known human history of over five millennia will also reveal real progress in knowledge and in gaining control over nature in a *measure* proportionate to his knowledge and his will for collective effort.

Bibliography

A. Primary sources

1. Ṛgveda (R.V)
2. Yajurveda (Y.V)
3. Atharvaveda (A.V)
4. Aitareya Brāhmaṇa (A.B)
5. Kauṣṣlaki Brāhmaṇa (K.B)
6. Taitllrṣya Brāhmaṇa(T.B)
7. Jaiminṣya Brāhamaṇa (J.B)
8. Śatapatha Brāhmaṇa (S.B)
9. Tśa Upaniṣad
10. Kaṭha Upaniṣad
11. Kena Upaniṣad
12. Praṣna Upaniṣad
13. Muṇḍaka Upaniṣad
14. Māṇḍukya Upaniṣad
15. Taittlrṣya Upaniṣad
16. Aitareya Upaniṣad
17. Chhāndogya Upaniṣad
18. Bṛhadāraṇyaka Upaniṣad
19. Śvetāśvatara Upaniṣad
20. Maitrāyaṇṣya Upaniṣad
21. Rāmayaṇa (Rām.)
22. Mahābhārata (Mbh.)
23. Matsya Purāṇa (Mat. P.)

24. Mārkaṇḍeya Purāṇa
25. Bhaviṣya Purāṇa
26. Bhāgavata Purāṇa (Bhāg.P.)
27. Brahma Purāṇa
28. Brahmāṇḍa Purāṇa
29. Brahmavaivarta Purāṇa
30. Vāyu Purāṇa
31. Viṣṇu Purāṇa
32. Vāmana Purāṇa
33. Varāha Purāṇa
34. Agni Purāṇa
35. Nārada Purāṇa
36. Padma Purāṇa
37. Liṅga Purāṇa
38. Garuḍa Purāṇa
39. Devṣbhāgavata Purāṇa
40. Bṛhannāradṣya Purāṇa
41. The Bible
42. The Gospel of St. Mathew (Mathew)
43. The Gospel of St. Mark (Mark)
44. The Gospel of St. Luke (Luke)
45. The Gospel of St. John (John)
46. The Revelation
47. The Pall Text Society Books (PTS)
48. Sacred Books of the East (SBE)
49. The Florentine Codex
50. Sahagun
51. Sacred Jain Texts
52. Avesta
53. The Epic of Gilgamesh (Gilgamesh)
54. The Koran

55. The Egyptian Book of the Dead
56. Ancient Middle Eastern Texts
57. The Theogony (of Hesiod)
58. The Homeric Hymns (Loebedn.)
59. The Orphic Hymns
60. Beowulf
61. Arthaśāstra of Kauṭilya
62. Manusaṃhltā
63. The Popol Vuh

B. Encyclopaedias

Brockhaus Enzyklopādie, Wicsbaden, 1968.

Dictionnuire de Spirituadite, Paris, 1967.

Dictionnuire de Theologie Catholique, Paris, 1932.

Dictionary of the History of Ideas, NY, 1973.

Encyclopaedia Americana, Connecticut, 1984.

Encyclopaedia Britannica, Macropaedia, 1974.

Encyclopaedia of Social Sciences, Macmillan, 1968.

Hasling's Encyclopaedia of Religion and Ethics, (ed.) Hastings, NY.

International Encyclopaedia of Religion. Macmillan, 1987.

Lexikon fur Theologie und Kirche, Freiburg, I960.

Lexikon Universalis, Paris, 1985.

C. Reference Books

Aiyappan, A., *A Case for a Sub-discipline: Brahminology*. Madras, 1983.

Anderson, A. J. O. & Dibble, C. E., (ed.), *Florenline Codex*. Utah, 1952.

Alkhin, B & R., *The Rise of Civilization in India and Pakistan*. Camb. Univ. Press, 1982.

Arulin, L, Le Rvi deufendur de Lq; roue solaireen revolution. Paris, 1975.

Asmusnen, J., P_V *Manichaean Literature*. NY. 1975.

Balyuzi, H. M., *Muhammad and the Course of Islam*. Oxford, 1976.

Baroja, J. C., *The World of the Witches.* Univ. of Chicago Press, 1973 ('63).

Baynes, C. F. (ed.), *I-Chmg.* Princeton, 1967.

Berger, P, A., *A Rumour of Angels.* Penguin, 1970.

Berger, P. L., *The Social Reality of Religion.* Faber & Faber, 1969.

Berger, P. L., & Luckman, T., The Social Construction of Reality. Penguin, 1967.

Bergman, F., *On Being Free.* Univ. of Notre Dame. Notre Dame& London, 1977.

Beteille, A., *Six Essays in Comparative Sociology.* Oxf. Univ. Press, 1974.

Beteille, *A., From Lineage to State.* Oxf, Univ. Press, 1984.

Bharati A., Great Tradition and Little Tradition. Delhi, Chowkhamba, 1978.

Bhattacharya, N. N., *The Indian Mother Goddess.* Calcutta, 1971. *History of Tantric Religion.* New Delhi, 1982.

Bianchi, U., *Selected* Essays on *Gnosticism, Duatism and Mysteriology.* Brill, 1978. Bianchi, u., Blecker, C.G., & Bausani, A. B. (ed.), *Problems and Methods of History of Religion.* Brill, 1972.

Blardesu, M., *Clefs pour la penste Hindoue.* Paris, 1972.

Biardeau, *M., Theore de la connaisearice of philosophie de la parole dans le brahmanisme classique. Paris, 1964.*

Bleeker, C. J., *The Sacred Bridge.* Brill, 1963.

Bloch, M., & Parry, J. (ed.). *Death and Regeneration of Life.* Camb. Univ. Press, 1982.

Blount, B. G., & Sanches, M. (ed.), *Sociological Dimensions of Language Change.* NY, 1977.

Bohling, A., *Mysterium und Wahrheit.* Brill, 1968.

Bohm, D., Causality and Chance in Modem Physics. Princeton Univ. Press, 1957.

Boon, A. J., *Other Tribes; Other Scribes.* Camb. Univ. Press, 1982.

Bom, M., *Natural Philosophy of Cause and Chance.* Oxf. Unvi. Press, 1951.

Boughton, G., *Primitivism and Related Idem in Philo-judacus.* Johns Hopkins Univ., 1946.

Bougle, C., *Essays on the Caste System* (tr. PocockD. F.). London, 1971.

Bayce, *M., A History of Zoroastrianism.* London, 1961.

Brandon. S. G. F., *The Saviors God.* Manchester, 1963.

Briffault; R, *The Mother* (3 vols.). London, 1969 (1st 1927).

Brock, R. van den. *The Myth of the Phoenix.* Brill, 1972.

Broek, R van den, Boarda, T, and Mansfield J., *Knowledge of God in the Graeco-Roman World.* Brill, 1988.

Broekington, J. L., *The Sacred Thread: Hinduism in its Continuity and Diversity.* Edinburgh, 1983.

Brown, C. M., *God as Mother.* U.K., 1974.

Bruce, L., *Priests, Warriors and Cattle.* Berkeley & London. Univ. of California Press, 1981.

Budge, E. A.W., *Egyptian Magic.* London, 1972 *The Hock of the Dead.* Chicago, 1901.

Cardona, C., and Hoenigawald, H. M. (ed.), *Indo-European and Indo-Europeans.* Philadelphia, 1979.

Carlton, E., *Patterns of Belief* (vols. 1 and II). London, George Allen & Unwin. 1971, 73.

Carpentier, J. (ed.), *The Uttarāhyānasūtra.* N. Delhi, 1980.

Cambell, A. L., *Mithraic Iconography and Ideology.* Brill, 1968.

Cambell, C. A., *In Defence of Free Will.* London, George Allen & Unwin, 1967.

Caspary, E. G., *Politics and Exegesis: Origin and the Two Sword.* UCLA Press, 1979.

Chakravarti, H., *Asceticism in Ancient India.* Punthl Pustak, Calcutta, 1973.

Cicero, M. T., (tr. Poteat, H. M.) *On Divination.* Univ. of Chicago, 1950

On the Nature of the Gods. Chicago, 1950.

On Duties. Chicago, 1950.

Cloffari, V., *Fortuna and Fate.* NY. Columbia Univ. Press, 1955.

Clark, G., *World Prehistory: An Outline.* Camb. Univ. Press, 1963.

Classen, H. J. M. and Skalnix (ed.), *The Early State.* London, 1978.

Cohen, J., *Chance, Skill and Luck.* Penguin, 1960.

Cornte, G. D., *Croyances, Rites, Institutions.* Paris, 1911.

Contenu, G., *Everyday life in Babylon and Assyria.* NY, 1954.

Cook, A. B., *Zeus: A Study in Myths, Mysteries and Religion.* 3 Vols. Camb. Univ. Press, 1914, 1925, 1940.

Conze, F., *Buddhist Thought in India.* London, George Allen & Unwin, 1962.

Cox, O. C., *Caste, Class and Race.* NY, 1970.

Carlton. E., *Patteras of Belief,* Vols. I and II, London, Allen & Unwin, 1972.

David, A. R., and Rosalie, A. O., *The Ancient Egyptians.* Routledge & Kegan Paul, 1982.

Dayal, H., *The Badhisativa Doctrine in Buddhist Sanskrit Literature.* London, 1932.

Derretl, J. D. M., *Religious Law and the State in India.* London, 1968.

Deshpande, M. M. and Hook, P. E., *Aryan and Non-Aryan in India.* Michigan, 1979.

Devasenapathy, V. A., *Of Human Bondage and Divine Grace.* Madras, Annamatai Univ., 1963.

Dhawan, B. D., *Mysticism and Symbolism in the Arunyakas.* Delhi, Gian Publishing House, 1988.

Dietrich, B. C., *Death, Fate and the Gods.* Univ. of London, 1965.

Dillon, M., *Celts and Aryans.* Simla, 1975.

Douglas, M. (ed.), *Witchcraft, Confessions and Accusations.* Tavistock, 1970.

Douglas, M. W., *Implicit Meanings. London, Roulledgede & Kegan Paul, 1975.*

Drower, E. S., *The Mandaeans of Iraq and Iran : Their Cults, Customs, Magic, Legends and Folklore.* Leiden, Brill, 1962.

Dubbs, J. P., and Whitney, D. D., *Cultural Context.* Allyn & Bacon Inc. Bost, 1980.

Dumézil, G., *Heur et Maiheurdu guerre.* Paris, 1969.

The Destmy of a King. Univ. of Chicago Press, 1973.

Dumont, L., *Religion, Politics and History in India.* Mouton, 1970.

Homo Hierarchicus. London, 1970.

Dutta, N. K., *Origin and Growth of Caste in India.* Calcutta, Firma K. L. Mukherjee, 1965.

Duverger, C., *La Conversion des Indiens de Nouveșle Espagne.* Paris, 1987.

Eiesenach, J. E., *Two Worlds of Liberalism.* Univ. of Chicago, 1981.

Eliade, M., *Shamanisan.* NY,1964.

Ociuitism, Witchcraft and Cultural Fashions. Chicago, 1976.

Yoga: Immortality end Freedom. Chicago, 3969.

Mephistophetes ct I'Andrcgyne. Paris, 1962.

Ellub, J., *The Ethics of Freedom.* Michigan, 1976.

Emerton, J. A., *Prophecy.* Berlin, NY, 1980.

Ergardt, T. J., *Faith and Knowledge in Early Buddhism.* Brill, 1977.

Fenerstein, G., *The Bhagavadștā.* New Delhi, 1980.

Fick, R., (tr. Maitra, S. K.). *The Social Organizations in North-East India in Buddhist Time.* Varanasi, 1972. (1st edn. 1920).

Finley, M. I., *The Ancient Economy.* London, 1973.

Fonlenrose, J., *Python.* Univ. of California Press, 1980.

Frankfort, H. H., *Ancient Egyptian Religion.* Columbia Univ. Press, 1950.

Frauwallner, E., Geschiete der indischen Philosophie. 2 vols. Salzburg, 1953–56.

Frazer, G. J., *The Golden Bough.* (2vols.) London, 1914, (3rd ed.).

Freedman, R. E., *Near Eastern Studies.* vol. 22. *The Creation of the Sacred Literature.* UCLA Press, 1981.

Freud, S., *Civilization and its Discontents.* London, 1955.

Fung, Yu-L'an., *A History of Chinese Philosophy.* Princeton Univ. Press, 1952.

Gasper, T. J., *Ritual, Myth and Drama in the Ancient Near East.* NY, 1950.

Geertz, C., *Islam Observed.* Yale Univ. Press, 1968.

Myth, Symbol and Culture. NY, 1971.

Ghosh, *A.*, *The City in Early Historical India.* N. Delhi, 1973.

Gimbutas, M., *The Gods and Goddesses of Old Europe. London, 1974.*

Glasenapp, H. von., *The Doctrine of Karman m Jain Philosophy. (tr. Glfford, G.B.),* Bombay, 1942.

Goetz, A and Sturtevant, A., *The- Hittite Ritual of Tunnawi.* Connecticut, 1938.

Goetz, R, and Morley, SG (ed.)., *Popol Vuh.* Oklahama, 1947.

Gonda, J., *Medieval Religious Literature in Sanskrit.* Weisbaden, 1977.

Goudrian, T., and Gouldner, A. W., *Maya, Divine and Human.* Delhi, 1978.

Graham, C., *World Prehistory: An Outline.* Camb. Univ. Press, 1963.

Grant, F. C. (ed)., *Hellenistic Religions.* NY, 1953.

Grant, R. M., *Gnosticism and Early Christianity.* Columbia Univ. Press, 1959.

Gnosticism, an Anthology. London, Collins, 1961.

Greene, W. C., *Moira.* Harper & Row, 1965.

Grobel, K., *The Gospel of Truth.* London, 1960.

Gronlngen, G., *The First Century Gnosticism.* London, 1967.

Gunther, D. S., *Hinduism Reconsidered.* Delhi, Manoharlal, 1989.

Gupta, B., *Magical Beliefs and Superstitions.* Delhi, 1979.

Gupta, C., *The Brahmans of India.* N. Delhi, 1983.

Gupta, U., *Materialism in the Vedas.* N. Delhi, 1987.

Gumey, O. R., *The Hittites.* Penguin, 1954.

Halbfass, W., *Tradition and Reflection.* Stale Univ. of NY Press, 1991.

Halbsberghe, G. H., *The Cult of Sol Invictus.* Brill, 1972.

Halliday, W. R., *Greek Divination.* Chicago, 1967 (1st edn. 1973).

Handiqi, K. K, *Yasastnaka and Indian Culture.* Sholapur, 1949.

Harrison, J., *Themis: A Study of Social Origins of Greek Religion.* Camb. Univ. Press, 1927.

Hawrkos, T., *Structuralism and Semiotics.* Methuen, 1977.

Hazra, R. C., *Studies in the Upapurāṇas.* Calcutta, 1958.

Herman, A. I., *The Problem of Evil and Indian Thought.* Motilal, 1976.

Hesiod (tr. Brown N. O.). *Theogony.* NY. 1953.

Hiltebeltel, A., *Purity and Auspiciousness in the Sanskrit Epics.* California, 1983.

Hoernle, R. (ed.), *Utāsagdasāo.* Calcutta, Asiatic Society, 1989.

Hondereich, T., *A Theory of Determination.* Oxford Clarendon Press, 1988.

Hooke, S. H., *Babylonian and Assyrian Religion.* London, 1953.

Hope, R., *The Book of Diogenes Laertes.* Columbia Univ. Press,1930.

Hsil, L. S., *The Political Philosophy of Confucius.* Beijing, 1932.

Hugo, A. R., *Sumerian Hymns and Prayers to God Ninih.* Pennsylvania Univ. Museum, 1911.

Hulin, M., *Le Principe de I'Ego dans la Pensée Indienne Classique la Notion d'Aharṇkāra.* Paris, 1978.

L'Hindouismc. Paris, 1978.

Ichiro, H., *Folk Religion in Japan.* Univ. of Chicago, 1974.

Kakar, S., *Shamans, Mystics and Doctors.* NY, 1982.

Kalupahana. D. G, *Causality the Central Philosophy of Buddhism.* Honolulu, 1975.

Kaveeshwar, G. W., *The Law of Karma.* Poona, 1975.

Karma and Rebirth. Poona, 1974.

Kayes, C. F., and Daniel, E. V., *Karma and Anthropological Inquiry.* Berkeley, Univ. of California, 1983.

Keith. T., *Religion and the Decline of Magic.* NY, 1951.

Klostermeier, K. K, *Mythologies and Philosophies of Salvation in the Theistic Traditions of India.* Wilfrid Laurier Press, 1984.

Kosambi, D. D., *An Introduction to the Study of Indian History.* Bombay, 1956.

Knox, Sir M., *Action.* London, G. Allen & Unwin, 1968.

Kramer, S. N., *Sumerian Mythology.* Philadelphia, 1944.

The Sumerians: Their History, Culture and Character. Univ. of Chicago, 1960.

Lacan, J., *The Language of the Self.* Baltimore, 1968.

Lacombe, O., indianite. Paris, 1979.

Larson, G. T. (ed.), *Myth in Indo-European Antiquity.* Univ. of California Press, 1974.

Law, B. C., *Heaven and Hell in Buddhist Perspective.* Delhi, 1973.

Lawrence, B. B., Shahrastani on Indian Religions. Hague, 1976.

Leach, E. R. (ed.), *Dialectic in Practical Religion.* Camb. Univ. Press, 1968.

Leach, E. R. (ed.), *The Structural Study of Myth and Totemism.* Tavistock Pub, 1967.

Leeuw, Van der., *Phenomenology of Religion.* 1956.

Lessa, W. A., and Vogt, E. Z. (ed.), *Reader in Comparative Religion.* London, Harper & Rowe, 1965.

Lewis, I. M., *Ecstatic Religion.* Penguin, 1971.

Lingat, R., *The Classical Law of India.* Illinois, 1958.

Long, A. M., *Hellenistic Philosophy.* London, 1986.

Lorenzen, D. N., *The Kūpṣlikus and Kālāmukhus.* N. Delhi, Thompson, 1972.

Lowe, M., and Blacker, C., *Divination and Oracles.* George Allen & Unwin, 1981.

Lukacs, G., (Ir. Livingstone, R), *History and Class Consciousness.* London, 1971.

Mackay, D. M., *Science, Chance and Prwidence.* Oxf. Univ. Press, 1978.

Madan, T. N., Non-renunciation: Themes and Interpretations of Hindu Culture. Oxf. Univ. Press, 1987.

Madden, F-H. and Hari, P. H. (ed.), *Evil and Concept of God.* Illinois, 1968

Mahadevan, T. M. P., *Time and Timeless.* Madras, 1954.

Malamoud, C., *La Mort, les inortes dans Icssocietes ancienres.* Paris, 1982.

Malik, S. C., *Indian Civilization: The Formative Period.* Simla, 1968.

Mandelbaum, S., *Society in India: Change and Continuity.* Univ. of California Press, Berkeley, 1972.

McDermott, M. (ed.)., *Village India,* Univ. of Chicago Press, 1955.

Mead, G. R. S., *Fragments of Faith: Forgotten Gnosticism.* NY, 1960.

Mead, M., *Culture and Commitment.* New York, 1970.

Mensching, G., *Structures and Patterns of Religion.* Motilal Banarasidas, Delhi, 1976.

Middleton, J., *Magic, Witchcraft and Curing.* NY, 1967.

Milton, S., *Man's Glassy Essence.* Indiana Univ. Press, Bloomington, 1967.

Mise, L.von., *Human Action* (3rd revised edition). Chicago. 1963.

Montogmery, J. A., *Ramaic Incantation texts from Nippur.* Pennsylvania Univ. Museum, 1917.

Moore, R.G. (ed.), *Tradition and Politicsin South* Asia. New Delhi, 1979.

Mowry, L, *The Dead Sea Scrolls and the Early Church.* Chicago, 1962.

Muir, R, *Witchcraft.* (1st edition 1969) London. 1975.

Mukherjee, B. N., *Mathura and its Society.* Calcutta, 1981.

Mumford, *L.,The City in History.* London. Seeker & Warburg, 1961.

Murty, K. S., *Metaphysics, Man and Freedom.* Asia Pub. House, NIY, 1963.

Nakamura, H., *A Comparative History of Ideas.* London & N. Y, 1986.

Narain, A. K. (ed.), *Studies in the History of Buddhism*, B.R. Publishing Corporation , 1980

Needham, J., *Yang Ch'ing k'un: Religion in Chinese Tradition,* Berkeley, 1961.

Neufeldt, R. W. (ed.), *Karma and Rebirth; Post Classical Developments.* Albany, 1986.

Neumann, E., *The Great Mother.* USA. Princeton, 1966.

Des Germanisclie Schicksalglaube. Berlin, 1939.

Neusner, J., *Judaism, the Evidence of the Mishnah.* Univ. of Chicago Press, 1981.

Nigg, W., The Heretics. NY, 1962.

Niyogl, Balaslev, A., *A Study of Time in Indian Philosophy.* Wiesbaden, 1983.

Ockham, W. (tr. Adams, M.M. & Kretzmann, N.), *Predestination, God's Foreknowledge and Future Contingents.* NY, 1969.

O'Flaherty. W. D. (ed.), *The Origins of Evil in Hindu Mythology.* USA, Univ. of California. 1976.

(ed.), *Karma and Rebirth in Classical Indian Traditions.* N. Delhi, 1983.

Olivelle, P., Renunciation in Hinduism. Vienna, 1986.

Oosten, J. G., *The War ofthe Gods.* London, Routledge & Kegan Paul, 1985.

Oppenhein, A. L., *Ancient Mesopotamia.* Chicago, 1964.

Pande, G. C., *Studies in the Origins of Buddhism.* Delhi, Motilal Banarasidas, 1979.

Parke, H. W., and Wormell, D. E. W., *The Delphic Oracle. 2* vols. Oxford, 1956.

Parrinder, G., *Avatar and Incarnation.* London, Faber & Faber, 1970.

Patrick, M. K., *The Greek Sceptics.* Columbia Univ. Press, 1929.

Perleman, M., *Classical Political Economy.* London, 1984.

Peterson, R. D., (ed), *Notes on Technology and Moral Order.* NY, 1962.

Pike. N. (ed.), *God and Evil.* Prentice Hall, 1964.

Pollard, J., *Seers, Shrines and Sirens.* London, 1965.

Pollard, W. C., *Chance and Providence.* NY, 1958.

Popper, R., *Thoughts in Public Life.* Open Books, U. K., 1980.

Potter, K. H., *Presuppositions in Indian Philosophy.* Prentice Hall, N. J., 1963.

Pritchard, J. B., *Ancient Near Eastern Texts.* Princeton Univ. Press, 1950.

Pressler, H. H., *PrimitiveReligion in India.* Christian Literary Society, 1971.

Preston, J. J., *Mother Worship.* Univ. of N. Carolina Press, 1982.

Puhvel, J., *Comparative Mythology.* Baltimore & London, 1987.

Radcliffe, R., *The Folk Culture.* Chicago, 1941.

Rai, J., *The Rural Urban Economy and Social Changes in Ancient India.* Varanasi, 1974.

Raphael, D. O., *Moral Philosophy. Oxf. Univ. Press, 1981.*

Recinos, G., and Morley, S.C. (tr.), *Popol Vuh.* Maya Univ. of Oklahama Press, 1947.

Soothsayer as Creator. Univ. of Oklahama Press, 1947.

Rickaby, Rev. J., *Free Will and Four English Philosophers.* London, 1906.

Ringgern, H., *Fatalism in Persian Epics.* Uppsala, 1952.

Studies in Arabian Fatalism. Uppsala, 1955.

(ed.), *Fatalism, Beliefs in Religion, Folklore and Literature.* Stockholm, 1967.

Rodhe, S., *Deliver Us from Evil.* Copenhagen, 1946.

Roger, J., *Relearn to Reason.* 198 UK.

Rowley, H. H., *Prophecy and Religion in Ancient China and Israel.* London, 1956.

Monastery and Guild. Delhi, 1986.

Rudolf, K., *Gnosis.* Edinburgh, 1983.

Salctore, R. N., *Indian Witchcarft.* N. Delhi, 1981.

Sanders, E. P., *Paul and Palestinian Judaism.* London, 1978.

Satprem, T., *The Vedas and Human Destiny.* Mysore, 1992.

Scheftelowitz, J., *Die Zeit ais Shieksalsgottkeit in der indischen and eranischen Religion.* Stuttgart, 1929.

Schubring, W., *The Doctrine of the Jains.* Motilal Banarasidas, Delhi, 1962.

Schweitzco, *A., Indian Thought and its Development.* London, 1951.

Selar, E., *Fray Bernadinode Sahagun.* Stuttgart, 1927.

3–, *Peasants and Peasant Societies.* Penguin, 1971.

Sharma, R. N., *Culture and Civilization as Revealed in Srautasūtras*. Delhi, 1977.

Sharma, R. S., *Indian Society: Historical Probings*. Delhi, 1977.

3–, Material Culture and Social Formation in Ancient India. New Delhi, 1963.

Shasta, K. A. N., *Gleanings on Social life from Avādanas*. Calcutta, 1945.

Sheridan, A., and Foucault, M., *the will to Truth*. NY, 1980.

Smart, N., *Doctrine and Argument in Indian Philosophy*. N. Jersey, 1967.

Smith, M., *Jesus the Magician*. NY, 1978.

Sontheimer, G. D. and Kulke, H. (ed.), *Hinduism Reconsidered*. Delhi, 1989.

Stcherbatsky, T., *Buddhist Logic*. New York, 1962.

Sleinsaltz, A., *The Essential Talmud*. London, Wiedenfeld and Nicolson, 1976.

Strawson, P. F., *Freedom and Resentment*. Methuen, 1974.

Slambaugh, J. E, *Sarapis under the Ptolemies*. Brill, 1972.

Stutley, M., *Ancient Indian Magic end Folklore*. Boulder, 1980.

Swanton, M., (tr.) *Beowulf*.

Swinburne, R., *The Concept of Miracles*. London, 1970.

Sundcn, ILJ., La *Theorie Personniene de la Religion*. Uppsala, 1940.

Teilhard, P., *Le Phenomenehumain*. Paris, 1955.

Thapar, R., *From Lineage to State*. Oxf. Univ. Press, 1964.

Thomas, L. V., *Anthropologic de lu mart*. Paris, 1975.

Thompson, L., *Challenge of Chance*. London, 1956.

Thompson, S., *Motif Intex of Folk Literature*. 6 vols. Indiana Univ. Press, 1955–1958.

Tillich, P., *Systematic Theology*. London, 1950.

Titter, J., Historisches Worterbuck der Philosophie Darmstadt, 1972.

Tokarey, S., *History of Religion*. Moscow, 1989.

Towler, R., *Homo Religiosus*. London, 1974.

Tucci, G., *The Theory and Practice of the Mandala*. Rider & Co. 1961.

Tulpule, S. G., *Mysticism in Medieval India*. Otto Horrassowltz, 1984.

Tylor, Sir E., *Primitive Culture*. London, 1871.

Unnik, W. C., Van, Newly Discovered Gnostic Writings. London, I960.

Upadhyay, G. P., *Brāhmaṇas in Ancient India.* New Delhi, 1969.

Vermaseren M., *Cybele and Attis.* London, 1977.

Vernant, J. P., *Myth and Thought among the Greeks.* London, 1965.

Walther, H., *The Religions of Mongolia.* Univ. of California Press, 1980.

Warder, A. K., *Indian Buddhism.* Delhi, 1970.

Watt, W. M., *Free Will and Predestination According to Islam.* Delhi 1970.

Widengren, G., Hochgottglauble in alien Iran. Uppsala, 1938.

Mesopotamian Elements in Manichiarasm. Leipzig, Uppsala, 1956.

Mani and der Manichaismus. Stuttgart, 1961.

Wilson, S., Saints and their Cults. Camb. Univ. Press, 1983.

Whitrow, G. T., *Time in History.* Oxf. Univ. Press, 1988.

Wolf, P. A., *Religion and Ritual m ChineseSociety*. Stanford Univ. Press, 1974.

Wolfson, H. A., Religious Philosophy: A Group of Essays. Camb. Moss., 1961.

Worsely, P., *The Trumpet Shell Sound.* London, 1968.

Young, R. F., *Resistant Hinduism.* Vienna, 1981.

Zaehner, R. C., *At Sundry Times.* London, 1958.

Zimmer, H., *Philosophies in India* (ed. Cambell, J.) N.Y., 1951.

D. Articles

Bhattacharya, H., "The Brahmanical Concept of Karma". *AR Wadin Comn.VoL,* Bangalore, 1954.

Biardcan, M., "Etudes dc mythologie hindoue". I & II in *Bulletin de I'Ecole Franaised' Exlréme-Orient,* 54 (1968), Paris.

Bayer, A. M., "Etude sur l'origine de la doctrine du Saṃsāra." *Journal Asiatique.* 9:18. Burk, C., "The letters of a sculptor". *Quarterly Review,* I984.

Chakravarly, G. N., "The Idea of Fate and Freedom in Mahābhārata". *Poonu Orientalist,20,* 1955.

Childe, V. G., "The Urban Revolution". *The Town Planning Journal,* vol. XXI, April. 1950.

Dumont, L., "World Renunciation in Indian Religions". *Indian Sociology,* vol. IV, I960.

Filliozat, J., "Taoismeet Yoga", *Journal Asiatique,* torne CCLVII, 1969, nos. 1, 2.

Fuller, C. J., 'The Hindu Pantheon and the Legitimation of Hierarchy", *Man,* vol. 23 no.1 March, 1988.

Fussman, G., "Pour uṇe problematique nouvelle des religions Indiennes anciennes". *Journal Asiatique.* tome CCLXV, 1977 f 1 & 2.

Gilhus, I. S., "Gnosticism - a study in liminal symbolism" *Namen.* XXI, 1984.

Goldman, R. P., "Karma, Guilt and Buried Memories: Public Fantasy in Traditional India." *Journal of the American Oriental Society,* vol., 105, no. 3. 1985.

Heesterman, J. C., "On the Origin of the nāstika", *Wiener Zeitschrift fir. Sud and Os-tasiens* Band II, 1959.

"Brahmin, Ritual and Renouncer". *Wiener Zeitschrift Sud and Os-tasiens,* Band VII, 1963.

"Non-violence and Sacrifice", *Indologica Taurinensia,* 12, 1984.

Induja, R., "Orientalist Construction of India." *Modem Asian Studies,* 20, 1986.

Lendtner, C., "Buddhist References to Old Iranian Religion".

A Green leaf: Papers in Honour of Prof. I. P. Asmussen, Leiden, 1988.

Madan, T. N., "Secularism in its Place". *Journal of Asian Studies,* vol. 46, no. l, Nov., 1987.

Mc Dermott, J. P., "The Kathavatthu Kamma debates". *Journal of American Oriental Society, 95,* 1975.

Naraharl, H. G., "Karma and Reincarnation In the Mahābhārata." *Annals of Bhandarkar Oriental Research Institute,* 27, 1946.

"On the Origin of the Doctrine of Saṃsāra." *Poona Orientalist,* 4, 1939–40.

Panikkar, R., "Time in India: Paradox of State and Motion". *East and West,* vol. 38, 1988.

"The Law of Karman and the Historical Dimension of Man". *East and West,* 22, 1972.

Pensa, C., "On the Purification Concept in Indian Tradition with special regard to Yoga". East *and West,* no. XIX, 1969.

Perrett, R. W., “Rebirth”. *Religion Studies,* vol. 23, 1987.

Ray, B., “Performative utterances in African rituals”. *History of Religions.* No. 13. 1973.

Reiner, E.,‘The Uses of Astrology”. *Journal of American Oriental Society,* vol. 105, No.4, 1985.

Ruegg, D. S., “Ahiṃsā and Vegetarianism in the History of Buddhism”. *Buddhist Studies in Honour of W. Rahula,* London, 1980.

Schmidt, H. P., “*The origin of Ahiṃsā.*” *Melanges d’ Indianisme a la memoire de L Renou,* Paris, 1968.

Smith, H. D., “Prāyaścitta in the Canonical works of Pancarātrāgama”. *The Adyar Litmery Bulletin,* 1966.

Smith, R.M. ‘Time in India: The Paradox of State and Motion.” *East and West,* vol. 38, Nos. 1–4 Dec, 1988.

Trigg, R., “Sin and Freedom”. *Religion Studies,* vol. 20, 1984.

Vrics, J. de, “Magic and Religion”. *History of Religion,* 1, 1962.

Wayman, A, “Studies in Yama and Māra”. *Indo-Iranian Journal,* No. III, 1959.

Zagzebski, L, “Divine Foreknowledge and Human Free Will”. *Religion Studies,* vol. 21, 1985.

Index